SERVING THE OLD DOMINION

MERCER
UNIVERSITY PRESS

Endowed by
TOM WATSON BROWN
and
THE WATSON-BROWN FOUNDATION, INC.

SERVING THE OLD DOMINION

A History of Christopher Newport University

1958–2011

PHILLIP HAMILTON

MERCER UNIVERSITY PRESS
MACON, GEORGIA

MUP/H836//P437

© 2011 Mercer University Press
1400 Coleman Avenue
Macon, Georgia 31207
All rights reserved

First Edition

Books published by Mercer University Press are printed on
acid-free paper that meets the requirements of American
National Standard for Information Sciences—Permanence of
Paper for Printed Library Materials.

Mercer University Press is a member of Green Press
Initiative (greenpressinitiative.org), a nonprofit organization
working to help publishers and printers increase their use of
recycled paper and decrease their use of fiber derived from
endangered forests. This book is printed on recycled paper.
ISBN   9780881462647 (cloth)
          9780881462654 (paperback)
Cataloging-in-Publication Data is available from the Library
of Congress

CONTENTS

ACKNOWLEDGMENTS

There are many people I would like thank who helped me in the production of this book. First, I'd like to thank Christopher Newport University President Paul Trible who commissioned me to write a comprehensive history of the school. At all stages of the book's preparation he provided me with a great deal of support as well as the freedom to explore all aspects of CNU's story. Many members of the university's community—both past and present—provided me with extremely valuable and helpful accounts of their experiences. The university's ex-presidents, James Windsor, Jack Anderson (who sadly passed away in 2009), and Anthony Santoro, were gracious, patient, and helpful with my many questions. Cecil Cary Cunningham, the widow of CNU's first president, H. Westcott Cunningham, also gave me important insights into Christopher Newport's early days.

Colleagues who assisted me with their recollections include Sam Bauer, Bill Brauer, Ronnie Cohen, Harold Cones, Rick Cheney, Jim Cornette, Douglas Gordon, Kara Keeling, Cheryl Mathews, Mario Mazzarella, Patty Patten, Jay Paul, Cindi Perry, Carol Safko, Susan St. Onge, Mark Reimer, Dick Summerville, George Webb, Jane Carter Webb, Ed Weiss, and Barry Wood. Laura Puaca of the history department read several of the book's early chapters and provided me with helpful feedback. Recent CNU students also contributed to this project, especially those who enrolled in my Spring 2008 history seminar entitled "Researching Christopher Newport University." The members of this class—Jessica Achorn, Chris Allen, Tim Coddington, Jeff Eckert, Zeh Hale, Jenna Heggie, Kate Judkins, Dan Moore, David Porter, Holli Sawyer, Hunter Snellings, Jordan Taylor, Ashley Tingler, and Chris Waltrip—each wrote valuable papers about the University's past that often enlightened me and occasionally pointed me in new directions. Several other CNU students—Liz Healy, Lindsay Newman, and Samantha Wessel—served at various stages as research assistants for the project, and their help was immeasurably important, especially in terms of their reviewing the wealth of information in the university archives. The staff of the Trible Library was also cooperative and helpful throughout the book's research and production, especially Susan Barber and Amy Boykin. I'd like to thank Johnnie Gray of the Trible Library as well as Bruce Bronstein and Jesse Hutchinson of the Office of Communications and Public Relations for their assistance with the book's illustrations. Former state delegate Alan Diamonstein also graciously sat down with me to share his insights into Christopher Newport's development. Others who assisted me in the volume's production as well as provided valuable advice and guidance include: James Axtell, Shirley Fields Cooper, Elsie Meehan Duval, Sean Heuvel, John Quarstein, and Peter Wallenstein. Thank you all!

Finally, I especially want to express my deepest appreciation and gratitude to my family—my wife Chris, and two sons, Tommy and Jake—for their love, support, and patience as I wrote *Serving the Old Dominion* over the past several years.

Part I

On An Upward Trajectory (1958–1971)

King Meehan, Deputy Commissioner for the Peninsula Industrial Committee.

Lewis A. McMurran Jr., who introduced the legislation to create Christopher
Newport College in March 1960.

H. Westcott Cunningham in front of the Daniel School in 1961.

(above) The Daniel School shortly after the commencement of classes in the Fall of 1961; (below) Several of CNC's first instructors: from left to right: (bottom row) Ernest Rudin, Faye Greene, Allen Tanner, and L. Barron Wood Jr.; (top row) Augustin Maissen, James Liston, Robert Vargas, and Robert Ursy

Professor Georgia Hunter leading a biology class in a second floor classroom in the
Daniel School Building in 1961

CNC's first Student Government Association leaders – from left to right: James Cornette (president), Howard Clark (vice president), Charlotte Anderson (secretary), and Patrick Baldwin (secretary).

1

"A College from Scratch"

The Lunch on 12 May 1958

On Monday, 12 May 1958, John Scozzari, assistant to the College of William and Mary president Admiral Alvin "Duke" Chandler, had lunch with a businessman from Newport News, Virginia, named E.J. "King" Meehan. Meehan headed a local civic group called the Peninsula Industrial Committee (PIC), an organization dedicated to bringing businesses to the Hampton Roads area. Their discussion at lunch focused on education in the region and, during their conversation, Meehan gave Scozzari a memo entitled "A Proposal for an Expanded Educational Program on the Virginia Peninsula." Meehan pointed out that the Hampton-Newport News region had grown rapidly since the end of World War II, yet no institution of higher education existed on the Peninsula south of Williamsburg. Thus, Meehan and the PIC proposed that a two-year college be established, and they wanted President Chandler's support. Scozzari returned to his office that afternoon and wrote to Meehan, thanking him for the meal and promising to give Chandler the memo.[1]

This lunch marked the beginning of Christopher Newport College (CNC). Twenty-two months later, in March 1960, the Virginia General Assembly passed legislation creating CNC as a two-year branch of the Colleges of William and Mary. In the years that followed, the school

---

[1] John Scozzari to E.J. "King" Meehan, Williamsburg, 12 May 1958, University Archives, The Paul and Rosemary Trible Library, Christopher Newport University, Newport News, Virginia.

developed in ways that few people had originally anticipated. In September 1961, CNC opened its doors in an abandoned elementary school in downtown Newport News and began to serve several hundred students from Hampton Roads. Ten years later, the college became a four-year institution with a student body composed largely of local urban residents, many of whom worked full-time and commuted to the school to attend both day and night classes. In 1977, Christopher Newport formally severed its ties to the College of William and Mary and became an independent public institution with its own governing board of visitors. Fourteen years later, in 1991, the college started to offer graduate classes and soon thereafter became Christopher Newport *University* (CNU). In 1996, former US senator Paul Trible became CNU's fifth president, whereupon he began a major transformation that moved the university away from its vocational studies and programs, and toward creating an undergraduate curriculum firmly grounded in the liberal arts. Instead of serving primarily older "nontraditional" students and local commuters, CNU became a predominantly residential university that aimed to educate high-achieving traditional-aged students drawn from throughout the Old Dominion. Trible also revitalized the midtown Newport News campus by overseeing a $500 million building campaign that included new dormitories, academic buildings, and a state-of-the-art performing arts center. As a result, by the end of the twenty-first century's first decade, CNU had transformed itself into a highly selective public university focused on high academic standards, solid undergraduate teaching, and close attention from faculty to student development.

A close examination of Christopher Newport over five decades reveals a great deal not only about the university's development, but also about changes within the surrounding Peninsula community as well as within American higher education in general. As a result, *Serving the Old Dominion: A History of Christopher Newport University* focuses on three overarching themes: First, it tells the story of the university's growth and progress over the years, highlighting the fact that CNU has *always* been a highly unique institution. From its start, the school has been filled with dedicated staff and faculty members who have paid close attention to classroom teaching and student success over the years. Nevertheless, the school has never stood still; indeed, change has characterized every decade of its existence, and one of the main purposes of this book is to tell this important story of both continuity and change. Second, the book examines CNU's history in the broader context of the Hampton Roads region. Throughout its history CNU has generally maintained close and fruitful relationships with political and civic leaders in Newport News as well as with leaders in other local municipalities. When these relationships have been strong, the university has been successful, but whenever these ties became strained—as they occasionally did over the years—the school suffered difficulties and hard times. Third, although a unique story in many respects, CNU's evolution has at many points reflected the broader historical trends present in American higher education. In other words, changes in the university's academic standards, the mores and values of its students and faculty, and the policies of administration leaders have always been influenced by the larger patterns found in higher education across the nation. Thus, the story of Christopher Newport University also tells us much about the general development of American colleges and universities during the past half-century.

Background — American Higher Education and the Hampton Roads Area (1945–1960)

The Virginia General Assembly created Christopher Newport College in 1960 because of important circumstances rooted in the outcome of the Second World War. America's participation in that conflict revolutionized and helped to create the modern system of higher education present in the United States today. Several elements contributed to this transformation. First and foremost was Congress' passage of the Serviceman's Readjustment Act of 1944, better known as the GI Bill of Rights. This statute offered returning veterans a package of government-provided benefits designed to assist their reintegration back into civilian life following the war. A key provision was the promise to provide servicemen with free tuition as well as money for books and basic living expenses. By 1950, more than two million veterans had enrolled in two- and four-year institutions of higher learning. As university administrators across the country watched their enrollment figures skyrocket (in some cases, more than double), they sought more public funding for new classrooms, laboratories, and other student/faculty facilities.[2]

Another source of transformation—slower to develop, but equally as important—was the baby boom. Beginning in 1946, birth rates in the United States dramatically increased. Indeed, because the United States entered an extended period of prosperity after World War II, American couples married earlier, divorced less often, and had more children. Improved medicines developed during the conflict—penicillin, for instance—also improved infant morality rates. As a result, from 1946 to 1964, American families had 3.2 children on average, with seventy-six million babies being born overall. Educators and public policy makers realized that a significant portion of this baby boom "bubble" would eventually reach the nation's already-crowded colleges and universities.[3]

Finally, federal policy contributed to the post-World War II transformation of higher education. In 1946, President Harry Truman established the Commission of Higher Education to examine the role of colleges and universities in preserving American democracy. Because a well-educated American citizenry was essential in order to preserve the nation's position in the world, Truman charged Commission members with finding "ways and means of expanding educational opportunities for all young people."[4] The Commission mainly recommended that the US devote significantly more political attention and financial resources toward providing a post-secondary education to all who desired it. Although the Commission's report brought the federal government into the national dialogue about higher education, Congress in the late 1940s and 1950s directed few federal resources toward implementing the Commission's goals. Therefore, the aim of expanding access to higher education remained largely a state and local responsibility throughout this period.[5]

Like most states, Virginia expanded its system of higher education even before World War II ended. Among the nine public institutions

---

[2] John R. Thelin, *A History of American Higher Education* (Baltimore, Maryland: Johns Hopkins University Press, 2004), 263–65.

[3] Eric Foner, *Give Me Liberty! An American History* (New York: Norton, 2005) 2:944.

[4] The Commission's recommendations are quoted in Thelin, *History of Higher Education*, 268.

[5] Thelin, *History of Higher Education*, 269–70.

present in 1941, the College of William and Mary and the University of Virginia were the state system's flagships. Rapid population growth, though, made new colleges essential. From 1940 to 1950, Virginia's population grew 25 percent from 2,644,250 to 3,318,680 people. Thus, the state in 1944 turned a small, private, African-American junior college into a public institution called the Norfolk Division of the Virginia State College. It joined the all-white, two-year, Norfolk Division of the College of William and Mary, which had been founded in 1930. These Hampton Roads-area colleges later became Norfolk State University and Old Dominion University respectively. The General Assembly later established Clinch Valley College (later University of Virginia at Wise) in 1954. Two years after that George Mason College was founded in northern Virginia as a two-year branch of the University of Virginia. Despite these additional institutions, Virginia's colleges and universities remained overcrowded and unable to accommodate many of the qualified students and ex-G.I.s applying for admission.[6]

In the 1950s, there was no college present on the Virginia Peninsula below Williamsburg, although the region experienced some of the state's heaviest population growth. The Cold War between the US and the Soviet Union in large part sparked this increase. Home to the Newport News Shipbuilding and Dry Dock Company (today Huntington Ingalls Industries), Peninsula workers constructed numerous civilian tankers as well as many naval warships, including Essex-class and later Nimitz-class aircraft carriers. The military also expanded its presence in the area. Langley Air Force Base and forts Monroe and Eustis were expanded and, in the wake of the Soviet launch of Sputnik in 1957, NASA established the Langley Research Center to work on Project Mercury.[7] As a result of these activities, the region enjoyed its greatest period of prosperity. The cities of Newport News and Hampton saw rapid economic growth as did Warwick County, a ten-mile semi-rural strip of land that stretched along the James River. New stores opened along Washington Avenue in downtown Newport News and, with the growing availability of

---

[6] Peter Wallenstein, *Cradle of America: Four Centuries of Virginia History* (Lawrence: University Press of Kansas, 2007), 375–76.

[7] Wallenstein, *Cradle of America*, 386; John V. Quarstein and Parke S. Rouse, Jr., *Newport News: A Centennial History* (Newport News, Virginia: City of Newport News, 1996), 144.

automobiles, suburban shopping centers opened north of downtown.
The Hilton Shopping Center, for instance, opened in 1953, and the
Newmarket Shopping Center followed just three years later. As the
region grew, more and more residents also moved away from the
Peninsula's congested southeastern tip and into new suburban
developments located in the less crowded Warwick County
(reincorporated as the City of Warwick in 1952).[8]

As these developments unfolded, local leaders contemplated the
Peninsula's long-term future. Some individuals argued that all of the
region's municipalities—Newport News, Hampton, Elizabeth City, and
Warwick—should combine into a massive urban and suburban area that
would be able to compete economically with Norfolk and Richmond in
terms of attracting new businesses and workers. Although parochial
rivalries ultimately prevented a Peninsula union, the citizens of Newport
News and City of Warwick voted on 16 July 1957 to combine or
"consolidate," thus creating a new elongated seventy-five square mile
municipality along the James River. After much discussion, civic leaders
decided to simply call the new city by the better-known name of
"Newport News." Consolidation created a number of opportunities for
development, but new problems also came with the combination. People
and businesses within the new municipality were still overwhelmingly
concentrated in the "downtown hub" and few substantial highways
linked the long and narrow township together. The primary concern,
however, remained economic competition from surrounding
communities. Post-World War II urbanization across the Hampton
Roads region had produced a number of thriving cities including
Norfolk, Virginia Beach, and Portsmouth. By the end of the 1950s, these
municipalities were all competing with one another for businesses, jobs,
and workers, as well as for state and federal resources.[9]

King Meehan, Lewis McMurran, and the Establishment
of a College on the Peninsula

As civic leaders contemplated how best to develop Newport News
in this competitive environment, they realized that a college was an

---

[8] Quarstein and Rouse, *Newport News: A Centennial History,* 158.
[9] Quarstein and Rouse, *Newport News: A Centennial History,* 165.

essential component. In particular, members of the civic-business group called the Peninsula Industrial Committee (PIC) saw a two-fold need for an institution of higher learning: One, it would serve the educational needs of the region's growing population, and two, it would help to attract new businesses and talented workers to the area. Founded in 1945 and composed of a forty-five-member board, the PIC's initial mission was to ensure that the area's economy remained prosperous following the Second World War. After the First World War, the Peninsula had fallen into a steep and long-lasting depression because of the dramatic drop in military spending that occurred during the 1920s and 1930s. In order to avoid a repetition of that history, committee members worked to expand the Peninsula's economic base beyond the defense industry. Between 1945 and 1960, the PIC successfully attracted a number of new businesses to Newport News, including Union Carbide and the Tidewater Garment Company. As a result, the Peninsula became much less dependent upon the ups and downs of military budgets.[10] The lack of a college, however, remained a significant liability.

In early 1958, King Meehan was a deputy commissioner on the PIC. Already troubled by the Peninsula's lack of a college, Meehan learned that spring that Norfolk leaders were lobbying members of the General Assembly for a new four-year state college in their city, even though a branch college of William and Mary, the Norfolk Division, already existed there. Meehan further discovered that the Norfolk Junior Chamber of Commerce was funding a federal study to examine the idea, and it planned to present the government report to the state legislature.[11] As a result, Meehan contacted John Scozzari and requested that they meet for lunch. As the pair discussed Meehan's memo at their meeting, he explained that the Peninsula had grown significantly since 1945, but business and civic leaders worried about sustaining this growth into the future. Not only were additional industries needed, but the PIC also wanted to entice "a comparatively high class of employees" to the area, "from semi-skilled mechanical up through highly skilled technical and scientific personnel." And one of the most "important criteria"

---

[10] Quarstein and Rouse, *Newport News: A Centennial History*, 148–50.
[11] Elsie Meehan Duval, "The Man that I Married," photocopied unnumbered scrapbook about King Meehan. Ms. Duval was Meehan's wife until his death in 1977.

businesses and workers use to evaluate a potential relocation site was its "education system." Although elementary and secondary schools figured into the mix, Meehan and the Peninsula Industrial Committee found that a "greater interest is shown in the facilities available for higher education."[12] Even though there were colleges located *near* the Peninsula, they were currently bulging with students and were difficult to reach given the region's inadequate road system; therefore, Meehan sought President Chandler's help to create a new college—not in Norfolk—but on the Peninsula. As promised, Scozzari passed the proposal to Chandler, who read it over that summer. In September, the William and Mary president picked up the telephone and called Meehan. The two men agreed that "it would be appropriate at this time to make a survey of the educational needs" of the Peninsula, "particularly insofar as the relationship of education to the cultural, industrial, and commercial needs of this area are concerned."[13]

After their conversation, Meehan formally surveyed Peninsula business leaders in order to build an even stronger case for a local college. He asked particularly about the educational challenges workers who wished to pursue additional training confronted. The answers Meehan received were helpful: almost all the leaders he contacted explained that the lack of a college or university made attracting and keeping talented and ambitious workers very difficult. Henry J.E. Reid, Director of the NASA research facility at Langley, for instance, wrote that the lab had tried to work with the University of Virginia and Virginia Polytechnic Institute to arrange for essential technological classes needed by his workers, but this proved impossible due to the "usual residency requirements" of both universities. Reid, therefore, suggested that any future plans for the Peninsula include a new branch college of an "existing higher educational institution...."[14]

Meehan then wrote to William McFarlane, the acting director of the State Council of Higher Education in Virginia (SCHEV), to urge that an "educational survey of the Tidewater area" be conducted. McFarlane

---

[12] King Meehan, "A Proposal for an Expanded Educational Program on the Virginia Peninsula," 15 May 1958, University Archives.

[13] Alvin "Duke" Chandler to King Meehan, 10 September 1958, University Archives.

[14] Henry J.E. Reid to King Meehan, 26 September 1958, University Archives.

agreed that a "disinterested evaluation" was certainly necessary given the "complex structure of the Tidewater community." Meehan also sought support from Dr. S.V. Martorana, a high-ranking official with the US Office of Education. In his letter, Meehan described the Peninsula as an industrialized area filled with businesses that required "highly skilled and technical personnel." However, because many of these workers periodically needed additional higher education courses to upgrade their skills, the lack of a local college was "our greatest handicap." Indeed, many businesses that sought a skilled labor force simply avoided the Peninsula instead "prefer[ing] to locate in a university neighborhood." Martorana responded that his office was already preparing a study of the educational needs of the Hampton Roads area, due primarily to the earlier request from the Norfolk Junior Chamber of Commerce.[15]

The federal official's response set off alarm bells within the PIC. Recognizing that Norfolk leaders were "driving hard for a [new] four-year college," commission members worried that their rivals across the water would get federal support for a new institution. Thus, some response had to be crafted. One commissioner, Louis Purdey, suggested that "a committee [be] set up" to make the strongest case possible to state and federal officials for a Peninsula college. But it could not just be any group of concerned citizens. Rather, it had to "be a real top-level committee," meaning a very select group of powerful local leaders. Purdey circulated the names possible members, but at the top of his list was Lewis A. McMurran, Jr.[16]

Everyone in Hampton Roads in the late 1950s recognized Lewis McMurran's name. Not only was he one of the most important citizens of Newport News, but he was also one of the most powerful members of the Virginia House of Delegates. Born in 1914, McMurran belonged to an old Virginia family that traced its lineage back to the famous Randolph clan. Because of his family's heritage, McMurran possessed a deep love of history—he had even purchased a mid-eighteenth century house called Tazewell Manor located in Williamsburg, which he then moved to

---

[15] King Meehan to William McFarlane, 2 February 1959, and King Meehan to Dr. S. V. Martorana, 15 April 1959, University Archives.
[16] Louis C. Purdey to J.C. Biggins, 12 June 1959, University Archives and "CNC Awaiting Decision," *Time-Herald*, 27 December 1967.

Newport News and had rebuilt along the banks of the James River. McMurran also owned the Colonial State Bank that had financed a great deal of the Peninsula's post-World War II development. Sometimes called "Lord Lewis" because of his formal and courtly behavior, he possessed an enormous sense of civic duty. In 1946, for instance, McMurran had helped to organize a six-day Golden Jubilee festival celebrating Newport News' establishment as an independent city a half-century before. Eleven years later, he led the enormously successful celebrations surrounding the 350th anniversary of the founding of Jamestown. In 1948, McMurran won election to the House of Delegates, where he quickly established himself as a legislative leader because of his wisdom, moderate temperament, and gentlemanly behavior toward all.[17]

Given McMurran's prominence in both Hampton Roads and Richmond, the chairman of the PIC, J.C. Biggins, invited him on 30 June 1959 to join the "top level committee" they were forming. He informed McMurran that Norfolk was "already quite a bit ahead of us," and, therefore, Peninsula leaders would have to act quickly. Two days later McMurran accepted.[18] McMurran later explained that he had multiple motives in joining the committee: he certainly realized that the Peninsula needed a college, but he also wanted to protect his beloved College of William and Mary. In short, McMurran believed that a new college on the lower Peninsula would essentially "free Williamsburg from being overrun by Newport News students." Indeed, if growing numbers of such students came to dominate the old college's student body, it would "damage...what William and Mary had developed into" (that is, it being one of the nation's premier public liberal arts universities).[19]

---

[17] Quarstein and Rouse, *Newport News: A Centennial History*, 146; Jane Carter Webb, ed., *Voices: An Essay in Photographs, Poems and Stories In Celebration of Christopher Newport College's Twenty-Fifth Year* (Newport News, Virginia: The Sailing Association Press, 1986), 15. On McMurran's purchase of Tazewell Manor, see Jon Kukla, *Mr. Jefferson's Women* (New York: Knopf, 2008).

[18] William H Bowditch and J.C. Biggins to Lewis McMurran, 30 June 1959, and Lewis McMurran to J.C. Biggins, 2 July 1959, University Archives.

[19] Lewis A. McMurran, interview with Jane Carter Webb, 15 November 1985, transcript, University Archives.

On 2 September 1959, members of the group met for the first time and called themselves the Peninsula Committee for Higher Education. They named Lewis McMurran as their "Permanent Chairman" and discussed the educational situation throughout Hampton Roads. All agreed there existed "an urgent need for developing study opportunities" for Peninsula residents. If the state established a school, however, it must not be a traditional four-year residential college. Indeed, they acknowledged the growing "national trend" to set up "branch or junior colleges at principal population centers."[20] Such a school, they believed, would perfectly suit the Hampton-Newport News region where many potential students worked full-time but frequently needed to augment their professional skills and training. A college on the Peninsula, moreover, could be started quickly if the city of Newport News made an "existing school building" available to serve as a "temporary" location while a "permanent site" was found and developed.[21]

When the federal study on education in the Tidewater was publicly released in December 1959, McMurran's committee had strongly influenced its final conclusions. In fact, McMurran himself later admitted, "we manipulated the report so that it recommended the establishment of Christopher Newport."[22] At its outset, the report stated, "programs [of higher education] should not be developed on more than one campus [in the same municipality] unless justified." Thus, because a college already existed in Norfolk, a new institution there was not recommended. On the other hand, the needs of the Peninsula—referred to as "North Hampton Roads" in the study—were clear and manifest. In fact, the report stressed that the Peninsula's projected population growth of "persons between 18 and 21" would likely triple between 1959 and 1973. Therefore, the US Office of Education strongly recommended a "2 year college" be established in the Hampton-Newport News area, one

---

[20] On this trend, see Thelin, *History of Higher Education*, 299–300.

[21] Peninsula Committee for Higher Education, Minutes of Meeting, 2 September 1959, University Archives.

[22] Lewis A. McMurran, interview with Jane Carter Webb, 15 November 1985.

that would "offer a comprehensive program of general studies and organized occupational curriculums."[23]

Armed with the federal government's recommendation, local leaders and area legislators immediately set to work to make the new school happen. In mid-January 1960, the Newport News City Council voted that, if a new junior college were established, it could use the John W. Daniel Elementary School as a temporary location until a permanent campus could be selected and buildings constructed. Council members, moreover, approved an initial grant of $25,000 to begin repairs to offices and classrooms. One councilman, J. Fred Christie, explained to the Newport News morning paper, the *Daily Press*, "If we're going to continue to grow industrially and economically, we have to have this two-year college." This was, he added, "a golden opportunity." Council members were so enthusiastic that Christie even predicted that any new junior college in Newport News certainly "will grow into a four-year college in a very few years."[24] Lewis McMurran, meanwhile, went to work in the General Assembly in Richmond. Not only did the state delegate point out the positive recommendations contained in the federal study and Newport News' commitment to loan the Daniel School to a new junior college, but he also reached out to state delegates in Petersburg. Petersburg leaders themselves had long wanted a junior college established in their city in order to serve its growing population. In order to gain political support among delegates from central Virginia, McMurran sponsored legislation to create *two* new junior colleges—one in Petersburg and one on the Peninsula—both of which would be "divisions" of the Colleges of William and Mary. On 3 March 1960, the General Assembly passed McMurran's bill unaltered and sent it to Governor J. Lindsay Almond, Jr., who signed it.[25] Hence, a college located on the Peninsula—albeit one yet without a name—was born.

---

[23] William H. McFarlane, "Observations Concerning Post-High School Education Needs in the North Hampton Roads Area," 18 November 1959, University Archives. These notes were made by McFarlane, the director of the State Council of Higher Education, after having previewed an advanced copy of the federal study.

[24] "Council Okays Elementary School as Location for 2-Year College," *Daily Press*, 19 January 1960.

[25] *Acts of Assembly, 1959/60* (Richmond, 1960), 190; Webb, *Voices*, 2.

Building a School from Scratch

On 4 July 1960, William and Mary's Dean of Admissions and Student Aid, H. Westcott Cunningham, sat working in his office. Although a holiday, President Chandler had wanted someone present from the admissions staff in case a potential student dropped by or called with a question. At three o'clock, Chandler himself called Cunningham and asked to see him right away in his office. "I'd like to ask you if you'd consider something," he told Cunningham when the latter arrived. Although Cunningham had heard about the General Assembly's creation of two new junior colleges the previous spring, he had not given the news much additional thought, but Chandler's request that afternoon changed everything. He asked Cunningham to take on the job of director of one of the colleges—and Chandler wanted an answer in three days.[26]

In 1960, H. Westcott "Scotty" Cunningham was only thirty-eight years old, but he had had a wealth of experience that prepared him to lead a new school. Born in 1922 in Elizabethtown, New Jersey, he attended William and Mary before World War II and fell in love with Tidewater Virginia. When the war came, he served in the Pacific theater as the skipper of a Navy PT boat. Patrolling the waters of New Guinea and the Philippines, Cunningham's wartime exploits provided him with a keen understanding of people and essential leadership skills. Not only did he gain the habit of command, but he also learned how to solve problems quickly and to deal effectively with different types of individuals. After the war, Cunningham returned to William and Mary so that his wife, Cecil Cary, could finish her studies. In the meantime, he took a temporary job as an assistant on the college's admissions staff. Enjoying both the work and the Tidewater area, Cunningham remained at the college after his wife completed her bachelor's degree. Called back into the Navy during the Korean conflict, he served as a military briefer to the Secretary of the Navy in Washington, DC. When that war ended, Cunningham returned to Williamsburg and became the college's Dean of

---

[26] H. Westcott Cunningham, "Christopher Newport College: A Look Backward ... and Ahead," *Daily Press*, 16 June 1963; H. Westcott Cunningham interview with Jane Carter Webb, 28 April 1986, transcript, University Archives.

Admissions and Student Aid.[27] President Alvin Chandler, himself a Navy man, came to trust and respect Cunningham's talents and thought him perfectly suited to create a college from scratch. Chandler, moreover, rightly sensed that Cunningham was ready for a new challenge after seven years as Dean of Admissions.[28]

Traveling to both Petersburg and Newport News before making his decision, Cunningham saw that Petersburg had significant advantages. The location for the future junior college—eventually called Richard Bland College—had already been selected, and there were existing buildings on the site that could be converted into academic offices and classrooms. At Newport News, on the other hand, "there was nothing," as Cunningham himself later confessed. "Not a blade of grass, not a paperclip, not an inkling of a piece of property." But after visiting with city leaders, he said, "I liked the looks of what I saw ... in terms of potential growth and the vigor of the community." Moreover, "the promise of support" from local leaders seemed genuine, especially with their pledge to loan and rehab the Daniel School. Finally, the Newport News college would be located near the James River, and Cunningham (as a Navy man) could not resist the water. Thus, on 7 July, Cunningham informed Chandler that he would lead the Peninsula college.[29]

In September 1960, shortly after the William and Mary Board of Visitors officially named Cunningham the college's director, he got to work. The task before him was daunting. Scheduled to open in twelve months, there was no school to speak of other than the director himself, and Cunningham still had to perform his responsibilities as William and Mary's Dean of Admissions. The first person he hired to help him was Nancy Ramseur, who served as the college's first registrar. Together they wrote the school's initial catalog and, after the first director of Richard Bland College backed out of the job, Cunningham and Ramseur wrote the catalog for that school as well. Cunningham and Ramseur were soon joined by business manager Tom Dunaway. With their offices located on William and Mary's campus, Cunningham and his tiny staff began

---

[27] "Temporary Job after Wartime Duty Results in Directorship of Peninsula's Junior College," *Daily Press*, 9 September 1962.

[28] Cunningham, interview with Webb, 28 April 1986; James Windsor, interview with Phillip Hamilton, 7 June 2007, University Archives.

[29] Cunningham, interview with Webb, 28 April 1986.

soliciting applications for faculty positions. To solicit these applications, Cunningham had called college administrators throughout the state asking if they knew of instructors who might want to relocate and teach in the Tidewater. Twelve applications arrived on his desk and eight were eventually hired.[30] Among the faculty members that first year was twenty-three-year-old L. Barron "Barry" Wood. Originally from the Peninsula, he had just completed a master's degree in English from the University of Pennsylvania. In the spring of 1961, however, he already had job offers from Clemson and Ohio University. But after sitting down with Cunningham and discussing the possibility of teaching at a brand new college, Wood found himself intrigued and accepted.[31]

In addition to the faculty, Cunningham and Ramseur had to process incoming student applications. Expecting an initial class of approximately two hundred, applications slowly arrived during the spring and summer of 1961. Because only freshmen courses were to be taught that first academic year, only recent high school graduates were accepted. Cunningham wanted these first CNC students to possess three things. They should: 1) have an academic record of "superior achievement;" 2) be involved in "extra-curricular activity" beyond the classroom; and 3) show evidence of "good moral character."[32] The first student accepted was a 1960 graduate of Warwick High School named James Cornette. Although admitted to the College of William and Mary for the fall 1960 term, Cornette decided to wait a year once he learned about the new junior college. A piano player of talent and ability, Cornette earned money giving piano lessons to neighborhood children. Thinking that he might want to go to a music conservatory instead of a traditional liberal arts school, he decided to apply to CNC in order to take his general education courses. As a result, Cornette wrote Cunningham in September 1960 asking if his William and Mary application could simply be transferred over to the college in Newport News. Cunningham

---

[30] Cunningham, interview with Webb, 28 April 1986; Windsor, interview with Hamilton, 7 June 2007.

[31] Barry Wood communication to Phillip Hamilton, 15 March 2008, University Archives.

[32] Christopher Newport College Catalog, vol. 1, no. 1, 1961–62, 17–18.

replied several days later, "Sure, easy as pie ... you're admitted."[33] Although Cornette was the first student admitted, Cunningham realized he would not be the last. There is an approaching "tidal wave of college-age students" in the Hampton Roads area he told the *Daily Press* the following year. In the spring of 1961, more than 2,400 students had graduated from local high schools, many of them anxious to pursue college or university work. Thus, while the size of the first-year class would be modest, Director Cunningham knew that many more local students would follow in the steps of that first class.[34]

Before the faculty could occupy their offices and students could enter their classrooms, though, the John W. Daniel School had to be completely overhauled. Built in 1899, the cavernous four-story structure was located in the downtown area on Washington Avenue between Thirty-first and Thirty-second streets. The Newport News Public School system had abandoned the building several years before because of age and due to population shifts northward. Strongly committed to making the new junior college a success, however, Mayor O.J. Brittingham and the city council had already pledged to Cunningham the use of the school for five years. They also increased the city's financial commitment for renovations to $125,000.[35] It was only when Cunningham first entered the building, however, that he realized the magnitude of the restoration job ahead of him. After getting the key from the main school office, he and his wife went down to have a look:

> I opened the door and walked in. Well, of course, it was a typical old, old school, with ceilings that looked to me to be forty feet high, and I suspect they were at least thirty feet high, huge central corridor, rooms with wooden floors, great state of disrepair, plaster hanging from the walls, lighting fixtures askew. I walked into a classroom right across the hall, and it had an old, pockmarked green blackboard in it. Scribbled

---

[33] James Cornette, interview with Phillip Hamilton, 25 September 2007, University Archives.

[34] "$1,941,170 Request Presented Almond, Budget Advisers To Begin Construction of Christopher Newport College," *Daily Press*, 15 August 1961; see also "College Accepts 47 Pupils," *Daily Press*, 12 April 1961.

[35] Cunningham, "Christopher Newport College: A Look Backward ... and Ahead," *Daily Press*, 16 June 1963; on the closing of the Daniels Elementary School, see "Peninsula Begins Push for Community College," *Times-Herald*, 19 January 1960.

across the board in yellow chalk was, THEY OUGHT TO BURN THIS PLACE.[36]

Cunningham immediately solicited bids from local contractors to perform repairs, but they came in far higher than the funds the city had provided. Therefore, in order to bring costs down, Cunningham himself drew up plans to fix the classrooms, set-up laboratories, and repair faculty and administrative offices. Hiring the local construction firm of W.M. Jordan Company to actually perform the work, he refurbished and equipped the school for less than $120,000.[37]

Starting the college's library proved to be an equally difficult assignment. Having no books to start with, Cunningham called librarians at William and Mary, Old Dominion College, and the Richmond Professional Institute (later Virginia Commonwealth University) asking for any books which they had in duplicate or no longer needed. As a result, several hundred volumes came in. Creative accounting on Cunningham's part also helped start the library's collection. When he discovered that he had $4,000 left in his rehab budget, he immediately thought about the library's needs, but the money provided by the city was only to be spent on construction and furniture. Cunningham concluded, however, that books were most certainly "furniture in a college" and so he spent the remaining funds on books.[38]

At the time Cunningham formally assumed the job as director in September 1960, the school had been given the name Christopher Newport College, after the seventeenth-century English mariner. Christopher Newport (1561–1617) is today best known to historians for having commanded the three-ship fleet that founded the Jamestown colony in 1607. Though overshadowed by the more colorful John Smith, Newport was one of the most accomplished sailors of his age and he possessed an extraordinary knowledge of the waters of the New World. In fact, he had already crossed the Atlantic Ocean thirteen times before he took command of the Jamestown expedition. During the summer of 1960, Cunningham, President Chandler, and Lewis McMurran probably discussed possible names for the college together, although it is unclear

---

[36] Cunningham, interview with Webb, 28 April 1986.
[37] Cunningham, interview with Webb, 28 April 1986.
[38] Cunningham, interview with Webb, 28 April 1986.

who initially suggested Christopher Newport. Once the name was put forth, however, all three men agreed it was a perfect choice. Both McMurran and Cunningham were lovers of history, while Chandler and Cunningham were both former Navy veterans. Thus, they enthusiastically put the name forward and, by September 1960, the name Christopher Newport College was official.[39]

During the summer of 1961, as student desks arrived, and in-between trips to Richmond to testify before educational and budget committees in the General Assembly, Cunningham drafted Christopher Newport's initial "Statement of Purpose." He explained that the United States had "undergone one of the largest population explosions" in its history. As a result, there was a "desperate need" for affordable "[higher] educational opportunities of an academic and terminal nature." Hence, the General Assembly had created Christopher Newport College. This college was to serve the "higher educational needs of the Lower Peninsula" by offering two years of high quality instruction to Virginia's future "doctors, lawyers, engineers, teachers, scientists, and business executives." Once provided with a solid academic foundation, these students would then be able to successfully complete their undergraduate studies elsewhere. The college, moreover, would help the Peninsula meet its "critical" need for personnel "in the technological and semi-professional scientific and engineering fields." Thus, Cunningham expected CNC to produce "certified specialists" in a wide variety of job categories, including chemistry, mathematics, and contracting. Finally, the director pointed out that CNC had the potential to become "the cultural apex" of the Peninsula, and, under his leadership, he pledged that the school would make "every effort" to provide programs of "notable speakers, fine music, and stimulating art exhibits." Above all, Cunningham stressed, "Quality has to be a watchword" at CNC.[40]

---

[39] For more information about how the name Christopher Newport was selected, see Cunningham, interview with Webb, 28 April 1986, and Lewis A. McMurran, interview with Webb, 15 November 1985.

[40] Christopher Newport College of the Colleges of William and Mary, Statement of Purposes and Programs, July 1961, University Archives. The last statement about "quality" is from "'New Guard' of Colleges Said Arising," Daily Press, undated article, most likely 1962 or 1963.

"A College is Born:" The First Academic Class (1961–63)

On 16 September 1961, the Newport News *Daily Press* ran the headline "Newport College Registers First Class Smoothly." The reporter explained how 155 students had the previous day registered for the semester with classes set to begin on Monday, September 18. Cunningham pointed out that the day "was ideal from the standpoint that everything had worked out exactly as planned." The director, however, likely did not use the word "ideal" to describe his experiences two days *before* registration when state inspectors had combed through the Daniel School to check the building's just-completed overhaul. Begun the previous April, the rehabilitation had turned the near-dilapidated structure into four floors of workable college-space. The basement held the college library of four hundred books (although there was space for up to three thousand volumes) and a reading room; the first floor included administrative offices as well as several classrooms; on the second floor, there were two laboratories for science classes, a conference room, additional classrooms, and several offices for the faculty; the third floor held the building's four-hundred-seat auditorium along with six lecture halls. While the building lacked air conditioning, when its large windows were opened, cooling breezes from the James River wafted through the rooms. Finally, the old school playground located in back of the building had been bulldozed and paved over in order to create additional parking spaces.[41]

Although Cunningham had thought he was "way ahead of the game" in getting things set, the state's electrical inspector came up to him after going through the building. "I'm sorry," he told the director, but there were "a lot of problems" and "I don't think we're going to allow you to open this place." Aghast that a year's work was about to go "down the drain," Cunningham cried, "WHY?" The inspector said, "Well, I just don't think the power you have coming into this building

[41] "Newport College Registers First Class Smoothly," *Daily Press*, 16 September 1961; "Building Pleases Dean," *Daily Press*, September 1961; "CNC Awaiting Decision," *Times Herald*, 27 December 1967; Wood communication to Hamilton, 15 March 2008; Cornette interview with Hamilton, 25 September 2007; Timothy Coddington, "The Creation of a Lower Peninsula Institute of Higher Education," unpublished undergraduate research paper, "Researching CNU" history seminar, Spring 2008, University Archives.

can handle the load that this building can generate." Cunningham took the man to another room so that they could talk alone and tried to explain that different college activities—such as classes, laboratory work, office tasks, etc.—did not all take place simultaneously, but occurred at different times of the day; thus, the building would never draw its full electrical capacity at one time. The inspector seemed dubious, but finally agreed. When he left, however, he warned, "Whatever you do, Mr. Cunningham, don't turn all the lights on in this building at the same time."[42]

Because of Cunningham's persuasiveness, registration proceeded and went smoothly. Of the 155 students who signed up for classes (eventually this number rose to 179 due to late registrations), 60 percent were male and most were from Hampton and Newport News, although several students were from Smithfield, Matthews, and York County.[43] The curriculum they took was basic and straightforward—courses in the core liberal arts disciplines, including biology, chemistry, English, history, mathematics, and modern languages. Vocational courses, ironically, were not offered that first academic year. Because of limited funds and the corresponding expense of such courses, Cunningham decided to delay their implementation. Thus, although the college's first catalog stated, "it is the purpose of Christopher Newport College to afford certain opportunities for training of a terminal nature," it added that "it is anticipated that ... vocational courses will be offered in future years."[44] Few such courses, however, ever materialized. This was, in part, because of ongoing concerns about expense, but also due to the fact that Cunningham himself seemed determined to keep the college rooted in the liberal arts. When later asked by the *Daily Press* what the overarching goal of CNC should be, Cunningham replied without hesitation, "Quality education." In fact, he stressed, "most of our students plan to go on to further studies." Therefore, instead of focusing

---

[42] "'Captain' Steers Steady Course," *Times Herald*, 7 June 1968; Cunningham, interview with Webb, 28 April 1986.

[43] "Newport College Registers First Class Smoothly," *Daily Press,* 16 September 1961. See also Cunningham, "Christopher Newport College: A Look Backward ... and Ahead," *Daily Press*, 16 June 1963.

[44] Christopher Newport College Catalog, vol. 1, no. 1, 1961–62.

on terminal programs, CNC "must see that [students] are prepared for the four-year colleges."[45]

On 18 September 1961, classes at Christopher Newport College began. Cunningham later recalled that when the bell rang that first morning, "chills" went "up and down my spine and all I could think of was, 'A college is born.'"[46] In the fall of 1961, public-survey polls revealed that most college students across America pursued higher education basically for three reasons: in order to "get ahead," to find a spouse, and/or they viewed college simply as a rite of passage into adulthood.[47] But CNC's first student body was different. Many students felt as if a fortunate opportunity had landed in their laps and they wanted to make the most of it. James Cornette remembered an intense sense of camaraderie among those first students. "We knew that this was something special that came to us—very beneficial, very unexpected, and we wanted to succeed."[48] On the first day of classes, however, he and other students learned that they were going to have to work hard in order "to succeed" because the college's eight instructors had collectively decided that high-quality teaching and rigorous academic standards were essential if the college was to get off on the right foot. Not only would these things establish important precedents, but they were important also because so little else about the Daniel School resembled a real college. One faculty member realized, "This game [i.e., teaching in a once-abandoned elementary school] won't work unless you play at your top." Moreover, without a library to speak of and with little equipment for classrooms, only serious, first-rate instruction could make the new college successful.[49]

Christopher Newport's history and government professor, Robert Usry, was especially important toward this end. In 1961, Usry was, at fifty-five, the oldest member of the faculty, with teaching being his

---

[45] "Temporary Job after Wartime Duty Results in Directorship of Peninsula's Junior College," *Daily Press*, 9 September 1962; see also Webb, *Voices*, 3.

[46] Cunningham, interview with Jane C. Webb, 28 April 1986.

[47] Thelin, *History of Higher Education*, 254–56.

[48] Cornette, interview with Hamilton, 25 September 2007, University Archives.

[49] Wood communication to Hamilton, March 2008. On the limited equipment available to instructors, see Shirley Fields Cooper interview with Phillip Hamilton, 8 January 2008.

second career. A successful businessman and owner of the Madison Craft Shop in Williamsburg, Usry decided in the late 1950s that he wanted to teach history. Therefore, he enrolled at William and Mary and earned a master's degree. While at the college, he got to know Scotty Cunningham, who was impressed by Usry's formidable demeanor and intelligence. Soon after he became CNC's director, Cunningham contacted Usry and asked him to join the faculty. Tall, grey-haired, and craggily faced, Usry daunted and intimidated those first year students who entered his classroom. Always well-prepared with organized, insightful, and intellectually challenging lectures, Usry let his students know in no uncertain terms that this was not a high-school class. Although he insisted on high academic standards, Usry also helped to establish CNC's reputation for possessing a caring faculty. Within weeks of the semester's beginning, Usry informed several of his struggling pupils that he would tutor them outside of class until they mastered the material to his satisfaction. In short, if they put forth the effort, he would help them to succeed.[50]

Another crucial instructor that first academic year was Barry Wood. At twenty-three he was the college's youngest faculty member, and his youth and energy deeply influenced many students. James Cornette, for example, later said that Wood changed his life that first year. Although Cornette had initially planned on a music career, he was dazzled by Wood's English literature class—indeed, Wood "was electric in class" and, as Cornette remembered:

> [Wood] never read from prepared notes, as far as we could tell. He would pursue ideas with a great deal of imagination and wit and play acting and role-playing in his presentations.... And the power of his words ... [revealed to us] the richest understanding of what literature is— an expression of the culture and the longings of humanity. He made that come alive in ways I had never seen before. I think that the turning point for me was the class that I took with him, the survey of English literature, especially the survey of English Romanticism, which is where I spent

---

[50] Cornette, interview with Hamilton, 25 September 2007; "Heart Attack Fatal to Robert M. Usry," *Daily Press*, 15 January 1971. For more information about Robert Usry and the History Department, see David Porter, "Changes in Latitudes, Changes in Attitudes: The Globalization and Expansion of the CNU History Department, 1960–2008," unpublished undergraduate research paper, Fall 2008, University Archives.

most of my energy as a [graduate] student later.... I mean Blake, Keats, Shelly, Wordsworth, and Coleridge. He brought them alive in ways I couldn't imagine possible.[51]

The college's three science professors—Graham Pillow (physics), Georgia Hunter (biology), and Jane Byrn (chemistry)—in many respects had the greatest challenge as teachers that first year. Because lab equipment was in such short supply, experiments had to be few and basic. As a result, these instructors were forced to be especially creative in how they conveyed information and scientific principles. Both Pillow and Hunter, for instance, designed multiple group projects and hands-on activities for students. These exercises not only taught key concepts, but, as one student later put it, they "kept these classes interesting." Despite the fact that experiments were minimal, the courses were rigorous (or "so hard" as this same student recalled).[52]

Instructors' grade books during that first year—and, indeed, in subsequent years in the 1960s—also reflected the college's academic rigor. Many professors recorded numerous F's and even more early withdrawals once students realized the amount of work their classes required. Some instructors also taught "life lessons" to their students— even to their best students. James Cornette received one grade of B during his two years at Christopher Newport, given to him by Robert Usry in a history class. When the pair discussed the grade, Usry frankly admitted that Cornette really deserved an A. But he told the young man, "I didn't want you to get the wrong impression.... Sometimes people are going to be unfair to you and this is an object lesson in unfairness." He finished by explaining that while "straight A's are wonderful, ... it is what goes into the production of the grades that is really important."[53] The difficulty of the academic work was further reflected in CNC's student retention. Although enrollment at the college rose from 179 to 210 in the spring of 1962, only 72 of these students returned for their second year of classes in the following fall semester. Most of the non-returning students left either because they realized that college in

---

[51] Cornette, interview with Hamilton, 25 September 2007.

[52] Cooper, interview with Hamilton, 8 January 2008.

[53] Wood communication to Hamilton, 15 March 2008; Cornette, interview with Hamilton, 25 September 2007.

general was not right for them or they transferred to institutions with less stringent academic standards. Despite the fact that CNC's early retention rate was weak, Cunningham told his instructors to continue demanding the best. He insisted that high quality instruction was the only way students would later succeed at four-year institutions, and it was paramount for the college's long-term success that it be viewed as a serious school with a substantive academic program.[54]

Despite the high attrition rate, the returning Christopher Newport students were serious and took their studies very seriously. Even their daily dress habits reflected an earnestness toward their class work. CNC students of the early 1960s typically wanted "to look sharp," as one of them later put it. Hence, they dressed for class as if going to work: many men wore jackets and ties while females dressed professionally in skirts and blouses. No one yet wore denim jeans to school. When many of these same students later transferred to four-year institutions, such as William and Mary and Old Dominion College, they saw a much more casual dress code in place. Therefore, a number of them became convinced that they had acted like "a bunch of eggheads" or the "original geek squad" while at CNC.[55]

Although academically serious, early CNC students also tried to create an active student life. In some respects, this was initially easier than it would be later on. Because all Christopher Newport students that first year were recent high school graduates from the Hampton Roads area, many knew one another before attending the college. Moreover, like many of their professors, they understood that their actions were establishing long-lasting precedents. One of the first things they did toward this end was to convince Director Cunningham to give them some space in the Daniel School basement near the library to serve as a student lounge. After Cunningham agreed, a number of students came in one weekend with paint and brushes in order to put up curtains and paint the walls. Soon afterward they opened and operated a small snack

---

[54] "Newport College Enrollment Tops States' 2-Year Units," *Daily Press*, 15 September 1962.

[55] Cornette, interview with Hamilton, 25 September 2007; Cooper, interview with Hamilton, 8 January 2008.

bar so that students could get candy bars, chips, or sodas between classes.[56]

Several student clubs and extracurricular organizations also began during the first academic year, including a German club, a bowling team, and a chapter of Circle K, the collegiate service organization associated with the Kiwanis. The latter group performed service projects aimed at helping the needy in Newport News and Hampton. Several students started a newspaper called *Chris's Crier* (it would later take the name *The Captain's Log*). Printed on several mimeographed sheets of paper, it kept students informed about school news and activities. Finally, the students wanted to establish a student government and they elected a special committee to draw up a constitution. After contacting student government associations at other Virginia colleges asking for advice, the committee drafted a plan that the student body as a whole then approved. Afterwards, the students elected James Cornette as the first president of CNC's Student Government Association (SGA). As head of SGA, Cornette and other officers met regularly with Scotty Cunningham to discuss such issues as parking, student fees, and possible campus speakers and activities.[57]

As the first academic year came to a close, everyone felt a great deal of satisfaction. A large number of students had worked hard and, although most would not be returning, many had succeeded in their studies. They had formed friendships and had begun student organizations that would have a lasting impact on the college. Cunningham and his staff were also proud in the spring of 1962. Running a college in the Daniel School had proved a challenge, but they had made it work. For instance, CNC's two janitors—a man and woman both named Odell—had somehow kept the enormous building clean; in particular, the custodians had struggled with how to deal with the old coal furnace in the basement. Although the furnace itself was no longer in use, built-up coal dust periodically blew out of the heating ducts. Thus, on many mornings, faculty and administrators could actually write their names on their desks in the dust that had accumulated

---

[56] Cornette, interview with Hamilton, 25 September 2007.
[57] Cornette, interview with Hamilton, 25 September 2007. Editions of *Chris's Crier* are located in the University Archives.

overnight. But students and staff remembered that "He Odell" and "She Odell", as they were called by business manager Tom Dunaway, always kept the rooms clean and generally helped things to run smoothly. As business manager, Dunaway had also kept things running smoothly. Always armed with a ledger and pencil, he could tell Cunningham where every penny spent had gone. Members of the faculty were justifiably proud as well. They had successfully begun a new college in a nineteenth-century school and had established what proved to be a lasting tradition of tough and demanding academic standards combined with caring, creative, and innovative teaching.[58]

The future looked promising. Enrollment numbers certainly demonstrated the need for the college—not only did enrollment grow 18 percent from the fall of 1961 to the spring of 1962 (from 179 to 210 students), but many individuals were also clamoring for summer classes. After discussing the possibility with local educators and community leaders, Cunningham offered a summer session of classes for both current Christopher Newport students and college students who lived in the area but attended other institutions during the regular academic year. More than two hundred students enrolled in the classes offered that first summer.[59] Another move Cunningham made was to establish an evening college for the fall 1962 term. An evening college had been planned from the start and was created in order to better serve nontraditional-aged students who worked during the day, but who wished or needed to enhance their academic credentials. During registration that September, 519 students signed up for classes. Nancy Ramseur told the *Daily Press* that 329 students had registered for day classes, while the other 190 had enrolled in the evening school. Thus, only one year after opening, Cunningham announced that Christopher

---

[58] Webb, *Voices*, 16; James Windsor communication to Hamilton, 15 May 2007, and Windsor, interview with Hamilton, 7 June 2007.

[59] "CNC Enrolls 225 Students for Summer," *Daily Press*, 15 June 1962. The number 225 is likely low. The text of this article stated that school officials expect "about 350 to 400 students" to enroll.

Newport had become the largest two-year, state-supported college in Virginia.[60]

To serve this larger and more diverse student body in 1962 and 1963, Cunningham hired ten new faculty members to join the eight returning "veterans." Among the new teachers was 30-year-old James Windsor, a Korean War veteran and William and Mary graduate. Like many already on the staff, Windsor had known Cunningham before Christopher Newport had opened.[61] Not only had Cunningham admitted Windsor to William and Mary when the former was Dean of Admissions, but Windsor had also worked part-time as a lifeguard at the Williamsburg Country Club to which Cunningham and his family belonged. Thus, the two men had gotten to know and like one another. Furthermore, Cunningham thought Windsor's talents and personality would fit in perfectly at the new school. During the summer of 1960, the pair had a chance meeting at William and Mary's campus center. As Cunningham later recalled, Windsor told him:

> ...that he was completing a graduate degree and that he would be so occupied for a year but that he would like to come to Christopher Newport in its second year, and I practically told him on the spot that he was going to be hired and that he would be the dean of students.... He was getting a degree in pastoral psychology, he had leadership experience in the military, he was a very genuine and sincere person, and he was also a person I thought had ambition and somebody who might be after my job some day.[62]

When Christopher Newport began its second year, Windsor taught several psychology courses as well as ran the college's new counseling center designed to help guide students through their academic studies— something clearly needed given the first-year retention rate. All of the professors, though, continued to emphasize high standards and creative teaching. One new student that year was Shirley Fields, who lived in the

---

[60] "Newport College Enrollment Tops States' 2-Year Units," *Daily Press*, September 1962. See also "Six Instructors Nominated for Newport College Staff," *Daily Press*, 20 March 1962.

[61] "Six Instructors Nominated for Newport College Staff," *Daily Press*, 20 March 1962; Windsor interview with Hamilton, 7 June 2007.

[62] Cunningham, interview with Webb, 28 April 1986. On Windsor's work as a lifeguard, see Windsor interview with Hamilton, 7 June 2007.

Buckroe section of Hampton. Fields decided to come to CNC both because of its low tuition of $300 per semester and its nearby location. Thus, she could take a city bus every day from her home to the downtown campus. Like students from the previous year, though, Fields found the work to be much more difficult than she had first imagined. The quality of the teaching, however, had an enormous impact on her. Both James Windsor and Robert Vargas, the college's mathematics professor, were "very tough" but "delightful" instructors. Although she did not initially like English, Barry Wood made her literature class "so exciting" that Fields actually began reading Shakespeare's plays on her own. Fields and other students continued to be dazzled by Wood's class lectures. When discussing John Milton's *Paradise Lost* in one of the fourth-floor classrooms, for instance, Wood vividly played the part of Satan. Toward the end of class, he suddenly ran to a large open window and threw himself out. Horrified and shocked, students gasped and screamed, at which point Wood popped his head up, revealing that he had only leapt onto the fire escape.[63]

When the second academic year ended, the SGA organized a large school dance at the Hampton Country Club in order to celebrate their successes. SGA even hired the well-known Al Katz Jazz Orchestra to play. Several weeks later, in June 1963, students received their associate degrees in a ceremony led by Director Cunningham. Although some students had vaguely hoped that third- and fourth-year classes might be offered for the coming fall term, most realized that their time at CNC had come to an end. In his remarks to this first class, Cunningham thanked them all for "laying the foundation" for high academic standards and achievement at the college, and he wished them well in their future endeavors.[64]

Several days later, the director wrote a column for the *Daily Press* entitled, "Christopher Newport College: A Look Backward … and Ahead." Cunningham pointed out that the staff, faculty, and students had all made a wonderful start for the new college. Indeed, there was

---

[63] Cooper, interview with Hamilton, 8 January 2008; James Cornette, lecture/discussion to History Class "Researching CNU," 4 February 2008.

[64] Cornette, lecture/discussion to History Class "Researching CNU," 4 February 2008.

much praise to go around. The college's eighteen full-time faculty as well as its sixteen part-time members had done a superb job educating students in the classroom and in supporting them in "the first stirrings of an extracurricular program" of clubs and service organizations. Cunningham also praised those students who were moving on. He noted that sixty CNC students had been accepted at four-year institutions, including class president James Cornette who had been accepted (again) by the College of William and Mary. Finally, the director thanked both the City of Newport News and the General Assembly for their support for the college. He pointed out that the state legislature had to date appropriated $400,000 to CNC for equipment purchases and capital construction projects and had voted $56,000 for new books for the library. As a result, CNC's library had grown from a collection of four hundred books to ten thousand volumes by the spring of 1963. The city had also responded "enthusiastically to the first call for assistance." Not only had the city donated the Daniel School and funds for conversion to the college, but it had also recently purchased land to the north upon which a new and permanent campus would be built. Thus, Cunningham looked backward with pride but he also looked ahead with confidence that even more successes lay in the future.[65]

The period of 1958–1963 was filled with remarkable accomplishments relating to Christopher Newport's establishment. Although born primarily because of national trends relating to the baby boom, the college never would have been created nor would it have succeeded without the strong and enthusiastic support of Peninsula political and business leaders. Lewis McMurran's support, in particular, was key. His political acumen combined with his formidable reputation gave the local community a powerful advocate in Richmond. And his advocacy not only led to the college's creation, but it also led to the General Assembly's strong financial support throughout its early years. H. Westcott Cunningham's leadership of CNC was also crucial to the college's short- and long-term successes. As director, he had a clear vision of creating a high-quality, two-year college that would focus on superior teaching and rigorous academic standards. Thus, Cunningham

---

[65] Cunningham, "Christopher Newport College: A Look Backward ... and Ahead," *Daily Press*, 16 June 1963.

made sure that he hired a faculty committed to teaching and student success. And, finally, the first CNC students were tremendously important. Recognizing the value of higher education and appreciating this new school, they took their studies seriously and many of them succeeded. Therefore, all looked forward to additional successes and expansion as the college began to create a permanent campus and a larger academic program.

2

A Changing College Amid Changing Times

H. Westcott (Scotty) Cunningham's task as Director of Christopher Newport in 1960 was to get the new college up and running. By the summer of 1963, he and his faculty had had two years of successes at the Daniel School in downtown Newport News. The initial class of students had successfully completed their associate degrees and many had moved on to four-year colleges. Christopher Newport College, moreover, had gained a reputation for academic rigor and caring instruction. Thus, Cunningham and his staff prepared for the next phases of the college's development: establishing a permanent campus, expanding the size and composition of its student body, and developing the academic curriculum in order to satisfy a broader constituency of students. Furthermore, Cunningham thought it essential for CNC's long-term success to become a four-year institution, which could serve the higher educational needs of the entire Peninsula community.

During CNC's growth throughout the 1960s, higher education institutions across the United States experienced extraordinary changes. Colleges and universities greatly expanded in terms of size and mission. Moreover, students born of the baby boom reached out—sometimes forcefully—for a greater voice in politics, culture, and education, and Christopher Newport's development during the years 1963 to 1971 mirrors this larger pattern. Although CNC experienced neither dramatic unrest nor violence, its administrators, faculty, and students were keenly aware of the political and social upheavals taking place elsewhere. CNC students wanted more say in their education as well as more control over their dress, manners, and lifestyles. Nevertheless, they were largely satisfied with Scotty Cunningham's leadership and their professors' instruction. Thus, they rarely protested events beyond the campus. They tended rather to focus pragmatically on completing their educations and moving forward onto their careers.

Cunningham's calm, deliberate, and focused stewardship proved particularly important to CNC's ongoing rise in the 1960s. His cool and unruffled management style reassured legislators in Richmond that the college was in good hands. His steady demeanor, moreover, provided students with reassurance in a period of rapid change. Indeed, Cunningham was determined to provide them with excellent teaching and meaningful classroom experiences, but he also wanted to establish the new school upon a firm, long-lasting foundation. Therefore, after the permanent campus opened in midtown Newport News in 1964, Cunningham carefully oversaw the expansion of the school's academic curriculum and meticulously supervised the growth of the faculty and student body. Most importantly, Cunningham adamantly believed that the new college needed to "step up" from a two-year to a four-year institution as soon as possible. He realized that only bachelor degree-granting status would ensure ongoing support from the local community as well as adequate funding from state leaders in the capital. Consequently, Cunningham's tenure in these years proved to be momentous to the school's long-term health—and not just in the 1960s, but for decades to come.

The Shoe Lane Controversy: 1961–63

In 1960, when the Newport News City Council offered Christopher Newport College the use of the Daniel School, everyone knew the arrangement would only be temporary. Therefore, even before the school opened in downtown, Newport News, CNC, and William and Mary officials all began discussing where the college's permanent campus should be located. Several factors were paramount in everyone's mind. First, because CNC was a commuter school, the site had to be near the newly constructed I-64 Interstate Highway. Second, city bus service had to be available for both students and staff. Third, because the future campus needed to be accessible to students from throughout the

Peninsula, officials wanted the campus in the midtown area of Newport News.[1]

By early 1961, they had picked several sites for consideration. The first one was in an area known as Oyster Point upon a surplus piece of federal government property straddling the city boundaries between Newport News and Hampton. The second site was several miles to the southwest near the James River Bridge, and the third locale was situated north of the bridge, about half-way between downtown Newport News and Williamsburg on a plot of land along a street named Roy's Lane. The fourth and final location was a three-minute car ride south, near the intersection of Warwick Boulevard and Shoe Lane, directly adjacent to the exclusive James River Country Club and near Riverside Hospital, the city's main medical facility. Because the city planned to purchase the land and then deed it to the state, the seven-member City Council insisted that the new campus had to be located entirely in Newport News. This eliminated the Oyster Point site due to its shared boundary with Hampton. When college officials and city leaders considered the other locations at a planning meeting, Alvin Chandler spoke up. Chandler had recently left the presidency of William and Mary, after having been appointed by the General Assembly to a new position called the "Chancellor of the Tidewater Colleges of Virginia." It was a largely honorific position where he oversaw a newly created system of state institutions located east of Richmond, including Christopher Newport College.[2] Chandler urged city leaders to eliminate the location near the James River Bridge. He explained that when he was president of William and Mary in the 1950s, he had overseen the expansion of its Norfolk branch college then simply known as the Norfolk Division (today's Old Dominion University). Because the college was located in downtown Norfolk, Chandler had had a difficult time acquiring additional lands adjacent to campus. To avoid this headache with CNC, he urged the city to purchase as large and as open a plot of land as possible. Because the

---

[1] H. Westcott Cunningham interview with Jane Webb, 28 April 1986, University Archives, Christopher Newport University.

[2] This system of the Tidewater Colleges only lasted several years and was discarded by the state in 1962.

site near the bridge was smaller than the others under consideration, he
urged that it be abandoned. The city council readily agreed.[3]

Thus, city and college officials had narrowed their choices to the
two sixty-acre tracts along Warwick Boulevard, separated by roughly a
mile of roadway. The Roy's Lane plot had a great deal to recommend it.
It was open, undeveloped, and located at a high and dry elevation. There
were no natural boundaries or barriers to worry about, and future
buildings could easily be linked into the city's utilities and sewerage
system. Best of all, the Roy's Lane tract was relatively inexpensive,
valued at $121,000. The Shoe Lane site had several similar advantages: it
was open, relatively undeveloped, had no natural impediments that
might complicate future construction plans, and city utilities and
sewerage were available. Two factors, however, complicated the Shoe
Lane site. First, it was more expensive. The Newport News tax office had
collectively appraised its thirty-four separately owned parcels at
$235,000. Second, the properties belonged to the members of a small but
long-established African-American community. The owners' ancestors,
who were descendents of slaves, had obtained these lands starting in the
1880s, where they and their families had remained ever since.[4]

In early 1961, as Newport News and college officials continued their
private discussions, rumors started to spread throughout the Peninsula
that the city government was interested in the properties near Shoe Lane
as a possible location for the college. When members of the small black
community learned of the city's interest, they were immediately
suspicious of the city's motives. And they had every reason to be
suspicious. Racial tensions throughout Virginia had been high
throughout the 1950s and into the early 1960s. The difficult struggle over
public school integration, beginning with the Supreme Court's *Brown*
decision, had caused considerable discord in all regions of the state. The
Old Dominion's political establishment, moreover, led the fight to halt

---

[3] Cunningham interview with Webb, 28 April 1986; James Windsor interview with
Phillip Hamilton, 5 June 2007; Lewis McMurran interview with Jane Webb, 19
November 1985; Barry Wood communication to Phillip Hamilton, 15 March 2008.

[4] Minutes of Public Hearing and Special Meeting of the Council of the City of
Newport News, 29 May 1961; "City Council Set to Select Jr. College Site at Special
Meeting Scheduled for Today," *Daily Press*, 29 May 1961; Barry Wood interview with
Phillip Hamilton, 28 July 2008.

implementation of the high court's judgment. Adopting Senator Harry Byrd's strategy of blatant noncompliance, better known as "massive resistance," state leaders passed laws specifically designed to thwart the court and, in 1958, Governor Lindsay Almond seized and temporarily closed the public schools of Warren County, Charlottesville as well as six white schools in Norfolk after they had been ordered by federal courts to accept black students. The following year, moreover, local officials in Prince Edward County in central Virginia closed their entire public school system in order to avoid a federal court integration order, and the county's schools remained closed until 1964. Although Newport News leaders and the city's long-time school superintendent, R.O. Nelson, did not go to the extreme lengths of Prince Edward County, they supported efforts to block integration. Furthermore, local members of the General Assembly had backed many of the anti-integration statutes passed by the state legislature. Thus, by 1960, the year Christopher Newport College was created, not one public school in the city had been desegregated.[5]

The city's attempt to maintain the racial status quo was hardly surprising, as Newport News itself had had a long and deep history of racial division. Pulitzer Prize-winning author William Styron, who grew up in the Hilton section of Newport News in the 1930s, remembered the Peninsula as "a thoroughly and severely segregated society."[6] The Ku Klux Klan had a significant presence within the city during the 1920s and 30s—for example, three thousand people participated in a public Klan rally in 1924. Seven years later, the Klan organized an equally large

---

[5] On Harry Byrd's strategy of "massive resistance," see James W. Ely, Jr., *The Crisis of Conservative Virginia: The Byrd Organization and the Politics of Massive Resistance* (Knoxville: University of Tennessee Press, 1976); Peter Wallenstein, *Cradle of America: Four Centuries of Virginia History* (Lawrence: University Press of Kansas, 2007) 344–59; and Ronald L. Heinemann, John G. Kolp, Anthony S. Parent, Jr., and William G. Shade, *Old Dominion, New Commonwealth: A History of Virginia, 1607–2007* (Charlottesville: University of Virginia Press, 2007), 330–49. Also useful is Numan Barley, *The Rise of Massive Resistance* (Baton Rouge: Louisiana State University Press, 1969). On the closing of Norfolk public schools, see Thomas C. Parramore, Peter C. Stewart, and Tommy L. Bogger, *Norfolk: The First Four Centuries* (Charlottesville: University Press of Virginia, 1994), 362–76, and Mary C. Doyle, "From Desegregation to Resegregation: Public Schools in Norfolk, Virginia 1954–2002," *The Journal of African American History* 90, no. 1/2 (Winter, 2005): 64–83.

[6] John V. Quarstein and Parke S. Rouse, Jr., *Newport News: A Centennial History* (Newport News, Virginia: City of Newport News, 1996) 179–80.

march along Washington Avenue through the heart of the downtown commercial area.[7] Although the Klan's influence had declined by the 1950s, whites in general were determined to preserve this system of racial segregation.

Because of this past history, the Shoe Lane community naturally viewed the city's actions warily. One resident named William Walker, Jr., was particularly suspicious. Not only was he involved in local civil rights activities, but he was also a real estate agent and developer.[8] Having moved to the Shoe Lane area in the late 1950s, Walker soon thought that he could finance and construct a "quality subdivision" within Shoe Lane's largely undeveloped interior acreage specifically for middle-class black families who were leaving the city's downtown region. He particularly wished to build homes much like the open-style ranch structures going up throughout the neighboring Hidenwood and Riverside subdivisions. News about Walker's plan, however, began circulating throughout Newport News at approximately the same time Christopher Newport College began searching for its permanent campus. The idea of a densely settled African-American community in the heart of a largely white, upper-middle class section of the town—to say nothing of the fact that it would be directly next to the James River Country Club—unnerved some on the city council. Walker's involvement in civil rights activities must also have worried a city council generally committed to the racial status quo.[9]

In early 1961, therefore, soon after the city publicly expressed its interest in possibly acquiring the Shoe Lane tract, Walker and others in the Shoe Lane community responded. They formed the Morrison Property Owners Association in order to express their solidarity and

[7] Quarstein and Rouse, *Newport News: A Centennial History*, 120–21. On the general issue of the Klan's presence in urban areas in the early twentieth century, see Kenneth T. Jackson, ed., *The Ku Klux Klan in the City, 1915–1930* (New York: Oxford University Press, 1967).

[8] For more information about Walker, see "Targeted Thrift was a Source of Pride, But Sand Lost Money Seven Years in a Row," *Daily Press*, 14 February 1989; "Peaceful Changes—Newport News Native Helps to Create a Community Where Equality Becomes a Reality for All," *Daily Press*, 26 July 1990; "William R. Walker, Jr., 92, Dies," *Daily Press*, 28 February 2004.

[9] "City Council Set to Select Jr. College Site at Special Meet Scheduled for Today," *Daily Press*, 29 May 1961.

(above) Aerial shot of the Shoe Lane tract looking south, published in the *Daily Press* during the controversy (Courtesy of the *Daily Press*). (below) Christopher Newport Hall shortly after opening in the Fall 1964

Scotty Cunningham with Governor Mills Godwin. The governor addressed CNC students and faculty during campus dedication ceremonies in September 1965 (Courtesy of the *Daily Press*)

Students preparing for a dissection lab in Gosnold Hall in the mid-1960s

Student members of the "Dramatic Workshop" in 1965.

(above) Coach "Bev" Vaughan (far left) with the 1967-68 CNC basketball squad.
(below) Christopher Newport's campus in the late 1960s. This photograph was taken from Shoe Lane.

President Windsor (right) giving Wayne Martin Barry the first bachelor of science diploma awarded by Christopher Newport College in 1971.

speak with one voice, and they hired William Walker's younger brother, Philip Walker, and his law partner, W. Hale Thompson, to represent them before the city. William Walker also wrote to the William and Mary Board of Visitors pleading that its members not become "an accessory" to "a criminal land steal."[10]

On 29 May 1961, the city council met in order to give citizens an opportunity to voice their opinions and to make their final decision between Roy's Lane and Shoe Lane. One hundred-and-sixty people attended the meeting, with half of the attendees being black and the other half white, according to the newspapers. So many spectators showed up that extra folding chairs had to be brought in, yet still the overflow audience lined the back wall of the council chamber. Among those in the crowd were the Walker brothers, W. Hale Thompson, and other members of the Morrison Property Owners Association. Mayor Brittingham opened the meeting by welcoming the crowd and asking citizens to limit their remarks to five minutes. The mayor assured everyone, however, "the Council will listen to the views and comments of each."[11]

Philip Walker rose and spoke first. He stated that he and members of the Morrison Association certainly wanted what was "best for the city of Newport News" and, in his view, the Roy's Lane tract was clearly the better choice for all in the community. He pointed out that officials with the College of William and Mary had publicly stated that either of the two sites was acceptable to them. Unlike Shoe Lane, however, the Roy's Lane tract was not controversial. On the other hand, the Shoe Lane

---

[10] W.R. Walker, Jr. to the Board of Visitors of the College of William and Mary, 17 May 1961; Davis Young Paschall Papers, Swem Library Special Collections, The College of William and Mary. The Shoe Lane property owners called themselves the Morrison Association because, throughout the nineteenth century, this section of Warwick County was known as Morrison. In 1882, moreover, around the time African Americans first moved to the area, a predominantly black Baptist church was located on what would later become Warwick Boulevard. The church was known as the First Baptist Church Morrison, "First Baptist Church Morrison, History," (http://www.fbcmorrison. org/History/tabid/58/Default.aspx; accessed 18 March 2009).

[11] Minutes of Public Hearing and Special Meeting of the Council of the City of Newport News, 29 May 1961; "Council Votes 5–2 for Shoe Lane Location for Christopher Newport Junior College: 5-Man Group to Set Final Boundaries," *Daily Press*, 29 May 1961.

owners "have no intention of consummating a negotiated sale of their property" and "[s]ome have stated that they are prepared to carry any condemnation action through the highest appellate courts available to them." Finally, the projected differences in costs—$235,000 for Shoe Lane versus $121,000 for Roy's Lane—made the latter site the obvious choice. Before he sat down, Walker forthrightly addressed the racial issues involved. He explained to the council that, while many homes were available to "other groups" in midtown Newport News, "very few are available to the Negro population." Therefore, "[i]t has been the hope of many citizens that Shoe Lane could become just one area where we could buy and build homes."[12]

W. Hale Thompson took the floor next and continued with the theme of race. He began by stating that, if the issue was based on "reason," "there could not be any question" about which site was best— Roy's Lane. But , he added, "I believe this to be an emotional question of race." Indeed, "[t]his was in order to eliminate the possibility of negroes[sic] building homes in the area." Labeling the city's actions "a dangerous policy," he warned council members that African Americans in Newport News had to live somewhere. They were not about to leave the city "because we like it as you do." Therefore, "[i]f you keep us throttled, where will we go?" Answering his own question, Thompson said they would then have to buy homes in the surrounding all-white Hidenwood and Riverside neighborhoods. (The *Daily Press* reporter pointed out that this statement "could have been interpreted as a threat.") Finishing his remarks, Thompson concluded, "If race has nothing to do with it, what keeps you from buying the Roy's Lane site?"[13]

After several whites speakers voiced opinions both in support and opposition to the Shoe Lane tract purchase, a member of the council, Marvin Murchison, produced two typewritten pages. Before reading them, he announced that the council members had "weighed heavily" all the factors involved and "there is [sic] no racial thoughts in our minds." He then read a proposed resolution calling upon the city to purchase the

---

[12] Ibid.; "Shoe La. Property Selected as Site for New College," *Times-Herald*, 30 May 1961.
[13] Ibid.

Shoe Lane tract. Without any further debate or explanation, the council approved the measure by a 5–2 margin. As soon as it was over, Councilman J. Fred Christie (who had voted "nay") said, "You have seen democracy in action. The majority rules." Turning to the Walker brothers, W. Hale Thompson, and the other opponents of the Shoe Lane purchase, he added, "Bitter as this decision may be, I ask you to join hands with us now in our efforts to make Christopher Newport one of the best colleges in Virginia."[14]

The resolution passed that afternoon not only selected Shoe Lane, but it also created a five-man commission, including several council members and the city manager, J.C. Biggins, to oversee the purchase of the tract's thirty-four separate parcels of land. Although the city council hoped to move quickly, the process took nearly eighteen months to complete, in part because the Shoe Lane property owners—true to their word—adamantly refused to sell. Moreover, delays occurred because of the city's less-than-forthright dealings with the black community. In the summer of 1961, the commission outlined the specific boundaries they wished to buy, a process that expanded the tract's size to seventy acres. The commission then extended formal offers to the owners "based on real estate appraisals." However, likely in an effort to bring down the projected costs, the commission decided to use long-outdated appraisals. Throughout the spring of 1961, the council had publicly stated that it estimated the collective value of the Shoe Lane properties to be $235,000. Yet when the specific offers were made the commission used City of Warwick real estate assessments from the mid-1950s to set their prices. These appraisals collectively valued the properties at only $186,855. The council's efforts to undersell the community only made the owners dig in their heels even more firmly. At an October 1961 meeting, City Manager Biggins informed council members that none of the city's offers

---

[14] Minutes of Public Hearing and Special Meeting of the Council of the City of Newport News, 29 May 1961; "Council Votes 5–2 for Shoe Lane Location for Christopher Newport Junior College, *Daily Press*, 30 May 1961; "Shoe La. Property Selected as Site for New College," *Times-Herald*, 30 May 1961. As if to underscore the tense racial situation nationwide, the *Daily Press* on the day after the City Council meeting noted the trek of the Freedom Riders with the headline "Montgomery Witnesses Relate Police Apathy in Race Rioting." The *Times-Herald* headline on the same topic was "Beating of Jailed 'Freedom Rider' is being probed."

had been accepted. After learning of the collective value of these initial offers, City Attorney Harry Nachman spoke up and warned the full council about "the importance of having fair valuations on properties when bona-fide offers are made." Afterwards, the council decided to hire a professional appraiser named George C. Karam to independently assess the land's value.[15]

Throughout the late fall of 1961 Karam visited the Shoe Lane properties and drew up formal appraisals for all thirty-four plots. Upon completion of his assessments, he informed the city that his final numbers had come in at $363,930 or more than $177,000 above the previous buy-out price. Stunned at the figures, council members shelved the purchase for six months until new city council elections were completed in mid-1962.[16] On 25 June 1962, the council finally took up the Shoe Lane purchase again. The council meeting that day once more overflowed with citizens of both races, including the members and attorneys for the Morrison Association. After the proceedings opened, the council publicly revealed Karam's estimates for the first time and discussed their ramifications. Councilman Robert B. Smith expressed considerable skepticism about the figures, stating that $4,000 per acre was the "standard" price for land in midtown Newport News. A number of white citizens attending the meeting were also upset when they heard the figures. A local lawyer named Bryan Palmer referred back the initial $186,000 assessment, stating, "Let us not assume that because the first offers were refused that they are necessarily far from a 'fair price.'" He pointedly asked the council, moreover, if it was really prepared to accept the opinion of "one man [Karam] against that of the [City of Warwick] real estate board." Palmer finished by reminding the council that it "is

---

[15] City Council Resolution, 353, 29 May 1961; Minutes of Regular Meeting of the Council of the City of Newport News, 16 July 1962. The city council not only repeatedly used Karam's services, but it also occasionally thought his appraisals *too low*. In February 1962, for instance, Karam appraised a gas station near Huntington High School that the city was purchasing at $16,500. However, "after a careful survey" of the property, both the council and the city manager determined that $19,000 would actually be a "fair and equitable" price; Minutes of Regular Meeting of the Council of the City of Newport News, 12 February 1962.

[16] Minutes of Regular Meeting of the Council of the City of Newport News, 8 January 1962.

morally obligated to the citizens" to complete this purchase.[17] After Palmer sat down, Biggins "threw out for consideration" the idea that the city should conduct an entirely new appraisal. When William Walker heard this, he could no longer contain himself. He rose and, in an angry reference to Palmer's comment about "moral obligations," said the "underlying reasons for purchasing this site ... are not very moral at all." Speaking "vigorously," according to the city council minutes, Walker said the entire purchase was "purely a matter of race." Indeed, it was due to the "considerable bias against his people in the good neighborhoods." W. Hale Thompson immediately echoed Walker, arguing that the council's actions were obviously racially motivated and they were "driving the best minds out of the city." Furthermore, he claimed that three council members had privately admitted to him "there was no question but that race was involved." Although Thompson refused to name the council members publicly, he promised that he would in court, which is where he said his clients would next "fight the acquisition." After Thompson sat down, a clearly frustrated Councilman Smith proposed that the city manager "be authorized to employ one, two, or three appraisers as he sees fit" to reevaluate the properties' worth. By a four to one vote, the council approved.[18]

City Manager J.C. Biggins, therefore, ordered Newport News Chief Appraiser J. Harold Gray to conduct the new assessments. Gray and his staff immediately got to work and submitted their appraisals in August. The new figures came in at $290,555. At the city council meeting that month, Biggins pronounced them "the most realistic" and advised the council to move forward with offers. Although the council largely agreed with the manager's opinions about moving forward, the new mayor, Donald Hyatt, said he first wanted to speak with the William and Mary Board of Visitors, perhaps in order to give several new council members some political cover to deal with this now very contentious issue. He and

---

[17] Minutes of Regular Meeting of the Council of the City of Newport News, 25 June 1962; "Negroes Charge Race Issue Factor In Land Purchase For College: Council votes for reappraisal of 70-acre tract by 4-to-1 margin," *Daily Press*, 25 June 1962.

[18] Ibid.; "Biggins' Retirement Poses Big Task for New Council," *Times-Herald*, 26 June 1962. This was the last meeting for five councilmen who had not run for reelection. Five new councilmen, including the new mayor Donald Hyatt, officially took their seats on 1 July, 1962.

other members also likely wanted the college's formal imprimatur supporting the acquisition before the city formally seized the land.[19]

The meeting with William and Mary's board took place on Saturday morning, 15 September. During the session, Mayor Hyatt asked board members if any of them "may have changed your minds or opinions on the [Shoe Lane] site." William and Mary Chancellor "Duke" Chandler interjected into the discussion that he had considered the acquisition of Shoe Lane a matter long "settled." However, if the city did not take the properties, problems would follow. As another board member pointed out, William and Mary had already asked the state government for $456,000 to build Christopher Newport's first academic building. But its request had specified that construction would take place upon the Shoe Lane site. If that site fell through, however, the college would have to go back to the state in order to request a new financial authorization for construction at some other location. Because the Assembly would not be in session again until January 1964, seventeen months in the future, Chandler concluded, "This would complicate the thing tremendously."[20] When the city council members emerged from the meeting, they held a brief news conference in which they made three points to waiting reporters: one, they planned to move forward with the purchase; two, William and Mary's Board found the Shoe Lane property acceptable; and three and most importantly, if that specific site was not purchased, $456,000 in state funds already appropriated to Christopher Newport College for construction of its first building would have to be returned to the state unspent.[21]

When the council met two days later, on 17 September, Mayor Hyatt welcomed yet another "overflow audience" of close to two hundred citizens, including once more the lawyers and members of the Morrison Association. As soon as the Shoe Lane purchase was taken up, City Manager Biggins played what he thought was the city's trump card:

[19] Minutes of Regular Meeting of the Council of the City of Newport News, 13 August 1962; "Council Deadlocks 3–3 On Naming Redevelopment Authority Member," Daily Press, 14 August 1962.

[20] Minutes of the Board of Visitors of the College of William and Mary, 15 September 1962.

[21] "Shoe Lane Site for College Set for Council's Approval Monday," Daily Press, 16 September 1962.

if this particular site was not purchased quickly, it "would result in a two-year delay in [the] construction" of the college's first permanent building. The reason was that "the appropriation and authorization [to the college] ... had been made by the Legislature" solely on the basis of the college obtaining the Shoe Lane tract. As soon as Biggins made this point, W. Hale Thompson rose and scoffed at the city manager. He "was familiar with the Act which provided ... [CNC with] the money," he said, "and there was no reference as to the Shoe Lane Tract." Upon hearing this, Councilman Harry Atkinson spoke up and confessed that that "was true," but added that William and Mary itself had specified the Shoe Lane site when it had requested construction funds from the General Assembly. Thus, he concluded, "if there was a change in site they would have to go back to the legislature and tell them." As everyone in the room knew, the General Assembly was not scheduled again for seventeen months.[22]

Sitting in the audience, William Walker, Jr., saw the writing on the wall and decided to again speak out. He said that he fully realized that the "Council will carry out the commitment of the City" and take the Shoe Lane site. But, in his mind, this was "wrong" as it amounted "to the confiscation of the properties." He and others in his community, however, would just "have to live with this," because, he added (perhaps sarcastically), "this decision ... was reached in a democratic method." He then turned to the other bone of contention, the appraisals valuing the properties. He reminded council members that they had hired "the most qualified person" to provide a fair valuation of this land, George Karam. But his figures were "not accepted." Instead, the city turned to "the bat boy"—a disparaging reference to Chief Appraiser J. Harold Gray—who had conveniently provided the city with a much lower figure. Walker finished by once more asserting that the entire acquisition was "wrong" but said (again, perhaps sarcastically) that those in the Shoe Lane community "would have to be good sports." Afterwards the council took two roll call votes; the first motion stated that the city would purchase the properties on the basis of the Karam appraisal of $363,930. It was defeated by a 5–2 vote. The second motion

---

[22] Minutes of Regular Meeting of the Council of the City of Newport News, 17 September 1962.

called for acquiring the properties using Gray's lower figure. It passed by a 4–3 vote. Afterwards, the council ordered the city manager to immediately make new offers.[23]

Following the meeting, Biggins quickly sent out offers to the Shoe Lane property owners and, by the council's meeting one month later on 22 October, almost all of them had been turned down. Indeed, Biggins had only one acceptance in hand along with eighteen rejections. Therefore, he told the council that "in order to expedite the project, condemnation proceedings should be authorized" at once. Everyone had anticipated this request, and the motion passed unanimously with neither debate nor discussion. By the following spring, the Shoe Lane properties had indeed all been taken by the city and, in August 1963, the city formally deeded the land to the College of William and Mary.[24]

Building a Permanent Campus

Despite the controversy, the purchase made considerable sense for the college. The size of the site at seventy acres would allow the school's infrastructure to grow as its student body expanded. In the early 1960s, no one knew exactly how large CNC would became during its first decade of existence, but everyone realized that the number of high-school graduates in Hampton Roads was rapidly rising and that the state's four-year institutions would, consequently, remain under considerable enrollment pressure for many years to come. After CNC's first two successful academic years, moreover, college officials understood that its growth would likely continue as well. With these assumptions in mind, Cunningham and his staff developed a master

---

[23] Ibid. The closeness of the final vote was due to one councilman, B.E. Rhodes, voting "nay" because he insisted that the council itself ought to determine the value of each of the thirty-four parcels of land. The city council minutes reveal Rhodes was not in sympathy with the black residents at Shoe Lane.

[24] Minutes of Regular Meeting of the Council of the City of Newport News, 22 October 1962, 19 November 1962, 11 February 1963, *Daily Press*, 15 September 1963, A. Jane Chambers, Rita C. Hubbard, Lawrence Barron Wood, Jr., eds., *Memories of Christopher Newport College: The First Decade—1961–1971, In Words and Pictures* (Gloucester Point, Virginia: Hallmark Publishing Company, 2008), 16. In 1982, William Walker, Jr., was appointed by Governor Charles Robb to the Christopher Newport College Board of Visitors. Governor Gerald Baliles appointed Walker to a second term in 1986. He died in 2004 at the age of 92.

plan of eight buildings to be erected between 1964 and 1972. Five structures were planned for a first wave of construction between 1964 and 1968: 1) a humanities building, 2) a science hall, 3) a library with an attached wing for administrative offices, 4) a gymnasium (that would initially serve as a campus auditorium), and 5) a pre-professional and business studies hall. Cunningham then hoped to oversee the construction of the remaining three buildings between 1968 and 1972: 1) a campus center, 2) a pre-engineering hall, and 3) a technical institute building, which would allow the school to begin offering terminal vocational programs. The total cost for the eight buildings, he estimated, would be approximately nine million dollars.[25]

Cunningham proved remarkably successful at obtaining capital funds from the General Assembly for the first wave of campus building. When appearing at legislative committee hearings in Richmond, he was articulate, comfortable, and well prepared. Typically modest, Cunningham later claimed that anyone could have done what he did. "If you were willing to go to Richmond and do your homework," he explained, "[with regard to] statistics, population figures and so on, you would get money for buildings." But Cunningham was also not afraid to speak out publicly when politicians threatened his plans. For instance, when funds for the science building were eliminated by Governor Albertis Harrison in the 1964–66 biennium budget, Cunningham immediately called the Newport News *Times-Herald*. The governor, the director told the paper, had "badly mangled the capital outlay budget." That money must be restored if Christopher Newport was to remain "a forward-moving college." After hanging up the phone, Cunningham drove to Richmond and testified before both the House and Senate budget committees. With calm and forceful logic, Cunningham stated why CNC needed the science building and the funds were restored.[26]

[25] Christopher Newport College Capital Outlay Study, 15 September 1960, University Archives; Cunningham, "Christopher Newport College: A Look Backward ... and Ahead," *Daily Press*, 16 June 1963; "Newport College to Ask $3 Million Building Outlay," *Daily Press*, 9 December 1964; "CNC Awaiting Decision," *Times-Herald*, 27 December 1967.

[26] "CNC Director 'Lobbying' For Science Bldg," *Times-Herald*, 1 January 1964; "Newport College to Push for Science Building Fund" *Times-Herald*, 10 January 1964; "Christopher Newport's Claim," *Times-Herald*, 16 January 1964; "'Captain' Steers

Ongoing financial support from the city of Newport News, moreover, proved crucial for the development of the Shoe Lane campus. Cunningham later explained that the city possessed "exuberance" for the college during the 1960s. Indeed, he remembered that after each building appropriation from the General Assembly, he went to the mayor and city council asking "'Will you put in roadways for us?' 'Will you put in a parking lot here?' 'A parking lot there?' All of which they did!" he recalled in amazement. The city's contribution to the campus' infrastructure development totaled an additional $125,000.[27]

The first building constructed at Shoe Lane was Christopher Newport Hall, later renamed the Lewis A. McMurran, Jr. Hall. Cunningham planned for it to be the school's humanities building, but initially it would also house the library. CNC hired a local architect named Forrest Coile, Jr., to design the structure. Coile proposed an architectural style that he called "contemporary oriental," featuring unique, pagoda-like rooflines that hinted at Asian structures.[28] W.M. Jordan Company, the firm that had rehabilitated the Daniel School several years earlier, came in with the lowest bid of $320,000, and thus was awarded the contract in September 1963.[29] Breaking ground shortly afterwards, the company finished construction in time for the fall 1964 semester. The 24,000 square-foot building contained ten classrooms, including a 223-seat lecture hall, fourteen faculty and administrative offices as well as space for the library and a student lounge. In the two academic years that followed, Christopher Newport operated at *both* the Shoe Lane campus and the Daniel School, where science classes and labs continued to meet.[30]

Steady Course," *Times-Herald*, 7 June 1968; see also "Area Praised for Support Given College," *Daily Press*, 10 November 1964.

[27] "CNC Awaiting Decision," *Times-Herald*, 27 December 1967.

[28] Jane Carter Webb, ed., *Voices: An Essay in Photographs, Poems and Stories In Celebration of Christopher Newport College's Twenty-Fifth Year* (Newport News, Virginia: The Sailing Association Press, 1986), 4–5.

[29] "State to Award Final Area Contracts Today," *Daily Press*, 19 September 1963.

[30] The Christopher Newport College of William and Mary, Announcements, Sessions 1964–65, vol. 4, no. 1 (May 1964) 12. Christopher Newport Hall was formally dedicated on 11 September 1965 with Lieutenant Governor Mills Godwin praising CNC, saying that many students "could not have attended college if [this] college had not come to them," *Times-Herald*, 11 September 1965.

During these years, additional buildings on the master plan were constructed. After Christopher Newport Hall opened, Cunningham thought the science building should be next. Forrest Coile again designed the structure, and once more he proposed the "contemporary oriental" style. W.M. Jordan Company again won the contract with a bid of $617,000. When the 42,000 square-foot building opened in September 1966, courses in chemistry, physics, biology, and mathematics were taught in its ten classrooms and nine laboratories. Called simply the "science building" during construction, Cunningham decided prior to its completion to name the structure after Bartholomew Gosnold, one of Captain Christopher Newport's chief lieutenants in the Jamestown expedition. A noted explorer before Jamestown, Gosnold had discovered (and named) Cape Cod and Martha's Vineyard in 1602. Hired by the Virginia Company five years later, he commanded the *God Speed* and was Newport's second-in-command during the expedition. A popular leader among the settlers, Gosnold died only four months after landing in Virginia.[31]

By fall 1966, all Christopher Newport classes were held on the Shoe Lane campus, and the Daniel School was formally returned to the city of Newport News. Nevertheless, students still had to deal with construction on campus. Two additional buildings constructed that academic year were Ratcliffe Gymnasium and the John Smith Library, both of which opened in the fall of 1967. Ratcliffe Hall was named after another lieutenant of Christopher Newport, Captain John Ratcliffe (d. 1609), who had command of the ship *Discovery* and served as Jamestown's second governor. The gymnasium's opening allowed the college to establish a physical education department and to require all students to take four semester hours of physical education classes. The new facility also permitted the college to inaugurate intramural and intercollegiate sports programs. Thirty-three-thousand square feet in size, it included faculty offices, classrooms, and two gymnasiums, one large enough accommodate one thousand spectators for indoor athletic

---

[31] On the construction of Gosnold Hall, see "Newport College to Push for Science Building Fund," *Times-Herald*, 10 January 1964; "Enrollment At CNC up 30% to 436, *Daily Press*, 25 September 1964; "Newport College Science Building Contract Signed," *Daily Press*, 29 October 1964.

events.[32] The Captain John Smith Library opened that same semester. Named in honor of the Jamestown expedition's most famous member, the library's completion allowed the college's 19,000-volume collection to be moved out of the first floor of Christopher Newport Hall. Moreover, attached to the 32,000-square-foot building was a wing of administrative offices, into which Cunningham and other college administrators soon moved.[33]

Given his remarkable success in gaining state funds for CNC's first four buildings, Cunningham wanted to keep the momentum going. Therefore, as soon as Ratcliffe Gymnasium and the Smith Library opened, the director submitted a $1.25 million budget request to Governor Mills Godwin for two additional buildings: $425,000 for a pre-professional academic hall and $825,000 for a campus center that Cunningham hoped would encourage student-life activities.[34] The first signs of the financial crisis that would later rock the nation in the 1970s, however, were already starting to manifest with sudden reductions in state contributions to higher education. While Governor Godwin included the pre-professional building in his 1968–70 budget sent to the General Assembly, he rejected Cunningham's request for the campus center as too costly. Godwin would only authorize $34,000 to draw up architectural plans so that the campus center could be built at some unspecified future date. During the General Assembly's 1968 session, moreover, legislators made CNC's capital funds entirely contingent upon passage of an $81 million state bond initiative that was to go before voters in November 1968. Although the bond referendum eventually passed, Cunningham had to cope with new problems that emerged at the end of the decade. He found, for instance, that the college already

[32] The Christopher Newport College of William and Mary, Announcements, Sessions 1971–72, vol. 2, no. 1, 18; see also "Newport College To Submit Plans for Library-Administration Bldg," *Daily Press,* 7 July 1966; "Summer Bulletins at CNC," *Times-Herald,* 27 March 1968.

[33] CNC, Announcements, Sessions 1971–72, vol. 2, no. 1, 18. For more information about the building and opening of the Smith Library, see "CNC Gets Unexpected Okay to Plan Library, *Daily Press,* 14 April 1966; "Library-Administration Building Planning Gets Green Light at College," *Daily Press,* 31 May 1966.

[34] "CNC Fund Requests Due Today," *Daily Press,* 19 September 1967. See also "New Classroom Plans for CNC," *Daily Press,* 23 May 1967 and "CNC's Proposed Building Approved," *Times-Herald,* 10 June 1967.

needed to upgrade its relatively new existing buildings. Because of rapid growth in the summer school program, the college badly needed air-conditioning in Christopher Newport and Gosnold Halls. Furthermore, Cunningham had to deal with the growing impact of inflation on construction costs. In its 1970–72 biennium request, the college asked for an additional $98,000 simply to finish construction on the pre-professional building. The director again solicited state funds for a campus center, but inflation had driven up its base cost from $825,000 to $972,340. While CNC received $160,000 for the air-conditioning as well as money to complete the pre-professional building (that opened in 1970 as Wingfield Hall, named after Captain Maria Wingfield), the governor and General Assembly again rejected the campus center as unfeasible.[35]

In addition to Cunningham's growing difficulties over capital funds, residents in the neighborhoods surrounding Shoe Lane had started to complain about the construction activities, noise, and dust they had had to endure. Neighbors especially objected to the growing number of cars traveling along Shoe Lane. As a result, residents formed the Shoe Lane Area Civic League so that their voices could be heard. Although Cunningham occasionally spoke to the group in order to ease their concerns, its members requested that the city formally conduct a traffic study to see if the roadway infrastructure surrounding the campus could handle any additional buildings. Despite these problems, CNC's campus had, by the decade's end, made an impressive start. From a near-open plot of land in 1963, Christopher Newport possessed five functioning academic buildings by 1970, and the campus itself served more than 1,700 full- and part-time students. [36]

---

[35] "Local College to Get First Bond Funds," *Times-Herald*, 7 December 1968; "Christopher Newport College Enters Bid for $1.8 Million," *Daily Press*, 6 June 1969. For more information on the construction of Wingfield Hall, see "College Seeks Solid Spot," *Times-Herald*, 10 February 1969; "New Building Site Found by Newport, *Times-Herald*, 22 February 1969; "CNC Building is Approved by Governor, *Times-Herald*, 29 April 1969.

[36] "Cunningham Sees Four Year Newport College in Future," *Daily Press*, undated clipping, likely from 1964. Student figures from Office of Institutional Research, Christopher Newport University.

Building Upon Success – Academic Life in the 1960s

Ever since Christopher Newport College's inaugural semester with 171 students in fall 1961, its enrollment had grown at a strong and rapid pace. The biggest reason for CNC's growth remained first and foremost tied to the coming of age of the baby boomers and the ongoing overcrowding at all of Virginia's four-year colleges and universities. The Peninsula's population, moreover, continued to grow throughout this period, especially with an increasing number of military personnel assigned to regional bases. Most years, therefore, showed significant increases in class sizes. When Christopher Newport Hall opened in the fall of 1964, for example, day-college enrollment had jumped to 436, a gain of almost 30 percent over the previous academic year. The night college grew rapidly as well. That same fall semester, 330 students enrolled in evening classes—also a 30 percent annual rise.[37] During the next academic year of 1965–66, enrollment in both the day- and night-colleges grew by another 30 percent, with the total student population reaching 1,026 by year's end. Although enrollment numbers leveled off between 1966 and 1968, CNC students who attended during these years took significantly more classes on average than those CNC students who had enrolled in the early 1960s. As a result, the college's full-time equivalency numbers (FTE's) jumped dramatically. For instance, in 1965–66 when the school enrolled 1,026 students, its FTE stood at 535; two years later during the 1967–68 academic year, CNC's total head count remained virtually unchanged at 1,093, but its FTE had grown 25 percent to 666. Thus, as the end of the decade approached, Cunningham pointed out that CNC was "by far" the state's largest two-year educational institution.[38]

Through the 1960s, the Christopher Newport student body was a diverse one, with students differing considerably in age and ambitions. They attended the school, moreover, for a variety of reasons. With few exceptions, the day-college students tended to be traditional-aged young

---

[37] "297 Enter CNC Evening College, *Daily Press*, 16 September 1964; "Enrollment AT CNC Up 30% to 436," *Daily Press*, 25 September 1964; see also "Christopher Newport Sets Fall Term," *Daily Press*, 1 August 1963.

[38] "CNC's Enrollment Mirrors Growth of Virginia Colleges," *Times-Herald*, 16 July 1968. Enrollment numbers are from Office of Institutional Research, CNU.

A History of Christopher Newport University, 1958–2011   53

men and women who came to CNC for the same reasons the first
students had come in 1961: they liked Christopher Newport's location on
the Peninsula, its small size, and low tuition (that was $150 per semester
in 1965–66 and which, if adjusted for inflation, would equal $1,025 in
2011). As the decade progressed and as the times changed, new reasons
appeared. By 1965, students who wished to transfer to William and Mary
began saying that they liked CNC's "strong reputation" for solid
academics; furthermore, some male students attended Christopher
Newport as "a way to avoid the draft."[39] The night-college students, on
the other hand, were typically much older. Its students were generally 25
to 35 years old, and a few even older. Many had belonged to the military
and were taking several courses to enhance their job skills.
Consequently, only about half of these night students planned to go on
and complete their bachelor's degree.[40]

As CNC grew in size, its curriculum expanded. Class offerings were
generally limited from 1961 to 1963 and consisted largely of introductory
courses in the liberal arts. After Christopher Newport Hall opened,
Cunningham added a broader array of classes. Therefore, between 1964
and 1967, as additional instructors joined the faculty, new courses were
added to the catalog in disciplines such as biology, business, English, the
humanities, mathematics, modern languages, and philosophy. An ROTC
program offered in cooperation with William and Mary began in 1966.
Once Ratcliffe gym opened the following year, the college required
students to complete four semester hours (in four separate, one-hour
courses) in physical education, with classes offered in basketball,
wrestling, gymnastics, and bowling.[41]

As the college expanded its academic curriculum, Cunningham also
wanted to add new vocational programs designed to enhance the
professional skills of those students who did not necessarily want or
need to complete a bachelor's degree. In November 1964, he told the
Daily Press that, as a two-year college founded to serve the entire

[39] "Freshmen Are Pleased with College Choice," Captain's Log, 20 October 1965.
[40] "Evening College Enrollment Rises," Daily Press, 12 September 1964; and
"Enrollment At CNC Up 30% to 436," Daily Press, 25 September 1964.
[41] Christopher Newport College of William and Mary, Announcements, Session
1967–68, vol. 7, no. 1, 44–45; "Enrollments Upped by 400 Fresh Fosh," Captain's Log, 14
September 1965. In 1970–71, the four-hour requirement was dropped to two hours.

Peninsula, CNC had a responsibility to provide "the community [with] what is needed." Therefore, he wanted to offer certificate programs in office management, computer programming and operation, and executive secretarial work.[42] But neither Cunningham nor the faculty seemed especially anxious to implement such offerings. In fact, during the 1960s, only one truly vocational program was ever implemented—a "middle management program." Begun in 1968, the course of study was designed specifically to help students attain entry-level managerial positions with local retailing and wholesaling businesses.[43] The lack of a wide array of vocational programs had two general causes: First, because Cunningham always envisioned CNC as a four-year college, he concentrated mainly on the careful development of its academic program; in other words, vocational studies were clearly a secondary priority. Second, in 1966, Governor Mills Godwin and the General Assembly created the state's new community college system. As a result, thirty-three two-year colleges opened across Virginia in 1968, including one in Hampton. Therefore, Cunningham likely concluded that CNC did not need to be all things to all people upon the Peninsula, especially because vocational programs would be offered at the new community colleges, including the one on the other side of the Peninsula.[44]

As the college's curriculum expanded and came into sharper focus, its reputation for academic rigor grew stronger. When located at the Daniel School in the early '60s, CNC's dropout rates were high and its freshmen retention low. The reason, in part, was preparation. Many admitted students simply were not ready for college-level studies. But CNC instructors also demanded hard work from their students. These trends continued well into the 1960s. In the fall 1965, for instance, seventy-four of Christopher Newport's 435 day-college students were forced to withdraw because of inadequate academic performance. Furthermore, many students—even those who passed their first year's

---

[42] "Area Praised for Support Given College," *Daily Press*, 10 November 1964; see also "Bright Future for CNC Seen by Cunningham," *Daily Press*, 18 August 1964; and "Service Role of CNC Cited by Cunningham," *Daily Press*, 7 October 1964.

[43] "New Management Plan Slates September Debut," *Times-Herald*, 26 March 1968, and "CNC Plans Middle Management Program," *Times-Herald*, 2 May 1968.

[44] Windsor interview with Hamilton, 5 June 2007. On the creation of the Virginia community college system, see Wallenstein, *Cradle of America*, 376–77.

classes—transferred elsewhere because of CNC's academic difficulty. One sophomore admitted that many students left simply to "attend easier schools like Old Dominion." Nancy Ramseur told the *Daily Press* that many high school graduates had come to CNC under the mistaken impression that it was easy. "This is one reason we call it a two-year college and not a junior college."[45] Students who remained, however, generally appreciated the demands their professors made upon them. A student editorial in the *Captain's Log* in December 1965 noted with considerable satisfaction that CNC "is gaining in reputation in the community for being a difficult but enlightening institution." Students especially appreciated that those who completed two years at CNC had little trouble transferring to four-year colleges, including William and Mary.[46]

In additional to maintaining high academic standards, professors continued to provide undergraduates with close and caring instruction. Throughout the 1960s, many baby boomers across the nation bitterly complained about the large impersonal "multiversities" they attended. These were enormous state universities with tens of thousands of students, oversized classes, and uncaring administrators. Thus, many undergraduates said they felt treated "only as a number."[47] In contrast, Christopher Newport typically had small classes that allowed professors to provide students with much more attention than they would have received elsewhere.[48] Robert Usry, in particular, remained an important presence on campus in this regard. His formidable demeanor conveyed the seriousness with which the faculty hoped students would take their academic studies. In the classroom, moreover, Usry demanded excellence from all who were enrolled. But he genuinely liked and respected his students, once telling the *Captain's Log* that most of them appeared "eager to learn" and "enthusiastic" about their course work.[49]

---

[45] "Christopher Newport's Day Enrollment Totals 325," *Daily Press*, 3 February 1965; "CNC Is Anxious to See 'Grades,'" *Times-Herald*, 29 December 1967.

[46] "Toward Excellence," *Captain's Log*, 15 December 1965.

[47] Thelin, *History of American Higher Education*, 306–08.

[48] James Cornette interview with Phillip Hamilton, 25 September 2007.

[49] "Faculty Members Seen as Pleased with CNC's New Atmosphere, Students; Windsor Cites Need," *Captain's Log*, 17 November 1965.

Usry also worked hard with students outside the classroom. He served as faculty advisor to new student clubs, and he continued his practice of tutoring any student in need of help. On several occasions throughout his tenure, Usry even took students into his home near the Shoe Lane campus in order to help them complete their course work. One student named Patrick Garrow, lived at the professor's home for a year and a half, along with two other male students. Garrow had had a difficult home life, few resources, and even fewer career prospects other than working at the Newport News shipyard. His father had died while he was in high school, and his mother had remarried just as Garrow started at CNC. His mother's remarriage had turned Garrow's home into "a zoo," as he later recalled, and the young man found that he just "couldn't study there." Because of his unsettled home life, Garrow's first semester midterm grades were "miserable." He thought about dropping out of college to enter the workforce. But Usry talked to him about his home life, academic studies, and career ambitions. After hearing the young man's dilemma, the unmarried Usry invited Garrow to room at his house in the Hidenwood neighborhood next to campus. Along with two other CNC students, Garrow paid the professor monthly room and board, and there he found the quiet and the social structure he needed to succeed. Garrow later remembered that Usry "had no TV and the radio was older than he was. The entire entertainment was a pool table, and he limited you to two games a night." Garrow admitted, though, "He [Usry] is the reason I made it through CNC." The young man later attended the University of Georgia where he earned both a bachelor's and master's degree in anthropology, before becoming a full-time archeologist for the state of North Carolina.[50]

Cunningham himself recognized that a number of CNC students faced not only difficult home lives and situations, but that they were also putting themselves through college. Therefore, he sought to help. In the fall of 1966, the director created the Student Employment Service specifically to help Christopher Newport undergraduates find part-time

---

[50] Patrick Garrow interview with Jane Carter Webb, 19 November 1985, University Archives; see also Webb, *Voices,* 36–39. Since the mid-twentieth century, evidence points to more and more teachers having social interactions with their students, see Thelin, *History of American Higher Education,* 225–26.

jobs either on campus or with area businesses. The service quickly became a vital resource for students struggling to find income to pay for their educations. By the spring 1969 term, nearly two hundred students participated in the program. Thirty-five had found work on campus as library and laboratory aides, secretarial helpers, and as coaches of intramural sports teams. More than 150 other students were placed in jobs with local businesses.[51] Cunningham also actively worked with community leaders to establish tuition scholarships for talented and needy students. Indeed, he spoke to numerous civic groups about the needs of CNC students and urged local leaders to create scholarships to help young people complete their educations. By 1967, fourteen tuition scholarships had been established for both needy and meritorious students. The Civitan Club of Newport News, for example, established a scholarship paying $300 per academic year to a graduate of a Peninsula-area high school that was to be awarded "on the basis of character, need, and ability."[52]

As the school and its curriculum expanded, Cunningham greatly increased the size of the college's faculty. In 1963, CNC's instructional staff stood at seventeen full-time professors; by the fall of 1967, that number had grown to thirty-seven teachers.[53] Moreover, a growing number of part-time instructors were hired each year. From the start, Cunningham preferred to hire people through informal means. He wanted, above all, good teachers who could instruct students in a clear, interesting, and dynamic manner. For instance, he hired a communications professor named Rita Hubbard in 1965. A mother of four children and a stay-at-home mom, Hubbard had met Cunningham when both were volunteering for a local group called the National Conference of Christians and Jews. After Hubbard mentioned that she had earned a master's degree from Johns Hopkins University,

---

[51] Christopher Newport College of William and Mary, Announcements, Session 1967–68, vol. 7, no. 1, 51; "Collegians Can Earn Cash," *Times-Herald*, 19 April 1969.

[52] Christopher Newport College of William and Mary, Announcements, Session 1967–68, vol. 7, no. 1, 49–51. On Cunningham speaking before local groups, see Cunningham interview with Webb, 28 April 1986.

[53] Christopher Newport College of William and Mary, Announcements, Session 1967–68, vol. 3, no. 1, 11; Christopher Newport College of William and Mary, Announcements, Session 1967–68, vol. 7, no. 1, 15–17.

Cunningham explained how he constantly kept his eyes open for qualified instructors whom he believed would be a good fit for the college. "Before I knew it," Hubbard recalled, "I was on the telephone with the coordinator of the evening college." Hired after an on-campus interview, Hubbard taught in the evening-college for two years and then switched to CNC's day college in 1967.[54]

Although Cunningham paid close attention to building a strong faculty, not all professors were effective teachers. In 1965, the *Captain's Log* ran an article about the faculty's teaching techniques. While students rated most professors "well above average," there were several complaints. Students told the college paper that a few professors merely read the course textbook aloud during classes. Several other instructors spoke to students in such a stultifying manner that it seemed they were "lectur[ing] at the wall."[55] Although Cunningham tried to weed out weaker instructors, he also had to work hard to keep his most effective professors, especially those with doctorates in hand. In the early and mid-1960s, there was a nationwide shortage of qualified college and university professors. Therefore, many academics with PhDs found themselves receiving multiple job offers from prestigious institutions. This situation naturally made Cunningham's task of building a solid faculty at a two-year college in Newport News all the more difficult. Jean Scammon, for instance, joined the faculty in 1963 to teach courses in modern languages, and she proved a popular instructor. Holding a PhD from the University of Kansas, however, Scammon left after only one year for a tenure-track professorship at the University of Rhode Island. To retain good faculty, therefore, Cunningham tried to encourage loyalty to the institution. Toward this end, he and his wife, Cecil Cary Cunningham, frequently entertained faculty members in their Newport News house, and the director always made sure that the door to his office on campus was open to faculty who had concerns about matters in or out of the classroom.[56] Furthermore, Cunningham tried to provide

---

[54] "Peninsula Woman Combines Homemaking, Teaching Roles," *Daily Press*, 25 February 1968.

[55] "Survey Exposes Need for Student, Faculty Dialogue over Techniques," *Captain's Log*, 15 December 1965.

[56] Cunningham interview with Webb, 28 April 1986; Cecil Cary Cunningham interview with Phillip Hamilton, 12 January 2008.

opportunities to faculty for career advancement. Throughout the decade, for instance, he approved generous leaves-of-absences to instructors who wished to return to graduate school to earn their PhDs. Faculty who took advantage of this, however, sometimes never returned. Professors Fred Brewer of the biology department and Robert Vargas of Mathematics both received leaves of absences in 1964 in order to work on their terminal degrees. Neither instructor, though, ever returned to the college to teach.[57] Adding to Cunningham's difficulties was the fact that Christopher Newport's faculty were the lowest paid among Virginia's state-supported schools, receiving on average 16 percent less than instructors at other state colleges and universities.[58] Despite these problems, his efforts to ensure that the faculty overall was of a high caliber, loyal to the institution, and generally close-knitted paid off in terms of student satisfaction and success.

Campus Life at Shoe Lane

For the two years that CNC was located at the Daniel School, student life was centered in the small student lounge in the building's basement. After the college moved to the midtown Newport News campus, however, social activities and events quickly multiplied. Nonetheless, students found it difficult to construct a robust campus life at a commuter college. Those students who attended the evening college generally worked full time and often had families. Thus, they rarely took part in activities outside of class. Many young people at the day college, meanwhile, continued to socialize with friends from high school. Consequently, charges of "student apathy" filled many campus publications throughout the decade. Scottie Fitzgerald, the president of the Student Government Association in 1965–66, lamented that the college lacked spirit and, thus, she urged everyone to become more involved. "No one thinks much of a school," she lectured, "whose students aren't proud of it."[59] Four years later, charges of student apathy

---

[57] "College Adds 2 Professors to Its Faculty," *Daily Press*, 13 March 1963; "Board Approves Plans For Science Building At Newport College," *Daily Press*, 15 June 1964.

[58] "Christopher Newport Faculty, Salary Lowest In Virginia, Report Reveals," *Daily Press*, 7 January 1970.

[59] "Scottie Supports SGA," *Captain's Log*, 10 March 1965; see also "Student Participation a Must in College," *Captain's Log*, 28 October 1964.

continued, although the tone had become more pointed. "If you are one of these apathetic students who do not care for this college," a student editorialized in the *Captain's Log* in 1969, "then we feel sorry for you. If you do not have the time for a basketball game, a dance, or anything else planned by the student government, then maybe you won't have time for the society you will be entering. Think about it."[60]

Despite such charges, the range of student activities outside the classroom gradually expanded from 1963 to 1970. The Student Government Association attracted the most active and involved students, with their main focus on organizing social events both on and off campus. In the spring of 1965, for example, SGA put together the college's first "Activities Week," which included an all-campus showing of the movie "The Mouse That Roared," a swim party, and a dance—each on separate evenings. This event eventually evolved into CNC's Homecoming celebration as well as its annual Spring Festival.[61] Another annual event, which began in 1963, was the selection and crowning of "Miss Christopher Newport College." Elected by the students in December, the winner was officially announced and crowned every year at the college's Christmas Formal Dance. Miss CNC then usually took part the following spring in the "Miss Hampton Roads" contest.[62]

As SGA worked to create a more lively campus life, part-time English department instructor Frances Kitchin started the "Dramatic Workshop" club in 1965, which later evolved into the college's theater program. Seven students joined the organization in its first year, and they performed a pair of one-act historical plays written by Kitchin herself. One was entitled "Spring 1622," a drama that examined the seventeenth-century Powhatan Indian uprising against the English; the other play, entitled "Cold Harbor," was set in Civil War Virginia during the 1864 battles outside of Richmond. Pleased at the "tremendous

---

[60] "Are You Apathetic? Think About It," *Captain's Log,* 31 October 1969.

[61] "Scottie Supports SGA," *Captain's Log,* 10 March 1965.

[62] "Sheilah Cassidy Crowned Miss CNC," *Captain's Log,* 18 December 1963; "Frances Enters Pageant," *Captain's Log,* 10 March 1965; "Miss Whitaker Named Miss CNC," *Times-Herald,* 24 January 1969. Evelyn Whitaker was apparently the last Miss CNC. In 1969, amid changing times, CNC instead began electing a "Winter Queen," who was announced during homecoming activities annually held every February; on this change, see "Winter Queen," *Captain's Log,* 1 December 1969.

interest" in the club, Kitchin recruited additional students the following year. In 1965–66, they performed a holiday spoof called "A hillbilly Christmas Carol," followed by a spring performance of Archibald MacLeish's Pulitzer Prize-winning verse drama entitled "J.B." As a result of Kitchin's early efforts, student interest in the drama program continued at CNC throughout the rest of the decade and into the 1970s.[63]

Students also wrote and edited several campus publications. In 1964, for example, sophomore Shirley Fields oversaw twelve students in the production of the college's first yearbook called *The Trident*. Although they lacked a faculty advisor, the students wrote copy, gathered photographs, designed the layout, and secured advertisers. They also dedicated the yearbook to Director Cunningham for his "steadfast service" and "constant help" given to all CNC students.[64] In following years, after physics professor Graham Pillow agreed to serve as advisor, yearbook staffs produced larger and more heavily illustrated volumes. In January 1966, English students published the first edition of a literary magazine called *The Undertow*. Featuring short stories, poems, and essays written by CNC students, it continued to be published into the following decade.[65] The college's newspaper, the *Captain's Log*, began publication in 1963. With approximately twenty students on staff, they published a four-page edition every other week throughout most of the decade. The paper contained campus news, information on upcoming student programs, and columns/editorials about contemporary events (both within the community and across the nation).[66]

---

[63] "She's Successful in Two Roles—Artist, Director," *Daily Press*, 23 February 1965; "CNC Dramatic Club Presents Two One-Act Historic Plays," *Captain's Log*, 10 March 1965; *Trident* 1964–65, vol. 2, 32; *Trident*, 1965–66, vol. 3, 51.

[64] *Trident* 1963–64, vol. 1, 6, 52; Shirley Fields Cooper interview with Phillip Hamilton, 8 January 2008.

[65] "New Literary Magazine, 'Undertow,' Will Be Published by Student Body," *Captain's Log*, 20 October 1965; *Trident* 1965–66, vol. 3, 49. English professor, and later Dean of Faculty, Stephen Sanderlin served as the faculty advisor to the student editors.

[66] *Trident* 1964–65, vol. 2, 25. The *Captain's Log* ran from 1963–67. In 1967, however, its publication was suspended for two years, likely for financial reasons. In October 1969, the paper resumed publication, and it continues to be published to the present; see "CNC Prints First Edition of Newspaper," *Times-Herald*, 13 October 1969.

Student clubs formed a large part of campus life at CNC during the 1960s. In addition to the Bowling Club and Circle K (both of which had started at the Daniel School), a number of new organizations began after the Shoe Lane campus opened, including several religious clubs. The Christian Science Club and the Baptist Student Union, for instance, met regularly on campus throughout these years. Ecumenical by design, members frequently invited non-churchgoers as well as students of other denominations to their meetings and to participate in discussions. In 1967, several students began a chapter of the Newman Club, named after Catholic Cardinal and scholar, John Henry Newman. Students in the organization not only performed community service projects, such as providing free tutoring to local school children and sponsoring a toy drive every Christmas, but they also organized a number of campus-wide parties and dances open to all CNC students.[67] Chapters of both the Young Democrats and Young Republicans started on campus in the fall of 1964. During the election campaign of that year, each organization put up posters, held rallies, and "stimulat[ed] political awareness among students."[68] Circle K, the collegiate service organization associated with the Kiwanis, was probably the most active CNC club of the decade, especially in performing service projects to benefit both the community and the college. Its members, for instance, once organized an all-day trip to Williamsburg for a group of local boys from the Portsmouth Boys Home. Touring the colonial city's historic area, Circle K members afterwards brought the boys back to campus for a party. At the end of the day, each child received a gift donated by a local retailer. Circle K members also participated in various campus-service projects such as keeping the grounds clean as well as helping to pack and move the college's nineteen thousand books to the John Smith Library when it opened in the fall of 1967.[69]

---

[67] "Scottie Calls Attention to Some Organizations," *Captain's Log*, 28 April 1965; "Spotlight on Organizations: Newman Club," *Captain's Log*, 12 December 1969.

[68] *Trident* 1964–65, vol. 2, 30–31; "Scottie Calls Attention to Some Organizations," *Captain's Log*, 28 April 1965.

[69] "CNC's Circle K Assists on Numerous Projects," *Daily Press*, 30 May 1966; "Books More Books Ready For Transfer," *Times-Herald*, 25 November 1967; see also "Circle K Arranges to Public Weekly Announcement Sheet," *Captain's Log*, 23 March 1966.

Athletics became an important part of CNC student life during the 1960s. When the Shoe Lane campus opened in the fall of 1964, for instance, the Student Athletic Association was founded in order to oversee a college intramural program. The only sport that initial year was flag football. Every Sunday afternoon from mid-October to early December six teams played on the athletic fields of Ferguson High School, next door to the Shoe Lane campus. Advised by Dean of Students James Windsor and Professor Robert Usry, the intramural program grew steadily over the years until, by 1969, several hundred young men and women participated annually, both as players and coaches. The program also sponsored a variety of sports, including basketball, volleyball, softball, and gymnastics.[70]

The college also supported an intercollegiate sports program that, too, began during the first year at Shoe Lane. In the fall of 1964, freshman Ted McFalls started a petition calling upon Christopher Newport to establish a men's outdoor track team. After a number of students signed, mathematics professor Raoul Weinstein volunteered to serve as the team's coach. A delighted Scotty Cunningham agreed to financially support the effort. Practicing throughout the spring of 1965, the team's first track meet took place on April 3 when the men competed against the Frederick Military Academy and the Apprentice School from the Newport News Shipyard. Later that same month, SGA organized a campus vote to select a team name. From among such choices as "the Founders," "the Colonials," and "the Seafarers," students voted to call their team "the Captains."[71]

As the Ratcliffe gymnasium neared completion in 1967, students and some faculty lobbied administrators to support the creation of a basketball team. Although it promised to be more expensive than track, Cunningham supported the move. Thus, the team's creation was announced in March 1967, and shortly afterwards William and Mary assistant coach, Randall Beverley "Bev" Vaughan, Jr., was named to head

---

[70] "Linkous, SGA Secure Change in Dress Rules," *Captain's Log*, 27 April 1966; "Intramural Program in Full Swing," *Captain's Log*, 14 October 1969; *Trident*, 1964–65, vol. 2, 33; *Trident* 1967–68, vol. 5, 65.

[71] *Trident* 1967–68, vol. 4, 58; Student Government Association, Meeting Minutes, 9 April 1965, University Archives, Christopher Newport University; "Scottie Calls Attention to Some Organizations," *Captain's Log*, 28 April 1965.

CNC's basketball program. Vaughan's inaugural season in 1967–68, however, proved to be a difficult one, with the team achieving a record of 8–11. The season's highlight, though, came in December when the Captains' first victory ever came over George Mason College with the score 83–73. Vaughan would successfully coach the basketball team until 1981, compiling an impressive career record of 204–128. He also served serve until 1987 as CNC's first athletic director.[72]

The 1967–68 academic year also saw the start of female field hockey—CNC's first women's intercollegiate sport. Coached by Professor Lillian Seats, a physical education instructor, the team took to the field that year with nineteen players. While they occasionally competed against four-year colleges like William and Mary, the team consisted of only freshmen and sophomores. Thus, it mainly played local high school teams, such as Gloucester, Warwick, and Hampton Roads Academy. Two years later, in 1969, a women's intercollegiate basketball team started to compete. However, in this period before Congress' landmark Title IX legislation of 1972, most athletic activities at the college predominately focused on male students.[73]

"The Times Are a Changing:" Christopher Newport College and "the '60s"

The *Trident* in 1964–65 began with the lyrics of Bob Dylan's famous hit "The Times Are a Changing." The song, in part, had said:

> Come mothers and fathers
> Throughout the land
> And don't criticize

---

[72] "CNC Names Vaughan As Cage Coach," *Times-Herald*, 20 March 1967; "Captains Defeat George Mason College, 83-73, For First Win; Hipple Stars," *Daily Press*, 10 December 1967; see also Jeff Eckert, "A Brief History of CNU Basketball," unpublished undergraduate research paper, "Researching CNU" history seminar, Spring 2008, University Archives. In 1968, CNC also began an intercollegiate men's golf team; see "Chowan Golfers Crush CNC, 17–1," *Daily Press*, 23 April 1968.

[73] *Trident* 1967–68, vol. 4, 65; Holli Sawyer, "The History of Women's Athletics at Christopher Newport College/University," unpublished undergraduate research paper, "Researching CNU" history seminar, 4; Christopher Newport College of William and Mary, Announcements, Session 1969–70, vol. 9, no. 1, 10.

What you can't understand
Your sons and daughters
Are beyond your command.[74]

Dylan's ballad—soon regarded as the anthem of a rising generation—seemed an odd song to include in CNC's yearbook. Indeed, the college's students generally were more conservative and pragmatically focused on studies and career goals than their more affluent counterparts at the College of William and Mary and the University of Virginia. Nevertheless, the song's inclusion indicates that the times were, in fact, changing for CNC students as well as for many others throughout the nation. Although Christopher Newport's campus was largely free of protests and demonstrations throughout these years, students' lives were certainly changing, especially in terms of dress, attitudes, and viewpoints. As a result, the events that changed the nation so profoundly clearly influenced many aspects of life on the Shoe Lane campus.

The Vietnam War more than any other event of "the '60s," most directly affected and changed the lives of CNC students, especially its young men. The conflict's impact on campus life, however, was initially minimal. The *Captain's Log* did not even mention the war until October 1965, shortly after President Lyndon Johnson had escalated America's troop commitment in Southeast Asia. As a result of the president's order, many male students suddenly became concerned with the status of their student draft deferments. That October, several male freshmen openly admitted to the college paper that they had enrolled at CNC merely "as a way to avoid the draft." One of these was Michael Engs, the first African American to enroll at CNC. Engs attended not to break the color barrier—rather he took classes at CNC only after being rejected by twelve other colleges and having no other way to avoid military service.[75] The following year, several dozen male students took a

---

[74] *Trident* 1964–65, vol. 2, 1.
[75] "Freshmen Are Pleased with College Choice," *Captain's Log*, 20 October 1965. Concerning Michael Engs's attendance at CNC, see A. Jane Chambers, Rita C. Hubbard, Lawrence Barron Wood, Jr., eds., *Memories of Christopher Newport College: The First Decade—1961–1971, In Words and Pictures* (Gloucester Point, Virginia: Hallmark, 2008), 194–99.

voluntary student-deferment test administered across the nation as well as on CNC's campus. The students hoped that strong results would permit them to maintain their deferment status with local draft boards.[76] At this point in the war, though, students did not yet feel compelled to openly criticize or condemn American foreign policy. In fact, most campus news about the conflict involved philanthropic efforts by students to help soldiers stationed overseas. In 1966, for instance, Circle K organized a campus-wide blood drive, with all donations flown to Southeast Asia to save the lives of wounded American servicemen. That same year, moreover, the Student Government Association worked with local high schools to collect more than ten thousand paperback books for US soldiers across the Pacific.[77]

Several years later, after Vietnam had deeply divided the nation and the generations, CNC students were fully aware and informed of the political upheaval. Most of them, however, took a passive role in the growing student protest movement. For instance, when millions of other college students across the country took part in the "Vietnam Moratorium Day" on 15 October 1969 to call for the war's end, CNC students seemed unmoved. SGA President William McGlaun said he would participate if anyone else was interested. A few students eventually drove up to Williamsburg to take part in the demonstration on William and Mary's campus. The only CNC activity associated with the Moratorium was "a discussion on Vietnam" sponsored by the Newman Club.[78] In early 1970, as the war started to wind down, students' political passivity became even more pronounced. In February

---

[76] "Educators Doubt Tests," *Times-Herald*, 28 March 1966; "Restrained Sigh of Relief Basic Reaction to Deferment Testing," *Daily Press*, 15 May 1966.

[77] "Bloodmobile to Pay Campus Visit under Auspices of Circle K Club," *Captain's Log*, 23 February 1966; "Circle K Backs Blood Drive," *Times-Herald*, 2 March 1966; "College Students Aid Blood Drive," *Daily Press*, 5 March 1966; "Christopher Newport's Circle K Assists on Numerous Projects," *Daily Press*, 30 May 1966; "Books-Books-Books—All for Vietnam," *Daily Press*, 4 June 1966; "Books for Soldiers in Viet Nam," *Daily Press*, 12 September 1966. Interestingly, the campus blood drives sponsored by Circle K in 1967, 1969, and 1970 did not mention Vietnam. Perhaps the war had become too controversial by that point for the drive to be associated with an increasingly unpopular war.

[78] "CNC Unlikely to Take Part in Vietnam Moratorium Day," *Daily Press*, 15 October 1969; "Moratorium: It Ain't Easy," *Captain's Log*, 31 October 1969; "Spotlight on Organizations: Newman Club," *Captain's Log*, 12 December 1969.

of that year, two sophomores attempted to start a campus chapter of the Student POW-MIA Action Committee, but the attempt failed "due to a lack of student interest."[79] The killing of four Kent State University students by Ohio National Guardsmen in early May 1970 sparked concern, but again no protests. James Windsor, on the eve of taking over as the new head of the college, made note of this fact, telling a reporter from the *Daily Press*, "I think it's news worthy that the students here [at CNC] have been so restrained ... when campuses elsewhere have been experiencing extreme difficulties."[80]

The campus unrest movement of the 1960s involved many issues other than Southeast Asia. Students across the nation protested over free speech, governance at colleges and universities, and the rights of the poor in communities surrounding their campuses. As with Vietnam, CNC students again demonstrated a keen awareness about these larger issues but little inclination toward activism. Indeed, the only campus protest of the era came in late 1968 and involved the issue of students' dress habits. On November 21, approximately ninety female students organized and staged a "sit-in" on the second floor of the Smith Library. The protest concerned the college's dress code, which then specifically prohibited women from wearing slacks in the building. Although female students had been allowed to wear slacks to classes for several years, the dress code remained unchanged for the library and was enforced by the college librarian Bette Mosteller. Therefore, the ninety women—all dressed in slacks—entered the library, sat down, and refused to leave until their opinions were heard and a petition had been submitted to Dean James Windsor. Tipped off beforehand about the protest, Windsor fully realized that the dress code regulation was outdated and immediately ordered it rescinded. "A student's dress and general appearance is considered to be a matter of personal taste," he told the

---

[79] "'The World is Watching'—POW-MIA Action Committee," and "No Time to Spare? For Once in Your Life Give a Damn," *Captain's Log*, 20 March 1970.

[80] "Windsor New Acting CNC President" and "Crowd Remains Peaceful at Rally," *Daily Press*, 16 May 1970. CNC student Robert Clark did write a letter to the editor protesting not the Kent State killings, but the fact that, after the tragedy, Kent State's administration had closed the school for the remainder of the semester following the tragedy; see "Halt in Education An Added Tragedy," *Daily Press*, 8 May 1970.

Times-Herald. Thus, the paper afterwards ran the dramatic headline "Students Win at Library."[81]

Despite the library protest, several reasons existed for Christopher Newport's lack of student activism throughout "the '60s." As historian John Thelin recently pointed out, the scope of the 1960s campus-protest movement has, in general, been overestimated by scholars and the public. Although several large institutions experienced significant upheavals, hundreds of other colleges and universities remained calm and undisturbed. At CNC and most other institutions, habits of dress, manners, and hairstyles were certainly changing. But these transformations occurred amid a general pattern of normalcy, with classes, sports events, and music recitals all being held with neither disturbances nor protests.[82] The specific type of student who attended CNC during the decade more specifically contributed to this lack of activism. Many students were older, ex-army veterans; their main focus was education, not politics. They particularly wished to take advantage of the benefits of the GI Bill in order to finish their schooling as soon as possible.[83] This focus on completing their educations influenced not just veterans, but a significant number of other Christopher Newport students. In 1970, the new Dean of Students William Polis explained to the *Daily Press* that CNC students were "somewhat older than on the average college campus, many with very determined attitudes. They're serious; they're going to make it. They demand much of their instructors. And when it comes to campus unrest, their attitude seems to be: 'Nothing had darn well better stop me from graduating in June.'"[84]

---

[81] "Library Laws Protested," *Times-Herald*, 21 November 1968; "Newport Staged a Sign-in, Not a Sit-in," *Times-Herald*, 22 November 1968; "Library Changes Sought," *Times-Herald*, 26 November 1968; "Students Win at Library," *Times-Herald*, 9 December 1968; on Windsor being tipped off early, see Windsor interview with Hamilton, 5 June 2007. CNC's dress code had started to become more liberal in 1966; see "Linkous, SGA Secure Change in Dress Rules," *Captain's Log*, 27 April 1966; these changes entitled students for the first time to wear "bermuda length shorts" on campus, but "with the understanding that high standards of personal appearance will be maintained."

[82] On the campus protest movement, see Thelin, *History of American Higher Education*, 309–10.

[83] "Today's Veteran Shoots for Dean's List Grade," *Times-Herald*, 6 January 1967.

[84] "Today's Youth Seeking Independence But With Limitations," *Daily Press*, 9 October 1970.

Scotty Cunningham's leadership further contributed to the lack of strife. Always sensitive to the views of others and accustomed to dealing with many types of people throughout his career, he decided to reach out to young students in order to let them know that he understood many of their concerns. Cunningham had pragmatic reasons to keep the campus calm and quiet. He realized that, in many states, student protests had led state legislatures to look much more critically at funding and appropriations for public colleges and universities. Thus, he did not want any campus controversies to jeopardize CNC's funding from Richmond. He consequently always made sure that he was accessible to students so that he could hear complaints and answer questions. When he spoke to the press, moreover, he made sure that he conveyed—if sometimes awkwardly—that he grasped what young people wanted. In 1968, for instance, he talked about the "new breed" of students then filling America's college classrooms. These were "academically aware and socially conscious" young people. In order to reach them, Cunningham said, "[c]ollege administrators have got to be tuned in and turned on if they're to be effective today."[85] Moreover, he perceptively realized that his students wanted not only to be heard, but they also wanted a role in college affairs. Toward this end, he ordered faculty committees to start including student representatives among its members. As a result, ten of the college's fifteen standing committees had a student representative by 1969, including the key committees on academic affairs and student activities.[86]

Becoming a Four-Year College and An End of an Era

From the day he took the job as CNC's director in 1960, Scotty Cunningham envisioned Christopher Newport becoming a four-year college. Aware that demographic trends in the country and on the

---

[85] "'Captain' Steers Steady Course," *Times-Herald*, 7 June 1968; see also "Colleges Charged with Irrelevance," *Times-Herald*, 17 October 1969, and Cunningham interview, 28 April 1986. On state legislatures looking more critically at funding for higher education in the 1960s, see Thelin, *History of American Higher Education*, 249, 312.

[86] "Cunningham Sees Local Board for CNC," *Times-Herald*, 29 June 1970; "Students' Voice in Affairs Cited for CNC Freshmen," *Daily Press*, 11 September 1970; "College SGA Head Pleased at Nixon Aides' Attitudes," *Daily Press*, 15 October 1970.

Peninsula favored such a step, he also understood that state and local
leaders would support four-year status *only* if the college first proved
itself as a two-year institution. Therefore, he always made sure that he
hired the best teachers and administrators he could find. Cunningham
furthermore maintained good relations with the local community. He
later estimated that he spoke to "nearly three hundred groups,
breakfasts, lunches, and dinners" during just his first-year-and-a-half as
CNC's director. Throughout the decade, moreover, he socialized
regularly with the Newport News city council members as well as with
state delegates and senators from the Hampton Roads area.[87]

In 1966, with the college solidly established and its reputation
growing, the opportunity emerged to begin heading toward degree-
granting status. That year a state legislative committee called the Higher
Education Study Commission published a landmark report that
transformed Virginia's educational landscape. Called the Bird Report
after its chair State Senator Lloyd Bird, it proposed the creation of a
statewide system of community colleges as well as raising both George
Mason and Christopher Newport to four-year status "in the near future."
With regard to CNC becoming a degree-granting institution, the report
pointed out the obvious educational needs of "the Northside of
Hampton Roads area." The region possessed a growing population and
numerous military personnel who needed access to higher education, all
of which made it imperative that a "distinctively urban
university...without highly selective admission policies" be established.[88] Governor Mills Godwin lobbied the General Assembly during
its 1966 biennium session for the complete enactment of the Bird Report.
Hampton Roads' delegation also vigorously supported the report. State
Senator Hunter Andrews of Hampton, for example, immediately
introduced a bill calling for CNC to become a degree-granting institution
as soon as a new community college was established on the Peninsula.
Within days, however, Lewis McMurran and several other Newport
News delegates started to worry that the Peninsula might not

[87] Cunningham interview with Webb, 28 April 1986; on Cunningham and how he
socialized with the Hampton Roads delegation to the General Assembly, James
Windsor to Hamilton, 15 May 2007.

[88] *Times-Herald*, 17 January 1966; "'Near Future' At CNC Now," *Times-Herald*, 28
December 1967; see also "CNC Awaiting Decision," *Times-Herald*, 27 December 1967.

immediately get one of the new community colleges. Therefore, McMurran convinced his colleagues to remove all restrictions preventing Christopher Newport from stepping up to four-year status. As a result, nearly everyone in the state thought that the transition would be quickly accomplished. CNC students were particularly excited at the prospect. An informal poll taken during the Assembly session revealed that 70 percent of students planned to remain at the college if it offered bachelor degrees.[89]

In April 1966, the General Assembly passed legislation formally creating the state's community college system, which included a branch campus for the city of Hampton. The legislation, however, contained no formal timetable for CNC's "step up" to four-year status. This absence stemmed not from any reluctance on the part of the General Assembly, but was due to William and Mary. To the surprise of many, its board of visitors had put on the brakes. In mid-February 1966, the board publicly stated that CNC should move to four-year status *only* on "the basis of [its] sound academic evolution." In short, more attention should first be given to such matters as "library resources, qualified faculty, and adequate enrollment." The board additionally urged the legislature to leave the determination of CNC's ultimate status to the parent college. Therefore, Lewis McMurran withdrew the formal "step up" timetable from the bill at the last moment.[90]

Despite this setback, most observers still expected four-year status to occur relatively quickly. In May 1966, for example, Director Cunningham ordered the faculty in several departments to prepare upper-level courses that could be offered to third-year students in the fall 1966 semester. The William and Mary Board, meanwhile, appointed Dean W. Melville Jones to serve as a coordinating officer between the

---

[89] "Finance Committee OK's Tax Bill; Peninsula Colleges Bill Submitted," *Daily Press*, 11 February 1966; "W&M Board Flashes 'Go Slowly' Sign in Creating 4-year Newport College," *Daily Press*, 13 February 1966; "Planned Bill Would Eliminate Two-year CNC Restrictions," *Daily Press*, 16 February 1966; "'Near Future' At CNC Now," *Times-Herald*, 28 December 1967; "Expansion Plans Await Politicians," *Captain's Log*, 23 February 1966.

[90] *Daily Press*, 13 February 1966; "'Near Future' At CNC Now," *Times-Herald*, 28 December 1967. For more information about the General Assembly's landmark 1966 session, see Wallenstein, *Cradle of America*, 369–70.

parent college and Christopher Newport. Jones arranged for a pair of reports to be prepared for the Southern Association of Colleges and Schools (SACS), the accreditation body for higher education institutions in the South. The reports—one to be a self-study by CNC faculty and the other to be written by William and Mary faculty—would provide tangible proof that Christopher Newport ought to be a four-year, degree-granting institution.[91]

As the months passed, however, this optimism for quick action faded. Although CNC's self-study report was submitted to SACS in April 1967, the William and Mary faculty report never materialized. The college's board of visitors, moreover, ordered Cunningham later that year to stop preparing upper-level courses for inclusion in the college's catalog and told him that absolutely no third-year classes should be offered to students. The director and other CNC officials grew nervous at these delays and actions. One reason for their apprehension had to do with Thomas Nelson Community College (TNCC), the new two-year school in Hampton. Throughout 1967, Hampton officials had moved with exceptional speed to construct and open the new school. Indeed, they had purchased land early that year with classroom buildings going up soon afterwards. As a result, classes were set to begin in the fall of 1968. CNC administrators recognized that Thomas Nelson posed a serious threat to Christopher Newport's enrollment numbers, especially because the state more heavily subsidized the new two-year school, thus TNCC's tuition was significantly lower. As a state school, however, Thomas Nelson's academic credits would easily transfer to all of Virginia's four-year public institutions. Without third- and fourth-year classes, Cunningham feared that the community college would hobble CNC's ability to attract new students.[92] Frustration grew as well among

[91] "CNC Eyes Independent Accreditation," *Times-Herald*, 14 March 1967; "'Near Future' At CNC Now," *Times-Herald*, 28 December 1967; "CNC Is Anxious to See 'Grades,'" *Times-Herald*, 29 December 1967. See Thelin, *History of American Higher Education*, 264–65, on how and why accreditation associations began in America in the years following World War II.

[92] "'Near Future' At CNC Now," *Times-Herald*, 28 December 1967; "CNC Is Anxious to See 'Grades,'" *Times-Herald*, 29 December 1967; "Nelson College Spells Trouble for Newport," *Times-Herald*, 1 February 1968; Cunningham interview, 28 April 1986. In terms of subsidies from the state, Christopher Newport received about 45 percent of its operating budget from the Virginia government, whereas TNCC was

CNC students who wanted to complete their degrees at the college. In May 1967, for instance, soon after William and Mary's board ordered third-year classes not to run, two students named Mike Haywood and Mike Joyce wrote a poem pointedly lambasting the parent college:

"The Student's Prayer"
Our father which art in Williamsburg,
Hallowed (?) be thy name?
A new kingdom come. A greater "will" be done
At Christopher Newport, as it was at Old Dominion!
Give us this year our separate status
And forgive us our excellence, as
We forgive your disdain.
And lead us not into oblivion; for
Thine WAS a kingdom that has lost
Its power and glory forever! Amen.[93]

Action on Christopher Newport's status finally came in early January 1968 during the winter meeting of the William and Mary Board of Visitors. During the gathering, the long-delayed report on CNC written by William and Mary faculty was confidentially presented to board members. After reviewing its findings, they announced that the earliest date for CNC to step up to four-year status would be 1972. Three criteria, though, first needed to be met: 1) CNC's library collection had to be significantly expanded in order to reach minimum standards for a four-year-college; 2) the college needed to hire a greater number of faculty holding terminal degrees; and 3) the full-time sophomore class had to consistently reach 250–300 students.[94]

William and Mary's restrictive conditions stunned both Christopher Newport officials and the entire Peninsula community. The requirement regarding the size of the sophomore class was especially troubling

---

scheduled to receive approximately 90 percent of its budget from the state, see "Christopher Newport To Seek $1,579,150 In Operating Funds," *Times-Herald*, 7 September 1967, and Cunningham interview, 28 April 1986.

[93] "Two CNC Students Express Sentiments," *Captain's Log*, 19 May 1967.

[94] "W&M's Intentions Outlines: An Independent CNC Possible In Time for 1970–72 Biennium," *Daily Press*, 7 January 1968.

because CNC's full-time sophomore class had numbered only around 100 students in fall 1967. With TNCC set to open the following autumn, getting to 250 seemed impossible to most. Ruth Mulliken, a psychology professor and director of the counseling program, told freshmen the day following the announcement to start looking somewhere other than CNC for their last two years of college.[95]

Cunningham was determined, however, to do what he could to change things. He later admitted, "I thought there was no tomorrow [in 1968]. I wanted a four-year college."[96] Therefore, he invited William and Mary President Davis Y. Paschall and Dean Melville Jones to campus so that they could explain the board's position more fully as well as hear from the local community. The director made sure that the meeting room in Christopher Newport Hall was filled to capacity with CNC supporters. Thus, on the day of the meeting, more than 150 people squeezed into Newport's auditorium room, including the Peninsula's delegation from the General Assembly, the city councils of Newport News and Hampton, local businessmen, CNC faculty, and students. As soon as the meeting opened, King Meehan rose to speak. The former head of the Peninsula Industrial Committee who had worked ten years before to establish the college, now told Paschall, "This argument of yours is like the arguments in the General Assembly against the James River Bridge. There can't be any traffic across a bridge that isn't built. Put a four-year college here, and the support will be forthcoming."[97] After Meehan sat down, applause filled the room. Taken aback by Meehan's confrontational tone and the crowd's support for his words, Paschall sputtered that building a bridge was not like building a sound academic institution.[98] Lewis McMurran then rose and also forcefully criticized William and Mary's slow timeline and restrictive criteria for CNC's step-up. He pledged to the audience, moreover, to get additional state appropriations for CNC so that the college could hire more faculty and create needed upper-level, third- and fourth-year courses. The Newport

---

[95] "Christopher Newport's Fight Is More Than Status," *Times-Herald*, 31 January 1968.

[96] Cunningham interview with Webb, 28 April 1968.

[97] Webb, *Voices*, 18.

[98] Memo from President Emeritus Davis Paschall to President John Anderson, 15 December 1986, University Archives.

News delegate finished by pointedly telling Paschall, "I hope the Board of Visitors—with money in hand—will find it possible to implement the decision for four-year status earlier than their resolution indicates."[99]

Peninsula leaders kept up the pressure in the weeks and months that followed. In February, McMurran successfully appropriated $245,000 in additional funds to CNC in order to support third- and fourth-year course work. The Peninsula Chamber of Commerce and Peninsula Industrial Committee, meanwhile, both issued official statements registering their "dissent" over William and Mary's policy on CNC's future. The *Times-Herald* published a lengthy article explaining that other public two-year colleges that had become four-year institution had not had these kinds of restrictions placed upon them. The piece also noted that George Mason's enrollment had surged *only after* it began to offer bachelor degrees. Finally, community residents continued to speak out loudly. One particularly unhappy Peninsula resident said that William and Mary's restrictions were "like a noose around CNC's neck."[100]

The intense lobbying paid off. When the William and Mary Board of Visitors met again in late May 1968, it rescinded its earlier restrictions and adopted a new resolution calling for CNC's elevation during the 1970–71 academic year. Third-year, junior-level courses could begin to be offered in 1969–70. Although the board reiterated the need for Christopher Newport to possess a qualified faculty and adequate library, it dropped the daunting requirement of a sophomore class of 250–300 full-time students. Rather, the board only vaguely referred to the need for "justifiable registrations" by 1970–71. After William and Mary's retreat, McMurran told the *Times-Herald*, "[T]he news is a delight to me,

---

[99] "On CNC Status: McMurran Raps Criteria," *Times-Herald*, 9 January 1968.

[100] "Christopher Newport's Fight is More Than Status," *Times-Herald*, 31 January 1968; "House Fattens CNC's Budget," *Times-Herald*, 26 February 1968 and "Peninsula Interests Jolted—McMurran Fumes," *Times-Herald*, 8 March 1968. For more information on the entire controversy, see "Meehan Attacks Schedule Set Up for Four Year CNC," *Daily Press*, 13 January 1968 and "Editorial [by unidentified CNC faculty member]," *Times-Herald*, 23 January 1968.

something that will mean great things, for the college and the entire community."[101]

Scotty Cunningham also basked in his hard-won victory. Not only did William and Mary move almost entirely in Christopher Newport's direction, the board also officially promoted Cunningham from Director to "Provost" of the new soon-to-be four-year college. The *Times-Herald*, furthermore, ran a glowing biographical article entitled "'Captain' Steers Steady Course," which detailed his eight-year tenure as head of the college and his tireless efforts to make it a degree-granting institution. The piece coincided with the news that Cunningham's "official portrait," painted by Lewis McMurran's youngest sister, Agnes McMurran Johnson, had recently been unveiled in a campus ceremony.[102]

The *Times-Herald* piece, however, did not simply look backward, but also forward as Cunningham reflected upon both American higher education and CNC's development in the years ahead. "Colleges have to get out of their ivory towers," he explained, "and offer programs that are meaningful for today's students." As a four-year college designed to serve the local community, Christopher Newport could no longer focus its efforts solely on preparing students to succeed at schools like William and Mary. CNC instead had to develop a broader mission to serve the *entire* community as well as create a more wide-ranging academic program. Cunningham particularly wanted to reach a greater number of Peninsula high school graduates with test scores "in the top 65% of the College Board." [103]

Toward this end, he organized a series of campus discussions throughout the 1968–69 academic year where he instructed his staff and faculty to think about how to recruit such students as well as the best ways to expand Christopher Newport College's reach as an institution. In the spring of 1969, after much debate and conversation, Cunningham told the press that the college was determined to "break away from the

---

[101] "Christopher Newport Granted Four-Year Status by 1970–71," *Times-Herald*, 1 June 1968 and "W&M Board Approves Four-Year Status for CNC During 1970–71," *Daily Press*, 2 June 1968.

[102] "'Captain' Steers Steady Course," *Times-Herald*, 7 June 1968. See also "Board Elects Cunningham As CNC's First President," *Daily Press*, 31 May 1969.

[103] "'Captain' Steers Steady Course," *Times-Herald*, 7 June 1968; "CNC Will Beef-Up Its Program for Urban Area Needs," *Times-Herald*, 5 March 1969.

traditional campus concept" in order to focus on the needs of the Peninsula's urban community. A traditional college, he explained, typically offered courses to students on a "take it or leave it" basis. "The urban campus," on the other hand, "goes out and sees what the community needs and plans its menu accordingly so more [people] can eat." After assessing the needs of the Peninsula, CNC officials determined that its curriculum "menu" would be a diversified one. Although bachelor degrees in the traditional disciplines of English, government, history, biology, and philosophy were planned, faculty and administrators also designed new, innovative programs to contribute to the needs of the community. The curriculum planning committee envisioned, for example, offering a special Bachelor of Science degree in business administration. Rather than train students "for Harvard's business school," CNC's degree would permit students "to step into jobs with Peninsula firms [on] the day they graduate." Cunningham and faculty also discussed creating a "pioneering, interdisciplinary degree in urban studies" to prepare graduates for civil service jobs with state and local governments. Finally, Cunningham wanted to expand the college's three-year nursing program (offered in cooperation with nearby Riverside Hospital) into a four-year BS degree so that nurses working for local medical facilities would be college graduates when they entered their profession.[104]

As planning for escalation to four-year status proceeded, the school began its final year as a junior college. The 1968–69 academic year, however, proved a difficult one in terms of enrollment numbers, largely because Thomas Nelson Community College had opened its doors. Due to its lower tuition of $135 per year (compared with CNC's $350 annual cost), the community college had more than 1,200 enrolled students in its first year, with the majority attending day classes. By contrast, CNC had only 169 freshmen enrolled in its day college in fall 1968. CNC's overall numbers dipped only slightly, however, as many more sophomores than usual returned with the intention of completing their bachelor's degree

---

[104] "CNC Will Beef-Up Its Program for Urban Area Needs," *Times-Herald*, 5 March 1969; "Cunningham Sees Local Board for CNC," *Times-Herald*, 29 June 1970.

at the college.[105] As predicted, CNC's enrollment grew significantly the following year when third-year classes started to be offered. On registration day in mid-September 1969, long lines wrapped around Christopher Newport Hall as many more students than usual signed up for classes. When Registrar Jane Pillow tallied the figures, she found that enrollment had jumped more than 38 % from the previous fall, with the total student body rising from approximately 1,000 to more than 1,400.[106]

In the autumn of 1969, as Cunningham began his tenth year as head of CNC, he possessed another new title. In its summer meeting, William and Mary's Board of Visitors officially named Cunningham Christopher Newport's first "president," both to acknowledge the school's move to four-year status and to recognize his instrumental role in taking CNC to this stage of its development.[107] The same semester Cunningham became president, however, the Pingry School in Hillside, New Jersey contacted him. Cunningham had graduated from the elite prep school in 1938 and now the school's board of trustees asked if he would come back as its headmaster. After offering him an attractive pay and benefit package—"far superior" to his CNC compensation—Cunningham accepted. He believed that he had received a marvelous education at Pingry and had several young children whom he wanted to educate there. Furthermore, Cunningham had long worried that Christopher Newport was becoming too closely identified with him alone. He realized, for instance, that many around the Peninsula called CNC "Scotty's school" at a time when, as he put it "the college really needed to be its own man." Therefore, on 3 February 1970, he submitted his resignation to be effective on 1 July of that year. In his resignation letter, he told the William and Mary Board of Visitors that Christopher Newport was now a healthy institution "with a devoted faculty, a solid student body, and a fine physical

---

[105] "Enrollment Rises," *Times-Herald*, 14 October 1968; "College Seeks Funds from Newport News," *Times-Herald*, 14 July 1969.

[106] "CNC Enrollment Swells," *Times-Herald*, 30 July 1969; "CNC's Switchboard Busy With Registration Queries," *Daily Press*, 2 September 1969; "CNC to Register About 740 Today," *Daily Press*, 7 September 1969; "CNC Registers 650," *Daily Press*, 18 September 1969; "CNC Registration at 1,312," *Daily Press*, 20 September 1969.

[107] "Cunningham Has New Title," *Daily Press*, 2 July 1969.

plant."[108] Several months later, on 12 June 1970, Cunningham presided over his last official ceremony when he presented twenty-two associate degrees at commencement exercises. He also formally opened the new pre-professional building, now called Wingfield Hall. As he packed up his office and looked over the college's seventy-five acres and five buildings, Cunningham wistfully told a reporter, "How many men have been this lucky—to help build something like this?"[109]

Cunningham was also pleased because he was handing the presidency off to his trusted friend and colleague, James Windsor. Windsor had been named "acting president" for one year by the William and Mary Board of Visitors the previous May. His appointment was designed to allow the college to conduct a nationwide search for Cunningham's permanent replacement. The thirty-seven-year-old Windsor was a good choice. He had had a long tenure with the school and was respected by both the faculty and student body. As an administrator, moreover, he had worked with Cunningham for many years and understood the many issues confronting the college. Thus, during Cunningham's final six weeks in office, the two men worked closely together to get ready for the transition.[110]

During Windsor's year as "acting president," CNC's enrollment continued to rise at a rapid rate. In September 1970, Nancy Ramseur reported that 1,094 students had signed up for day classes, an increase of 369 from the previous autumn; among that number were 178 juniors and 85 seniors. With the evening school's enrollment added in, approximately 1,800 students attended Christopher Newport during the 1970–71 academic year.[111] Several items of business kept Windsor

---

[108] "H. W. Cunningham Resigns," *Daily Press*, 4 February 1970; Webb, *Voices*, 18; Cunningham interview with Webb, 28 April 1986. See also "The Age of Cunningham," *Daily Press*, 5 February 1970 and "Cunninghams Preparing for Move: Cece Looks Forward to Their New Lives," *Daily Press*, 21 June 1970. For information about Cunningham's twelve-year tenure at the Pingry School from 1970–1982, see "Pingry Remembers Headmaster Cunningham," 27 July 2008 at http://www.pingry.org/about/articles/2007jul27cunningham.html.

[109] "CNC Becomes a Teenager," *Times-Herald*, 13 June 1970; "Cunningham Sees Local Board for CNC," *Times-Herald*, 29 June 1970.

[110] "Windsor Named Acting CNC President," *Daily Press*, 16 May 1970.

[111] "CNC Rolls Up 46 Percent," *Times-Herald*, 10 September 1970; "CNC Enrollment Stands at 1,094," *Times-Herald*, 23 September 1970.

especially busy. First, he worked on finishing his doctorate in psychology from the University of Virginia. Indeed, he spent almost every Monday and Tuesday that year driving back and forth from Charlottesville to take classes. Second, he labored hard to boost the library's collection. In April 1970, just before Cunningham's departure, SACS had sent a preliminary accreditation team to visit CNC in preparation for a full-scale visit scheduled for the following year—one that would evaluate the college for accreditation as a four-year institution. The team was appalled by the meager size of the library. Its twenty-five thousand volumes were only half of what was considered to be the absolute minimum for a degree-granting college. The SACS team, therefore, recommended "emergency measures" to bolster book buying. Toward this end, Windsor launched a $300,000 fund-raising drive for money to purchase additional volumes. Moreover, he worked with Jack Willis, William and Mary's liaison to CNC, in order to make the Swem Library's collection fully available to CNC students. Because of Willis's efforts Christopher Newport students gained full-borrowing privileges, and he even arranged for Swem's entire card catalog to be photocopied and placed in the Smith Library. These actions later proved crucial when the formal SACS team returned in 1971.[112]

Christopher Newport College held its first commencement ceremony in which bachelor degrees were awarded in June 1971. Wayne Martin Barry was first student to walk across the commencement platform in order to receive his Bachelor of Science diploma from President Windsor. Windsor also awarded nine other BS degrees as well as forty-five Bachelor of Arts diplomas. The commencement speaker that day was now-former Governor Mills Godwin, who congratulated both the students and the college itself. Christopher Newport, he said, had in its short ten-year history transformed itself into a vital institution that provided "an opportunity for all those willing to work toward a higher education."[113] The ceremony proved a happy occasion also because James Windsor had just been named the college's permanent president

---

[112] "Report from Visiting Committee from the Commission on Colleges, SACS," May 1970, University Archives; "CNC Drive Asks $300,000 for Library," Times-Herald, 18 March 1971; "College Plans Fund Drive to Buy New Books," Daily Press, 31 March 1971; Windsor interview with Hamilton, 5 June 2007.

[113] "First Four-Year Degrees Presented by CNC," Daily Press, 13 June 1971.

by William and Mary's Board of Visitors. The appointment delighted both faculty and students, as Windsor had provided strong and effective leadership over the previous academic year. Commencement, though, was bittersweet. Scotty Cunningham was still deeply missed by the entire campus community. More poignantly, students and faculty were all saddened by the recent death of Professor Robert Usry, who had died of a heart attack in January 1971 near the end of the fall term. In failing health for several years, the sixty-five-year-old history teacher had long suspected his end was near. In fact, two weeks before his fatal heart attack, he wrote up the final examinations for his classes and gave them to a colleague "just in case." Everyone at the college knew that replacing such a dedicated teacher would be difficult, if not impossible. Thus, as CNC's tenth year of classes came to a close, times continued to change and everyone saw that the college had begun to head in a very different direction.[114]

---

[114] "Heart Attack Fatal to Robert M. Usry," *Daily Press*, 15 January 1971. On Windsor's appointment as permanent president, see "Windsor Named New CNC President," *Daily Press*, 16 April 1971. On Usry's preparation of his final examinations shortly before his death, Mario Mazzarella Lecture to "Researching CNU" history class, 25 February 2008.

PART II

GROWING PAINS (1971–1995)

3

Dealing with the '70s

On 12 May 1973, the famous novelist and Newport News native William Styron returned to his hometown to give the commencement address to Christopher Newport College's third graduating class. The forty-seven-year-old Pulitzer Prize-winning writer spoke with both optimism and pessimism about the many changes that he and all in the audience had experienced in recent years. Styron listed, for example, the wondrous technologies that had emerged in just the previous quarter century: "Television ... Xerox. Transistors. The tape recorder. The passenger jet aircraft.... Satellites.... The computer. Frozen foods.... The pill. Interstate highways.... Electric typewriters." Yet Styron also reflected upon "the abrupt and devastating" changes that had occurred within his hometown, especially as the Peninsula's "lovely pine wilderness" disappeared "in the face of population pressures and sometimes explosive growth."

Styron admitted that "[c]hange is not new" to human civilization, "only new is its acceleration." Thus the current "breakneck" pace of change—particularly with the appearance of "B-52 bombers" and "Nuclear warheads"—confronted the CNC graduates with a troubling future: "The rapidity and ruthlessness of change presents the face of total chaos." Nonetheless, Styron refused to despair. Indeed, he believed the students should not "be intimidated or undone, for this scene can be exhilarating." Styron applauded the "new life style" that had emerged among young people in the 1960s and early 1970s. In contrast to the 1950's "stale smell of dullness and hypocritical respectability," this new style was "spirited and invigorated" with its "flamboyant color," "variety," and "gaiety." Thus, while the graduates were entering a world that possessed its share of "terrors and outrages," it was also a world of "exhilarating promise."[1]

William Styron's memorable commencement address that spring afternoon reflected Christopher Newport College's second decade of existence. As a new four-year school, CNC's faculty and students certainly felt great anxiety and uneasiness in the face of challenging times. The decade of the 1970s—with the bitter end of the Vietnam War, the Watergate scandal, and economic stagflation—witnessed great pain and apprehension across the nation. These years, moreover, saw a dramatic change in attitudes about higher education. As costs mounted and test scores fell, the public grew increasingly unwilling to provide ever more tax dollars for public institutions.[2] There was, furthermore, growing uncertainty about what the "college experience" was exactly supposed to be. In the 1960s, leaders in higher education embraced the ideal of "mass universal access." But this aim collided with the 1950's notion of college as a "rite of passage" and/or as a means to "get ahead" in life. The subsequent expansion of two-year community college systems only added to the confusion about what "going to college" really meant.[3]

Despite these concerns, CNC's faculty and students optimistically believed their institution possessed a future with great promise and possibilities. Under the leadership of James Windsor, CNC served the local community as well as sought to establish an identity wholly independent of the College of William and Mary. Positioning itself as an "urban college" on the Lower Peninsula, the college dramatically expanded its curriculum and faculty in order to handle a growing number of full- and part-time students. To generate as much of the "college experience" as possible, CNC also created a much wider array of student activities, ranging from additional athletic squads, to academic clubs, to social organizations.

---

[1] William Styron, Commencement Address, Newport News, Virginia, 12 May 1973, University Archives, Christopher Newport University.

[2] Peter Wallenstein, *Cradle of America: Four Centuries of Virginia History* (Lawrence, Kansas: University of Kansas Press, 2007), 377–78.

[3] John R. Thelin, *A History of American Higher Education* (Baltimore, Maryland: Johns Hopkins University Press, 2004), 211, 322.

Because of these countervailing forces, CNC experienced a decade of both progress and setbacks. The college certainly grew in size and its student body became more diverse. Yet the decade's hard economic times led to inadequate funding from the General Assembly, with CNC receiving the fewest dollars per student among Virginia's four-year colleges. This situation forced college officials to repeatedly raise tuition and to shift the burden for education increasingly upon students and parents, who themselves were often economically strapped. Thus, like the nation as a whole (and higher education in particular) CNC found the 1970s to be a mixed bag—one filled with sometimes "devastating change" in the present as well as "exhilarating promise" for the future.

James Windsor as Christopher Newport's Second President

On a snowy evening in the late 1970s, CNC president James Windsor caught a ride home with Professor Cheryl Mathews, who taught classes in sociology and social work. Both lived in Williamsburg, about fifteen miles up the Peninsula. As Mathews drove northward, however, the weather and roads worsened. Just before the turn-off into their subdivision, Mathews's car hit a patch of ice and slid into the oncoming traffic lane, whereupon the pair saw a fire truck with lights flashing barreling down the road at them. Just in the nick of time, however, Mathews's car gained just enough traction to the pull off the road. After the fire truck sped past, Windsor turned to Mathews and calmly said, "That was close." "Jim was *always* calm like that," Mathews remembered.[4]

James Windsor dominated Christopher Newport College throughout the 1970s, much as Scotty Cunningham had dominated the 1960s. His calm and tranquil demeanor in times of change and stress certainly helped the school successfully navigate the era's difficult economic climate as well as complete the transition of becoming an accredited, independent, four-year college. Windsor's background had prepared him well for the task. Born in 1933 in West Virginia, he had wanted to travel the world upon completing high school. Soon after graduation, though, he and some buddies saw a World War II movie starring John Wayne. Inspired by "the Duke," Windsor and his friends decided to join

---

[4] Cheryl Mathews, email communication to Phillip Hamilton, 6 June 2008.

the Marine Corps—a move they hoped would allow them to serve their country *and* see the world. Windsor signed his enlistment papers on 1 June 1950. Twenty-five days later, however, hundreds of thousands of North Korean and Chinese troops invaded South Korea, and the US suddenly found itself at war in East Asia. After basic training, Windsor's infantry battalion was sent across the Pacific. As a member of a weapons company equipped with machine guns and flamethrowers, Windsor remembered that "We were sort of the shock troops of the battalion and, when infantry units got bogged down, we were the ones who came through with this heavier equipment. So we had a lot of intense involvement, a lot of casualties." After rescuing a marooned tank crew three miles behind enemy lines, the military awarded Windsor a Naval Commendation Medal. Twice wounded, he escaped death "many times" and, as a result, learned to treat "every day [thereafter] ... as a bonus."[5]

Following the Korean War, the Navy stationed Windsor in Yorktown at the Naval Weapons Station. He liked the Hampton Roads area and applied to the College of William and Mary after his enlistment expired. Graduating four years later, Windsor then pursued a divinity degree from Colgate-Rochester Divinity School in New York, during which time he took a number of psychology courses. Increasingly interested in that subject, he returned to Virginia to earn a master's degree from Virginia Commonwealth University. In 1962, Windsor received a call from Scotty Cunningham, who knew him from his days at William and Mary. Cunningham asked Windsor to join CNC's staff in order to teach psychology courses. Windsor accepted at once and, throughout the remainder of the 1960s, he proved indispensable to the new college, teaching various classes, establishing the academic counseling center, and running the evening and summer schools. In 1966, moreover, Windsor became the college's Dean of Students.[6]

After establishing a stellar record and getting along with almost everyone on the Peninsula, Windsor seemed a natural choice to be

---

[5] James Windsor interview with Phillip Hamilton, 5 June 2007; "Windsor New Acting CNC President," *Daily Press,* 16 May 1970; "Windsor Named New CNC President," *Daily Press,* 16 April 1971; "Dialogue: James C. Windsor," *Daily Press,* 8 August 1971.

[6] James Windsor to Phillip Hamilton, 13 May 2007; "CNC President Sets an Example with Service," *Daily Press,* 24 June 1974.

James Windsor teaching a psychology class during his presidency in the early 1970s.

(above) Samuel Bauer of the Psychology Department in his office in 1972.
(below) George Webb performing an experiment for students.

Biology Professor Harold Cones, pictured in the *Trident 1971*.

President Windsor (far left) with Werner Von Bruan (far right). Von Braun was the commencement speaker at CNC's graduation in 1974.

CNC's campus in the early 1970s, looking southeast. Gosnold Hall is on the left; Christopher Newport Hall is in the center.

Members of the Black Student Association.

CNC students dancing during the History Club's "Renaissance Festivals". Professor
Mario Mazzarella also is participating (left background).

Former President Cunningham, Former Chancellor Alvin Duke Chandler, Rector Harrol Brauer with President Windsor at the college's independence celebration on July 1, 1977. They are standing before Christopher Newport's "academic mace" which is carried in all of the college's academic ceremonies.

"acting president" after Cunningham's departure. Windsor, though, expected the position to be only temporary. Indeed, he did not even apply the following year when William and Mary officials conducted a national search to fill the CNC presidency. After failing to find an acceptable candidate, however, the search committee approached the thirty-seven-year-old and asked him to serve as the college's permanent president. Although "somewhat reluctant," Windsor eventually accepted. "We had four-year status and accreditation, and a dozen major different projects coming," he later explained, "and I didn't think it was a good time to be changing presidents." His only condition was that he be allowed to complete his PhD in psychology at the University of Virginia. Everyone was delighted. A straw vote of the faculty overwhelmingly endorsed the decision. Local leaders, moreover, publicly expressed their enthusiasm. Not only did General Assembly delegate Richard Bagley of Hampton appear at the press conference announcing the appointment, but Lewis McMurran also attended and spoke earnestly about the new president's character and ability.[7]

CNC students were also delighted at Windsor's appointment. While "acting president," he had made it a point to reach out to students, to understand their views, and to stay accessible. Viewed as more approachable than the formal Scotty Cunningham, Windsor made sure that students saw him often. He frequently took walks across campus, ate lunch in the student lounge, and kept his office door open to all comers. And the students often came, sometimes in groups of ten to thirty, to discuss a variety of topics. Soon after his appointment, the *Times-Herald* reported that they appeared in Windsor's office not only "to rap about their campus gripes," but also to discuss "their future plans, the [Vietnam] war [and] all the topics that concern collegians today."[8] Like Cunningham, Windsor wanted to understand the members of the baby-boom generation. When a reporter asked him about "long-haired, bearded, jeaned students" who "scorn their parents' values and standards," Windsor replied with great sensitivity:

---

[7] Windsor interview with Hamilton, 5 June 2007; "Windsor Named New CNC President," *Times-Herald*, 16 April 1971; "CNC's President—He Seeks That Student Touch," *Times-Herald*, 27 April 1971.

[8] "CNC's President—He Seeks That Student Touch," *Times-Herald*, 27 April 1971.

All of us as parents must try very hard not to judge our children on superficial grounds. What he IS, or is BECOMING as a person is much more important than whether or not he wears long hair or a beard. Some parents' values, such as a preoccupation with material things, should be scorned. We should not assume the youngster is wrong when there is a discrepancy of values.... You can't knock "peace" and "love."[9]

Windsor's formal presidential inauguration took place on 13 October 1971. The new college head began his remarks to the audience with characteristic humility explaining how, according to the Peter Principle, "man is frequently promoted to his level of incompetence." After the laughter had died down, Windsor said in a more serious vain that he hoped CNC would become a model-four-year "urban college" under his leadership, one "dedicated to serving the educational needs of the metropolitan area," open to full- and part-time students of all ages, and with classes running "from eight o'clock in the morning until ten o'clock at night." This mission of serving the community was essential. The Hampton Roads area had grown significantly during the 1960s, and the college had grown with it. Indeed, CNC had gone from 171 students and eight faculty members in September 1961 to approximately 1,800 students and 69 members of faculty in 1971. Everyone in the audience that day expected this robust growth—for both the college and the community—to continue throughout the 1970s. With ongoing growth, Windsor predicted that CNC would have five thousand students by 1980 and speculated about the possible need for "a new campus in another region of the metropolitan area." He wished, moreover, to establish a Christopher Newport College Urban Affairs Center that would "become the instrument of our liaison with the community." In fact, such a center would ensure that the college remained a fundamental part of the Peninsula as well as true to its overall mission.[10]

---

[9] "Dialogue: James C. Windsor," *Daily Press*, 8 August 1971.

[10] James Windsor Inaugural Remarks, 13 October 1971, University Archives; "Windsor Sees Second Campus—CNC's 1980 Dream," *Times-Herald*, 13 October 1971. For more information on expected growth in college enrollment at public institutions in the 1970s, see "CNC May Be the State's Last New Four-Year Institution," *Times-Herald*, 26 October 1968. For additional information about Windsor's ideas for a CNC Urban Affairs Center, see *Times-Herald*, 13 August 1970. The Center never materialized, however, likely because of the economic crises later in the decade.

"The Urban Expression of William and Mary"
—Academic Life in the 1970s

James Windsor always understood that the means through which Christopher Newport would become a truly "urban college" would be by establishing a curriculum specifically tailored to the needs of the Hampton Roads population. Because he saw "no necessary conflict between liberal and vocational education," he proposed in his inaugural address that CNC "have both." This would produce "a student who is liberally educated no matter what his vocational specialty may be." Only this "successful alliance" could prepare the CNC graduate *both* "to make a living [and] ... to live a meaningful life." At the time of his remarks, administration officials and faculty members had already begun building a curriculum that would serve the wide-ranging needs of the Peninsula and students of varying ages with different career goals.[11]

Throughout the 1970s, no "typical" CNC student existed. Early in his presidency, Windsor decided to combine the day and evening schools, even though during the 1960s, Scotty Cunningham had kept the two schools as well as their students strictly segregated. To provide him and his staff with more flexibility in scheduling classes and faculty, Windsor decided to integrate the two. Although he required one-third of classes to be held in the evenings and on Saturday mornings, the decision transformed the college's academic life, with traditional and nontraditional students now sharing classrooms and socializing on campus to a much greater extent than before. Even though a substantial percentage of students continued to be recent high school graduates, Windsor recalls that "many there were in their early to late 20s" and already members of the work-force. "They were trying to improve their situation in their jobs." A significant number of married women who had had children and were preparing to reenter the workforce also attended CNC in greater numbers during these years. As a result, the student

---

[11] James Windsor Inaugural Remarks, 13 October 1971. For more information on CNC's mission during James Windsor's administration, see "Deans See Image-Building Their Task," *Times-Herald*, 8 September 1969; "Dean Musial Discusses Educational Identity of CNC, *Captain's Log*, 17 December 1973; "Educational Goals are Defined," *Daily Press*, 18 April 1974.

body reflected "a cross-section of the community which you get in an urban setting."[12]

Because Christopher Newport College's mission statement called for it to support the local community, CNC maintained an open admissions policy. Nancy Ramseur, director of admissions from 1969 to 1974, once told a gathering of Peninsula high school students that the college's central aim was "to serve good, average students with a solid background in academic studies." The only explicit requirement for admission was a high school diploma. For older nontraditional students, moreover, Ramseur and her admissions staff always took into consideration "the life-long learning needs of ... part-time, mobile student[s]."[13] This flexibility, combined with growing numbers of baby boomers coming of age, meant enrollments rose throughout the decade. In 1970–71, 1,826 full- and part-time students attended CNC; at the decade's end, this number had grown to nearly 4,000.[14]

The rapid growth in enrollment required the college to establish a curriculum both flexible enough for students to graduate in a timely fashion and substantive enough to prepare them for meaningful and satisfying careers.[15] Soon after the college gained four-year status, Cunningham (and later Windsor) adopted William and Mary's general education requirements with few variations. To be completed within the first two years of study, they were a standard mix of first-year English composition classes, along with courses in the humanities, social sciences, and natural sciences. Although a foreign language component required students to take Spanish, German, or French to the intermediate

---

[12] "'Christopher Newport Independence' Special Edition," *Daily Press*, 27 June 1976; Windsor interview with Hamilton, 5 June 2007.

[13] "Christopher Newport College Enrollment Swells, *Times-Herald*, 15 September 1969; "Attend Hometown College and Save, Peninsula Students Urged, *Daily Press*, 5 March 1970; "Aims and Purposes," Christopher Newport College Catalog, 1977–79, vol. 16, no. 1. See also "SGA Sponsor Open House on April 10," *Captain's Log*, 31 March 1975, about on-campus recruitment efforts for high school students from the Peninsula. This article explains how students were welcomed by President Windsor, watched a film about CNC, and then visited classrooms to view a lecture.

[14] "Christopher Newport May Need $2.5 million," *Times-Herald*, 26 April 1971; "Windsor to Step Down as Christopher Newport College Head," *Times-Herald*, 9 March 1979. Student numbers are from the Office of Institutional Research, CNU.

[15] Ibid.

level, they could test-out of it using language credits earned in high school. Finally, CNC students had to complete two, one-credit physical education courses. This general education core would remain in place at the college for a generation.[16]

In addition to setting distribution requirements, Windsor and the faculty oversaw a vast expansion in the number of academic majors the college offered. When he became president in 1970, CNC supported five majors—English, history, biology, psychology, and government—each of which had been drawn up by the faculty and approved by the State Council of Higher Education in Virginia (SCHEV). Shortly after Windsor took over, additional academic majors began to be added to the catalog. After a series of "rap sessions" with students, for instance, Windsor approved in 1972 the formation of a new communications department. As the catalog explained, the department was to "explore problems ... common to communications activities and media" with courses to be offered "in speech, writing, journalism, and cinema." By the mid-1970s, moreover, the college established new majors in French, Spanish, chemistry, and fine and performing arts. Given Windsor's desire that CNC offer both liberal *and* vocational studies, the number of academic majors the school offered had grown to twenty-six by 1980.[17]

Although CNC officials always insisted that this curriculum expansion simply served the needs of the local population, it was also part of a broader national trend toward a "new vocationalism" in American higher education. In the challenging economic times of the 1970s, students, parents, and state legislators across the United States demanded that college degrees lead not simply to educated individuals, but also to good-paying jobs.[18] An example of CNC's "new

---

[16] Christopher Newport College Catalog, 1970–71, vol. 10, no. 1; George and Jane Carter Webb email communication to Phillip Hamilton, 28 May 2008.

[17] "CNC to Improve Communication," *Times-Herald*, 25 July 1975; "CNC Slates French Degree for June 1973," *Daily Press*, 11 June 1972; "CNC Budget is Approved by WandM Board," *Daily Press*, 19 May 1974; Christopher Newport College Catalog, 1972–73, vol. 12, no. 1; Christopher Newport College Catalog, 1977–79, vol. 16, no. 1. In 1972, the college established a philosophy major in cooperation with the Department of Philosophy at William and Mary; see Christopher Newport College Catalog, 1972–73, vol. 12, no. 1.

[18] Jane Carter Webb, ed., *Voices: An Essay in Photographs, Poems and Stories In Celebration of Christopher Newport College's Twenty-Fifth Year* (Newport News, Virginia:

vocationalism" appeared in 1971 when the college created a business degree that required students to take courses in economics, accounting, and management. After it was approved by SCHEV, Windsor told the press that CNC business graduates would be well prepared to step into solid jobs with companies located on the Peninsula.[19] The following year, CNC created a Management Information Service degree, which called upon students to take an interdisciplinary mix of business and "scientific data processing" courses. Marshall Booker, a business professor and then-dean of faculty, explained that the college developed the program in "close cooperation [with] the Peninsula business community" which needed workers with skills in computer technology. In fact, the initial graduates of the Management Information Service major were employees of the National Aeronautics Space Agency (NASA) and the Newport News shipyards.[20]

The government degree also reflected the school's attempt to blend the liberal arts and vocational training. In 1969, a faculty-led curriculum committee created the bachelor's degree in government in order "to fulfill the college's obligations as an urban centered campus." Thus, major classes emphasized "local government and problems of urban areas." Government courses, moreover, provided opportunities for students "to step out of the textbook and into the actual world of government at work." The college, furthermore, developed a Bachelor of Science in Government Administration to permit students to focus on a number of specific career paths, such as urban management, law enforcement and corrections, and urban development and planning. Windsor explained the BS in Government Administration assisted students "in developing the intellectual comprehension, practical skills, and professional attitudes required by those seeking careers in the public

---

The Sailing Association Press, 1986), 21; Thelin, *A History of Higher Education*, 327–29; "CNC to Continue Its Basic Programs," *Times-Herald*, 12 March 1969; "Psych Degree Will Be Offered by CNC," *Times-Herald*, 13 March 1969.

[19] "Virginia Approves 2 More CNC Degree Programs," *Times-Herald*, 11 December 1969; Christopher Newport College Catalog, 1971–72, vol. 11, no. 1.

[20] "CNC Offers Three Computer Courses," *Daily Press*, 9 July 1969; "CNC to Add Eighth Degree," *Daily Press*, 18 May 1971; "Christopher Newport to Add Eight Degrees," *Times-Herald*, 24 May 1971. CNC continued its two-year middle management program in retail (mentioned in Chapter 2) throughout the 1970s (Christopher Newport College Catalog, 1972–73, vol. 12, no. 1).

sector."[21] Barry Wood, Assistant Dean for Academic Affairs during much of the decade, later remembered that the college's faculty members took the task of building the college's curriculum very seriously because, as professors at a four-year college, they realized they were now "fully responsible for preparing students to enter their own mysteries and curiosities—to find their bliss and their do."[22]

Remedial courses also became an increasingly prominent part of Christopher Newport's curriculum, especially by the mid-to-late 1970s. The reasons were both national and local in origin. Across the country, the failure rates for freshmen in introductory general education classes were growing at an alarming pace. College administrators, therefore, adopted remedial training simply to keep the doors to a college education open for more students.[23] Windsor himself ordered remedial courses at CNC for largely the same reasons: he wanted to keep the college's overall enrollment growing in order to demonstrate CNC's long-term viability to the community, but he also wished to expand higher education opportunities for Peninsula students, especially those with disadvantaged backgrounds. In particular, he wanted to increase the number of African-American students attending the college. In 1973, only 2 percent of CNC students were black. Part of the reason was the presence nearby of the Hampton Institute as well as lingering bitterness

---

[21] "Government Degree Outlined," *Times-Herald*, 11 March 1969; "CNC Will Offer New Degree In Public Service," *Daily Press*, 8 August 1972. A "law enforcement specialty" consisting of additional coursework in criminal law, juvenile delinquency, and legal evidence was later added to aid students who wished to become police officers directly upon graduation (see "CNC Expands Program in Law Enforcement," *Daily Press*, 23 August 1975; Christopher Newport College Catalog, 1972–73, vol. 12, no. 1.).

[22] Barry Wood to Phillip Hamilton, 15 March 2008. During his presidency, Windsor established a number of cooperative programs with other schools to expand Christopher Newport's range of degree offerings. He worked with Old Dominion University, for example, to set up cooperative programs in engineering and nursing. The engineering degree track permitted CNC students to take their first two years of pre-engineering courses with the college's physics department and then students would complete the final two years of the engineering BS at Old Dominion. The nursing program was designed for non-traditional students who wished to earn a BS in Nursing and required them to take only their last three semesters of course work at the Norfolk university ("CNC, ODU Engineering Program is Announced," *Daily Press*, 20 April 1976; Christopher Newport College Catalog, 1977–79, vol. 16, no. 1).

[23] Thelin, *History of American Higher Education*, 327–33.

in the African-American community over the 1962–63 taking of the Shoe Lane tract. Thus, to recruit more minority students, CNC admissions staff began talking to African-American high school seniors throughout Hampton Roads. Realizing that many of these students needed additional work in such subject areas of mathematics, writing, and reading, they suggested that the college create a "basic studies program" which would offer non-credit corrective courses during a student's first-year at the college. Windsor agreed, and in the fall of 1974, CNC formally established the basic studies department.[24]

To manage both the rapidly expanding curriculum as well as the growing number of academic departments, Windsor hired Thomas Musial in 1973 to be the college's Dean of Academic Affairs. Musial's central responsibilities were to deal with new curriculum proposals, oversee the faculty, and communicate with the public about Christopher Newport's academic mission. To accomplish these goals, Musial reorganized the college into five "academic divisions," each headed by a separate faculty "coordinator." While clear on paper, the new system proved cumbersome and ineffective in practice. The five coordinators lacked administrative authority, and their only true responsibility was to explain their division's needs to the administration. Musial, moreover, did not get along with many faculty members, who saw him as somewhat pretentious. In 1976, therefore, Musial resigned and left for St. Mary's University in Nova Scotia, Canada.[25] To replace him, Windsor turned to biology professor Robert Edwards. Viewed as fair and even-handed by the faculty, Edwards closely worked with Windsor to revamp and reorganize the college's structure. The five academic divisions Musial had created were scrapped and two new entities created—a Liberal Arts and Sciences division and a Social and Behavioral Sciences

[24] "CNC Committee Checks For Equality in Hiring," *Times-Herald*, 29 January 1975; Christopher Newport College Catalog, 1975–77, vol. 15, no. 1, and Catalog, 1977–79, vol. 16, no. 1; George and Jane Carter Webb, communication to Phillip Hamilton, 28 May 2008.

[25] "Three Promoted to New CNC Positions," *Daily Press*, 27 January 1971; "CNC President Appoints Dean of Academic Affairs," *Daily Press*, 20 July 1973; "Dean Resigns at CNC," *Times-Herald*, 24 August 1976; George and Jane Carter Webb communication to Hamilton, 28 May 2008. For an example of Musial communicating with the public, see his article "Educational Goals are Defined," *Daily Press*, 18 April 1974.

division. Two assistant deans possessing significant administrative authority were then appointed to head each school: William Parks of History as head of the Liberal Arts and Sciences division and James Moore of Government as leader of the Social and Behavioral Sciences division.[26]

Just as the academic curriculum expanded during the 1970s, the size of the faculty grew as well, rising from 69 to 102 full-time instructors over the course of the decade. Four-year status and rising enrollments made this expansion necessary. Because academic jobs in general were scarce throughout the decade, Windsor—like most college and university presidents searching for new professors—found an abundance of applicants with PhDs already in hand. In the 1960s, most new PhDs had three to four job offers upon leaving graduate school, which had made Cunningham's task of building a solid faculty extremely challenging. As the situation reversed, however, institutions could and did demand more highly credentialed applicants. Thus, Windsor hired many new faculty members who held their terminal degrees before walking onto the campus. In 1971, for instance, Samuel Bauer joined the psychology department with a PhD from the University of Illinois; two years later, the college hired Sanford Lopater with a doctorate from University of Virginia to teach psychology and George Webb with a PhD from Virginia Tech to teach physics.[27]

---

[26] "Assistant Deans Named," *Times-Herald*, 4 July 1977; George and Jane Carter Webb communication to Hamilton, 28 May 2008.

[27] Samuel Bauer communication to Hamilton, 6 June 2008; George and Jane Carter Webb communication to Hamilton, 27 May 2008; "New Faculty Members, Part I," *Captain's Log*, 22 October 1973. Concerning the overabundance of PhDs on the market, see Thelin, *History of American Higher Education*, 331–32. Cunningham and Windsor often sought to financially help established young faculty members who had master's degrees and who had proven themselves to be talented teachers, obtain their doctorates. For instance, the college assisted Mario Mazzarella in the history department in earning his PhD. An army veteran from Rhode Island, Mazzarella joined the faculty in 1969 as the college prepared for third- and fourth-year course work. Although he had a master's from the University of Rhode Island and had begun doctoral work at American University, Mazzarella had not completed his dissertation. Because he was an effective and dynamic teacher as well as active within the campus community, Windsor wanted to keep him on the staff. Hence the president offered him a two-year leave of absence which allowed the history professor to complete his doctorate and then return to the campus, "CNC Assists

Women filled many of the college's new faculty positions. This was due largely to the relatively new phenomena of "academic couples" in the academy. Indeed, a number of CNC's female professors had married other academics, most of whom they had met while at graduate school. As their husbands landed jobs at nearby institutions, these female instructors sought employment at CNC. And President Windsor eagerly hired a number of them. For instance, French Professor Susan St. Onge came to CNC in 1970 with a PhD from Vanderbilt after her husband had started teaching at William and Mary. This situation, though, sometimes worked in reverse. Samuel Bauer applied to CNC only after his wife had joined the William and Mary faculty. Due to the fact that the college in Williamsburg had a strong nepotism policy preventing his possible employment there, he decided to join CNC's staff.[28] Because the tight academic job market continued throughout the 1970s and into the 1980s, many of these new faculty members remained at Christopher Newport for their entire careers even though its salaries remained the lowest in the state. It was, Windsor later quipped, "a brotherhood of misery."[29]

Most professors who came to CNC in these years focused on teaching. As mentioned above, Windsor decided for administrative simplicity to integrate the day and evening schools, a move that transformed the experiences of both students and faculty. Indeed, CNC's diversity in the classroom increased significantly as both traditional and nontraditional students now took the same courses. Growing levels of

---

Faculty Toward PhDs," *Times-Herald*, 19 November 1969; Mazzarella's hiring was announced in the *Times-Herald* on 4 June 1969.

[28] Susan St. Onge, email communication to Hamilton, 25 February 2008; Samuel Bauer, communication to Hamilton, 6 June 2008; George and Jane Carter Webb communication to Hamilton, 27 May 2008. Other examples of women coming to CNC because of academic husbands include Jane Carter Webb of Tulane University, who was hired along with her husband and together they team-taught physics courses for many years. Theodora Bostick, with a doctorate from the University of Illinois, joined the History Department in 1970 soon after her husband, Darwin, had been hired by Old Dominion University to teach history.

[29] "CNC Faculty Salary Lowest in Virginia, Report Reveals," *Daily Press*, 7 January 1971; Windsor interview with Hamilton, 5 June 2007. Ironically, and counter to national trends, the average salaries of female CNC professors were higher than those of their male counterparts. In 1974, the mean salary for a male professor was $12,910 while a female instructor averaged $13,186; see "Average Salary for Women at CNC Above Those of Men," *Daily Press*, 17 November 1974.

student aid, moreover, such as Basic Education Opportunities Grants, or Pell Grants as they are commonly known today (named after US Senator Claiborne Pell), allowed more minority and underprivileged students to attend.[30] As a result of these changes, classrooms tended to be more informal than in the previous decade. Professor Albert Millar of the English department, for instance, joked in a 1971 *Captain's Log* article about an emerging "tradition" at CNC of both students and faculty being at least five-minutes late for every class. Students and instructors increasingly felt free to smoke and, as a result, custodians had to stock classrooms with fresh ashtrays each day. Professors sometimes even found babies and children in their classes, particularly when students' babysitters fell through. Faculty members generally understood these situations and tried to be as "kid friendly" as possible as long as the young visitors did not disrupt classroom activities.[31]

Many professors, moreover, found teaching in this diverse environment both challenging and stimulating. George Webb discovered CNC to be an enormous change from his previous experiences at Tulane University. Webb joined the college's faculty in 1973 after teaching for several years in New Orleans. Christopher Newport hired not only Webb but also his wife Jane Carter Webb, who held a PhD from Tulane and who had team-taught physics courses there with her husband. At Tulane, almost all of the Webbs' students had been traditional-aged, upper-middle class, and highly motivated to succeed. During their initial semester at Christopher Newport, though, they discovered that their students' ages ranged from 18 to 65 years old and motivation levels varied almost as greatly. However, the couple had decided that they would not "dumb down" their material—even in introductory courses— but rather they would teach at the same level as at Tulane. The first entry-level physics class they taught their initial semester met one evening per-week for three hours. After the first examination, though,

---

[30] Christopher Newport College Catalog, 1973–75, vol. 13, no. 1; Barry Wood interview with Phillip Hamilton, 24 July 2008; Windsor interview with Hamilton, 5 June 2007. On the growth of federal student aid in the 1970s, see Thelin, *History of American Higher Education*, 324–26.

[31] "No Ivy But … ", *Captain's Log*, 2 December 1971; Mathews email communication to Hamilton, 6 June 2008; Bauer communication to Hamilton, 6 June 2008; St. Onge email communication to Hamilton, 25 February 2008.

the couple realized that significant changes were necessary—especially after their 65-year-old student complained about the "C" he had received. "[W]ith grades like that," he said, "I can't get into graduate school." Another student went to George Webb equally unhappy. Referencing Webb's undergraduate degree from the Massachusetts Institute of Technology, the student protested, "Dr. Webb, I did not pay MIT prices and I do not want an MIT course." The couple discovered, furthermore, that a group of blue-collar workers from the shipyards resented being taught by a female professor, and the fact they drank beer before coming to class did not help matters. As a result, the Webbs altered their approach. They realized, for instance, that very few of their students had had trigonometry in high school; therefore, they tried to explain the required material in a more accessible fashion. At the same time, though, the couple frankly told students that without trigonometry, they were simply going to "have to work a little harder" in order to master key concepts. Because most of the students had grown up with a gritty understanding that there was no "free lunch" in life, they were indeed willing to work harder in order to succeed.[32]

Professors in other disciplines had similar experiences. Susan St. Onge recalled teaching a seventy-year-old nontraditional student named James Lane in her French classes. Lane had grown up in New York City during the Depression and had had to drop out of school because of financial hardship. But he made a life-long promise to himself to complete his college education at some point. After Lane retired in Hampton Roads, he enrolled at CNC and majored in French simply because he loved the language.[33] While older, nontraditional students such as Lane frequently attended the college, occasionally highly talented younger students also enrolled. In 1974, sixteen-year-old Nicholas Harper graduated from high school in Newport News. The youth not only graduated two years ahead of his counterparts, but he also had scored 1,460 on his SAT exams; thus he likely could have gone to almost any university in the nation. But Harper decided to attend CNC, where he majored in chemistry, with plans to eventually go to medical school. He completed his undergraduate degree in just two

---

[32] George and Jane Carter Webb communication to Hamilton, 27 May 2008.
[33] St. Onge communication to Hamilton, 25 February 2008.

years, in large part because "[t]he professors took time with me." Harper even found time to immerse himself into the college's social life outside the classroom. He worked as an aide for CNC's Parking Services and as a laboratory assistant for the chemistry department. Despite the age differences, Harper got along well with his fellow students. "We spend a lot of time [together] talking mostly about ourselves," he told the *Daily Press*, "We discuss the state of our world very rarely."[34]

These student success stories were accomplished throughout the decade in the face of difficult and constrained academic budgets. Samuel Bauer, for instance, was floored when he started teaching in 1971 to discover a $200 equipment budget for the entire year, a sum that would not even allow him to buy a single essential instrument. Therefore, he took the money, bought some wood, and constructed lab benches on his own time—benches which he used until his retirement in 2008. In order to properly instruct students in his psychology lab, however, Bauer had to beg and borrow vital equipment from other nearby colleges and universities.[35] Harold Cones, a biology professor who came to CNC in 1968, taught a summer oceanography course throughout the 1970s. Although CNC was surrounded by water, Cones received no money for a boat in which to conduct fieldwork. Therefore, he and his students attempted to save 2.4 million Sperry & Hutchinson Green Stamps in order to purchase a twenty-two-foot Aquasport, along with a built-in sea tank for specimens. Cones eventually obtained a boat (which was a donation), but he and his students never saved enough stamps for an outboard motor and the sea tank.[36]

Like many colleges and universities in the 1970s, CNC offered several experimental classes for students. In 1971, for example, six professors from four different disciplines (biology, economics, psychology, and sociology) taught a course entitled "Can Man Survive?" It provided students with an interdisciplinary look at the globe's environmental situation. Fifty students enrolled in the weekly class, with the professors and occasional guest speakers lecturing and leading class

---

[34] "He's 18 and a CNC Grad," *Daily Press*, 27 June 1976.

[35] Bauer communication to Hamilton, 6 June 2008.

[36] CNC Oceanography Students Saving for a Boat … Stamp by Stamp," *Daily Press*, 24 May 1970.

discussions. The following year, CNC participated in a University of California-project called "Courses by Newspapers." Underwritten by a National Endowment for the Humanities and called "America and the Future of Man," the two-credit class examined the many rapid changes experienced by the United States during that time. Twenty 1,400-word essays written by "distinguished world scholars" and published in local newspapers formed the course's core readings. Two CNC faculty members met periodically with the students to review the essays and discuss views about America's future.[37] During the nation's bicentennial celebrations, the history department sponsored a public symposium on the American Revolution. Bringing in historians from William and Mary, Colonial Williamsburg, and elsewhere, the scholars gave talks on various topics relating to the War for Independence. While open to the public, the college also arranged for CNC students to participate in the symposium for academic credit.[38]

Although most of the faculty's time was spent on teaching, many worked hard to remain active scholars, though generally with mixed results. At the decade's start, no explicit tenure requirements existed for CNC faculty, including those setting publication expectations, and many professors decided—with a heavy 4-4 teaching load—to remain simply teachers. However, as the faculty expanded (with many new instructors holding PhDs from prestigious institutions), more instructors wanted to publish regularly within their disciplinary field. Windsor encouraged scholarship among faculty members as much as possible, and several professors published books as well as obtained major research grants and wrote peer-reviewed articles for scholarly journals. But CNC had few research funds and even fewer sabbaticals available for faculty, both of which were (and are) essential for the completion of serious scholarly projects. Professor Jay Paul of English remembered when he arrived on campus in 1978 there was a culture "where faculty knowledge ruled, few

[37] Christopher Newport College Catalog, 1973–75, vol. 13, no. 1; "Christopher Newport, Times-Herald Offer New Plan in Higher Education," *Times-Herald,* 9 September 1972; Bauer communication to Hamilton, 6 June 2008.

[38] "Bicentennial Symposium Announced by CNC History Department," *Captain's Log,* 23 September 1974. To take advantage of the nearby Mariners' Museum, the history department also offered an evening course on maritime history, see "Mariners' Museum to Support College Course," *Virginia Gazette,* July 1971.

ideas surfaced and everyone roundly praised even the slightest notion of a [scholarly] accomplishment."[39]

The state of the library did not help matters. Throughout the 1970s, the Smith Library's collection grew in size—from twenty-four thousand volumes in 1970 to fifty-eight thousand in 1980—but it remained wholly inadequate for faculty to engage in serious research. Sam Bauer remembers his adjustment to Smith Library as "a trauma," especially after attending the University of Illinois, which boasted the second largest academic library in the country. Bauer's relationship with head librarian, Bette Mosteller, did not help matters. When Bauer wrote her a memo to complain about some of the library's policies, he quickly got on "Mosteller's @#*% list." In fact, Bauer remembers, "she never conversed with me again."[40]

Despite these realities, faculty collegiality remained strong. Susan St. Onge remembers CNC's faculty as being sort of like a "pick-up basketball team" during the decade. Professors' mailboxes were all located in Smith Hall, adjacent to President Windsor's suite of offices. This led to many informal discussions among instructors from different disciplines—who often taught in different buildings—and made acquaintances and friendships easier to form. Some departments made a point to have lunch together on a regular basis. The sociology department, for example, frequently gathered at a nearby restaurant called Sammy & Nicks. Although the grease in the French fries helped neither the department members' health nor waistlines, it allowed them to share their problems as well as enjoy each other's company. A number of professors from different departments also organized a "Gourmet

---

[39] George and Jane Carter Webb communication to Hamilton, 27 May 2008; Jay Paul communication to Hamilton, 14 March 2008. Examples of scholarship in the 1970s included Dr. St. Elmo Nauman, Jr., who published *The New Dictionary of Existentialism* in 1971, and Dr. Marshall Booker, who published an essay in *Principles of Economics*, which was published by George Mason University in 1974. See "CNC Professor's Work Published," *Daily Press*, 19 November 1971; "Public Seeks CNC Economist for Answers," *Daily Press*, 18 March 1974. Regarding Windsor encouraging faculty scholarship, he strongly supported the establishment of a Dean's Colloquia in 1977. It was designed to highlight the faculty's original research; see "Bauer to Inaugurate Colloquia," *Captain's Log*, 18 October 1977.

[40] Bauer, communication to Hamilton, 6 June 2008. On the size of the library, see "Psych Degree Will be Offered by CNC," *Times-Herald*, 13 March 1969.

Club" that met once a month over the years at various instructors' homes, where everyone pitched in to make special dinners. Finally, a campus pub called "The Wheelhouse" opened up in 1974 and permitted faculty members oftentimes to meet after class and unwind over a beer.[41]

Despite the overall social collegiality on campus, professional tensions among some faculty and between some departments did exist. These tensions typically surfaced at Friday afternoon faculty meetings in Christopher Newport Hall. Because the curriculum so frequently expanded and changed during the decade, these meetings were often long—typically running from 3pm to 7pm—and filled with, as one faculty member recalled, "a lot of discord, elocution, impatience, and dissatisfaction." Larry Sachs of the chemistry department, for instance, often held things up by closely reviewing all new courses and program proposals as well as catalog changes. He frequently delayed meetings simply in order to insert a comma or wordsmith a minor phrase. Other faculty members often went on too long making their points about particular issues, much to the frustration of colleagues. Chair of the biology department Jean Pugh had little patience with verbose professors and often launched brusque comments in order to rein them in. And she was not the only faculty member to do so. At one meeting, when a professor of accounting argued at length about the need to place all the business disciplines into a separate school—a proposal most other faculty members thought silly—Robert Saunders of the history department finally interrupted with the barb, "Have you all designed your flag yet??" Laughter ended the discussion, at least for the time being. But such comments reflected an emerging (and perhaps inevitable) division among faculty members as the college expanded and developed.[42]

Finally, commencement ceremonies became larger and more elaborate in the decade. In 1974, Windsor inaugurated a program of high-profile graduations held in the new Hampton Coliseum and

[41] George and Jane Carter Webb communication to Hamilton, 27 May 2008; Bauer communication to Hamilton, 6 June 2008; Mathews email communication to Hamilton, 6 June 2008; Jay Paul, email communication to Hamilton, 14 March 2008.

[42] George and Jane Carter Webb communication to Hamilton, 27 May 2008; Bauer communication to Hamilton, 6 June 2008; Mathews email communication to Hamilton, 6 June 2008.

featuring major national speakers. The president aimed to gain publicity for the school as well as to improve relations with the city of Hampton, which had been strained since the early 1960s when Newport News made sure CNC was placed entirely within its boarders. Windsor also held elegant post-graduation dinners at the James River Country Club with political and civic leaders from *both* Newport News and Hampton invited to attend. Over the years, prominent figures such as George McGovern, Ramsey Clark, Sam Donaldson, and Shirley Chisholm spoke to graduating seniors with crowds of more than three thousand people often in attendance. Occasionally, however, planning for the events proved difficult. In 1974, for instance, Windsor invited the German rocket scientist Werner Von Braun to speak at the Coliseum. Soon after the college announced the appearance, the president got a visit from Sam Jacobson, a leading figure within the Peninsula's Jewish community. "How can you insult the Jewish community by having a former Nazi speak," he yelled. After calming Jacobson down, Windsor invited him to the post-graduation dinner at the country club. Jacobson agreed, but found that the president had seated him next to the German scientist for the meal. Much to Windsor's relief, the two men got along fine and enjoyed each other's company. More importantly, the commencements in Hampton, which continued throughout the 1970s, brought the school national publicity as well as earned it strong political support from Hampton's General Assembly members.[43]

Coping with the '70s: Budgets, Constraints, and Construction

Throughout the 1960s, the Hampton Roads-area economy thrived due to rising populations as well as strong commercial and industrial growth. Robust defense spending tied to Vietnam and the ongoing Cold War also strengthened the region. But circumstances changed in the 1970s when the national economy faltered, especially with the shock of the Arab oil embargo and sharply rising energy costs. As the war in Southeast Asia wound down, moreover, defense spending declined along with Pentagon contracts to the Newport News shipyard.[44] In

---

[43] Windsor interview with Hamilton, 5 June 2008. See also Webb, *Voices*, 22 and "Ramsey Clark to Speak at May Graduation," *Captain's Log*, 22 March 1976.

[44] Wallenstein, *Cradle of America*, 386.

addition to these challenges, Newport News dramatically changed. In particular, the city's once-thriving downtown area along Washington Avenue rapidly declined, with commercial stores like Sears & Roebucks and Nachmans relocating to midtown Newport News, where suburban housing developments continued to grow. Although shipyard workers and city personnel remained at work in the downtown area, shoppers and tourists stayed away. The *Times-Herald* wrote as early as 1972, "People do not stay away from downtown because they are afraid to walk the streets. They stay away because there is nothing to do." By the end of the decade, Washington Avenue and its surrounding neighborhoods had become blighted and increasingly crime-ridden, filled largely with people who could not get out and small businesses struggling to survive. Those businesses in midtown Newport News, meanwhile, did reasonably well in the 1970s. Nearer to the city's new population center and Christopher Newport College, local leaders worked to expand commercial development in such areas as Oyster Point. These structural changes in the city would later greatly affect CNC's development and evolution. But, in the difficult years of the 1970s, these transformations—especially the deterioration of the downtown area—were perceived as irreparable losses.[45]

James Windsor faced additional challenges tied to economic change. Indeed, he had to confront a growing number of problems that other college and university presidents across the country were dealing with. In particular, as economic times grew more difficult, taxpayers and state legislatures became deeply reluctant to increase budgets for higher education. Moreover, inflation drove up construction, energy, and maintenance costs while the declining quality of high school graduates (as revealed by the growing number of failures in introductory college classes) made it more expensive to educate young people. Worst of all, college administrators – including Windsor—realized that these new realities were not transient issues, but chronic problems with which they would have to deal for the foreseeable future.[46]

[45] John V. Quarstein and Parke S. Rouse, Jr., *Newport News: A Centennial History* (Newport News, Virginia: City of Newport News, 1996) 188–94.
[46] Thelin, *History of American Higher Education*, 336.

In a retrospective booklet celebrating Christopher Newport's twenty-fifth anniversary in 1986, a faculty member wrote about the 1970s. No one, she said, initially saw that "the sunshine days [of the 1960s] were just about to end.... But in 1970, the money tap turned off and in Newport News downtown began to die. That was the world Jim Windsor stepped into and he did well to keep things going."[47] Indeed, Windsor did well not only to keep the college going, but he also helped it to expand in the face of challenging circumstances. The 1973–74 recession especially demonstrates how Windsor and the college weathered the economic crisis. The downturn of those years came in part because of the Arab oil embargo sparked by the United States' support for Israel in the Yom Kipper War. Following the oil stoppage, Americans had to deal with a rapid and sustained rise in energy prices. The end of the military draft in June 1973 (tied to the drawdown of troops in Vietnam) exacerbated the financial crisis for colleges. Because many young men had pursued higher education only to maintain their deferments, American colleges and universities afterwards suffered a drop in enrollment for the first time since the end of World War II. While this reality ultimately forced institutions to pay more attention to student needs and concerns, the most immediate impact was financial—fewer students meant fewer tuition dollars.[48]

CNC's leaders confronted all of these realities in the fall of 1973. That semester, Governor Linwood Holton ordered public colleges and universities to cut their budgets by 5 percent because of shortfalls in state revenues. The request upset and worried Windsor. He had previously told state officials that CNC's funding was already inadequate for a bachelor-degree granting institution. Indeed, it repeatedly received the lowest amount of money per student from the state's general fund. "The fact is," he told state leaders as early as 1971, "we are trying to operate a four-year-college on a two-year-college budget."[49] Holton's demand in 1973 for a 5 percent cut would force the college to return nearly $128,000. If that happened, Windsor predicted it would have a "crippling effect"

[47] Webb, *Voices*, 21.

[48] Christopher J. Lucas, *American Higher Education: A History* (New York, 1996) 283; Thelin, *History of American Higher Education*, 321–26.

[49] "Thrifty CNC Deserves Hike in Budget, Windsor Asserts," *Daily Press*, 23 September 1971.

on the college's operations. By curbing nearly all out-of-state travel and equipment purchases, and through negotiations with the governor's office, Windsor eventually reduced the cut to just $54,000.

Windsor also faced the problem of declining enrollment. Because the draft ended in mid-1973, CNC officials saw enrollments drop by nearly 10 percent in the spring of 1974, going from 2,544 students the previous autumn to just 2,313 that spring. The immediate impact was financial: nearly $42,000 in tuition money, which the college had anticipated and budgeted for, did not materialize.[50] In fall 1974, enrollments rose once more—but only by 4 percent—much less than had been expected. Furthermore, increasing inflation and a deepening national recession deterred many Peninsula students from signing up for classes. These developments forced Windsor to cut part-time adjunct faculty, raise average class sizes, halt equipment purchases indefinitely, and put a moratorium on all college hiring, even for replacement faculty.[51]

Because everyone at CNC tightened their belts in the 1970s, campus operations kept going without pause. Windsor's ability to work amicably and successfully with area legislators certainly helped the school through the difficult period. Lewis McMurran, for example, continued to be a staunch advocate for the college until his retirement in 1977. A number of younger Peninsula leaders who supported CNC, moreover, rose to positions of leadership and influence during the decade, including Hunter Andrews in the state Senate as well as Alan Diamonstein and Dick Bagley in the House of Delegates. All of these leaders liked and respected Windsor and looked out for Christopher Newport as best they could. Early in the decade, for instance, their support helped Windsor to secure $1.1 million to build a much-needed Campus Center. When it opened in November 1973, the building included a number of game rooms, a student lounge, a cafeteria, a campus pub (initially called "The Wheelhouse" and later renamed "The

[50] "CNC Cuts Will Save $54,000 for State," *Times-Herald*, 8 December 1973; "CNC Enrollment Dips," *Daily Press*, 7 February 1974.

[51] "CNC Feels Budget Pinch," *Times-Herald*, 4 October 1974; "CNC Starts Hunting for Ways to Cut Spending by 5%," *Daily Press*, 30 October 1974.

Terrace"), and a three-hundred-seat auditorium (which would eventually be named Gaines Theater).[52]

As the nation's economic doldrums worsened, the legislators worked hard to obtain as many state dollars as they could. Dick Bagley, for example, usually met with President Windsor before legislative hearings to discuss the college's financial needs and the president's testimony. During the hearings, furthermore, Bagley often asked Windsor "soft ball" questions. After the president had completed his budget statement one year, for example, Bagley solemnly asked, "Dr. Windsor, how is it you can run a college and produce good students and have good faculty members with less money than any of the others." Such efforts ensured that CNC received as much state money as was politically possible.[53]

Despite the strong political support from local leaders, capital spending on new buildings essentially stopped in the early 1970s, as the state government slashed construction dollars at all public colleges and universities. Basic maintenance and repairs, moreover, consumed the remaining capital funds. In 1973, for instance, the college spent a half-million dollars to install a desperately needed storm-drainage system in order to halt damaging floods that had long plagued the campus following heavy rains.[54] In 1975, moreover, the student body began to grow again with enrollment topping three thousand for the first time

---

[52] "CNC Awards $1.1 million Pact for Center," *Times-Herald*, 19 July 1972; "New Campus Center to Open This Fall, Something for Everyone," *Captain's Log*, 28 August 1973. Gaines Theater was almost eliminated by the General Assembly during appropriation meetings. Only the fast intervention of Lewis McMurran, Dick Bagley, and Hunter Andrews into committee appropriation talks got the money restored, Windsor communication to Hamilton, 13 May 2007.

[53] Windsor interview with Hamilton, 5 June 2007; Webb, *Voices*, 21.

[54] "Rain Reveals Need for Funds at CNC," *Times-Herald*, 24 May 1973; see also "Holton Pares CNC Capital Outlay Plans," 16 January 1974. Windsor had many capital projects in mind. In 1972, he unveiled a ten-year master plan that called for several new academic buildings, a dramatically expanded library, and the establishment of a second campus in midtown Newport News. Preparing for an enrollment of 6,700 students by 1982, Windsor told the Virginia Commission on Higher Education that his plan would cost approximately $12 million. The plan collapsed the following year, however, due to the national recession, see "CNC's Site Plan Goes to Board," *Times-Herald*, 23 September 1972; "CNC to Seek $12 million Next Decade," *Daily Press*, 31 October 1972.

that autumn. But, with all new construction halted, campus buildings quickly filled to capacity. Classrooms were used six days a week, day and night, while space for faculty offices ran out. Indeed, the college had to rent trailers simply to provide some places for the faculty. Located just north of Christopher Newport Hall, the dozen mobile units eventually became known as "Windsor Village."[55] The Smith Library also became a victim of the economic downturn with expansion plans deferred year after year. As a result, the building completely lacked shelf-space for new books and had little room for students. In 1975–76, the library had a seating capacity of only 205 for CNC's 3,000 commuters. Librarian Bette Mosteller, therefore, had to stack new books on windowsills and under reading tables while the students themselves studied in stairwells and sometimes on the floor.[56]

Tight budgets, revenue cuts, and ongoing inflation additionally forced Windsor to raise tuition. In 1972, CNC tuition was $20 per credit hour; by 1979, it had risen to $32 per credit hour. The college's nonrefundable "comprehensive fee," moreover, rose from $2 per credit hour to $7.50 during this same period.[57] To further cope with ongoing budget shortfalls, the president began raising private funds within the Peninsula community. Toward this end, he created the President's Advisory Council in 1973 made up of prominent Hampton Roads leaders, such as Harrol Brauer, Vice President for Sales at WECV-TV. These individuals both contributed funds to the school and helped the college identify other potential donors. Windsor also established the Christopher Newport College Endowment with an initial goal of $3,660,000. Finally, the president created an Annual CNC Fund Drive, initiated the "Captain's Crew" (to raise money for the athletic program), and hired a professional fundraiser whose job was to solicit financial contributions from alumni, businesses, and national and local philanthropic organizations.[58] These measures helped to place

---

[55] "Further Budget Cuts Could Hurt CNC," *Daily Press*, 12 November 1975.

[56] "CNC Waits for Addition to Cramped Library," *Daily* Press, 1 January 1976.

[57] Christopher Newport College Catalog, 1972–73, vol. 12, no. 1, and 1979–81, vol. 17, no. 1; "CNC Increases Tuition Fees," *Daily Press*, 11 January 1980.

[58] "CNC Told to Pass Hat as State Funds Dwindle," *Times-Herald*, 14 December 1973; "CNC Seeks Private Aid," *Times-Herald*, 17 May 1974; "CNC Endowment Proposed," *Times-Herald*, 15 November 1974; "Dr. Beal to Head CNC's Drive," *Times-*

Christopher Newport on somewhat stronger financial footing. Yet the college's straightened circumstances in terms of state funding made Windsor's job an extremely difficult one.

The Shaner Report

The so-called Shaner Report of 1973 emerged out of the decade's financial crisis. Donald Shaner was an efficiency expert and owned a consulting firm in Chicago, Illinois. In 1972, the General Assembly and State Commission on Higher Education hired his firm to examine Virginia's state university system and to recommend specific cost savings at each level of operation. Over a twelve-month period, Shaner visited all of the Old Dominion's public colleges and universities, including Christopher Newport; he and his team then wrote detailed reports and cost-analyses on each. The report dealing with CNC, confidentially released to Windsor in August 1973, was devastating. Shaner argued that CNC's leaders had abandoned the college's original mission to provide vocational training for the Peninsula's local work force; instead it had simply become a liberal arts college whose curriculum mirrored the mother institution of William and Mary. Because other higher education institutions throughout the Hampton Roads-area also offered liberal arts courses, Shaner predicted that CNC would remain small for the foreseeable future. He additionally argued that Christopher Newport's budget planning had been poorly executed and its long-term strategic planning was completely "inadequate." Therefore, the institution should "be closed as quickly as conveniently possible." CNC's full-time students, Shaner wrote, could be easily transferred to William and Mary, which the consultant discovered had an excess classroom capacity for two thousand additional students. Part-timers, meanwhile, could attend nearby community colleges and/or other local four-year colleges. While new faculty would undoubtedly need to be hired at William and Mary, the firing of CNC's classified employees and faculty-ranked administrators would annually save the

Herald, 22 June 1976; "CNC's Budget Approved," *Times-Herald,* 15 September 1978. The Annual Fund Drive was used to support a variety of efforts, such as student grants, faculty research, promotional information, and the Smith Library.

state $680,000. The state, furthermore, would not have to spend additional funds maintaining CNC's seventy-five acre campus.[59]

In early October 1973, Shaner's report leaked to the press. Because it was still officially classified by the General Assembly, Windsor told reporters that he could not speak publicly to the specific criticisms, except to say "if there is a rumor that CNC is going to be phased out, that rumor is false." Throughout the month, however, reports mounted that the state planned to close the college. As a result of the anxiety, Windsor called a college-wide campus meeting attended by hundreds of students, faculty, and staff. He assured the crowd that stories of CNC's demise were "nonsense" and that the best thing the students could do was to go to class and "be a credit to the college." The local community also expressed strong support for Christopher Newport. The Newport News Chamber of Commerce, for instance, passed a resolution that emphasized the college's "great value to the 300,000 people ... [of] the lower Peninsula."[60]

After he had calmed nerves on campus, Windsor traveled to Richmond to testify about the report before the State Council of Higher Education. Appearing with William and Mary President Thomas Graves, both men voiced their strong opposition to Shaner's analysis and recommendations. Graves argued that, while his college did have classroom space for CNC students, the two schools were vastly different. William and Mary admission standards were so rigorous that he believed few CNC students could actually gain admission. William and Mary, moreover, lacked dormitory space for two thousand additional students, and at that time there was little money in the state budget for

---

[59] Donald Shaner and Associates Report, 1973, University Archives. For information on the genesis of the Shaner Report, see "Secret Shaner Report Urges Abolishing CNC," *Daily Press*, 25 October 1973.

[60] "CNC Independence May Not Come Soon," *Times-Herald*, 3 October 1973; "Colleges to Stay Joined, 3 October 1973; "CNC Status—Cloudy or Not?" 5 October 1973; "Secret Shaner Report Urges Abolishing CNC," *Daily Press*, 25 October 1973; "President Holds Assembly: CNC Students Told Closure Nonsense," *Daily Press*, 27 October 1973; "Windsor Dispels Rumors of Abolishment," *Captain's Log*, 5 November 1973; "Chamber of Commerce Passes Resolution Supporting Christopher Newport College," *Captain's Log*, 10 December 1973. Windsor kept faculty informed through two memos, see "Memorandum To Faculty and Staff from James Windsor," 21 September 1973 and 25 October 1973, University Archives.

new ones. Windsor told the council that Graves was "absolutely right". The two colleges served "two different student bodies." Specifically with regard to CNC, it served an urban community and its students greatly needed the college's services. In fact, CNC needed additional classrooms, more faculty offices, and a larger library. Due to these "bitter differences of opinion between the consultant and college and university officials," council members ordered Shaner to revisit both campuses.

In November 1973, therefore, Shaner returned to CNC and met twice with Windsor. The consultant privately admitted that the real target of his recommendations had been the College of William and Mary. Shaner had been angered by President Graves's elitist attitudes as well as by the college's highly restrictive admissions policies. "They weren't acting like a public institution," Shaner complained, "and this was a perfect way to rattle their cage." At the conclusion of his second meeting with Windsor, Shaner told the local press that CNC was indeed a vital and necessary institution to the Peninsula community. He even publicly supported the college's request then before the General Assembly for five million dollars in capital funds needed to expand its facilities. As a result, when the council formally took up the report's recommendations in early January 1974 Christopher Newport's abolition was "summarily and unanimously rejected."[61]

Windsor looked back on the episode as having "strengthened" CNC because of the political support that arose both within the community

----

[61] "CNC Status—Cloudy or Not?" 5 October 1973; "Secret Shaner Report Urges Abolishing CNC," *Daily Press*, 25 October 1973; "Shaner Scheduled to Revisit CNC," *Captain's Log*, 12 November 1973; "Second Shaner Visit to CNC Appears Productive," *Captain's Log*, 3 December 1973; "Panel Rejects CNC Closing Proposal," *Daily Press*, 23 January 1974; James Windsor to Phillip Hamilton, 13 May 2007; Windsor interview with Hamilton, 5 June 2007. See also Webb, *Voices*, 39. In a history paper on the Shaner Report, CNU student Ashley Tingler reported "There were also accusations about Donald Shaner from other colleges and universities that said that Shaner had made numerous mistakes in his report. These show the report's unreliability and Shaner's lack of experience within education. Moreover, there were problems with the report that Shaner had done on Virginia Polytechnic Institution and Radford. It suggested that VPI and Radford merge together; this recommendation was disliked by both colleges, and the schools requested that they remain separate. This shows that CNC was not the only school dealing with problems from the Shaner Report," see Ashley Tingler, "The Shaner Report," unpublished undergraduate research paper, "Researching CNU" history seminar, Spring 2008, University Archives.

and among local leaders. The Shaner Report nonetheless did long-term damage to the college. In particular, it left a perception that Christopher Newport was expendable and much less important than the state's other public institutions. In April 1974, for example, only four months after rejecting Shaner's recommendation that CNC be abolished, the State Council turned down a proposal from the college to establish an academic major in physical education. The council specifically cited Shaner as the "main reason" for their veto. His report had stressed the duplication of many academic programs at Peninsula-area colleges. Thus, because William and Mary, Old Dominion University, and Norfolk State College all offered degrees in physical education, SCHEV argued that a similar degree from CNC was "unnecessary."[62] The Shaner Report also created a deep sense of inferiority and vulnerability among students and faculty—a sense of inferiority and vulnerability that lasted throughout the next decade.

From Student Unrest to Student Antics: Campus Life in the 1970s

Developing an active campus life at a commuter college is a challenge even in the best of times. Christopher Newport in the 1970s was no exception. Throughout the decade, college officials such as Dean of Students William Polis and a cadre of dedicated students attempted to create a robust campus experience. But most students—because they held outside jobs and/or had spouses and children at home—simply attended classes and left afterwards. As a result, charges of apathy and a lack of school spirit frequently appeared. A 1970 student editorial in the *Captain's Log* likened the "atmosphere" at CNC to a "glorified high school." Seven years later, a *Captain's Log* editor sarcastically wrote, "This school ought to offer a course on apathy for freshmen and transfer students."[63] Although these observations were not entirely inaccurate, student life did develop over the years with the initiation of many new

[62] "Physical Education Degrees Vetoed," *Captain's Log*, 8 April 1974.

[63] "CNC Fog," *Captain's Log*, 27 February 1970; "Apathy Cancerous and Spreading at Christopher Newport," 25 October 1977. Susan St. Onge observed that typically between her afternoon and evening classes during the hours of 5 and 7 p.m. she "was literally one of the only people on campus!" Not only was it "depressing," it was also "a bit scary," St. Onge email communication to Hamilton, 25 February 2008.

campus events and traditions. The opening of the Campus Center in 1973, moreover, permitted college-wide parties and concerts to be held, all of which brought more students (and oftentimes faculty) together outside the classroom.

When the decade began, many American campuses experienced considerable political and social unrest. While CNC students generally refrained from protests, demonstrations, and marches, the era's changing values and circumstances continued to be reflected on its campus.[64] One of the largest changes to come to the campus—and which was part of a nationwide phenomenon—was the growing presence of African-American students. Throughout the 1960s, few blacks attended Christopher Newport due to the presence of Hampton Institute and Norfolk State as well because of lingering bitterness over the purchase of the Shoe Lane tract. No full-time black instructors, moreover, taught at CNC. Nevertheless, the college remained open to African Americans from the start. Michael Engs, CNC's first black student who enrolled in 1965, remembered how Christopher Newport faculty members and students accepted people of color with "ease."[65] When the 1970s began, however, the number of African Americans on campus remained very few. In order to increase their enrollment, Windsor and his admissions staff started to actively recruit black students from Peninsula high schools. By 1972–73, ninety-six African Americans had begun to attend. The college, furthermore, sought to develop curricula and programs that would both educate and appeal specifically to African Americans. In the spring of 1973, for instance, history professor Robert Saunders offered a course entitled "Black History," which examined African-American culture across the generations in order to help all students gain "insights into the problems encountered in contemporary black-white relations." Six African-American and twenty-six white students enrolled in the

---

[64] Concerning the lack of unrest at CNC, Windsor told a magazine reporter in 1971, "We have not solved all of the problems of the campuses, but a good start has been made.... A great deal of good has come from some students' efforts.... I'm very proud of our students at CNC. They have not rioted or destroyed anything," "Dialogue: James C. Windsor," *Daily Press*, 8 August 1971.

[65] "First Negro Asks For Day Class At CNC," *Daily Press*, 28 August 1965; A. Jane Chambers, Rita C. Hubbard, Lawrence Barron Wood, Jr., eds., *Memories of Christopher Newport College: The First Decade, 1961–1971* (Gloucester, Virginia: Hallmark), 197–98.

class, which featured lectures and discussions dealing with racial issues throughout the nation's past as well as in the present. The college also sponsored a public lecture and discussion series called "The Black Man in Contemporary America." Featuring film presentations and lectures by professors from Norfolk State College and CNC, the series explored the challenges and barriers that confronted black males in the United States.[66]

In the spring of 1973, a number of African Americans at CNC formed the Black Student Association (BSA) in order "to provide an identity essential to Black students on a predominantly white campus; to provide cultural awareness; and to bring about a closer relationship between Black students, faculty, administration, and other students."[67] In the years that followed, the BSA sponsored a number of campus activities, including dances, movie nights highlighting films with African-American themes, and celebrations such as "Black Awareness Week" and "Black History Week." Hosting speakers, local choirs, documentaries, and round-table discussions, the group sought to "familiarize the college community with the talents and cultural contributions of blacks." Due to CNC's recruitment efforts and its more inclusive campus life, more than three hundred African Americas (or 10 percent of the total student population) enrolled in the college by 1977.[68]

Despite this progress, many blacks still felt out of place on campus. While some white-black friendships existed, most African-American students did not participate in CNC's extracurricular activities beyond the classroom. Some blacks, moreover, believed that "where white students are predominant, funds and facilities are ... better."[69] To help with this sense of isolation, Windsor created the post of minority student counselor in 1977 so that African-American students would have an

---

[66] "CNC Begins Black Lecture Series," *Captain's Log*, 10 October 1970; "Black Studies," *Captain's Log*, 6 March 1973.

[67] "BSA," *Captain's Log*, 2 April 1973.

[68] "BSA Dance," *Captain's Log*, 26 November 1973; "BSA Sponsors Black Awareness Week," *Captain's Log*, 3 February 1975; "BSA to Sponsor 'Black History Week,'" *Captain's Log*, 23 February 1976.

[69] "Blacks Feel Socially Isolated at CNC," *Times-Herald*, 16 September 1976; "Social Isolation Felt by Many at CNC; Social Problems Not Restricted to Blacks," *Captain's Log*, 27 September 1976.

official "with whom they can identify more closely" and who could serve "the needs of our minority enrollment."[70] Windsor's actions, combined with the ongoing campus activities of the BSA, led to more social integration and to an easing of tensions across the campus by the end of the decade.[71]

The women's rights movement grew in prominence among CNC's female students during the 1970s. This was, however, not an entirely new phenomenon. In 1968, more than ninety young women participated in the "sit-in" demonstration at the library protesting its out-dated dress code. Four years later, following Congress' passage of the Equal Rights Amendment (ERA), a group of CNC women formed "Equality," a club designed "to promote equal opportunity and treatment of men and women." In its first year on campus, its members established a "feminist library" housed in the Smith Library, and hosted an "open debate" for students and faculty about the controversial issue of abortion. The following year, club members changed their name to "Organization for Women's Equality" (OWE), and over the course of the decade, they sponsored numerous campus speakers, panel discussions, and workshops about such topics as the ratification of the ERA, sexual discrimination, and women's rights regarding jobs and employment. Several members also conducted research projects focusing on sexual discrimination within the Hampton Roads area.[72] Finally, as more women entered the workforce, OWE as well as the Student Government Association lobbied the college to set up an affordable and accessible daycare center. In 1973, therefore, a CNC daycare facility opened near

---

[70] "Student Counselor Post Created, Filled," *Daily Press*, 18 August 1977.

[71] On the activities of the BSA in the late-1970s, see "CNC Black Student Association Appeals to Blacks," *Captain's Log*, 15 November 1977; "Black-American History Month Comes to CNC," *Captain's Log*, 31 January 1978; "BSA to Present Cultural Festival Night," *Captain's Log*, 14 February 1978; "BSA Activities Prove Successful," *Captain's Log*, 6 February 1979; "Prominent Poet Encourages CNC's Black Students—Learn to Like Selves," 13 February 1979; "African-American History Month Concludes with Discussion," *Captain's Log*, 27 March 1979.

[72] "Equality," *Captain's Log*, 29 August 1972; "O.W.E. Now Recruiting," *Captain's Log*, 17 September 1973; "Women's Work to be Discussed in O.W.E. Workshop," *Captain's Log*, 17 January 1977.

campus at the Warwick United Church. Operating for several years, both students and faculty used the facility.[73]

Throughout the early 1970s, other important contemporary issues were discussed on campus, primarily through the Patrick Henry Forum, which featured a program of monthly speakers and discussions. Begun by government professor C. Harvey Williams, Mario Mazzarella of History, and Joseph Healey of Sociology, the forum tackled such diverse issues as population growth, revising Virginia's state constitution, Zen Buddhism, and the United States' ongoing involvement in Vietnam.[74] The forum's annual "Raft Debates," however, proved to be its most popular event. The premise of the Raft Debates was that, twenty-four hours after a nuclear holocaust, three survivors—represented by three professors from different academic disciplines—are stranded on a raft in the ocean with only enough food for one to survive. The three professors then had to debate among themselves whose discipline was the most worthy of the food. The applause of the several hundred students and faculty typically in attendance determined the winner. Students liked the Raft Debates so much that they continued throughout the 1980s, even though the Patrick Henry Forum itself ended in 1975.[75]

After the Campus Center opened in 1973, its three-hundred-seat theater often became the locale for many political debates and appearances. In October 1976, for instance, the lobbying group Common

---

[73] "Cowboy Bob's Column," *Captain's Log*, 6 March 1973; "Kids 'Sure Do' Like Day Care Center," *Captain's Log*, 24 September 1973.

[74] "Forum Unites Town and Gown," *Times-Herald*, 22 February 1971; "Patrick Henry Forum," *Captain's Log*, 23 September 1971; "Man Who Exposed 'Tiger Cages' Speaker at CNC," *Daily Press*, 2 November 1971; "North Ireland Problem Is Discussed Here," *Times-Herald*, 27 April 1972. The most prominent Forum speaker was William Kunstler, noted civil rights attorney and defense attorney for the "Chicago Eight," "Kunstler Will Speak at CNC on the American Indians," *Captain's Log*, 22 April 1974.

[75] "Patrick Henry Forum Sponsors 'Raft Debate,'" *Captain's Log*, 18 March 1974; "Cease Drinking the Salty Water of Authorities, Whether Priests or Scientists, Doctors, or Humanists," *Captain's Log*, 25 March 1974; "Patrick Henry Forum Closes," *Captain's Log*, 31 March 1975; "Raft Debate for Survival," *Captain's Log*, 17 November 1975; "Over 200 Attend Recent Raft Debate," *Captain's Log*, 24 November 1975; "Raft Debate Brings Scholars Together in Midst of Ocean to Solve the Problems of Survival," *Captain's Log*, 6 March 1979; "Nauman Gets the 'Raft,'" *Captain's Log*, 27 March 1980; "World Will End on September 20," *Captain's Log*, 14 September 1989; "Satan in Raft Debate," *Captain's Log*, 28 September 1989.

Cause sponsored a debate among several candidates running for the state's First Congressional District. One candidate was a local district attorney named Paul Trible. Several weeks later, Trible went on to win the seat. When he ran for re-election in 1978, his wife, Rosemary, represented her husband at a "Politics with Principles Forum" sponsored by the Christopher Newport Student Association. Film star Elizabeth Taylor also appeared in the campus theater. Then-married to Virginia's US Senator John Warner, Taylor came to CNC in 1979 in order to build political support for her husband in the Tidewater area.[76]

The Campus Center's theater served the Peninsula community in other ways. Many local organizations used the facility as a venue for their own performances, including the Norfolk Theater Company, the Peninsula Civic Opera, the Peninsula Community Theater, and the United Nations Association.[77] The decade's most important cultural program—both for the college and the community—was the Nancy A. Ramseur Memorial Artist-in-Concert Series. Nancy Ramseur, who had served as CNC's first registrar and director of admissions, tragically died in the spring of 1974 in an automobile accident during a vacation in England. Later that fall, Barry Wood and Rita Hubbard organized the series to honor their colleague. The series featured performances by well-known classical artists and groups, such as the Metropolitan Opera's baritone William Walker, the Israeli pianist Joseph Kalichstein, and the Royal Shakespeare Company. Well-attended throughout the years (often with standing-room only), the series ran until 2002.[78]

---

[76] "Congressional Candidates Meet at CNC," *Captain's Log*, 4 October 1976; "SA Invites Virginia Politicos to Speak in October," *Captain's Log*, 3 October 1978; "Attendance at Forum Embarrasses CNC," *Captain's Log*, 17 October 1978; "Elizabeth Taylor Warner Charms CNC Audience," *Captain's Log*, 18 October 1979; see also "Ford, Trible, and Byrd Win in a Straw Poll," *Captain's Log*, 1 November 1976 and "Warner, Trible Edge Out Competition in Christopher Newport Opinion Poll," *Captain's Log*, 7 November 1976.

[77] "World Affairs Forum Underway at CNC," *Captain's Log*, 9 September 1974; "Does Community Commitment Mean the Loss of Student Activities at CNC?" *Captain's Log*, 8 April 1974. CNC's mission is listed in the "Aims and Purposes" section of the Catalog, 1977–79, vol. 16, no. 1.

[78] Windsor interview with Hamilton, 5 June 2007; "Olivia Stapp, Mezzo-Soprano, Will Perform in CNC Theater," *Captain's Log*, 4 November 1974; "Artist-in-Concert Series to Begin October 10," *Captain's Log*, 6 October 1975; "Kalichstein Renders Outstanding Performance," *Captain's Log*, 12 April 1976; "Nancy A. Ramseur

The Christopher Newport Players, the college's theater troupe, also annually performed a variety of full-length and one-act plays in the center's theater. The Players mainly staged experimental avant-garde performances as well as serious works by such playwrights as Tennessee Williams. The high point for the group came in 1974–75 when they performed *Farewell Judas*, a play written by the Polish playwright I. Iredynski. The Polish embassy's cultural attaché came down from Washington, DC, to attend the performance. After seeing the show, he invited the CNC students to Poland to perform *Farewell Judas* in his homeland. In early 1975, therefore, the group traveled to Poland where they performed in Karkow, Wroclaw, and Warsaw.[79] Despite this triumph, however, most performances by the Players were greeted by indifference from students with the theater rarely even half-filled. When only fifteen patrons showed up for one production, CNC Theater Director Bruno Koch complained to the *Captain's Log*, "I think we have something culturally substantial to offer…. The problem is that no one is taking advantage of it." The roots of the problem, however, lay in the fact that CNC remained a commuter college; thus, most students had neither the time nor the opportunity to take part and support such campus events.[80]

Christopher Newport's Student Government Association (SGA) continued to operate throughout the decade, but it, too, had a difficult time. Few students participated in elections and even fewer were willing to serve in office. In the spring of 1974, for instance, only 188 CNC

Memorial Concert Series to Present Grammy-Award Winning Artists," *Captain's Log*, 13 September 1976; "Concert Series Begins Season," *Captain's Log*, 11 October 1977; "Celebrated Musicians Perform for CNC Concert Series, Soprano Opens," *Captain's Log*, 19 September 1978; "Artist-in-Concert Series Opens Sixth Year in October," 27 September 1979.

[79] "CNC Players Present Two by Tennessee Williams," *Captain's Log*, 11 December 1972; "*Farewell Judas* Will Open CNC Players' Season This Week," *Captain's Log*, 11 November 1974; "CNC Players Soon Embark for Poland," *Captain's Log*, 24 November 1974.

[80] "Despite Low Student Participation, Discouragement Is Not Allowed," *Captain's Log*, 21 November 1978; "CNC's One-Act Plays Are Ready for Prime Time," *Captain's Log*, 6 December 1979; "'A Funny Thing …' Hits the Mark," *Captain's Log*, 13 March 1980. For more information about CNC/CNU Theater over the years, see Kimberly Burbank, "Theater CNU," unpublished undergraduate research paper, "Researching CNU" history seminar, Spring 2008, University Archives.

students cast votes at a time when the student body stood at approximately 2,500. The *Captain's Log* reported that consequently "none of the Junior class offices were filled." In 1975–76, the college attempted an experiment of actually paying SGA officers in order to entice more students to serve; the student president, therefore, earned $690 that year, while each senator made $345. Windsor discontinued the trial the following year when student voting and participation failed to increase. Although CNC's status as a commuter college once again likely contributed to low student participation, other factors also may have played a part. In the wake of the Vietnam debacle and Watergate scandal, disillusionment with government at all levels probably led students to reject SGA and to shift their energies elsewhere. Many students throughout the decade, for instance, did participate in the production of the student paper, the *Captain's Log*. Despite the difficult economy, the college financially supported and published the paper twice a month during each academic year. As throughout the 1960s, a dedicated cohort of eighteen to twenty students annually wrote, laid-out, and edited the paper, which featured stories about student classes and campus activities as well as editorials containing faculty and student opinions.[81] English students, moreover, continued to publish *The Undertow*, soliciting works of art, poetry, short-story fiction, drama, and photography from the student body.[82]

In 1971, another group of students, describing themselves as "history freaks," began the History Club as a way to "channel their energy." Over the decade, they sponsored panel discussions and lectures on such serious topics as the Arab-Israeli conflict. They also took field trips to Monticello and to many of Virginia's Civil War battlefields. The club became especially well known across campus because it regularly

---

[81] "SGA Elections Returned; CNC Mascot Named," *Captain's Log*, 29 April 1974; "Should CNC Students Pay SGA Officers," *Captain's Log*, 26 April 1976; "Distrust of 'Establishment' Lead to Declining Support by Students," *Captain's Log*, 20 September 1977. See also "Are SGA Elections a Farce, or Are the Students?" *Captain's Log*, 25 March 1974; "Poor Attendance Plagues SGA Senate," *Captain's Log*, 16 February 1976; "SA Vice-President Blames Lack of Exposure to Student Apathy," *Captain's Log*, 11 April 1978.

[82] "Read This," *Captain's Log*, 7 February 1973; "Undertow to Offer $$ Prizes," *Captain's Log*, 20 January 1975; "'Undertow' Changes Name to Express the Flow of Literature," *Captain's Log*, 7 February 1978.

sponsored weeklong "festivals" celebrating medieval and Renaissance culture. Working with Professor Mario Mazzarella, club members designed the five-day events to provide their fellow students with "a broader understanding and appreciation" of this historical period. During 1976's Medieval Week, for instance, the club organized a costume exhibit, a historical "debate" (with each participant portraying a well-known figure in history), and a jousting tournament. The festival ended with a medieval banquet and a Commedia dell Arte held in the Campus Center. Although events sometimes only drew small crowds, the club continued to hold the festivals until the late 1970s.[83]

Throughout the decade, CNC athletic teams grew substantially in number. At the decade's start, Christopher Newport joined the Dixie Intercollegiate Athletic Conference and, from that point onward, "the Captains" competed only against other four-year colleges and universities. Because of Title IX, moreover, CNC started and supported new women's teams in basketball, tennis, golf, track and soccer. Although some called upon the college to also sponsor men's baseball and football squads, President Windsor firmly said no. With limited facilities and funds as well as because CNC could offer no athletic scholarships, additional sports were simply not possible.[84]

Basketball proved to be the decade's most successful and popular sport at the college. Under the ongoing leadership of Coach Bev Vaughan, the squad attracted fine players from throughout the

---

[83] "Psyching Out History," *Captain's Log,* 26 March 1973; "History Department to Present Five-Day Festive Celebration of Medieval Culture," *Captain's Log,* 22 March 1976; "Medieval Week Plagued by Poor Turnout, Lack of Knowledge," *Captain's Log,* 5 April 1976; "Medieval Week Celebrated at CNC," *Captain's Log,* 7 March 1978; "Renaissance Week Offers CNC Students a Glimpse Backward into 15th and 16th century Europe and Beyond," *Captain's Log,* 24 April 1979.

[84] "New Era Begins for CNC Basketball: Team to Play Only Four-Year Institutions," *Captain's Log* , 23 September 1971; "CNC Bids for Two Affiliations," *Captain's Log,* 16 January 1972; "CNC Will Keep Its Sports Modest, Windsor Declares," 23 November 1974; *Daily Press*; see also "CNC Uses Community Facilities for Physical Education Program," 24 September 1972, *Daily Press.* On the formation of the girls' basketball team, see "Girl Basketball Team Forms," *Captain's Log,* 24 September 1973. For more information about women's sports at CNC/CNU, see Holli Sawyer, "The History of Women's Athletics at Christopher Newport College/University," unpublished undergraduate research paper, "Researching CNU" history seminar, Spring 2008, University Archives.

Peninsula and earned winning records nearly every year. As a result, it drew spectators from across the campus and community. Indeed, the team periodically squeezed more than seven hundred fans per game into Ratcliffe Hall's tiny gymnasium. Because of the team's success and popularity, student leaders and administrators began the annual homecoming tradition with festivities and student social events organized around several basketball games every February. Probably the team's best player of the decade was Carl Farris, who played four years of outstanding basketball and set a variety of team records. In 1973–74, moreover, Farris was Christopher Newport's first athlete to be named an All-American by the National Association of Intercollegiate Athletics.[85]

While intercollegiate sports attracted a number of dedicated CNC students, even more participated in the college's intramural sports program. Begun in the 1960s, intramural squads expanded in number as the college itself grew in size. By the mid-1970s, hundreds of Christopher Newport students annually participated in eighteen separate sports, with basketball and flag-football the most popular. Throughout the decade, for instance, at least eleven men's basketball teams annually competed against one another, with typically 120 student-players on the rosters. Even male faculty members organized an intramural basketball team to play against the students; and sometimes their squad dominated entire seasons.[86] Although flag-football tended to be a male-only sport, a

[85] "CNC Captains Crush Greensboro Hornets in Opening Game," *Captain's Log,* 3 December 1973; "Dan Kooi Crowned Homecoming Queen, Abdicates to Susan Buckley," *Captain's Log,* 4 February 1974; "Carl Farris: CNC's First All-American," *Captain's Log,* 8 April 1974; "Captain's, Vaughan Logs 100th Win," *Captain's Log,* 20 January 1975; "Basketball Team Shoots for Capacity Crowds," *Captain's Log,* 18 October 1977; "Frenzied Mob Gathers in Ratcliffe Gymnasium to Support Captains," *Captain's Log,* 31 January 1978.

[86] "Intramural Basketball to Begin Soon," *Captain's Log,* 12 November 1973; "Sunday Marks Opening of Intramural Basketball," *Captain's Log,* 10 December 1973; "Intramural Sports Draw Participants and School Support," *Captain's Log,* 1 March 1977. See Christopher Newport College Catalog, 1972–73, vol. 12, no. 1 for a list of intramural sports. By 1974, the intramural sports program had grown so large that Windsor established an Intramural Sports Office, with two paid student-workers administrating things, "Intramural Sports Office Opens Doors," *Captain's Log,* 30 September 1974. Occasionally, the faculty men's basketball team would play the CNC Varsity female basketball team, see "Lady Captains Fall to Older, Taller Men's Faculty Team," *Captain's Log,* 10 April 1980.

group of female students attempted in 1974 to establish all-girl "powder puff" teams. Eventually two squads were cobbled together—one composed of freshmen and sophomores and the other of juniors and seniors. The girls' season ended abruptly, however, after only three games. Although the freshmen/sophomore team won the first game, the upperclassmen took the second contest. The final game proved to be the grudge match. Indeed, the game grew so rough that several girls left the field with black eyes and one exited with blood streaming from her nose. Hence, with the score tied 7-7, the game was called and the players decided to leave flag-football to their male counterparts.[87]

By the mid-1970s, with the Vietnam War and the draft having ended, student protests and marches on American campuses also largely came to an end. In fact, as the social atmosphere at colleges and universities became less-highly charged, student antics and pranks increasingly replaced political rallies and demonstrations. Once more, student life at CNC reflected these broader trends. In the spring of 1974, for example, at a time when streaking had become a national phenomenon, a wave of nude runners struck Christopher Newport. The first incident occurred one afternoon in March at the center of campus near Smith Hall. According to the *Captain's Log*, an unidentified male student ran up to the campus flagpole and "stood in nature's dress" for everyone to see. When a crowd gathered nearby and began clapping, the bare student gladly "accept[ed] the applause" of all. Later that same day, a group of male streakers disrupted a faculty meeting in Christopher Newport Hall. At the time, President Windsor had been discussing the college's budget when seven naked students ran in one door, dashed in front of the collected professors, and then exited out the other side of the room. After a moment of stunned silence, faculty members themselves began clapping and soon gave the seven a standing ovation with cheers of "nicely done."[88]

In addition to these antics, the opening of the Wheelhouse Pub in the Campus Center that same year began a time of growing socializing

---

[87] "Powder Puff Football Ends After Bloody Encounter," *Captain's Log*, 11 November 1974.
[88] "CNC Streakers Join Nationwide Phenomenon," *Captain's Log*, 18 March 1974; Windsor interview with Hamilton, 5 June 2007. See also "On Streaking, by President Windsor," *Captain's Log*, 18 March 1974.

among students on campus. Indeed, after it opened, the pub quickly became *the* meeting place for students to gather, share a beer and sandwich together, or meet with faculty members in a more informal setting. Various local musical groups also started to perform in the campus bar several evenings a month. In fact, the pub became so popular that, just two years after it opened, the college had to enlarge the length of the bar, add two beertaps, and greatly expand the food menu.[89]

The Campus Center and pub also became the locale for a growing number of campus parties. Because students often consumed alcohol (sometimes to excess), however, these events occasionally became rowdy and even destructive. The main campus celebrations each academic year were the annual Fall and Spring Fests. Begun in 1973 as a weekend of activities, the tradition eventually expanded into a weeklong festival of students (and many faculty) enjoying games, movies, concerts, and beer. The 1975 Spring Fest, for example, featured live music by a number of local bands that performed outdoors behind Christopher Newport Hall. Students also organized competitive activities among CNC's clubs, featuring such games as a "stumble foot derby," "a sensitivity awareness" match (sponsored by the Psychology Club), and a "beer-guzzling contest." Over the weekend, the party lasted all-night with concerts not wrapping up until 2 a.m., while movies ran in the Campus Center until dawn. As the sun came up, students enjoyed a breakfast of bacon and eggs before finally heading home.[90]

Campus life continued to develop when a new student-group formed in 1976. Taking the tongue-in-cheek named of "The Over-the-Hill-Gang" (OTHG), the club focused, not on academics, but on hanging out with friends, hosting campus parties, and playing pranks. Composed of an equal number of men and women, the OTHG regularly participated in intramural sports as well as homecoming activities. Indeed, two of its members (Rick Trotman and Donna Newsome) were

---

[89] "Rollings Has CNC Pub 'Rolling' with Help from His Friends," *Captain's Log*, 2 December 1974; "Wheelhouse Considered Success, New Morning String Band Will End Semester," *Captain's Log*, 9 December 1974; "New Dining Facilities Planned for Campus Center," *Captain's Log*, 10 January 1977.

[90] "SGA Schedules 'Spring Fest,'" *Captain's Log*, 7 April 1975.

named the King and Queen of the 1977 Homecoming Court.[91] The club also annually sponsored a "Taco Night" and a "Hog Dog Night." Held in the pub, these parties featured "limitless" tacos and hot dogs as well as "all-you-can-can-drink" beer. Typically attracting several hundred students, the revelry always culminated with the "Annual Chugging Contest," which was traditionally judged by three CNC faculty members. In 1979, for instance, Drs. Charles Behymer (then Dean of Student Affairs), St. Elmo Nauman, and Robert Coker judged the beer-drinking competition among the six men's teams and three women's squads.[92] The OTHG also sponsored a Toga Party (several months after the release of National Lampoon's *Animal House*) as well as a campus fund raiser based on the 1970s television hit *The Gong Show*, with the money going to the college's annual Fund Drive.[93] The Over-the-Hill-Gang's most popular event on campus, though, was its annual "wet t-shirt contest" held in the Campus Center cafeteria, adjacent to the pub. Begun in the fall of 1976, the event always drew hundreds of rowdy (mostly male) students who usually shouted "more water" at the nine or ten female contestants. A female student who attended the contest one year (but who was not a contestant) left the Campus Center saying the place was "full of animals." As with the "Chugging Contest," CNC faculty members typically judged the event.[94]

[91] "Over-the-Hill Gang Takes Homecoming Crown," *Captain's Log*, 31 January 1977.

[92] "OTHG Fiesta Great Success," *Captain's Log*, 22 November 1977; "OTHG Plays Host to Rowdy Mob," *Captain's Log*, 28 February 1978; "OTHG Draws 250 People to Pub for Hog Dog Fest and Chugging Contest," *Captain's Log*, 14 November 1978; "OTHG Chows and Chugs," *Captain's Log*, 18 October 1979.

[93] "TOGA!" *Captain's Log*, 10 October 1978; "Doane and Simmonds Ring Out First Place in OTHG Gong Show," *Captain's Log*, 3 April 1979.

[94] "Water Shortage, Only Problem at 'Wet T-Shirt Contest,'" *Captain's Log*, 6 December 1976; "Over-The-Hill-Gang Announces the Return of Two Special Events," *Captain's Log*, 14 March 1978; "300 Crowd into a Hot Cafeteria to Watch 8 Women Cool Off," *Captain's Log*, 4 April 1978; *Captain's Log*, 15 November 1979; "OTHG's Wet T-Shirt Contest Draws Large, Rowdy Crowd," *Captain's Log*, 17 April 1980. In 1979, a "best buns" contest was added with male student contestants, see *Captain's Log*, 15 November 1979. The Over-the-Hill-Gang's various traditions lasted until the early 1980s, after which its initial members graduated. In the early 1980s, moreover, Greek organizations began to dominate the campus's social life. Greek life on campus will be discussed in Chapter 4.

As the number of campus parties grew, however, incidents of violence and damage unfortunately increased as well. A dance sponsored by the Modern Language Club, for instance, ended with the arrival of the Newport News Police who came to campus to disperse the "rowdy attendees." Administration officials the next day found the Campus Center "looking like a disaster area" with beer and wine bottles scattered both inside and outside the building. The men's bathroom, moreover, had sustained significant damage with several broken sinks and water handles.[95] As a result of the vandalism, Dean of Student Affairs William Polis imposed tighter controls on parties, such as limiting the number of outside guests CNC students could bring to campus. He required the pub, moreover, to hire an adult to check CNC I.D.'s, while student organizations themselves had to hire security personnel to patrol all parties at the Campus Center with more than 100 attendees. Although violence and vandalism periodically occurred afterwards, these measures greatly reduced the number of such incidents.[96]

Breaking the Bonds: Independence from the College of William and Mary

Even before James Windsor became president, rumors existed that Christopher Newport College would sooner rather than later gain its independence from the "mother college" of William and Mary. When the school became a four-year institution and its student body expanded, such rumors gained momentum. In 1972, the *Times-Herald* ran a prominent article headlined "CNC Appears Ready for Independence." The reporter gave three reasons: First, the college had long possessed "a fairly free hand" in its day-to-day operations and Windsor himself had administrative "authority roughly comparable to the William and Mary president." Second, Virginia's State Council of Higher Education had issued a report several years earlier entitled "Plan for the '70s," which

---

[95] "Dance Plagued with Property Destruction, Litter, Misconduct," *Captain's Log*, 17 February 1975.

[96] "Outsiders Cause Problems at Dances," *Captain's Log*, 17 March 1975; "CNC Student Association Vice President and Two Others Sustain Injuries in Brawl," *Captain's Log*, 5 December 1978; "Dean Reiterates Restrictions for Dances and Activities," *Captain's Log*, 16 January 1979.

had called for the elimination of all state branch colleges. Finally, in 1972, the General Assembly granted George Mason University and Mary Washington College their independence from their "mother college," the University of Virginia. It seemed to most observers, therefore, that CNC's independence was only a matter of time.[97]

The following year, Windsor took a step toward independence when he established the "President's Advisory Council." As mentioned, the council was composed of prominent business and civic leaders from throughout the Peninsula and chaired by Harrol Brauer. The president hoped the body would not only raise money for the college, but also serve as a pseudo-board of visitors. He particularly wanted its members to lobby state leaders to support CNC's eventual independence. Indeed, one of the council's first actions was to approve and endorse a "planning statement" sent to the State Council of Higher Education calling for independence as soon as possible. Explaining that, as an "urban, non-residential" college, Christopher Newport was "clearly different" from William and Mary. Because each college possessed different student bodies and different professional and academic programs, CNC should, therefore, become an "autonomous institution with its own governing board" no later than 1 July 1974.[98] Days after the advisory council sent the statement to the State Council, however, the press learned of the Shaner Report. In the wake of its recommendation to abolish the college, SCHEV rejected CNC's proposal and informed Windsor and council members that its affiliation with William and Mary would continue.[99]

In addition to the State Council, William and Mary officials and Lewis McMurran also balked at separation. President Thomas Graves did not wish to see the tie end in large part because his college got credit for educating all students on the Peninsula through its affiliation with CNC. This connection politically protected William and Mary's elite status, especially with the state legislature. Members of William and

---

[97] "CNC Appears Ready for Independence," *Times-Herald*, 17 February 1972.

[98] "CNC Split Will Come-Eventually," *Times-Herald*, 12 October 1973; "CNC Apparently to Remain as William and Mary Branch," *Captain's Log*, 6 February 1974. For more information on the President's Advisory Council, see "CNC Seeks Private Aid," *Times-Herald*, 17 May 1974.

[99] "CNC Apparently to Remain as William and Mary Branch," *Daily Press*, 6 February 1974.

Mary's Board of Visitors repeatedly made this same point at their meetings. Lewis McMurran also wanted the affiliation to continue, but for different reasons. McMurran had a deep and profound sense of history, particularly Virginia history. Several times he went to Windsor's office to discuss independence from a historical perspective, telling the president, "I don't think it's good for a young college to separate itself from the ancient College of William and Mary." In short, CNC's future would be stronger and brighter by maintaining its formal affiliation with a mother college established in 1693 rather than simply being a brand new institution out on its own.[100]

To deal with these roadblocks, Windsor took direct action. In May 1975, he attended a William and Mary Board of Visitor's meeting where he argued strongly for CNC's independence. He bluntly told board members that his college's "'branch' status" equaled "a second-class status" to most observers. Even though CNC had achieved independent accreditation as a four-year college in 1971, the ongoing William and Mary tie had created "the implication that [the college] is not ready to stand alone." Windsor further stated that the board of visitors barely spent any time on CNC matters during its meetings. This was not out of negligence, he realized, but simply due to "a matter of time." Nonetheless, this lack of attention had created a leadership vacuum for the college. Furthermore, the present arrangement provided CNC with no financial benefits, as the schools' appropriations and budgets were already completely separate. Finally, Windsor appealed to the board's own self-interest. He told its members that CNC independence would mean "[y]ou will have one less college to govern, [and] a few less resolutions and enclosures to consider." Concluding with an analogy, Windsor said, "Like a child who gets separated from his family as he grows, Christopher Newport has slowly evolved an identity of its own." The president's performance greatly impressed William and Mary officials. Indeed, he convinced President Graves and all board members present to support the college's independence. Although they pointed out to Windsor that it was the responsibility of "the General Assembly to

---

[100] Windsor interview with Hamilton, 5 June 2007.

initiate separation procedures," they would no longer publicly oppose such actions.[101]

Legislative action, however, required Lewis McMurran being brought on board. Indeed, no one in the legislature would act before "Lord Lewis" had taken a position. In 1975, however, McMurran was still not ready for separation. Therefore, Windsor carefully prepared to change his mind. That fall, the president called upon the advisory council, the CNC Alumni Association, and the Peninsula Chamber of Commerce to all issue resolutions calling upon the General Assembly to vote for CNC independence by 1 July 1976. Each group agreed, and their resolutions pointed out that the college would significantly benefit by having its own board of visitors dedicated solely to Christopher Newport affairs. Windsor also convinced Alan Diamonstein, a General Assembly delegate from Newport News who was then growing in stature and prominence, to publicly assert that he would "go along with the wishes of [CNC's] administration" on the matter of independence.[102]

McMurran still balked, however, and sought to find some middle ground that would allow CNC to "have what it wants and still keep the benefits of the tie with William and Mary." He suggested that the board of William and Mary could, perhaps, increase in size by seven members, all of whom "would be oriented toward CNC." Advisory Council Chairman Brauer, though, told Windsor that such a proposal was unworkable in his mind. To break the impasse, the president organized a lunch with McMurran, Brauer, and all other local members of the General Assembly in attendance. The meeting initially did not go well. Throughout the meal, McMurran continued to say that he just could not be a part of the college's separation from William and Mary. Finally, fellow House Delegate Ted Morrison spoke up, "Lewis, I know how you feel. But the people [of the Peninsula] have spoken and we just don't have the right to stop it." Morrison's point struck home. After pondering the issue for several moments, the father of Christopher Newport College at last agreed and said that he would introduce the necessary

---

[101] President James Windsor Remarks to the William and Mary Board of Visitors, 3 May 1975.

[102] "Alumni Back Solo CNC," *Times-Herald*, 6 November 1975; "College Advisory Council Supports Separation from William and Mary," *Daily Press*, 14 November 1975; Windsor interview with Hamilton, 5 June 2007

legislation.[103] True to his word, on 26 January 1976, McMurran submitted a bill to the General Assembly to formally separate CNC and William and Mary. The entire Hampton and Newport News delegations were listed as co-sponsors. The legislation specifically called for the formal creation of a Christopher Newport Board of Visitors to be appointed by the governor on 1 July 1976, with complete independence taking place one year later on 1 July 1977. The legislation sailed through the various committees and was passed by the full General Assembly on 5 March 1976.[104]

In June 1976, after Governor Mills Godwin signed the legislation, he appointed twelve men to make up CNC's first board of visitors. The list included Harrol Brauer, who soon afterwards was elected the college's first rector. One name left off the governor's list, however, was King Meehan, the man who had launched the Peninsula's drive for a college eighteen years earlier. Meehan had been an active member of Windsor's President's Advisory Council and a vocal proponent of independence from William and Mary. But, in 1976, he was bed-ridden, suffering from cancer, and not expected to live long. He anticipated, however, being named by the governor to CNC's first board because of his many contributions to the institution. When he discovered, however, that Mills had not appointed him, either because he, Meehan, did not hold a bachelor's degree or due to his ill health, he was devastated. His wife, Elsie, later remembered the profound hurt and disappointment she saw on his face when he learned that he had been passed over.[105]

---

[103] "CNC Split Awaits McMurran," *Times-Herald,* 13 January 1976; Windsor interview with Hamilton, 5 June 2007. See also "CNC-WandM Tie Doesn't Bind," *Times-Herald,* 6 October 1975; "Separate CNC Endorsed," *Times-Herald,* 22 November 1975; "SGA Referendum Results Positive," *Captain's Log,* 24 November 1975; "Advantages Outweigh Disadvantages in W&M, CNC Separation Issue," *Captain's Log,* 1 December 1975; "Senate Approves Support for Independent Status," *Captain's Log,* 12 January 1976; "Windsor: W&M's Just a Name," *Times-Herald,* 16 January 1976.

[104] "CNC Independence Before Legislature," *Times-Herald,* 27 January 1976; "Christopher Newport—William and Mary Bill Clears Committee," *Danville Register,* 30 January 1976; "Newport College Bill Advances," *Richmond Times-Dispatch,* 30 January 1976; "Milestone Achieved in CNC Separation Quest," *Captain's Log,* 2 February 1976; see also Webb, ed., *Voices,* 5.

[105] Elsie Meehan Duval interview with Phillip Hamilton, 20 April 2008.

On 1 July 1977, however, the college as a whole celebrated its independence with a formal academic procession and ceremony in which the resolution separating the school from William and Mary was officially read and presented to the new board of visitors and President Windsor. Professor Stephen Sanderlin, the senior member of CNC's faculty, carried the college's new mace of walnut and sterling silver in the procession. Engraved with the name of the college's two presidents and rector, the mace signified CNC's new institutional independence. Brauer delivered the main address to the gathered faculty, staff, and guests where he explained that "[CNC's] challenge is to create a new tradition.... Today a new and greater institution exists. It is prepared to rise imbued with that indomitable spirit and energy by which it has been guided."[106] The following year, CNC awarded an honorary degree to Lewis McMurran during its spring commencement exercises. Everyone praised the delegate for his long "leadership in public affairs" which had made such "an outstanding contribution to the Peninsula community." President Windsor especially lauded McMurran for his stewardship over the years specifically with regard to Christopher Newport, ranging from chairing the founding Peninsula Committee for Higher Education in 1959 all the way to sponsoring the legislation creating an independent institution in 1976. Windsor concluded that the state delegate, who had just retired after twenty-eight years in the General Assembly, certainly deserved to be known as "the Father of Christopher Newport College."[107]

Toward the 1980s and an Uncertain Future

Throughout the public ceremonies and celebrations of 1976–77, President Windsor and the new board of visitors had also been meeting behind closed doors to discuss the college's short- and long-range plans. The most immediate concern involved obtaining capital funds to begin long-neglected campus construction projects as well as getting rid of

---

[106] "Christopher Newport Sets Independence Rites," *Daily Press*, 25 June 1977; "CNC Gains Independence," *Captain's Log*, 22 August 1977.

[107] Christopher Newport College Graduation Booklet, 14 May 1978; "Lifetime of Distinguished Service Earns Founding Father Honorary Degree in Law," *Captain's Log*, 21 March 1978.

Windsor Village, the dozen mobile trailers located just north of Newport Hall. The board also wanted to expand the campus by purchasing some of the homes, small businesses, and vacant lots surrounding it. The additional acreage would allow the college to build several badly needed parking lots and create a new access road directly onto Warwick Boulevard.[108] The board and Windsor also had to deal with long-term recruitment issues. College enrollment nationwide began declining in the mid- to-late 1970s. The end of the military draft and the tail end of baby boom generation led to a dip in the nation's college and university enrollment of 175,000 students in 1975–76. As mentioned above, this decline hurt CNC at a time when adequate state funds were hard to obtain and tuition hikes in a dismal economy led many to defer college altogether.[109]

Windsor's energetic lobbying efforts for capital funds finally began to pay off toward the decade's end. By the late 1970s, state officials began to publicly acknowledge CNC's needs for additional classroom buildings, library space, and administrative offices simply in order to continue its academic mission. In 1977, for instance, SCHEV Director Gordon Davies told the General Assembly that CNC only had 67 percent of the space it needed given its current enrollment as well as future projections. Hence, he recommended that the state provide funds for a new four-story "office-instructional" building. Davies also pointed out that the Smith Library should be expanded to accommodate student needs. The General Assembly supported both projects and construction on the library expansion began in 1978. The following year, ground was broken for the four-story structure that would eventually be simply called the Administration Building.[110]

---

[108] "CNC Board of Visitors Votes Brauer Rector," *Captain's Log*, 20 September 1976; "Board of Visitors Begins Planning," *Captain's Log*, 18 October 1976; "CNC Looks to Future after Separating from Its Mother Institution," *Captain's Log*, 22 August 1977.

[109] On the decline of college enrollment nationwide, see Thelin, *History of American Higher Education*, 321.

[110] "State Staff Favors CNC Projects," *Times-Herald*, 19 July 1977; "High Bids Delay CNC Library Work," *Times-Herald*, 5 April 1978; "Space Problems Plague CNC," *Daily Press*, 18 August 1978; "CNC Tuition to Rise," *Daily Press*, 12 May 1979; see also "Lack of Space Could Hold Up CNC Expansion," *Daily Press*, 9 November 1979.

These two projects helped to alleviate many of the college's spatial problems and permitted Windsor at last to remove the dozen trailers from campus. But the president recognized that even more needed to be done in terms of construction. He wanted, for instance, a new and up-to-date science building as well as a major addition to the Campus Center. But Windsor possessed an even bolder vision for CNC. Believing that the college ought to be the community's cultural center, and understanding that he needed to attract more students in these difficult times, he proposed two major projects that (if implemented) would have fundamentally changed Christopher Newport: 1) a 350-bed student dormitory, and 2) a 1,900 seat performing arts center. The idea for a dormitory was first introduced in 1977 by a CNC alumnus named Jay Epstein. Epstein had purchased land adjacent to the college and had asked administration officials to help him fund the construction. Windsor liked the idea as more and more students had been requesting assistance with housing needs. A dormitory, moreover, could help the college attract students from outside the immediate Hampton Roads area.

Confident that he could fill at least one dorm, Windsor took Epstein's proposal to the board of visitors. Although board members liked the idea, the project became a victim of growing tensions with the college's surrounding neighbors.[111] In the fall of 1977, as Epstein's dorm plans took shape, the board had also discussed building a new access road directly onto Warwick Boulevard, which would have required purchasing some additional private lands. These plans, however, brought the college into conflict with the Rev. Marcellus Harris, Jr., the pastor of the predominantly black First Baptist Church Morrison, located on Warwick Boulevard and directly next to the college. When Harris learned of CNC's plans for both the road and the dormitory, he formed a neighborhood committee designed to protect his church as well as the homes and properties immediately surrounding the campus, many of which belonged to African-American members of his congregation. After

---

[111] CNC Board of Visitors Minutes, 8 December 1977; "Dormitories Questioned for Private Owner," *Captain's Log*, 6 December 1977; "CNC Dormitory Project Rejected by Board," *Captain's Log*, 18 January 1978. See also "Student Senate to Probe Student Opinion on Dorms," *Captain's Log*, 15 March 1976.

learning of the creation of the neighborhood committee, Windsor went to the church to explain that CNC had no plans "to take" their homes. But he did tell them that if they wanted to sell, "they ought to let us know because we might be an interested buyer." However, in the wake of these tensions, and because everyone remembered the racial controversies surrounding the original purchase of the Shoe Lane tract, Windsor and the board temporarily halted Epstein's idea for a dormitory and the new access road.[112]

The following year, Windsor and the board of visitors returned to the idea of a campus dormitory, but decided to construct the building on land already owned by the college so as to avoid further controversy with the college's neighbors. After drafting a feasibility study, Windsor submitted the proposal for a 350-bed facility, financed through general revenue bonds, to the State Council of Higher Education. Council Director Gordon Davies, however, rejected the idea out of hand, stating that CNC was a commuter school and he saw no need to alter its basic mission. If a dorm was built, he further pointed out Christopher Newport might start competing for students with George Mason University and James Madison College. Resentful at how Davies had pigeonholed CNC as simply "a commuter school," Rector Brauer told the press he would seek to "better inform" SCHEV about the college's potential for expansion. He pledged, moreover, to try and overturn the decision in the General Assembly. Despite Brauer's efforts, SCHEV's decision stood—at least for the time being.[113]

Windsor's other project—a 65,000-square-foot performing arts center with seating for 1,900 people—was also scuttled at the end of the decade. The president had envisioned the center as a multi-purpose facility serving the needs of both the college and the Peninsula. Indeed, it would be the venue for college graduation ceremonies, public lectures,

---

[112] CNC Board of Visitors Minutes, 8 December 1977; Windsor interview with Hamilton, 5 June 2007; "History of First Baptist Church Morrison," http://www.fbcmorrison.org/history (accessed 19 March 2009).

[113] "Dormitories Seriously Considered," *Captain's Log,* 17 October 1978; "Dormitories Are Upcoming Reality," *Captain's Log,* 16 January 1979; "CNC Won't Get Dorms, Might Get a Track," *Captain's Log,* 19 September 1979; "State Approves New Track and Campus Center Addition," *Captain's Log,* 27 September 1979; William Brauer interview with Phillip Hamilton, 13 November 2008.

concerts, professional theater troupes, as well as symphonies and operas. The center would also serve the college's academic mission, housing the fine arts department and providing classroom and office space for students and faculty. Working with Newport News City Manager Frank Smiley, Windsor thought the project held great promise and, with the support of the board of visitors, he had architectural plans drawn up. Like the plan for the dormitory, however, the performing arts center never materialized. Some members of the city council felt that, if Newport News funds contributed to the project, the center ought to be located in the ailing downtown area. Hence council members refused to support it. The state, moreover, had few funds available for such a project. As a result, the idea for an arts center would have to wait another quarter century until the opening of the Ferguson Center for the Arts in 2004.[114]

In early 1979, James Windsor decided to step down as president of Christopher Newport College in order to return to the classroom. Considering himself always to be a "reluctant president," he announced his decision to the campus community in March to be effective at the end of the calendar year. While Windsor genuinely looked forward to teaching once again, he also looked back with satisfaction on a number of meaningful accomplishments. During his presidential tenure, the school's student population had doubled in size, rising from 1,800 in 1970 to nearly 4,000 in 1979. Despite a difficult local and national economic climate, moreover, he had always secured sufficient funding in order to keep the college expanding. Indeed, when he left the presidency, the state provided nearly two-thirds of CNC's annual operating budget, the highest percentage ever. He had overseen a dramatic expansion of the curriculum, moreover, and, in one of his last administrative acts, supervised a major reorganization of the faculty into two separate schools—the Business and Economics Division and the Liberal Arts, Science, and Education Division. Above all, Windsor had skillfully negotiated with William and Mary and state officials to secure Christopher Newport's independence with its own board of visitors.

[114] CNC Board of Visitors Meeting Minutes, 8 November 1979; "Christopher Newport Plans Projects for Arts, Athletics," *Daily Press*, 13 June 1979; Barry Wood communication with Phillip Hamilton, 15 March 2008.

Leaving the presidency had its humbler moments, however. After a one-semester sabbatical with which to prepare to reenter the classroom, Windsor began teaching in fall 1980. He recalled that during the second week of classes, a student in his introductory psychology course came up to him and said, "Dr. Windsor, someone in the class said you used to be president of the college. Is that true?!" Laughing about it years later, Windsor admitted his surprise at how fast "the glory" of the presidency had faded.[115]

In the summer of 1979, the CNC Board of Visitors announced that John "Jack" Anderson, then acting president of Columbus College in Georgia, would replace Windsor. Like the out-going president a decade before, Anderson would face challenges upon taking office. Even though independence had been achieved in 1977, the school still searched for a larger mission at the decade's end. With his dormitory and performing arts projects, Windsor had tried to expand the school's mission beyond the narrow confines of it simply being "a local commuter college." But both efforts had failed. Furthermore, many people in 1979 still remembered the Shaner Report. Despite the fact that its recommendations had been officially rejected, the fact that CNC's abolition had even been proposed had made the college seem vulnerable and unneeded. Students sensed this vulnerability and perceived inferiority. In September 1979, for example, a *Captain's Log* editorial claimed that many students viewed CNC as a "second rate" college and, as a result, "worr[ied] that the degree they get here won't carry much weight." The writer concluded that students had to stop "send[ing] out

---

[115] "Poor Faculty Salaries Cited," *Times-Herald*, 8 December 1978; "College Plans Reorganization," *Daily Press*, 9 March 1979; "Windsor to Step Down as CNC Head," *Times-Herald*, 9 March 1979; "Dr. Windsor Steps Down," *Daily Press*, 12 March 1979; "President Windsor Announces Resignation to Return to Teaching and Counseling," *Captain's Log*, 13 March 1979; Windsor interview with Hamilton, 5 June 2007. After his one-semester sabbatical, Windsor taught psychology at CNC for two years until 1983 when he retired from the college. Several years later, he became president of Atlantic University in Virginia Beach, Virginia, an institution founded by the Edgar Cayce Foundation and which offered courses in transpersonal studies. Its curriculum blended modern psychology with New Age research. For more information on Windsor's post-CNC career, see "Profile: Jim Windsor," *The Williamsburg Advantage*, 16 November 1983 and "Ultimate Question in Pursuit," *Richmond Times Dispatch*, 6 September 1988.

messages to this effect." The faculty also felt uneasy about CNC's "inferiority" and "second-rate" status. French professor Susan St. Onge remembered feeling that way in 1979 when shopping in Hilton Village barely two miles from campus. When St. Onge paid for an item with a bank check, the clerk asked for her place of employment. After St. Onge replied "Christopher Newport College," the puzzled clerk looked up and responded, "What's that?"[116]

---

[116] "Captain's Commentary," *Captain's Log*, 6 September 1979; St. Onge communication to Hamilton, 25 February 2008.

4

CHALLENGES AND CHANGES

H. Westcott Cunningham came back to the Peninsula in the early 1980s to work once more for the College of William and Mary, this time as its director of alumni relations. Soon after his return, he visited the original location of Christopher Newport College on Thirty-second Street and Washington Avenue. He found, however, not the "very busy active mercantile community" present throughout the 1960s, but an array of dilapidated buildings and "boarded up" storefronts. The economic difficulties of the 1970s—highlighted by the collapse of the downtown area—had had a "corrosive" effect on everyone in Newport News, Cunningham later told an interviewer, including "the people involved in the college." The former CNC president, despite having lived in New Jersey for the previous twelve years, fully understood the growing pains Christopher Newport had experienced throughout the past decade as the nation, region, and higher education itself changed. But he also grasped that difficulties likely lay in the future for the college. "The first blush was over," he explained. CNC had certainly "begun to stabilize" as an institution, with four-year-status in 1970-71 and independence from William and Mary in 1977. Ongoing economic challenges, however, posed uncertainties for the future, especially with regard to adequate funding from the General Assembly and sufficient enrollment by Peninsula students. Moreover, what vision—other than simply being a mid-sized commuter school—would sustain the college into the future? President James Windsor's failure at the decade's end to garner support in Richmond for a campus dormitory and college performing arts center revealed the difficulties in carving out a new and independent identity.[1]

The challenges Cunningham identified in his interview manifested fully during the 1980s and early 1990s, as the college experienced additional—and sometimes painful—transitions. Two presidents, John "Jack" Anderson and Anthony Santoro, led CNC throughout these years, and both men strengthened the school in important ways. In particular, they reaffirmed the college's central focus on providing quality and caring classroom instruction by strengthening the curriculum and increasing the size of the faculty. Furthermore, the college physically expanded with the purchase of Ferguson High School and achieved university status with the inauguration of graduate-level courses in several disciplines. Despite these accomplishments, both Anderson and Santoro confronted problems associated with ongoing economic difficulties on the Peninsula and in Virginia, as well as with stagnating student enrollments nationwide. Each president, moreover, had to deal with changing perceptions about higher education in general, and what many perceived as an unclear institutional mission. Thus, although the college made progress in these years, faculty and students alike generally viewed Christopher Newport as an institution adrift and confronting an uncertain future.

A Man from Georgia—Jack Anderson and "the Anderson Era" (1980–1986)

In the summer of 1979, Rector Harrol Brauer announced that forty-seven-year-old John "Jack" Anderson would become Christopher Newport College's third president, replacing the retiring James Windsor. Originally from Ohio, Anderson had an extensive background in higher education. After earning a doctorate from Ohio State University in psychology, he taught at the Rochester Institute of Technology and Florida State University. In 1963, he began working at Columbus College—now Columbus State University—where over the years he had served as a dean, academic vice president, and, ultimately, acting president. Brauer told the press that "a combination of things" made

---

[1] H. Westcott Cunningham interview with Jane Carter Webb, 28 April 1986.

Anderson stand out among two hundred applicants as a good choice for Christopher Newport. His seventeen years of experience at Columbus College were particularly valuable, especially because the Georgia state school resembled CNC in important ways—it was a commuter college that served mainly working-class students of all ages from the local community.[2] During his interviews for the position, moreover, Anderson articulated a bold vision for CNC that called for the college to maintain its core mission of providing a high-quality undergraduate education for local students, but he also wanted to add several master's degree programs to serve students who already had a bachelor's degree. The incoming president knew from his experiences at Columbus College that undergraduates often returned to their alma mater for additional professional and post-graduate training when it was offered. Thus, if CNC became a comprehensive undergraduate *and* graduate degree-granting institution, it would have a self-sustaining source of new students. To step up to the magisterial level, Anderson said that he would take the college's strongest undergraduate departments and use them to create a select number of master's degree programs. Impressed with his record and vision, the board of visitors offered Anderson the job without hesitation.[3]

Several days after Brauer's announcement the Newport News afternoon paper, the *Times-Herald*, published an article about the presidential-selection process. It ominously pointed out that CNC's 106 faculty members were unhappy because they had not been involved in the presidential search. Although the paper editorialized that "[i]t always has been ... bad practice to let people select their boss," the article presaged a difficult relationship between the new president and a faculty that had had a large hand in governing the institution over the previous

[2] "CNC Picks Leader from Ga. College," *Times-Herald*, 8 August 1979; "College Appoints Georgia Educator New President," *Daily Press*, 9 August 1979; "Board of Visitors Appoints New President to Assume Office January. 1, 1980," *Captain's Log,* 6 September 1979; John Anderson communication to Phillip Hamilton, 21 June 2007; Jane Carter Webb, ed., *Voices: An Essay in Photographs, Poems and Stories in celebration of Christopher Newport College's Twenty-Fifth Year* (Newport News, Virginia: The Sailing Association Press, 1986), 25.

[3] "Christopher Newport's President Busy Selling His School's Role," *Daily Press*, 9 November 1980; Anderson communication to Hamilton, 21 June 2007; John Anderson interview with Phillip Hamilton, 13 November 2007.

decade. Matters became further strained when the faculty learned, three months after Anderson's appointment, that he was still under consideration for the presidency of Columbus College. When a *Times-Herald* reporter asked him if he would take the job in Georgia if offered, he breezily answered, "I doubt it." Although Anderson did withdraw his name just days later, CNC's faculty strongly disliked his off-handed comment.[4]

In January 1980, Anderson arrived in Newport News to begin his tenure as CNC's third president. He spent several days meeting and getting to know faculty, students, and administrators. He then traveled up the road to Richmond to meet with Hampton Roads' local legislators as well as the key chairmen of the finance and education committees in the General Assembly, all of whom were then putting together the state's biennium budget. The trip had a major impact on the new president's thinking and outlook. Much to Anderson's dismay, he learned that the state's largest education institutions, such as the University of Virginia and Virginia Tech, had full-time lobbyists in the state capital almost year round. These officials, moreover, often worked closely with powerful legislators who were often alumni of the school. Such contacts allowed these universities to secure the most state funds and political favors. "The smaller institutions [like CNC]," Anderson remembered, "relied on their presidents who had mostly academic backgrounds with little exposure to political reality."[5] Anderson learned, furthermore, that few General Assembly members were open to CNC becoming anything more than it already was—a mid-sized, four-year commuter college serving the Peninsula community. In the course of his meetings, several legislators even brought up the 1973 Shaner Report that had recommended CNC's closure. Although closing the school seemed unlikely, consolidation with another institution seemed a reasonable possibility to many. For instance, many people thought that Old Dominion University's president, Alfred B. Rollins, wanted a greater presence in Hampton Roads, and some even speculated that he

---

[4] "Decision for CNC," *Times-Herald*, 13 August 1979; "CNC Chief 'Doubts' He'd Renege," *Times-Herald*, 12 November 1979.

[5] Anderson communication to Hamilton, 21 June 2007.

President John "Jack" Anderson (right) speaking to CNC graduates in 1984. Richard Summerville (left) is standing next to the president.

(above) The Science Building, with its open corridors, after its opening in 1984. (below) The parking lot west of the Campus Center in the 1980s. A shortage of parking spaces for students was a problem throughout the decade and into the 1990s.

Lamont Strothers, at 6'4", played for CNC during the late 1980s and early 1990s. He later had a brief career in professional basketball.

President Anthony Santoro shortly after his arrival on campus.

President Santoro with Shin-ichiro Nagashima and Keizo Yamaji of Canon, and Lloyd U. Noland Jr. of the Noland Company at the dedication of the Tea House in September 1989. Canon and the Noland Company contributed funds for the Tea House's reconstruction.

(above) Christopher Newport's first dormitory under construction. The building would later be named the Carol K. and Anthony R. Santoro Residential Hall.
(below) CNU Cheerleaders celebrating after the public unveiling of the school's new "Christopher Newport University" sign on Shoe Lane.

envisioned CNC one-day becoming the Peninsula branch-campus of ODU.[6]

Anderson returned to campus uncertain about CNC's future, and even wondering if the college he now led would survive as an independent institution. That spring semester, moreover, he learned that the school stood on precarious financial ground. Soon after he returned from Richmond, Anderson met with the college's Budget Director Jim Eagle who told the president that there were few financial controls over spending and that the college is soon "going to go broke." After his conversation, Anderson walked over to see CNC's Vice President for Financial Affairs, a man named Cal Hones, to discuss matters further. After some prodding, Hones reluctantly admitted there were problems. He then showed Anderson his "secret drawer," from which he pulled a two-inch stack of unpaid bills. Hones said there simply was not enough money in the current fiscal budget to pay these vendors. Angry at having been kept in the dark, Anderson quipped, "Cal, we have a place for persons who did that in Georgia—they're called jails. And I'm not going to jail."[7]

As Anderson delved deeper into CNC's finances, he learned that few limits existed on faculty spending. Department chairs, for instance, possessed full authority to purchase anything they needed and usually spent their funds as quickly as possible. When money ran out, Hones typically raided the library's book-purchasing fund. A related problem involved faculty members teaching course overloads. Because the college's salaries were the lowest in the state system, many professors taught an extra course per term to make ends meet—essentially creating a 5-5 teaching load for themselves. Several chairs even turned down offers to hire new faculty members because they themselves feared losing the opportunity to teach additional courses. Many professors also taught during the summer. Faculty pay for these additional classes was based upon a professor's seniority and salary level. However, like all courses at CNC during this period, the overload and summer classes ran

---

[6] Anderson interview with Hamilton, 13 November 2007; Anderson communication to Hamilton, 21 June 2007. See also Alfred Rollin's interview at Old Dominion University website at http://www.lib.odu.edu/special/oralhistory/oduhistory/rollinstranscript.html (accessed 12 July 2010).

[7] Anderson interview with Hamilton, 13 November 2007.

no matter how few students were enrolled. Thus many courses had only three or four students registered in them, but they went forward anyway. Therefore, student tuition often did not even cover the cost of the instructor. Hence the system essentially drained additional funds from the college.[8]

After sizing up the situation, Anderson realized that he had to tighten up the college's fiscal controls. The school had simply grown too large over the previous decade to be held together through informal procedures and fuzzy lines of authority. Anderson, therefore, held meetings with staff and faculty members to inform them that a strict system of managerial controls would soon be established so that the college's leadership could make sound financial decisions.[9] Toward this end, he promoted Jim Eagle to Vice President for Financial Affairs and made Cynthia Perry the college's new budget director. A graduate of William and Mary, Perry had worked in the budget office since 1979 and had proven to be a skilled and talented worker. Anderson also hired Richard Summerville to join CNC as Dean of the Liberal Arts and Sciences Division. Summerville came to Virginia from Armstrong State College in Savannah, Georgia, where he had built an impressive record as chair of a large and talented mathematics department. Summerville not only brought keen administrative skills to Christopher Newport, but he also possessed the ability to work comfortably within CNC's already-established administrative culture. These abilities led Anderson to promote Summerville to Vice President for Academic Affairs just two years after his arrival on campus.[10] With Eagle and Summerville in place—whom Anderson referred to as his fiscal and academic "think tank"—he implemented a more top-down managerial structure for the college. He met with his administrative leaders every Monday. "We

---

[8] Ibid., Richard Summerville interview with Phillip Hamilton, 8 January 2008.

[9] Anderson interview with Hamilton, 13 November 2007; George and Jane Carter Webb communication to Phillip Hamilton, 27 May 2008.

[10] Anderson interview with Hamilton, 13 November 2007; Cynthia Perry interview with Hamilton, 4 June 2009. Richard Summerville would remain at Christopher Newport until 2007. He earned a master's degree from Washington University in St. Louis and a PhD in mathematics from Syracuse University. After post-doctoral work at Syracuse, he joined the faculty at Armstrong State College in the fall of 1970; Summerville communication to Hamilton, 10 December 2007.

would have two agenda items," he remembered, "one, this week and, two, what's coming up next week that we could use to further the enterprise."[11]

To place the college on a sounder financial footing, Anderson created the Christopher Newport College Educational Foundation in May 1980. Although the college had held annual fund drives throughout the Windsor years, it never systematically raised donations from alumni, major community figures, or local corporations. The foundation's initial board, led by Harrol Brauer, consisted of members of the board of visitors as well as Hampton Roads business leaders who strongly believed in CNC's mission. During its first twelve months, the foundation raised more than $85,000.[12] Anderson also appointed Barry Wood as the college's first director of development. His efforts brought additional funds into the foundation. For instance, he convinced Preston and Suzanne Greene (a brother and sister) to donate $200,000 to establish the Wallace and Mabel Greene Scholarship in honor of their parents. The gift allowed CNC to grant annually three full academic scholarships to its top students. Three years later, John Gaines, a Newport News resident who frequently used the Smith Library, donated $100,000 in appreciation. The college responded by naming the Campus Center's auditorium the John W. Gaines Theater. By 1986, the Educational Foundation's assets topped $650,000, and its annual income provided money for library books, athletic equipment, and student scholarships.[13]

With the college's finances taken care of, Anderson turned his attention to the faculty. Like most college and university presidents nationwide, Anderson believed that too much power had moved into "the hands of the faculty" during the previous decade. Although excellent teachers, most professors did not understand the broader

---

[11] Anderson interview with Hamilton, 13 November 2007; Anderson communication to Hamilton, 21 June 2007; George and Jane Carter Webb communication to Hamilton, 27 May 2008.

[12] "CNC Establishes Foundation," *Daily Press*, 9 May 1980; "CNC Starts Fund Drive," *Daily Press*, 27 January 1981; "Money Challenge a Success," *Captain's Log*, 4 February 1982; "Christopher Newport College Begins $425,000 Drive," *Daily Press*, 20 February 1984; Anderson communication to Hamilton, 21 June 2007.

[13] "CNC Gets $200,000 Donation," *Times Herald*, 9 November 1983; "Theatre Named for Donor," *Captain's Log*, 5 December 1986.

institutional perspectives of administration officials. Thus, Anderson felt his office needed to assert itself more forcefully for the good of the college. Crucial in his thinking was a bitter lawsuit between CNC and Professor St. Elmo Nauman. A philosophy professor, Nauman had taught at CNC since the 1970s. In addition to his usual teaching load of four courses per semester, he typically taught one or more additional courses at night in order to earn extra money. Anderson thought this wrong and ordered Nauman to stop. Refusing to be cowed, the professor had friends ghost sign adjunct contracts for him. After this was discovered, he began teaching night courses at other colleges in the Hampton Roads area. After Anderson learned of the instructor's moonlighting, he fired him. Nauman, though, sued the college to get his job back. The case was settled out of court, but Christopher Newport had to pay him a financial settlement as part of a permanent separation agreement. After the lawsuit, Anderson contacted the state attorney general's office and requested help rewriting CNC's College Handbook. With state government lawyers assisting him, Anderson imposed more stringent controls on the faculty over such issues as hiring, firing, and teaching loads. Anderson also convinced the board of visitors to require student evaluations in all CNC classes and for the evaluations to be used in instructor reviews for retention, tenure, and promotion. Although the process sometimes proved difficult and contentious, all parties eventually approved the handbook that Anderson had largely drafted.[14]

The president took additional steps to end faculty members teaching overloads. Realizing that most professors taught extra classes because of below-average salaries, he asked Richard Summerville to explore ways to boost faculty pay. Working with the State Council of Higher Education and administrators from other public colleges and universities, Summerville helped to establish the state's faculty-salary benchmark system. It created, for each public institution in the Old Dominion, a "peer list" of twenty-five similar colleges and universities from around the nation. Under the plan, faculty-salary appropriations to

---

[14] Anderson communication to Hamilton, 21 June 2007; Barry Wood interview (by phone) with Phillip Hamilton, 6 June 2008; Summerville communication to Hamilton, 10 December 2007; "CNC Teachers Plan Protest of Rule Book," *Daily Press*, undated newspaper clipping, ca. 1983.

each school were pegged at the sixtieth percentile of the salaries on the peer list. After the legislature adopted the benchmark system in 1985, CNC's faculty received three annual raises of 10 percent, 10 percent, and 12 percent. As these increases in income occurred, the desire to teach overloads courses among the professors quickly evaporated. The salary increases, moreover, made it easier for Anderson and Summerville to recruit new, highly qualified faculty members.[15]

Beyond administrative reforms and changes, Anderson made sure that campus construction continued throughout his presidency. The Administration Building was completed during his first year in office, opening in late 1980. Thereafter, the building housed the president's administrative team, the registrar's office, as well as several academic departments. Anderson also wanted money for a CNC Performing Arts Center. After learning of Windsor's experiences, he realized that that was unrealistic, but he did secure funds for an expansion to the Campus Center and money for a desperately needed science hall.

Everyone cheered when these appropriations came through. The Campus Center expansion permitted many additional student activities to take place on the Shoe Lane campus. However, the science hall—later simply called the "Science Building"—seemed jinxed from the beginning, leading many to later dub it as "Anderson's Folly." Indeed, even the initial $3.2 million appropriation in March 1980 came as a mistake. The state had meant to deny Anderson's funding request, but it was erroneously listed as an approved budget item. As a result, state leaders let the project go forward. Although the building had initially been designed with considerable input from the science faculty, Anderson later changed its fundamental layout in an attempt to expand its usable space. In particular, he redesigned the building so that offices and hallways would open onto an open-air exterior walkway. While pleasant in the spring, the exposed walkway proved problematic in other seasons. It caused classrooms to be exceedingly hot in the summer and cold in the winter. On windy and stormy days, moreover, rain, leaves, and dirt blew in from the outside. Construction problems, furthermore, led to lengthy delays. In October 1982, for instance, within months of the

---

[15] Summerville communication to Hamilton, 10 December 2007; "10% Raises Proposed at CNC," *Daily Press*, 17 April 1985.

building's scheduled opening, several cement panels shifted for some unknown reason and appeared "cockeyed" to observers. Deemed unsafe by city inspectors, the work had to be completely redone. Thus, the building did not open until the fall of 1984, eighteen months behind schedule. Even when the Science Building opened, few people liked it. Biology Professor Harold Cones told the *Captain's Log* within weeks of the start of classes that "there are big pools of standing water upstairs and a couple of rooms could take on water with heavy rainstorms." That winter, moreover, several people slipped and fell on that ice that had formed along the outside corridor. Cones predicted to the reporter, "I wouldn't be surprised if, in a couple of years, we are going to the state to get [the building] closed in." Cones' prediction proved accurate as CNC sought money in 1985 to close in the Science Building's exposed corridors. State funds, however, were not appropriated until 1994.[16]

Despite Anderson's successes in obtaining money for the Campus Center and Science Building, the early 1980s coincided with yet another steep economic recession that pushed national unemployment above 10 percent. Although the Hampton Roads economy benefited from increased defense spending inaugurated by the Reagan Administration (particularly in the Newport News shipyards), the Peninsula and the state of Virginia struggled financially. Ongoing efforts to revitalize New-

---

[16] "Board Approves CNC Budget," *Daily Press*, 14 September 1979; "Science Building Addition Stirs Up Controversy," *Captain's Log*, 1 November 1979; "CNC Awaits State Verdict," *Daily Press*, 7 March 1980; "Christopher Newport's President Busy Selling His School's Role," *Daily Press*, 9 November 1980; "Christopher Newport Breaks Ground for Addition; Board Approves Tuition Hikes," *Times Herald*, 18 December 1981; "Crooked Wall Panels Worry CNC," *Daily Press*, 29 October 1982; "Science Building Opens," *Captain's Log*, 23 August 1984; "One and a Half Years Later, Science Hall Ready," *Daily Press*, 26 August 1984; "CNC Examines Renovation Needs," *Daily Press*, 28 September 1984; "CNC Shows Off Science Building," *Daily Press*, 20 October 1984; "College Glass," *Times Herald*, 14 March 1985; "Science Building to Be Renovated," *Captain's Log*, 11 April 1994; Cheryl Mathews communication to Phillip Hamilton, 6 June 2008; George and Jane Carter Webb communication to Hamilton, 27 May 2008. On the addition to the Student Center, see "Campus Center Addition Nears Completion," *Captain's Log*, 25 August 1983. The college also purchased in 1983 an official presidential residence for Anderson to be used during his tenure in office and by all future CNC presidents until 2009, see "CNC Buys Home for Its President," *Times Herald*, 8 January 1983; "CNC Now Provides Presidential Housing," *Captain's Log*, 27 January 1983.

port News' downtown region, moreover, floundered with businesses fleeing to Oyster Point in the city's midtown near CNC's campus. As local leaders and Hampton Roads representatives in the General Assembly attempted to deal with these complex changes, finding adequate funds to support the college proved increasingly difficult.[17]

Shifting attitudes within the legislature about the state's responsibility for higher education made the situation worse. In the early 1980s, the Assembly coped with its budget difficulties by shifting the costs of higher education to Virginia's students and parents. While public funding of colleges and universities continued, it covered less and less of the true cost of a bachelor's degree. CNC, moreover, fared worse than other schools, particularly because the State Council of Higher Education adopted a per-student funding formula based upon an institution's official "mission" and the number of full-time students it had. As a commuter college with many part-time pupils, CNC received the least state support of any college in the Old Dominion. In the 1982–83 academic year, for instance, the college received only $2,687 for each full-time student enrolled, whereas the state averaged $4,067 per pupil. Anderson and the board of visitors could only cope with these developments by dramatically raising student charges. Thus, tuition rose 18 percent in 1983 and another 9 percent in 1984.[18] The board and Anderson toyed with the idea of raising the faculty's teaching load as a way to ease financial pressures, but ultimately decided against this draconian step.[19]

Christopher Newport's funding problems may have also been linked to difficulties Anderson had with some leaders in Richmond. Ever since his arrival in 1980, Anderson disliked Virginia's system of public

---

[17] John V. Quarstein and Parke S. Rouse, Jr., *Newport News: A Centennial History* (Newport News, Virginia: City of Newport News, 1996), 202–07.

[18] Christopher Newport College Catalog, 1979–81, vol. 17, no. 1; Christopher Newport College Catalog, 1983–84, vol. 19, no. 1; Christopher Newport College Catalog, 1985–86, vol. 21, no. 1. See also "CNC Increases Tuition, Fees," *Daily Press*, 11 January 1980; "CNC Might Raise Tuition Fees by 15 Percent Next Fall," *Times Herald*, 13 October 1981; "CNC Tuition Hike Cut," *Daily Press*, 16 April 1982; "Higher Fees Recommended for Christopher Newport," 23 February 1984; and "CNC to Raise Tuition, Fees in the Fall," *Times Herald*, 27 February 1985.

[19] "CNC May Increase Teaching Loads," *Times Herald*, 7 June 1983; "Faculty Disputes Need for Teacher RIF," *Daily Press*, 12 June 1983.

higher education where individual presidents and other top
administrative leaders directly lobbied the General Assembly for money.
Having worked for seventeen years in the highly centralized Georgia
state system (where it was actually illegal for a college president to
discuss higher education matters with state legislators), Anderson
struggled with the Old Dominion's decentralized arrangement, as well
as with the complicated political waters in Richmond. He fortunately
struck up a lasting friendship with Alan Diamonstein, who was a key
member of the House of Delegates' appropriations committee. Referring
to Diamonstein as "the coach," Anderson constantly sought his help and
advice.[20] The president's relationship with Hunter Andrews, however,
proved more difficult. Presidents Cunningham and Windsor had
periodically had their trouble dealing with the quick-tempered state
senator from Hampton, but things became more strained when
Anderson took over, partly because their relationship got off on the
wrong foot. Soon after arriving in Virginia, Anderson called Andrews to
invite him to come to his office on campus for a get-acquainted visit.
Thinking that the new president should come to *his* office in Hampton,
Andrews was deeply insulted. Anderson made matters worse by
repeatedly telling the state senator that Georgia's education system was
far superior to the Virginia system. Indeed, the Old Dominion's way of
doing things, Anderson said, allowed the state legislature to play
favorites. As he later put it, "the institutions with the bigger guns were
more likely to prevail. The peasants got what was left." Andrews neither
forgot nor forgave Anderson for these criticisms.[21]

Despite these financial and political difficulties, Anderson moved
forward with his plans to turn Christopher Newport into a comprehensive university that would offer several graduate programs at the
master's level. Given the professional needs of the local community and

---

[20] Webb, *Voices*, 25. Ted Morrison, Dick Bagley, and Herb Bateman were also
strong supporters of CNC during Anderson's tenure, see Anderson communication to
Hamilton, 21 June 2007.

[21] Summerville interview with Hamilton, 8 January 2008; Anderson interview with
Hamilton, 13 November 2007; George and Jane Carter Webb communication to
Hamilton, 27 May 2008. Anderson openly admitted that his actions sometimes grated
those in power: "I pissed people off" with that "procedural tone in my voice," he said;
Anderson interview with Hamilton, 13 November 2007.

the large number of CNC graduates living in Hampton Roads, the president firmly believed that advanced-degree programs would be successful. To better access potential demand on the Peninsula, Anderson had a questionnaire developed and mailed to local residents in the fall of 1981. The eight hundred returned surveys predicted "a large demand" for master's programs in three specific areas: Business Administration, Education, and Computer Systems Science. Therefore, the college began preparing graduate proposals in these three subjects and submitted them to the State Council of Higher Education in June 1983.[22] Three months later, the State Council sent a Status-Change Visiting Committee to campus, and its meetings with faculty and administrators went well. Several months later, however, the entire State Council sent a negative recommendation on the proposals to the General Assembly. Their report cited duplication between CNC's proposed programs and those currently in place at William and Mary and Old Dominion University. SCHEV also noted shortcomings in both CNC's library and the academic credentials of its faculty. Many observers on campus ascribed the rejection to Gordon Davies, SCHEV's powerful head. Davies had previously been hostile to changes in CNC's role and position in Virginia higher education. Despite SCHEV's negative report, Peninsula representatives in the House of Delegates strongly supported CNC's change of mission and, with their political backing, the graduate proposals successfully passed the entire House in January 1984. In the Senate, passage also seemed likely, especially after the proposals passed the Senate Education Committee with a positive recommendation. However, when the applications came before the Senate Finance Committee chaired by Hunter Andrews, they were unexpectedly defeated by a two-vote margin.[23] In the wake of this loss, Anderson settled for half a loaf. He negotiated with William and Mary officials for

---

[22] "Grad Programs Proposed for '83," *Captain's Log*, 3 December 1981; "Three Graduate Programs Proposed for Fall," *Captain's Log*, 8 September 1983; "CNC Official Seek to Improve Library," *Times Herald*, 6 October 1983; Anderson communication to Hamilton, 21 June 2007.

[23] "Three Graduate Programs Proposed for Fall," *Captain's Log*, 8 September 1983; "CNC Supports Plan for Engineering Center in Hampton: ODU Graduate Classes OK'd," *Daily Press*, 24 December 1985; Webb, *Voices*, 26; Anderson communication to Hamilton, 21 June 2007.

the latter school to transfer its part-time MBA program to CNC's campus in the fall of 1985. Although the graduate instructors would be William and Mary faculty and students in the program would earn a William and Mary degree, the president hoped that offering the courses on CNC's campus would be a first step toward Christopher Newport eventually owning the program.[24]

Soon after Anderson completed his negotiation with William and Mary over the MBA program, the college received another shock. In January 1986, Governor Charles Robb's Secretary of Education Donald Finley announced a new initiative designed to assist public colleges and universities with rising enrollments. He planned to increase their state funding by withdrawing staff and faculty positions from institutions with stagnant or declining enrollments. Because CNC's student population had drifted lower in the mid-1980s—dropping from 4,398 in 1983 to 4,089 in 1986—Finley told Anderson to cut thirty-two positions, or 10 percent of the college's workforce. The announcement stunned the college. The president immediately traveled to Richmond and angrily told legislators that Finley was playing "Robin Hood in reverse" and he predicted that the personnel cuts could possibly send CNC into an irreversible "death spiral."[25]

The defeat of the graduate programs combined with the new threat of significant staff cuts set off a chain of events that ended with Anderson's resignation several months later. Faculty members who were already frustrated with his leadership over a number of matters went public with their concerns. On 30 January 1986, a *Daily Press* article headlined "Stress Quality, Not Quantity, Teachers Say," featured history professor James Morris blasting Anderson for weak and ineffective management. "In the early '70s," Morris said, "there wasn't any question of [CNC's] mission." It was "to provide Peninsula residents with a high-quality undergraduate education." However, "[t]oday if someone asked

---

[24] "William and Mary, CNC Plan Graduate Business Program," *Times Herald*, 4 January 1985; "CNC's Students Offered Masters Program," *Captain's Log*, 17 January 1985; "New Era of Cooperation Begins with MBA Program," *Captain's Log*, 3 October 1985; CNC Board of Visitors Minutes, 26 February 1985.

[25] "State Likened to Reverse Robin Hood," *Times Herald*, 20 January 1986; "College Takes Stand Against Budget Cuts," *Captain's Log*, 23 January 1986; Anderson interview with Hamilton, 21 June 2007.

me what is CNC, where are we going, I have to say I don't know." Morris also stated that academic standards were "slipping" due to efforts to boost the college's stagnant enrollment. English professor Douglas Gordon agreed. Chair of the Faculty Advisory Committee, he stated that the school should focus on improving its undergraduate curriculum before attempting again to establish graduate programs.[26]

Morris and Gordon spoke not only to the press, but also to the board of visitors, which had gathered that month specifically to discuss Anderson's performance. Gordon told the body that "there was no articulate plan for the school's future" and, in his mind, the president should not continue to lead the college. Board member Irwin Drucker was himself unhappy with the caliber of education at the college and, during the four-hour meeting, wondered aloud why stronger undergraduate programs had not yet been developed.[27] Meanwhile, a separate faculty committee, then drafting the college's self-study review for its ten-year re-accreditation by SACS, declared that Anderson was not the right man for the job. Their report stated that "serious problems are perceived in the Office of the President by the faculty" and that Anderson was "aloof and condescending to faculty members." He was, moreover, "unwilling to involve them in significant decision-making."[28]

The board of visitors met two months later to talk further about Anderson's performance. To many observers, the meetings themselves were a clear indication that the president had lost the confidence of many board members. Thus, on 25 March 1986, Anderson announced his resignation effective at the end of the calendar year. He told reporters at a press conference, "Now I'm firmly convinced we need a type of president who is a visionary." Although Anderson's presidency ended

[26] "Stress Quality, Not Quantity, Teachers Say," *Daily Press*, 30 January 1986; "Faculty Advisory Committee Says Mission Statement Needs New Focus," *Captain's Log*, 6 February 1986.

[27] "Stress Quality, Not Quantity, Teachers Say," *Daily Press*, 30 January 1986; "Faculty Advisory Committee Says Mission Statement Needs New Focus," *Captain's Log*, 6 February 1986; George and Jane Carter Webb communication Hamilton, 27 May 2008.

[28] "Study Critical of CNC President's Leadership," *Times Herald*, 30 April 1986. Several months after this self-study was submitted, SACS criticized the faculty for not "respect[ing] the integrity of the Office of the President," see "Give Respect to CNC Head, Report Says," *Daily Press*, 26 June 1986.

amid a host of difficulties and divisions, the *Daily Press* published an editorial several days later that placed his tenure in a broader context. Although Anderson may not have been the visionary leader CNC needed, he had created "a firm foundation" for his successors. He had overseen a budget which had grown from $6 million to $11 million per annum; several new buildings and additions to existing structures were completed under his watch; he had established the Educational Foundation and helped it grow to more than $650,000; and, finally, Anderson had centralized and rationalized purchasing and personnel practices, an essential task for a college of CNC's size.[29] After his presidency and a one-semester sabbatical, Anderson returned to teaching. In the fall of 1987, he joined the faculty in the School of Business, where he taught for fifteen years. In 2002, he moved over to the Department of Psychology before retiring in the Spring 2003 at the rank of Distinguished Professor.[30]

Academic and Student Life in the 1980s and Early 1990s

Academic and student life at Christopher Newport College from 1980 to 1995 had a number of general continuities with the 1970s; but some gradual changes and transformations also marked these years. The composition of the student body during the 1980s closely resembled the mix of students from the previous decade. Those who attended Christopher Newport continued to be largely a mix of traditional and nontraditional students. The eighteen- to twenty-two-year-old pupils generally had more diverse educational goals: some wished only to start their academic careers at CNC and then transfer to more prestigious universities. Many others wished to complete their undergraduate studies at the college from start to finish, while still others attended

---

[29] "CNC's Anderson Resigns from Post of President," *Daily Press*, 25 March 1986; "College President Announces Resignation," *Captain's Log*, 27 March 1986; "CNC's John Anderson," *Daily Press*, 29 March 1986; Anderson communication to Hamilton, 21 June 2007. For more on these issues, see "CNC President Ends Term at Graduation Today," *Daily Press*, 11 January 1987.

[30] Anderson communication to Hamilton, 21 June 2007. John "Jack" E. Anderson died on 26 August 2009 at the age of 77; see "Anderson, Former CNU President, Dies, *Daily Press*, 29 August 2009.

merely because of family pressures to continue with their education after high school. Many of CNC's older nontraditional students, on the other hand, returned to college either to complete their bachelor's degrees or to gain additional career training. In fact, a significant number of CNC's nontraditional students arrived on campus with previously earned bachelor's degrees already in hand; most of them came back to college in order to pursue alternative career paths. A trucking company owner, for example, came to Christopher Newport during these years in order to earn a degree in mathematics so that he could become a high school teacher. Another nontraditional student, after having struggled through "a bunch of jobs" with only a high school degree, came to the college to major in business with the hope of "do[ing] something that I *like* to do instead of something that I *have* to do to survive."[31]

To meet the demands of such students as well as the needs of the local community, CNC continued to expand its undergraduate curriculum. The college, for instance, established a Bachelor of Science degree in physics in 1985. The driving force behind its creation was Lewis McMurran himself, who had long wanted to the college to have a high-quality program in the discipline. When Department Chair George Webb started planning the major, though, he did not want to duplicate William and Mary's program, which typically prepared students for graduate school. Therefore, he organized a task force of nineteen local business leaders and together they developed a physics curriculum that would produce graduates with the professional skills that Peninsula companies needed. With McMurran's and the business community's support, SCHEV approved the program.[32] Two years later, the college also inaugurated a four-year nursing program in cooperation with Riverside Hospital. The new program allowed students to earn their bachelor's degrees as well as their license to practice in the medical field at least one

---

[31] Richard Summerville communication to Phillip Hamilton, 10 December 2007; Tisa Ann Mason, "The Commuters' Alma Mater: Profiles of College Student Experiences at a Commuter Institution" (PhD Dissertation, The College of William and Mary, 1993), 182. For more information on student experiences during this period, see Webb, *Voices*, 41 and "Super Woman: Betty Smith," *Daily Press*, 25 May 1989.
[32] George and Jane Carter Webb communication to Hamilton, 27 May 2008.

year sooner than in other nursing programs in the Hampton Roads region.[33]

The college also established its Honors Program during the 1980s. The program started because of a 1978 symposium organized by Dean of Admissions Keith McLoughland entitled "What Does it Mean to Be Educated." Both McLoughland and then-Academic Vice President Bob Edwards had grown increasingly concerned that the collage paid too much attention to its weakest students (primarily through the basic studies department), with little or no special attention being directed toward CNC's strongest pupils. Therefore, in the fall of 1980, with the support of President Anderson and the board of visitors, they helped to establish a formal Honors Program with its initial participants called "Styron Scholars," after the famous Newport News author. Headed by a faculty-led Honors Council, students needed a 3.0 GPA and a combined SAT score of 1000 for admission. Once accepted, they enrolled in a series of more challenging and rigorous classes, and then graduated from CNC "with distinction."[34]

As the Honors Program grew and developed, the number of CNC students majoring in business rose at an extraordinary rate. Reflecting national trends born in the hard economic times of the 1970s, CNC students increasingly wanted degrees that they perceived as "practical." The pattern was, as SCHEV officials put it at the time, "typical of what we're seeing across the state and nationwide." In 1976–77, for example, the number of business majors at CNC jumped to 28 percent of the overall student body. By 1980, that number had risen to 38 percent. The major's popularity led to the creation of the School of Business and

---

[33] "Program to Pump New Life Into Nursing School," *Daily Press*, 4 July 1986; Christopher Newport College Catalog, 1987–88, vol. 22, no. 1. On earlier efforts to establish this program, see "College, Hospital Hope to Offer Nursing Degree," *Times Herald*, 18 June 1982 and "12 Colleges Oppose CNC-Riverside Program," *Times Herald*, 4 November 1982.

[34] "CNC Adds Honors Program," *Daily Press*, 8 January 1980; "An Overview of the Styron Scholars Program: Their Inspiration and Challenge," *Captain's Log*, 25 September 1980; George and Jane Carter Webb communication to Hamilton, 27 May 2008. For information about the 1978 symposium, see "CNU Says Goodbye to Beloved Mentor," *Captain's Log*, 19 June 1995. McLoughland died of cancer in 1995. See also "Styron Scholars in Profile," *Captain's Log*, 8 October 1982.

Economics in 1979.[35] Professor Ronnie Cohen, hired to teach business law in 1983, recalled that her students throughout the era were mainly older individuals and, therefore, "the culture in the business school was very professional/practitioner-oriented." Because of CNC's open admissions policies, student abilities varied widely. Nevertheless, most of them worked diligently in the classrooms despite the heavy demands upon their time due to family responsibilities and/or outside jobs.[36]

While more and more students entered the School of Business—the "practical side of the house" as President Anderson once called it—a serious disciplinary imbalance developed within the faculty. In the early 1980s, for instance, the business school had only twenty-one professors on staff. Given the number of students enrolled within its majors, however, its faculty should have numbered at least thirty-nine. The number of humanities and social science majors, meanwhile, dropped during these years. Thus, many professors in these departments lacked a sufficient number of students for their courses. The college eventually solved the problem in two ways: first, it hired more part-time adjuncts to teach business classes; and second, it asked humanities and social science professors to teach courses outside their disciplines. Realizing that they might be let go if they did not do so, many volunteered. Sociology Professor Joseph Healey, for example, taught introductory computer programming courses while French Professor Susan St. Onge volunteered to teach English composition classes.[37]

Despite these changes in students' academic interests and priorities, the college retained its reputation for high teaching standards inside the classroom, and friendliness and comaraderie on campus.[38] Indeed, CNC faculty continued to focus on teaching with care and concern, and students continued to appreciate that fact. After formal student

---

[35] "CNC Business Students Face Larger Classes" and "Enrollment Called Typical," *Times Herald*, 24 April 1980; Christopher Newport College Catalog, 1979–81, vol. 17, no. 1; Ronnie Cohen communication to Phillip Hamilton, 5 March 2008.

[36] Cohen communication to Hamilton, 5 March 2008.

[37] "CNC Business Students Face Larger Classes," *Times Herald*, 24 April 1980; "Professors Retrain in New Fields," *Daily Press* , 1983.

[38] Summerville communication to Hamilton, 10 December 2007; *The Captain*, Christopher Newport College Yearbook, 1988; "Local Students Surveyed on CNC's Image and Reputation," *Captain's Log*, 22 October 1981.

evaluations were introduced in the mid-1980s, large numbers acknowledged that most professors were approachable, friendly, and helpful. Students especially liked that the faculty generally tried to learn and remember their names.[39] As always, they enjoyed the "entertaining" instructors the most. In 1983, the *Captain's Log* even compiled a list of "the five most entertaining professors at CNC." At the top of the list was Douglas Gordon, who had arrived at the college in 1980 after having taught at Austin Peay State University in Tennessee for several years. Hired initially to teach in Basic Studies, he soon joined the English department where he taught courses on Shakespearean literature. A formidable personality, Gordon made the plays of the Bard come alive for students in the classroom. He also became an important presence on campus outside the classroom. In 1987, for example, Gordon played the title role in the theater department's production of *Oedipus*.[40] Above all, students respected those teachers who intellectually challenged them, especially since so many of them had saved money to pay for college themselves. The physics program, in particular, developed a strong reputation for demanding high-quality work from its majors. A professor once overheard a major telling a group of students, "Man that's a hard HARD department. You gotta be one of those Chinese guys to make it there."[41]

Despite the college's inability to construct a performing arts center, important cultural events and experiences continued to occur on campus outside the classroom. The ongoing Ramseur Series presented numerous classical musical performances in the Campus Center for both students and members of the Peninsula community.[42] Many outside speakers,

[39] Tisa Ann Mason, "The Commuters' Alma Mater," 188–89. On the introduction of student evaluations, see George and Jane Carter Webb communication to Hamilton, 27 May 2008; see also "Faculty Senate Wants Students to Sign Evaluations," *Captain's Log*, 2 March 1992 and "Signing Teacher Evaluations Not Popular," *Captain's Log*, 6 April 1992 for an attempt by some faculty to have students sign their evaluations.
[40] "Who's Who Among Entertaining Profs," *Captain's Log*, 7 April 1983; Christopher Newport College Yearbook, 1988, 80.
[41] George and Jane Carter Webb communication to Hamilton, 27 May 2008.
[42] For information about the Ramseur Series throughout the 1980s, see "Artists-in-Concert Series Opens Season on October 4," *Captain's Log*, 25 September 1980; "Ramseur Series Begins Eighth Season, *Captain's Log*, 22 October 1981; "Agenda of

moreover, appeared on campus. Author Victor Herman, for instance, spoke in 1982 about his experiences in a Siberian gulag during Joseph Stalin's reign of terror.[43] The History Club periodically sponsored special panel discussions entitled "The Meeting of the Minds." Based on Steve Allen's famous PBS program, faculty members portrayed important historical figures from different eras, such as Albert Einstein, Susan B. Anthony, and Adolph Hitler. They then collectively discussed a wide range of historical topics and issues.[44] Finally, the famous Raft Debates of the 1970s continued into the '80s and remained a popular event for both students and faculty.[45]

Intercollegiate athletics played a larger role in campus life in the 1980s and into the 1990s. In fact, when long-time athletic director and men's basketball coach Bev Vaughan retired in 1987, CNC's athletic program had grown to seventeen intercollegiate sports, including baseball and sailing. Track proved to be Christopher Newport's most successful program during these years. Under Coach Vince Brown's impressive leadership, the team attracted extraordinary athletes for a Division III squad and won nine straight Dixie Conference titles.[46] Both

---

Music Department to Offer a Wide Variety," *Captain's Log*, 10 September 1982; "1983–84 Ramseur Series Announced," *Captain's Log*, 25 August 1983; "Ramseur Concerts Opening Saturday," *Captain's Log*, 7 November 1986.

[43] "Herman to Lecture on Exile in Russia," *Captain's Log*, 15 October 1982.

[44] "Meeting of Minds," *Captain's Log*, 7 May 1981.

[45] "World Will End on September. 20?" *Captain's Log*, 14 September 1989. To exhibit student art, the college established the Falk Gallery named after Jean Falk who had contributed $100,000 to the college, see "College Gets New Art Gallery," *Daily Press*, 14 May 1989 and "CNC Gets $100,000 for Music," *Times Herald*, 15 January 1985. In 1991, the college gave Falk an honorary degree; see "CNC Speaker Challenges President," *Daily Press*, 13 May 1991.

[46] "Track Team Captures Dixie Conference Title," *Captain's Log*, 24 April 1986; "CNC Athletic Director Resigns," *Daily Press*, 20 June 1987; "CNC Track Coach Rakes in Success," *Daily Press*, 25 January 1990. For stories about several exceptional track athletes, see "Davis on Way to Iowa," *Captain's Log*, 11 May 1982 and "CNU Runner's Career Ends in Blaze of Glory Wilder Claims Tops National Title," *Daily Press*, 8 June 1995. President Anderson, a long-distant runner, often practiced with the track team during his presidency; see Anderson communication to Hamilton, 21 June 2007. On the establishment of the baseball team, see "Baseball Season Underway," *Captain's Log*, 18 February 1982 and "Baseball Team Makes History," *Captain's Log*, 8 April 1982; on the establishment of the Sailing Team, see "Sailing Becomes Newest Varsity Sport at CNC," *Captain's Log*, 11 September 1985. In 1989, CNC inaugurated the

the men's and women's basketball teams also consistently earned winning records. In 1986, for example, both squads won the Dixie Conference championship, and players on each team gained All-American honors.[47] The most notable player from the 1980s and '90s was Lamont Strothers. Originally from Suffolk, Virginia, the 6'4" Strothers arrived on campus in 1986 and, during his college career, set every individual record possible on the basketball team, including scoring 2,709 points and averaging 23.4 points per game. During his senior year in 1991, he was named Division III Player of the Year and won his third All-American title. The team itself won the Dixie Conference Championship that season with a record of 21–4. Later that year, the Golden State Warriors of the NBA drafted Strothers, and he eventually played with both the Portland Trail Blazers and the Dallas Mavericks.[48]

Like the intercollegiate program, intramural sports remained a vital part of campus life at CNC. During the 1980s, more than 2,400 students participated every year in activities ranging from flag football to volleyball to golf. Sometimes teams and players even took their activities on the road. During Spring Break 1987, the intramural department sent twenty-two CNC students to Daytona Beach to compete in the National Intramural Collegiate Sports Festival. Fielding teams in volleyball, swimming, golf, and laser tag, CNC's squads collectively finished in the top ten among the dozens of schools participating nationwide.[49]

Athletic Hall of Fame and inducted former Athletic Director Bev Vaughan and the following student-athletes: Bobby Arnette (basketball), Andrew Bell (soccer), Edna Davis (track), Carl Farris (basketball), Linda Richardson (basketball), Andy Waclawski (basketball); see "First Inductees Honored," *Captain's Log*, 26 January 1989.

[47] "Captains, Lady Captains Win Dixie Conference," *Captain's Log*, 27 February 1986 and "Steward and Moore Earn All-American," *Captain's Log*, 3 April 1986.

[48] On Strothers's career at CNC and brief career in professional basketball, see "Captains Rewrite History—Strothers Gives Exclamation Point," *Daily Press*, 17 February 1991; "At Week's End," *Daily Press*, 6 July 1991; "Wish Comes True for Strothers, Portland Activates Former CNC Star," *Daily Press*, 8 January 1992; "Briefs: Strothers Playing for Greek Team," *Daily Press*, 11 December 1992; "NBA Briefs: CNU-Star Signs Celtics Contract," *Daily Press*, 2 October 1993. In 2006, Strothers returned to the Hampton Roads region to coach basketball at Bethel High School, see "Strothers Gets Chance to Lead, *Daily Press*, 23 September 2006.

[49] Christopher Newport College Yearbook, 1988, 108; "Intramural Spring Breakers Come Back Big Winners," *Captain's Log*, 9 April 1987.

Although everyone considered CNC's sports program extremely successful, student participation in campus life outside of athletics proved uneven. As during the 1970s, some students became deeply involved in campus affairs while many others simply went home after class. In the early 1990s, Tisa Mason, long-time Director of Student Life, wrote a doctoral dissertation entitled "The Commuters' Alma Mater." Mason's thesis looked at student life at Christopher Newport College and analyzed the reasons why some students actively participated in campus life while others did not. Although some students invariably complained among themselves about there being "nothing to do" at CNC "because it was a commuter college," Mason found through formal questionnaires and interviews that most actually realized there were many activities on campus, including student clubs, lectures, concerts, and other extracurricular activities. One student explained, "Most people are aware of the extra programs. That's one good thing I can say... there are definitely a lot of extracurricular programs here at Christopher Newport if you want to be involved." Those students who simply came to class and left, however, remained uninvolved largely because they were older nontraditional students who had outside jobs that made extracurricular activities unfeasible. Other students, however, avoided campus life because of personal insecurities. One unnamed traditional-aged student told Mason that CNC was "kind of harsh" in the sense that "if you're just a regular student ... [and] you don't really have too many friends, nobody want[s] to talk to you." Thus, it was easier to go home after class and socialize with old friends from high school.[50]

One aspect of CNC's campus life that involved *all* students was parking. Throughout the 1980s, parking spaces remained in short supply, and students frequently and vocally complained. When the decade began, there were only four permanent and two temporary parking lots, an amount totally inadequate to the number of students then enrolled at the college. Despite repeated requests to the state government for additional funds to build more, the General Assembly refused. Thus students felt they had no choice but to park illegally along

---

[50] Mason, "The Commuters' Alma Mater," 202–03, 234–36. On student complaints about "nothing to do," see "On Life," *Captain's Log*, 19 November 1981. On attendance at sports events during the 80s, see Cohen communication to Hamilton, 5 March 2008.

all available curbs and even directly on the athletic fields behind Ratcliffe Hall. To help solve these problems, President Anderson established a Committee on Traffic Control. Although the body met frequently, its only tangible action was to convince the president to turn forty-five "faculty only" parking slots into "student only" spaces.[51]

Once, anger over the issue actually bubbled into a vocal student protest. During the Founders' Day festivities of 1989, Governor Gerald Baliles visited the campus. When one of the main parking lots was closed to accommodate the governor's entourage, several dozen students led a protest to express their frustration. The demonstration became so loud and raucous that an aide to the governor came over and yelled at the students for creating bad press for the college. During the following decade, however, parking problems eased when the state allocated more resources to build several additional CNC lots.[52]

If the 1970s represented a time of generally raucous campus parties, the 1980s signified a period when things gradually calmed down and alcohol usage declined. New federal and state laws were the main reasons for the change. In 1984, President Ronald Reagan signed the Uniform Drinking Age Act, which mandated that all states adopt twenty-one as the legal drinking age within five years or lose federal transportation funds. Virginia's legislature responded and increased its drinking age in 1987. Attitudes about the use of alcohol and its potential dangers also changed during the decade. Indeed, campus alcohol awareness campaigns grew more serious and substantive as the years passed. For instance, the Campus Program Board organized its first "Alcohol Awareness Day" in 1982, just as perceptions were starting to change. Held during Fall Fest, participants did not discuss the dangers of alcohol abuse, but only "different aspects of alcohol." The Campus Board, moreover, followed up the event that same evening by showing the movie *Animal House* to students.[53] A decade later, however, students

---

[51] "Parking Problem," *Captain's Log*, 17 September 1981; "CNC Parking," *Captain's Log*, 24 September 1981; "Proposal Creates More Parking Spaces," *Captain's Log*, 29 October 1981.

[52] "Founders Day Protest," *Captain's Log*, 28 September 1989; "New North Parking Lot Opens for Use," *Captain's Log*, 15 February 1990; "Santoro Opens All Lots: Parkers Pleased," *Captain's Log*, 12 September 1994.

[53] "Fall Fest Spans Two Days," *Captain's Log*, 24 September 1982.

and administrators clearly took the issue much more seriously. In 1992, the school sponsored an active campus chapter of BACCHUS ("Boost Alcohol Consciousness Concerning the Health of University Students"), and every fall its members organized "Alcohol Awareness *Week*." The series of activities that year included a staged drunk driving "accident," followed by a mock trial of the guilty party. After a week of such educational events, the Newport News City Council awarded the BACCHUS chapter a special city proclamation recognizing the students for their important contributions and service to the community.[54]

These changes significantly influenced CNC's campus culture. As drinking ages rose, for instance, the pub in the Campus Center started to emphasize food items over alcohol by expanding its menu and prohibiting the sale of pitchers of beer.[55] The Student Association, moreover, sponsored numerous alcohol-free events so that *all* CNC students would "feel they are welcome." Some student events did continue to offer alcohol, but only under highly restrictive conditions. While many applauded the more mature attitude regarding alcohol, the changes had a negative impact on student participation and attendance at campus functions. Indeed, throughout the late '80s and early 90s, once-popular student events—such as Fall and Spring Fests—suffered from increasingly lower attendance. Mike Rich, head of the Campus Program Board in 1986–87, complained about the low attendance at many of the events that the board had organized. Commenting specifically on the law increasing the drinking age to twenty-one, he said, "It hampers it, of course."[56]

[54] "BACCHUS Presents Alcohol Awareness Week," *Captain's Log*, 19 October 1992

[55] "CNC Rules Change Due to New State Drinking Laws," *Captain's Log*, 25 August 1983. On student reactions to these changes, see "Students Air Grievances at 'Suggestion Session,'" *Captain's Log*, 4 October 1984 and "Terrace Makes Changes after Student Forum," *Captain's Log*, 11 October 1984.

[56] Christopher Newport College Yearbook, 1987, 7; "SA Considers Alternatives for Drinking on Campus," *Captain's Log*, 11 September 1986; see also "Students Only Want to Drink Beer," *Captain's Log*, 3 April 1986. On the toned down Fall and Spring Fests, "One 'Super' Weekend" and "Pies and Profits, Chicken and Christopher, Barnstorff and Blue Rays Highlight Springfest," *Captain's Log*, 23 April 1987; "SGA to Sponsor Fall Fest on Saturday," *Captain's Log*, 22 September 1988; "Fall Fest Kicks Off With Booths and Bands, *Captain's Log*, 11 October 1990; "R'Octoberfest Bands Keep CNU Rockin," *Captain's Log*, 25 October 1993. The 1988 CNC Yearbook also complained about "low attendance" at campus events; see p. 102.

Although alcohol consumption at college-sponsored events declined, student drinking hardly ended. If CNC's traditional-aged students reflected national trends, drinking actually *increased* in the late 80s and early 90s.[57] Perhaps not coincidentally, CNC's Greek system of fraternities and sororities expanded significantly immediately after the hike in the state's drinking age. In fact, the number of Greek chapters on campus and student membership within them *doubled* between 1987 and 1993. The Greek system at CNC had begun in 1970 with the founding of the Chi Psi Omega, which was soon followed by several additional fraternities and sororities. Student participation in Greek life, though, remained very small. In 1979, things began to change when Kappa Nu opened CNC's first off-campus fraternity house. Although the brothers were soon forced to move because of city ordinance violations, it marked the beginning of Greek organizations establishing an off-campus presence.[58] The number of Greek chapters varied throughout the '80s and '90s, but typically there were between four and six active fraternities and two to four active sororities at CNC; each chapter also usually had between thirty and forty student members. The recruitment of new brothers and sisters, typically called "rush," occurred at the start of each academic year, with fraternities holding special parties called "smokers," and with sororities hosting "teas" and/or special theme parties for potential members. After a week of rush activities, the chapters extended invitations (or "bids") to students to join. Pledging activities usually took place during the remainder of the fall term and consisted of nine or ten weeks of service projects (for example, serving as the "clean-up crew" for college events) and initiation pranks (such as being required to carry a fish on a pole all day).[59] Most students who joined the Greek system at

<hr>

[57] On this trend, see "Young Collegians Drinking More: Survey Cites Excess of Underage Students," *Daily Press*, 21 May 1993. Christopher Newport students, however, were not cited in this article.

[58] "Kappa Nu Opens CNC's First Frat House, *Captain's Log*, 4 October 1979; "Kappa Nu Is Forced to Seek New Home for Fraternity," *Captain's Log*, 7 February 1980. On the doubling of Greek organizations, see Mason, "The Commuters' Alma Mater," 207.

[59] On Greek rushing and pledging activities at CNC, see "The Life and Times of Sigma Pi's Alpha Pledge Class," *Captain's Log*, 19 November 1981; "Sorority Rush 1991, a Memorable Event," *Captain's Log*, 12 September 1991; "1992 Greek 'Rush' Commences," *Captain's Log*, 7 September 1992.

CNC were white, between the ages of eighteen and twenty-two, and were seeking a more "traditional" college experience. On campus, Greek chapters typically participated in the annual Fall and Spring Fests, as well as took part in philanthropic activities. During the fall 1984 semester, for instance, the sisters of Delta Sigma Theta organized a special basketball game to raise money for Alzheimer's disease and a clothes drive to benefit Friendship House (an organization dedicated to helping the needy and homeless of Newport News). In the early 1990s, the brothers of Pi Lambda Phi served lunch three times a week at St. Vincent's Back Door Kitchen, raised money for the March of Dimes, and helped to organize the annual Special Olympics celebration.[60]

A non-Greek organization that also succeeded and grew in the 1980s and 1990s was the United Campus Ministry. Established in 1981, it sought to connect CNC students to local churches and, when necessary, provide them with spiritual counsel. Despite concerns among some professors about separation of church and state issues, funds to support the campus ministry were provided by local churches. These monies permitted the college to hire a part-time campus minister, as well as bring a chapter of Intervarsity Christian Fellowship to CNC. Over the years, the chapter participated in both local charity efforts as well as the annual Fall and Spring Fests celebrations.[61]

The presence of African-Americans students on campus marked a point of continuity with the 1970s. For instance, throughout the 1980s, they comprised approximately 10–11 percent of CNC's total student population, just as in the previous decade. The Black Student Association

---

[60] "Sorority an Active Part of Campus Life," *Captain's Log*, 8 November 1984; "Fraternity Notes Accomplishments," *Captain's Log*, 27 January 1992. Regarding philanthropic activities, "Unusual Events Sponsored During Spring Fest Week," *Captain's Log*, 7 May 1981; "Gamma Phi Beta Receives Award for Philanthropy," *Captain's Log*, 14 September 1992; "Angels Needed for the Homeless," *Captain's Log*, 17 April 1995; "Greeks Go All Out," *Captain's Log*, 6 November 1995. For more information about Greek life in general at CNC/CNU, see David Porter, "Greek Life at CNU: Bucking the Stereotypes," unpublished undergraduate research paper, "Researching CNU" history seminar, Spring 2008, University Archives.

[61] "CNC Plans to Establish Campus Ministry This Fall," *Times Herald*, 30 May 1980; "Brown Bag Lunches Open to All Students and Faculty," *Captain's Log*, 16 November 1984; "One 'Super' Weekend," *Captain's Log*, 23 April 1987; "SGA to Sponsor Fall Fest on Saturday," *Captain's Log*, 22 September 1988; George and Jane Carter Webb communication to Hamilton, 27 May 2008.

(BSA), moreover, remained active on campus. In February 1981, the club celebrated Black History Month by organizing a "Great Kings of Africa" exhibit and setting up a "Wall of Respect" in the Campus Center lobby. The latter was to be "a source of community education that expresses various forms of art and history inherent in the Afro-American culture." However, despite the presence of large numbers of black students and the BSA, there is little evidence that whites and blacks participated together in a significant way outside of class. For example, the BSA "encourage[d]" other CNC clubs to participate with it in a campus-wide event it sponsored one year called "Ethics Day," but none apparently did, and this pattern remained in place throughout the decade. In 1988, the CNU Yearbook staff summed up the Black Student Association, by then renamed the Multicultural Student Association, as "Silent but strong, the Multicultural Student Association did not participate in a number of activities, but its presence was known on campus." Therefore, while racial tensions were muted in campus life, black and white students seem to have rarely socialized or collaborated together.[62]

Despite this reality, CNC administration officials worked hard over the years to encourage academic success for its black student population. In 1983, both administrators and faculty noticed that, while African Americans comprised around 10 percent of all students, they had significantly lower graduation rates. Indeed, from 1979 to 1983 only 3 percent of students in CNC's graduating classes were black. Virginia's Office of Civil Rights noticed this, too, not only at CNC but also at other public colleges and universities across the state. Concluding that administrators were "not doing enough" to help minority students, it called upon higher education officials to do more to help them succeed. In response, CNC established "the Transition Project." Designed by Professors Richard Butchko, Joseph Healey, and Marshall Booker, it aimed to "boost the self-confidence of twenty black incoming freshmen through a program involving four faculty members and four peer tutors to counterbalance any negative aspects of [the students'] social, family or

---

[62] "BSA Marks Black History Month with Various Activities," *Captain's Log*, 12 February 1981; "The Captain," CNC Yearbook, 1988, 85. See also "BSA 'Shows' Off," *Captain's Log*, 4 December 1980. See Mason, "The Commuters' Alma Mater," 206 for more analysis on this point. For information about CNC's first predominately black fraternity, see "Catching the Wave," CNC Yearbook, 1987, 59.

academic life that may keep them from succeeding." Through a weeklong series of workshops dealing with test anxiety, taking class notes, and successful study habits, it sought to teach these incoming students "to become problem solvers" on their own.[63] Two years later, the college also created the Female Minority Adult Learners Program in order "to recruit, retain, and improve performance for black female adult learners."[64] By the decade's end, these and other efforts had paid off. Not only had African-American graduation rates ticked upward, but black enrollment overall at CNC had risen to 15 percent, in line with the demographics of Newport News in general.[65]

Amid the evolution of the college's academic and campus life in the 1980s, the most tragic event of that decade involved the unsolved murder of two Christopher Newport students named Keith Call and Cassandra Hailey. On 10 April 1988, the pair had been on their first date together. After leaving a party at University Square Apartments near campus at 2 a.m., the couple disappeared. Police found Call's empty car the next morning parked at a scenic overlook on the nearby Colonial Parkway. The case eventually garnered national attention when it was featured on the television show *Unsolved Mysteries*. Although the students' bodies were never found, the FBI and local police theorized that the couple had been victims of a serial killer who operated along the Parkway between 1986 and 1989, during which time six other people had been murdered.[66]

---

[63] "Project Helps Minorities Adjust to College Life," *Captain's Log*, 1 September 1983. See also "BSAP Developed at CNC," *Captain's Log*, 10 September 1981; "Desegregation Successful," *Captain's Log*, 15 September 1983, "Bell Wants MSA Involved," *Captain's Log*, 12 February 1987.

[64] "Stuckey Directs Minority Program," *Captain's Log*, 7 November 1985. See also "At CNC, Older Minority Women Get a Little Motherly Attention," *Times Herald*, 18 March 1986.

[65] "CNC, ODU Surpass Black Goals," *Daily Press*, 17 May 1989. See also "CNC Names 3 Blacks to Faculty; Total is Now 4 of 109," *Times Herald*, 15 October 1987.

[66] For information on this case, see "Killings Were Up in 1988," *Daily Press*, 8 January 1989; "Pennsylvania Detectives 'On Track' in Case of Family of Missing Students," *Daily Press*, 3 February 1989; "Television Program to Show Story on Parkway Mysteries Murders, Disappearances Featured," *Daily Press*, 7 September 1989; "Mysterious Cases Trouble Parkway Legend, Fear Long a Part of Life on River's Edge," *Daily Press*, 8 April 1990; "Mom of Missing Student Seeks Answer to Mystery," *Daily Press*, 26 July 1990. In 2006, the *Daily Press* looked back on this case, see "Cases

Searching for a New President and a New Vision

In 1986, Professor Rita Hubbard chaired CNC's Publications and Commemoratives Committee tasked with overseeing the school's twenty-fifth anniversary celebration. The planning occurred, however, during a dismal year for the college. The state had imposed severe budget and staffing cuts, while the General Assembly had rejected two key college proposals: one to establish graduate programs and a second to build a student dormitory. Meanwhile, disagreements among faculty, administration leaders, and board members culminated that spring with the resignation of President Jack Anderson.[67] Hubbard worked closely with Jane Carter Webb throughout the year of planning. In fact, the latter edited a commemorative booklet about Christopher Newport entitled *Voices*. Although Webb attempted to portray CNC as "a sturdy self-sufficient institution with smoothly running internal processes," her booklet really illustrated a deep sense of uncertainty and insecurity as people across campus looked to the future. For example, Webb interviewed several college leaders during her research, and her questions occasionally belied the grim state of faculty and staff morale. She asked President Anderson shortly before his resignation if he thought that "we [are] headed on the downward slope?" and followed with the query, "Aren't you sick of this place?" While *Voices* reflected the faculty's gritty pride in educating middle- and working-class Peninsula students, it also demonstrated resentment at being at the bottom of Virginia's higher education system, with particular antipathy directed at nearby William and Mary and its supposed elitism. One story written by an unnamed professor, for instance, was entitled "She Remembers a Student." It discussed a local African-American female who enrolled at CNC as a freshman. The professor recalled her as a "gentle little thing, timid, but very bright."

Still Unsolved: Colonial Parkway Killings Haunt Twenty Years Later," *Daily Press*, 16 October 2006.
[67] "CNC Plans 25 Year Celebration," *Captain's Log*, 25 September 1985. For more information about the 25th anniversary celebration, see "CNC Searches for Motto and Song," *Captain's Log*, 20 November 1985; "Winters' Music Voted In," *Captain's Log*, 23 January 1986, "Should CNC Have Dorms?" *Captain's Log*, 4 September 1986 and "25th Anniversary Commemorative Convocation Program," 19 September 1986, University Archives.

There weren't too many black students around at the time. She seemed to appreciate the attention, so I kept up with her, even though she wasn't in my department, somebody talked her into going up to William and Mary one year, and so when I saw her in the hall much later, I was surprised, and I said, "Mary, what are you doing here? Didn't you like William and Mary?" "I'll tell you how it was," she said. "We all got back from Christmas, and one girl said, 'Ah did mah reSEARCH in Austria ovah Christmas. What did YOU do, Mary?' and I said to myself, I don't belong here—I'm going back to CNC. So I did."[68]

The twenty-fifth-anniversary celebration culminated on "Founders Day," 19 September 1986, with a two-and-a-half hour convocation held, unfortunately, under a "sweltering sun." The keynote address that day was delivered by the well-known *Washington Post* columnist William Raspberry, who called upon faculty, staff, and students to "bring honor and reputation to the college" in the days ahead. Afterwards, attendees munched on a lunch of pulled pork and shrimp while listening to the CNC Jazz Band.[69] The celebrations certainly portrayed an institution that had been extremely successful in educating local students, many of whom had few other options in going to college; but it also pointed to a growing uncertainty about the school's long-term mission and growing doubts about its future direction.[70]

Three months after Founders' Day, Anthony R. Santoro, Jr., visited Christopher Newport's campus to interview for the job as the college's fourth president. One of 203 applicants for the position, Santoro, along with his wife, Carol, stayed in Newport News for three days. Then president of St. Joseph's College, a Catholic institution in Standish, Maine, Santoro charmed both the board of visitors and the faculty. With

---

[68] Webb, *Voices*, 41. Concerning Webb's questions to Anderson, see Anderson interview with Jane Carter Webb, 6 February 1985.

[69] "25th Anniversary Commemorative Convocation Program," 19 September 1986, University Archives; "Seek Own Identity CNC Told on 25th," *Daily Press*, 20 September 1986.

[70] Indeed, many people throughout Hampton Roads still thought of CNC as a community college and, into the 1980s, local high school students came to campus, not to study, but simply to "hang out" at the Smith Library. On the stigma of being thought a two-year college, see "All I Want Is a Room Somewhere," *Captain's Log*, 4 December 1980 and "Dance Draws Large Crowd," *Captain's Log*, 11 September 1980. On high school students "hanging out" at the library, see "ID Check Implemented at Smith Library," *Captain's Log*, 6 April 1987.

a PhD in history from Rutgers University, he reassured the faculty that, although he had been an administrator throughout most of his career, he understood their concerns as professors and needs as scholars. He jokingly explained, moreover, that he would have little problem dealing effectively with politicians in the Virginia General Assembly. "Anyone who has dealt with the Catholic Church, particularly the nuns," he quipped, "certainly knows what politics is." Confident that Santoro's administrative experience and appealing personality would permit him both to strengthen the school's academic reputation and improve its financial situation, the board offered him the job.[71]

In April 1987, Santoro officially began his tenure as CNC's fourth president, with his formal inauguration ceremony taking place the following fall. His inaugural address laid out where he hoped to lead CNC by the year 2000. Stressing both continuity and change, he asserted that the college would continue to serve Peninsula commuter students of all ages through excellent teaching and close interactions with professors. In terms of changes, Santoro ironically returned to some of the ideas of his predecessors. First and foremost, he wanted to shift the curriculum's focus back toward the liberal arts—as was the case in the 1960s and 1970s—in order to develop "well-rounded and mature" students. Toward this end, he called for rigorous foreign language and history requirements. In an age of global integration, knowledge of a foreign language and world history were indispensable tools. Given Japan's increasingly prominent place on the global economic stage in the late 1980s, moreover, Santoro said that he thought a Japanese Studies program would especially benefit CNC graduates. He furthermore wanted to build a college dormitory—an idea first expressed by

<hr />

[71] "CNC President Chosen by Board," *Daily Press*, 18 December 1986; Santoro communication to Hamilton, 23 February 2009; Santoro interview with Hamilton, 24 March 2009; George and Jane Carter Webb communication to Hamilton, 27 May 2008; Summerville interview with Hamilton, 8 January 2008. Before his job as president of St. Joseph, Santoro had been an administrator at Briarcliff College and Ladycliff College, both in New York state. For more information on Santoro's background, selection, and initial vision, see "CNC President Stresses 'Open' Doors," *Daily Press*, 29 December 1986 and "CNC President Faces Fence-Mending Task," *Daily Press*, 29 March 1987. Between January and March 1987, Dr. George Healy served briefly as CNC's interim president, see "Board Picks Santoro, W&M's Healy in Interim," *Captain's Log*, 22 January 1987.

President Windsor—so that both Virginia residents beyond the Tidewater as well as out-of-state students could attend the college. Graduate programs at the master's level—the idea of President Anderson—were also needed, especially a Master's of Business Administration. Finally, Santoro demanded more racial diversity at CNC. Although the student body was 11 percent African American in 1987, the Hampton Roads region had a higher overall percentage of black residents. Moreover, no black professors were among the college's 108 faculty members. He vowed to change these statistics. In closing his address, Santoro predicted that CNC would be "the jewel in the crown" of Virginia higher education by the year 2000.[72] Everyone—from faculty and students to members of the local community—praised the inauguration address and had remarkably high hopes for Santoro's presidency. The *Daily Press* characterized him as "a man of personal dignity, warmth, and integrity." Faculty and staff certainly expected him to secure better salaries, new programs, and additional funds from the legislature and more respect from the higher education community in general.[73]

Given the extremely high expectations for Santoro's tenure, there were (not surprisingly) disappointments. Nonetheless, the new president made some important and lasting positive changes. One of his first goals upon taking office was to strengthen the faculty. Indeed, he not only wished to increase the number of black faculty members, but he also wanted to expand the faculty's size in general. Thus, during Santoro's tenure from 1987 to 1996, the faculty grew from 108 to 164 professors. Santoro also strengthen the faculty's academic credentials. Toward this end, he insisted after assuming office that all prospective faculty members possess the PhD or the appropriate terminal degree in their fields if they wished to be hired at CNC. Such credentials would now

---

[72] "Santoro Inaugurated as CNC's Fourth President," *Daily Press,* 20 September 1987; "Christopher Newport's Santoro Looks Optimistically to the Future," *Daily Press,* 20 September 1987; "CNC Welcomes New President," *Denbeigh Gazette,* 23 September 1987; Summerville interview with Hamilton, 8 January 2008. On the renewed emphasis on the liberal arts in the undergraduate curriculum, see "The Captain," CNC Yearbook, 1988, 38–41.

[73] "Editorial: A Man Well-Qualified," *Daily Press,* 20 December 1986; Summerville interview with Hamilton, 8 January 2008.

also be required for CNC professors already on staff who wished to be considered for tenure and/or promotion. Designed to enhance the college's academic reputation, the new hiring and promotion standards nonetheless created uneasiness among those professors who lacked their terminal degrees. Many instructors in the business school, for example, possessed only master's degrees along with certain professional certifications (such as the CPA); many realized that with these new requirements they would now likely be denied tenure and they left CNC as a result.[74]

Santoro also proposed the creation of a faculty senate, arguing that the college's professors needed a formal voice and role in the institution's governance, particularly over academic and curriculum matters. Several professors came out against the idea, however, arguing that such a body would concentrate power in the hands of only a few faculty members. Despite such fears, most professors liked the idea and thus the college's faculty senate was established soon afterwards.[75]

Santoro's most notable action, though, was his vigorous recruitment of African-American professors. Indeed, he publicly said that 20 percent of the college's faculty would be African Americans by the end of his presidency. Upon his arrival in 1987, Santoro had learned through conversations with local leaders such as Robert "Bobby" Scott, then a member of the General Assembly, that African-American students at CNC did not feel the school was doing enough to recruit black faculty members. Mistakenly believing that earlier indifference had caused the problem, Santoro went to CNC's vice presidents, deans, and department chairs, and forcefully told them:

> Here's what I'm going to lay down for you. I'm not going to abuse affirmative action, but we're going to actively recruit blacks for tenure-tract faculty and I will give preference to departments that show me a list of finalists with at least one black candidate on it. If you don't have a black on the list of finalists, I won't look at it. I won't ask you to hire the

---

[74] Santoro communication to Hamilton, 23 February 2009; Santoro interview with Hamilton, 24 March 2009; Cohen communication to Hamilton, 5 March 2008. On the number of faculty members, information from CNU Office of Institutional Research.

[75] George and Jane Carter Webb communication to Hamilton, 27 May 2008; Santoro communication to Hamilton, 23 February 2009. Santoro had also created a faculty senate during his tenure at St. Joseph's College.

black person, but he has to be a qualified person. And by some understanding you have to explain to me why you didn't hire the black person.[76]

To achieve his goal, Santoro ordered Richard Summerville, who had remained as vice president for academic affairs, to create several new teaching positions and to place job advertisements in such publications as *Black Issues in Higher Education.* The issue of blacks in higher education was a national concern in the 1980s, and Santoro was not the first to address the situation. Under President Anderson, for instance, CNC had energetically pursued black job candidates. Because few African Americans nationwide went into academics, they were highly sought after by prestigious institutions. Thus, CNC search committees found the black candidates they interviewed lured away by colleges and universities offering higher salaries, lighter teaching loads, and graduate programs. After many failed searches, the college set up a faculty exchange program in the early 1980s whereby an African-American professor from a nearby institution would teach at CNC for one year as a visiting professor. In 1984–85, for example, Professor Grace Stuckey, a black instructor from Norfolk State University, taught in the Department of Sociology and Social Work.[77]

Even so, by the fall 1988 semester, six new African-American professors had been hired, and eventually a total of twelve black faculty members would join CNC during Santoro's presidency. Although most later left the college because of better job offers from larger and more prestigious institutions, several remained and dedicated their careers to the college, including Shumet Sishagne in history, Harry Greenlee in

---

[76] Santoro interview with Hamilton, 24 March 2009. On Santoro's view that earlier "indifference" had lead to an absence of black professors, see "CNC Chief Seeks Out More Blacks," *Daily Press,* 17 April 1988.

[77] On Santoro's state goal of 20 percent of the faculty being African American, see "The Captain," CNC Yearbook, 1988, 36; and Santoro communication to Hamilton, 23 February 2009. On Anderson's earlier efforts to bring black professors to CNC, see "Dalton to Encourage Hiring of Black Professors at CNC," *Times Herald,* 31 January 1981; "Black Student Association Petitions CNC: Seeks Black Teachers," *Daily Press,* 2 February 1981; "Dr. Anderson Discusses Hiring Minorities with BSA," *Captain's Log,* 26 February 1981 "CNC Hopes Exchange Brings Black Professor," *Times Herald,* 8 October 1981; "Education Council Rejects CNC Request," *Times Herald,* 27 October 1981; "Program Brings New Professor to Sociology," *Daily Press,* 31 January 1985.

government, and Shelia Parker Greenlee in psychology. All three instructors, moreover, eventually became chairs of their respective departments.[78] Not everyone was happy with Santoro's aggressive hiring of African Americans, though, and he was subject to charges of reverse discrimination and some unwelcome national attention. In the spring of 1990, a faculty search for a vertebrate biologist generated eighty-eight applications. Only one, however, was from a black candidate, and he lacked the specific research and teaching subfields needed by the biology department. Even though many fully qualified applicants remained in the pool, Santoro unilaterally cancelled the search. Afterwards, search committee chair Dr. Edward Weiss informed the candidates, "It is with considerable disappointment and much frustration that I write to inform you that the search for a general biology/vertebrate biology position has been terminated by the administration due to the inability to find a viable black candidate." One of the rejected candidates sent Weiss's letter to the nationally syndicated conservative columnist James J. Kilpatrick. In a column printed nationwide, Kilpatrick argued that Christopher Newport's actions were "a sad example of racism in its naked form" and represented the "lunatic end that 'affirmative action' is taking us." He ended by publicly lambasting CNC for a decision that "went woefully, inexcusably wrong."[79] Santoro responded to the press inquiries that poured into his office by stating that Kilpatrick's assertions were "poppycock" and "yellow journalism." He also told the press that Weiss's letter had been "wrong" as it did not fully present CNC's hiring policies. Rather Weiss had made it seem that "the college only wanted to hire minority applicants." Despite the negative press attention, the controversy soon passed and Santoro continued his hiring policies.[80]

---

[78] Santoro interview with Hamilton, 24 March 2009.

[79] James Kilpatrick, "Affirmative Action Hiring at CNC Demonstrates Woeful Reverse Discrimination," *Daily Press*, 9 June 1990. The column was not only printed in the local *Daily Press*, but across the nation.

[80] "Columnist Bashes CNC Hiring Practice; Kilpatrick Charges Discrimination," *Daily Press*, 9 June 1990. The *Daily Press* wrote an editorial supporting CNC and Santoro; see "The Kilpatrick Column, *Daily Press*, 16 June 1990. See Robert Short's letter to the editor in the *Daily Press*, 26 June 1990 supporting the views of Kilpatrick.

At the same time the president sought to strengthen the faculty and bring more black professors to campus, he worked to develop the college's international ties, especially with Japan. Santoro focused on Japan not only because of that country's dramatic economic rise in the 1980s, but also due to the fact that the Japanese corporation, Canon, had recently opened a manufacturing plant in Newport News. Soon after the facility opened, Santoro met the president of Canon Virginia, Shinichiro Nagashima. Wishing to be a good corporate citizen while in the United States, Nagashima asked what his company could do to help Christopher Newport. Santoro responded by asking for money to set up a language lab, to which the corporate president agreed. Because of the presence of Canon on the Peninsula and his increasingly close relationship with Nagashima, Santoro soon submitted a proposal to the State Council of Higher Education that CNC be allowed to create a Japanese Studies Program, arguing "We feel it important ... to sensitize our population to Japanese commerce and culture." Following SCHEV's approval, the General Assembly followed up with $300,000 of seed money to get the program up and running. Initiated in 1988, Japanese Studies consisted of a mix of language classes as well as cultural studies and history courses.[81] The following year, Nagashima helped CNC establish formal relationships with Kansai Gadai University and Osaka International University in Japan in order to set up faculty and student exchanges.[82] In 1990, Monica Tornoff became CNC's first overseas exchange student and studied the Japanese language and society at Kansai Gadai University during the 1990–91 academic year.[83]

The relationship with Canon and the Japanese Studies Program, furthermore, led the college to acquire a full-sized reproduction of a sixteenth-century Kyoto Teahouse. In early 1989, Virginia Governor

<hr>

[81] "CNC Chief Seeks Out More Blacks," *Daily Press*, 17 April 1988. On Canon's opening in Newport News, see John V. Quarstein and Parke S. Rouse, Jr., *Newport News: A Centennial History* (Newport News, Virginia: City of Newport News, 1996), 209.

[82] "Santoro Visits Japan for a Week," *Captain's Log*, 2 November 1989; "Asian Trade Accord CNC Students Going to Japan," *Daily Press*, 1 January 1990; Santoro communication to Hamilton, 23 February 2009.

[83] "Japanese Exchange Program Takes Off; CNC Senior to Study in Asia," *Daily Press*, 22 August 1990.

Gerald Baliles saw the teahouse in an exhibit on Japanese life at the National Gallery in Washington, DC. When he learned the structure would be destroyed following the show, the governor asked Santoro if CNC wanted it in order to promote its Japanese program. Although Christopher Newport would need to raise $700,000 to pay for transportation and reconstruction costs, Santoro liked the idea. Believing the teahouse would enhance the college's international image as well as attract additional Asian businesses to Newport News, he convinced the board of visitors to accept the gift.[84] Santoro pledged, moreover, to raise the relocation costs among local business leaders. The teahouse, nonetheless, proved controversial and caused a flurry of "Letters to the Editor" in local papers from readers who were angry about the relocation costs. One Newport News resident, for instance, sarcastically predicted that CNC could hold classes in the tiny structure or even turn it into a dormitory: "After a full day of housing classes the teahouse would make a cozy little dorm. Tack up a blanket across the middle of the teahouse and the dorm could be coed.... Won't William and Mary be jealous!"[85] Despite the protests, Santoro and the board successfully raised the money and, throughout the spring and summer of 1989, Japanese artisans reconstructed the teahouse in a wooded lot south of the Campus Center. On 20 September 1989, Santoro, Governor Gerald Baliles, and officials from the Japanese embassy in Washington, DC, formally dedicated the teahouse and, afterwards, all participated in a traditional Japanese tea ceremony.[86]

---

[84] "CNC Close to Acquiring $700,000 Japanese Teahouse," *Daily Press*, 7 February 1989; "CNC Board Votes to Accept Teahouse School Must Raise Money for Move," *Daily Press*, 23 February 1989; "Tea House Complements Japanese Studies," *Captain's Log*, 23 February 1989.

[85] "Letter to the Editor: Santoro's Tempest in a Teahouse," *Daily Press*, 22 February 1989; see also the letters to the editor on the teahouse in the *Daily Press*, 2 May 1989.

[86] "Governor Lauds Teahouse During Dedication," *Daily Press*, 21 September 1989; "Governor at Teahouse Dedication," 28 September 1989. On fundraising to pay for the teahouse's construction, see "Teahouse Fund Raising Starts," *Daily Press*, 3 June 1989; "Work Under Way on CNC Teahouse Exacting Task is a Matter of Skill," *Daily Press*, 8 June 1989; "Prayers Said for Teahouse Japanese Rite Done at CNC, *Daily Press*, 23 June 1989. For more information about the Japanese Teahouse, see Jordan Taylor, "The Japanese Tea House in Virginia," unpublished undergraduate research paper, "Researching CNU" history seminar, Spring 2008, University Archives, and Quarstein and Rouse, *A Centennial History*, 209.

In the early 1990s, Santoro further expanded overseas study opportunities for students by developing formal exchange programs with several universities in China, and he created short-term travel opportunities for students and faculty to Latin America and the United Kingdom. In 1991, for instance, Santoro initiated the President's London Seminar during which he and several faculty members traveled to the capital of the UK for two weeks to teach students about particular aspects of British culture. Students learned about Victorian children's literature one year and about English gardening and horticulture during another. That same year, Christopher Newport opened an International Student House on campus designed to help CNC's foreign-exchange students from Asia and Latin America make the cultural and linguistic transition to American life.

During the early years of Santoro's tenure, Lewis McMurran's health deteriorated. Living several miles from campus at Tazewell Hall, he remained an important and influential figure throughout Hampton Roads even after he retired from the House of Delegates. In 1985, the college's board of visitors honored the delegate, whom everyone now referred to as "the father of Christopher Newport College," by changing the name of "Christopher Newport Hall" to "Lewis A. McMurran, Jr., Hall." When the former delegate died four years later at the age of 75, everyone honored him for his many accomplishments that had so greatly benefited Virginia and the Hampton Roads region. His death, however, also marked an important turning point. Always determined to preserve Christopher Newport College's fundamental mission of serving local undergraduate students from the Peninsula, McMurran had opposed the college's building a dormitory as well as establishing graduate-level programs. With his death, some of this resistance came to an end.[87]

---

[87] "Thirty-Year Legislator Lewis McMurran Dies," *Daily Press*, 18 July 1989; Parke Rouse, "McMurran: Gentleman-Scholar Who Served Newport News Well," *Daily Press*, 19 July 1989; Santoro interview with Hamilton, 29 March 2009. On the renaming of McMurran Hall, see McMurran interview with Jane C. Webb, 19 November 1985; "Newport Hall Gets a New Name," *Captain's Log*, 27 November 1985; "Students Don't Agree with Name Change," *Captain's Log*, 30 January 1986.

New Directions, New Buildings, and New Programs

In 1990, the year after Lewis McMurran's death, the General Assembly altered Christopher Newport's long-term trajectory in two ways. First, it approved the issuance of state bonds to permit CNC to build its first dormitory on campus and, second, the legislature formally backed the college's plans to offer several graduate programs at the master's level. These twin developments—discussed since the 1970s—represented significant milestones for Christopher Newport College and ones that later administrative leaders would build upon.

President Santoro envisioned a dormitory on CNC's campus almost as soon as he arrived in 1987. He supported the idea for a variety of reasons. Local students, for instance, had claimed for years they wanted a more traditional college experience and said they would live on campus if such opportunities existed. Santoro also saw that CNC's enrollment had leveled off. Indeed, despite vigorous recruitment efforts in Hampton Roads throughout the 1980s, the growth of Christopher Newport's student population had remained relatively stagnant. This was due to a number of factors. First of all, the baby boom generation had reached maturity, which meant a decline in high school graduates and fewer potential college students. Furthermore, other higher education institutions (such as Old Dominion University and George Washington University) had opened branch campuses on the Peninsula and engaged in aggressive student recruiting of their own. These developments limited CNC's ability to attract additional students. Given the paucity of state funding throughout the decade, this lack of student growth meant additional financial resources could only be obtained only through tuition hikes—an action that merely made community colleges or other schools more attractive to many local students. A dormitory, on the other hand, would attract those local students who indeed wanted a traditional college experience; more importantly, residential housing would permit CNC admissions personnel to recruit outside the Hampton Roads area.[88]

---

[88] George and Jane C. Webb communication to Hamilton, 27 May 2008. On efforts to bring a dormitory to campus during Anderson's presidency, see "CNC Needs Dormitories," *Captain's Log*, 27 September 1984; "Editorial: Dorms," *Captain's Log*, 11

Santoro started planning for the dormitory in late 1988. The college hired the architectural firm of Magoon and Guernsey, which drew up plans for a six-hundred-bed, $17 million facility to be located just north of Gosnold Hall. The General Assembly, however, rejected the proposal as too expensive. To lower the costs, college officials scaled back the dormitory's size to four hundred beds. Santoro also wanted to hire a private contractor who would put up the cash for construction in order to lower costs further. In particular, he approached Edwin Joseph, the head of Greater Atlantic Real Estate Property Management and a major donor to the college. During several rounds of negotiations, Joseph stated that he could build the dormitory at the cost of $9.2 million and lease the facility to CNC for thirty years in return for an annual payment of $900,680. After thirty years, full ownership of the building would revert to the college.[89] Soon after signing an agreement, however, the governor's office informed Santoro that it wanted the state government to fund the dormitory through bond sales. The president and the board agreed, though Joseph was angry at having his contract voided. After the plan to finance the dorm was finalized in the spring of 1992, W.M. Jordan Company won the contract to build a four-story, U-shaped building for four hundred co-ed students at a cost of $7.8 million. On 30 November 1992, state and college officials participated in a groundbreaking ceremony, with the building's opening planned for fall 1994.[90]

While college officials worked on the dormitory, they also again attempted to establish graduate-level programs in several areas. Santoro

September 1985; "General Assembly, Tax Reform May Stop Dorms," *Captain's Log*, 11 September 1986.

[89] "Definite Steps Taken in Dorm Plan," *Captain's Log*, 1 December 1988; "Dorm Committee Weighs Design," *Captain's Log*, 2 March 1989; "Dormitory on Campus Delayed Temporarily," *Captain's Log*, 1 February 1990; "Reduce Dorm Plan, CNC Told Board to Follow Lawmaker's Advice," *Daily Press*, 19 January 1990; "CNC Awaits State Consent for Dorm," *Daily Press*, 13 July 1990.

[90] "Dorm Process Getting Closer to Being Finished," *Captain's Log*, 20 April 1992; "Phase I of CNU Dormitory Estimated at $10.7 Million," *Captain's Log*, 31 August 1992; Santoro interview with Hamilton, 24 March 2009. On the undoing of the private contract with Greater Atlantic, see "Mr. Inside: Alan Diamonstein and the Power of Connections: Straddling Public-Private Line—Diamonstein Doesn't Prevail in Bidding War over CNU Dorm," *Daily Press*, 23 February 1994.

believed that graduate studies at CNC were essential for several reasons. First, too many people still thought of Christopher Newport as a community college. For instance, biology professor Harold Cones was once asked by a parent what her daughter should do after "she finished her two years" of community college at CNC.[91] At roughly the same time, then-Rector David L. Peebles inadvertently yet publicly referred to Christopher Newport as "the best community college" in the state. Raising the institution to university status would alter these public perceptions. Second, Santoro believed that many Peninsula residents wanted graduate programs available to them, especially if they could attend part-time. Thousands of CNC graduates lived in Hampton Roads, and, for personal and professional reasons, many wanted to pursue graduate degrees. Finally, state law mandated that salaries for faculty members would rise if CNC became a magisterial-degree-granting institution. Thus, graduate studies would boost faculty pay *and* morale.[92]

Knowing that Anderson had attempted and failed to establish a graduate program several years previously, Santoro first arranged to discuss his plans with William and Mary's President Paul Verkuil. Santoro explained that Christopher Newport wanted to set up master's degree programs in areas where faculty resources were in place and start-up cost would be minimal. In particular, he was considering graduate proposals in history, English, and education. Verkuil rebuffed Santoro, however, telling him that those programs would duplicate those offered at William and Mary. After the meeting, Santoro contacted Delegate Alan Diamonstein who supported CNC's efforts, but said that William and Mary's opposition posed a problem. Acting upon the Newport News delegate's advice, Christopher Newport officials submitted a dramatically scaled-down proposal that requested permission from SCHEV to offer only a master's degree in education for elementary, middle, and high school teachers. Although the State Counsel rejected the degree proposals aimed at elementary and high school instructors, it approved CNC offering magisterial degrees in mathematical and science training for middle school teachers. In January 1991, the House of

---

[91] "CNU Tries to Erase its Community College Image," *Daily Press*, 12 August 1993.
[92] Santoro interview with Hamilton, 24 March 2009.

Delegates passed the necessary legislation (sponsored by Diamonstein), with the Senate following suit in February. In fall 1991, therefore, Christopher Newport started to offer graduate classes in education.[93]

The following year, Diamonstein helped CNC secure approval for its second master's degree program, this one in applied physics. The Newport News delegate once more strongly supported the college's efforts and shepherded the legislation through the General Assembly. He supported the proposal for several reasons: First, the college's physics and computer sciences department headed by George Webb was highly regarded, exceptionally strong, active in research, and strongly committed to teaching. Second, the graduate degree would permit the college to have a greater presence at the US Department of Energy's Continuous Electron Beam Accelerator Facility (CEBAF), which was then under construction several miles from campus next to the Jefferson Laboratories facilities. The CEBAF aimed to explore physical matter at the quantum level and CNC's physics faculty and students had been involved with the project from its start. Dr. David Doughty, for instance, had earlier developed with three CNC undergraduates a triggering system designed to alert CEBAF scientists when an electron had collided with a nucleus. The two-year master's program was specifically designed for physicists, engineers, and computer scientists on the Peninsula who needed additional skills and knowledge for their jobs and careers.[94]

As the state legislature considered the proposal in applied physics, President Santoro decided that Christopher Newport College should change its name to Christopher Newport *University*. With the Master's of

---

[93] "State Panel Backs Offering Master's Degree at CNC," *Daily Press*, 4 January 1990; "CNC Planning New Degree Anyway," *Daily Press*, 23 February 1990; Santoro interview with Hamilton, 24 March 2009; Richard Summerville email communication to Phillip Hamilton, 20 June 2009.

[94] "CNC & CEBAF: A Symbiotic Relationship," *Captain's Log*, 16 March 1992; "A Matter of Degree: Master's in Physics Coming Soon to CNC," *Daily Press*, 23 March 1992; "Masters Program in Physics Packs a Powerful Punch," *Captain's Log*, 30 March 1992; "CNC Will Offer Master's in Physics," *Daily Press*, 13 May 1992; Santoro communication to Hamilton, 23 February 2009; George and Jane Carter Webb communication to Hamilton, 27 May 2008. In 1995, two new master's degrees were approved: environmental science and nursing; see "State Approves Two CNU Programs," *Daily Press*, 10 May 1995.

Arts in Teaching degree already in place and believing the new name would end confusion over Christopher Newport as a community college, the president initially sought approval from the CNC's faculty senate, Student Government Association, and the Alumni Society, all of whom enthusiastically backed the change. He then presented the measure to the board of visitors, which unanimously approved and then forwarded it on to the General Assembly.[95] Not everyone on campus, however, supported the name change. Some faculty members thought the administration had focused too much of its energy on these new graduate programs and not enough on undergraduate curriculum, faculty needs, and classroom equipment. English professor Douglas Gordon said, for instance, "CNC may not have as much concern for its [undergraduate] students as it has in the past." The *Daily Press* even chimed in on the name change. Urging readers to say the new name out loud, its editors wrote, "We can imagine the pitch to prospective students: 'We'll be seeing you … at *CNU!*' Groan…."[96]

The loudest protest regarding the name change, though, came from an unexpected corner: William and Mary's President Paul R. Verkuil. In a letter to the *Daily Press*, Verkuil stated, "As president of the most venerable 'college' in America, I have some reservations about Christopher Newport's desire to change its title to that of university." He said that he understood the college had been granted the right to award "a master's degree in education," but university status was only truly reserved for those institutions that awarded "the PhD or doctoral degree." Although Verkuil admitted "many true colleges" had in recent decades renamed themselves universities in order "to inflate their status," Christopher Newport ought not to follow their lead. "[A] single master's program," he sniffed, "does not a university make."[97]

The letter set off a wave of indignation across CNC's campus. Christopher Mancill of the Student Government Association called

---

[95] "Name Change May Be in CNC's Future," *Captain's Log*, 24 October 1991; "College Name Change Tops Agenda," *Captain's Log*, 31 October 1991; CNC Board of Visitor's Minutes, 23 October 1991, University Archives.

[96] "Changes Evoke a Variety of Responses," *Captain's Log*, 7 November 1991; for the *Daily Press* editorial, see "At Week's End: Capsules of Commentary on Recent Events," *Daily Press*, 26 October 1991.

[97] Paul R. Verkuil, "By Any Other Name?" *Daily Press*, 13 November 1991.

Verkuil's attitude "unwarranted, unfounded, and unkind." Economic professor Carl Colonna referred to the William and Mary president as an "academic snob," while Santoro responded with a *Daily Press* letter of his own. Claiming that he was "most disappointed" by his fellow president's letter, and especially with its "remarkable language," Santoro asserted that Christopher Newport had earned the designation "university," not only because it would soon be offering two graduate programs, but also because it "has a high percentage of faculty who hold terminal degrees, has a large student body, and is conducting a substantial amount of research." Santoro concluded, "It is unfortunate that others are discomforted by our progress, yet we at CNC must define our own vision."[98] Although Verkuil publicly refused to back down and, indeed, urged the CNC community to "lighten up," he phoned Santoro and privately told him that he, Santoro, had had the better of the exchange.[99]

Once CNC's proposed name-change made it to the General Assembly, it sailed through. Sponsored and strongly supported by Diamonstein, the legislation won passage in the House of Delegates in late January 1992 by a 96–3 vote.[100] Two weeks later, the Senate also overwhelmingly passed the bill, with Governor Douglas Wilder signing the legislation on March 4. With the name change to take effect on 1 July 1992, CNC's Bookstore immediately put everything with "Christopher Newport *College*" on it on sale. The following year, in May 1993, Judith Remsberg became the first student to graduate with a master's degree *and* a diploma that read *Christopher Newport University*.[101]

---

[98] Anthony Santoro, "CNU As It Should Be," *Daily Press*, 15 November 1991. On the responses of Colonna and Mancill, see "Verkuil Letter Irks CNC Campus," *Daily Press*, 14 November 1991.

[99] Santoro communication to Hamilton, 23 February 2009; Santoro interview with Hamilton, 24 March 2009. On Verkuil's final public comments on this, see "CNU? Verkuil Says 'Lighten Up,'" *Daily Press*, 15 November 1991.

[100] One of the "nays," however, came from Delegate George Grayson who was a William and Mary professor. Grayson argued on the House floor that the bill "makes a mockery out of the term 'university,'" see "CNC Moves a Step Closer to Becoming a University," *Daily Press*, 30 January 1992.

[101] "Old Logo Heads Out the Door," *Daily Press*, 6 March 1992; "First Class: Diplomas Say University," *Daily Press*, 10 May 1993.

Although the college's student enrollment only modestly increased in the late 1980s and early 1990s, adequate space for faculty and classes continued to be at a premium. Because funds for new academic buildings seemed unobtainable, President Santoro ordered short-term measures to maximize use of the college's existing facilities. In 1988, for example, construction workers enclosed McMurran Hall's breezeway and converted the space into new offices for English faculty. Several years later, the administration leased two-floors of the Newport News Savings Bank building, located along Warwick Boulevard two blocks north of the main campus. The space provided additional classrooms and faculty offices, although it occasionally posed a logistical problem for students and professors who only had ten minutes to shuttle between classes.[102]

To obtain even more needed space, Santoro also considered expanding into the residential neighborhoods surrounding campus. This was not a new idea. In 1979, President Windsor and the board of visitors drew up a master plan calling upon the college to acquire the private homes along the streets immediately adjacent to campus. President Santoro and the board reaffirmed this plan in 1989. However, they also reaffirmed the long-standing policy adopted by Windsor of not forcing unwilling homeowners to sell. Nevertheless, residents were nervous. "They've placed a stigma on our community," one resident complained to the *Daily Press*. Another asked who would want to move into a neighborhood slated for destruction.[103] Racial tensions regarding possible campus expansion also reemerged in June 1989 when a group of black homeowners filed a federal lawsuit alleging that CNC's master plan aimed at "the destruction of their community for the benefit of white students." The lawsuit proved particularly awkward for William

---

[102] "Construction to Continue to Early 1989," *Captain's Log*, 15 September 1988; "CNU Faces Growing Pains with Expansion," *Captain's Log*, 31 August 1992; "Bank Classes Pose Travel Problems," *Captain's Log*, 26 January 1993. On spatial problems elsewhere on campus, see "CNC Library May Soon Be All Booked Up," *Daily Press*, 18 January 1989 and "Need for Space Compelled Move," *Captain's Log*, 5 October 1989.

[103] "Residents Upset Over CNC's Plans for Expansion," *Daily Press*, 26 January 1989; "CNC Will Not Try to Buy Homes Unless Approached First," *Daily Press*, 20 January 1989. On the 1979 master plan, see "Lack of Space Could Hold Up CNC Expansion," *Daily Press*, 9 November 1979.

R. Walker, the real estate developer and civil rights advocate who had led the effort to halt the city's purchase of the Shoe Lane campus in the early 1960s. Now a member of the board of visitors, Walker said he understood both sides. "As homeowners, we're concerned about our property, but the college has to expand." In the spring of 1990, however, the issue faded when a judge dismissed the case before it went to trial.[104]

By that time, moreover, Santoro believed he had found an alternative solution to the college's space problem—one that would avoid expanding into its surrounding residential neighborhoods. The previous fall, the city of Newport News had announced plans to build a new high school in the city's Denbeigh area, several miles north of CNC's campus. This predominately white section of town had grown rapidly since 1970. The proposal, though, led many African Americans to charge that the now-largely black downtown area of Newport News was being ignored by city leaders. After learning of these debates, Santoro called City Manager Edgar Maroney to offer a possible solution that would benefit both the city and the college: the city could sell Ferguson High School—which was directly adjacent to the college—to Christopher Newport for $12 million. Because Warwick High School was located less than a mile away, most displaced students could easily be shifted there. The $12 million from the sale could then be used by the city to build a brand-new high school in the city's downtown area. Finally, the sale would solve CNC's spatial problems and reduce the growing tensions between the college and nearby local neighbors. Maroney liked the idea, and negotiations among the city's school board, college officials, and state legislators began soon thereafter.[105]

The talks eventually led to an agreement for the state to purchase Ferguson High School and its thirty acres from Newport News for

---

[104] "Black Homeowners Sue to Stop Newport News College's Growth," *Richmond Times-Dispatch*, 20 June 1989; "Homeowners Sue CNC Over Expansion Plans," *Daily Press*, 21 June 1989; "Lawsuit Against CNC Pending," *Captain's Log*, 5 October 1989. On the dismissal of the black homeowners' lawsuit, see "Lawsuit Trial Date Set Between CNC and Homeowners," *Captain's Log*, 26 April 1990; "Judge Dismisses Suit Against CNC, *Daily Press*, 10 May 1990.

[105] "Plan Would Sell Ferguson High to CNC," *Daily Press*, 16 November 1989; "CNC Plan for Ferguson: Use it for Classes, Offices," *Daily Press*, 17 November 1989; Santoro interview with Hamilton, 24 March 2009.

$10,833,000 and then to convey the property to Christopher Newport. While Alan Diamonstein strongly supported the project and helped to move the negotiations forward, Hunter Andrews's backing as head of the Senate Finance Committee proved especially important. Andrews's support for the project, though, only went so far. At a public event celebrating the purchase, the Senate Committee Chairman ceremonially handed President Santoro a giant check for the $10.8 million. But, as he did, he whispered into the president's ear that he better not ask for a dime for renovations of Ferguson or "this money is gone."[106]

As the Ferguson High School purchase moved forward during the early 1990s, the university's academics continued to change with the times. The emergence of the Internet, for instance, led to the possibility of online instruction. Professor George Teschner of the philosophy and religious studies department took the lead in utilizing the new technology. In 1992, he designed and offered CNU's first online course— an introductory religion class. Sensing that "distance education" might be a way to expand the school's enrollment, the administration asked Teschner to help create and oversee twenty new online courses that would be taught by various professors in different disciplines.[107] He agreed, and the courses started to run in 1994. Called "CNU Online,"

---

[106] For some of the articles dealing with Ferguson's sale to CNC, see "Officials Question Proposed High School Sale," *Daily Press*, 5 December 1989; "Newport News Board Approves Plan to Sell School," *Daily Press*, 21 December 1989; "Newport News Sells Ferguson to State, *Captain's Log*, 8 February 1990; "FHS, CNC, Neither? Questions Surface over Proposed Sale of Newport News' Ferguson High," *Daily Press*, 23 March 1992; "CNU and the Future: One Giant Step—Local College to Regional University," *Daily Press*, 20 October 1992; "Voters Pass GOB [General Obligation Bonds] Referenda, CNU Allocated $17.1 Million," *Captain's Log*, 9 November 1992; "Contract Signed for Ferguson," *Captain's Log*, 6 December 1993; "School Purchase Boosts CNU Size, *Daily Press*, 16 February 1995; Santoro interview with Hamilton, 24 March 2009. For more information about the purchase of Ferguson High School, see "Christopher Waltrip, "CNU: The College that Went Back to High School," unpublished undergraduate research paper, "Researching CNU" history seminar, Spring 2008, University Archives.

[107] "Virginia's College Cost Crunch: Technology May Offer Home for Some Savings," *Daily Press*, 23 September 1993; "Class Time? Just Click on the Computer— CNU Courses Entirely On-Line," *Daily Press*, 6 December 1993; "Dialing into Education: On-Line," *Captain's Log*, 21 March 1994. The John Smith Library began to purchase online informational databases in the early 1990s, see "Library Embraces Technology," *Captain's Log*, 24 January 1994.

university officials promised (actually over-promised) great things. Buck Miller, a professor in the government department who had partnered with Teschner, told the *Daily Press* that the online courses:

> ... will improve teaching and learning if only by eliminating some of the negatives of the traditional classroom. In a traditional setting, teaching success is measured not by how effective the teaching is, but by how popular instructors are with students. Students with handicaps or who are timid in classrooms may do poorly for those reasons. With the computer network, teaching and learning are removed from these distractions.[108]

Despite such hopes, problems soon emerged. CNU's computer system, for instance, quickly became overwhelmed by online traffic. Indeed, the university only had ten modems into which students could dial. Therefore, continuous busy signals became the norm, and many students could not get on at all. Nevertheless, the university pressed ahead with plans to expand the number of online classes in order to both serve more Peninsula students and to boost the school's enrollment.[109]

Campus Controversies and the End of the Santoro Era

Despite the unmistakable progress Christopher Newport made under Santoro's leadership, the university experienced several controversies during his tenure caused by a variety of factors, one being his strong personality and forceful management style. When he arrived at the college in April 1987, the campus community fully embraced him, hoping that he would prove as charming and intelligent as his initial interviews had indicated. Administration officials who started to work closely with Santoro on a daily basis, though, soon learned that he could be a demanding and occasionally single-minded boss. In public, however, the president remained a popular figure with both students on

---

[108] "CNU Instructors Just a Keystroke Away: Online Lets Students Skip Class Til Later," *Daily Press*, 11 August 1994. See also "CNU Unveils Class by Computer Pilot Program Linked to Internet," *Daily Press*, 10 August 1994.

[109] "On-line Problems Come to Light with Petition," *Captain's Log*, 10 April 1995; "This is CNU Online," *Captain's Log*, 18 September 1995; "Internet Access Difficulty for Students, *Captain's Log*, 9 October 1995. See also "Welcome to the Web," *Captain's Log*, 18 September 1995 and "On-Line Not Needed [Letter to the Editor]," *Daily Press*, 14 May 1995.

campus and the general public throughout Hampton Roads. But perceptions started to change in 1990 when a controversy arose over the employment contracts of forty non-teaching faculty and administrators. In November of that year, Santoro unilaterally, and without warning, altered the contracts of these personnel (mainly librarians, coaches, and deans). Beforehand they had been given annual contracts that guaranteed them at least six months notice if laid off or replaced. Santoro believed the policy too generous. Therefore, he replaced the contracts with "letters of appointment," which required the administration to give only thirty days notice of termination. Santoro publicly said it was "a better way to run a business." The decision, made with no faculty input, sparked outrage across campus. The faculty senate, for instance, called an emergency meeting attended by more than sixty professors, staff, and students. In addition to condemning the policy shift over contracts, professors also started to complain about how "morale was declining among faculty and staff while fearfulness over job security was rising." One unnamed faculty member told the *Daily Press*, "The trust that should exist [between an administration and faculty] has been destroyed." After the faculty meeting, the senate created a committee of five tenured professors to investigate Santoro and his management style. While the president ignored the investigation, he responded to the criticism over the personnel contracts by simply stating "[i]t is not their [the faculty's] concern."[110]

The senate committee's investigation took three months to complete and resulted in a fifty-page report based largely on answers to a questionnaire sent to all of the college's 350 faculty and staff members. Only 112 were returned; most respondents said that Santoro was not doing a good job as the college's chief administrator. Fifty employees, moreover, characterized the president's management style as "vindictive, autocratic, dictatorial, or intimidating." Although Santoro did not publicly respond to the report, the board of visitors reviewed the

---

[110] "CNC's Santoro Tightens Policy on Staff Discharges: Year Contracts to be Scrapped," *Daily Press*, 14 November 1990; "No-Contract Policy Worries CNC Staff, Students," *Daily Press*, 17 November 1990; "Faculty Fights No-Contract Policy, *Captain's Log*, 29 November 1990; "Santoro Defends Policies at Town Meeting," *Captain's Log*, 6 December 1990. See also "CNC Controversy," *Daily Press*, 22 November 1990.

document and dismissed it. Board member Betty Levin, for instance, said the survey results were "long on feelings, rumor, perceptions and suspicions, but short on fact." Therefore, the board's only recommendation for Santoro was that "he [should] work on communicating better."[111]

Despite the board's strong backing for Santoro, faculty morale *was* declining in the early 1990s. Santoro's management style accounted for some of the problems, but ongoing budget shortages and declining support from Richmond posed more serious dilemmas. Indeed, Virginia's state government experienced repeated revenue shortfalls during the first half of the 1990s and responded with significant budget cuts, especially in higher education. In 1990, newly inaugurated governor Douglas Wilder found a $1.5 billion deficit upon entering office. To deal with the financial gap, he cut college and university budgets across the board, with Christopher Newport losing 5 percent of its state funds. At the same time, the General Assembly repealed a law that had granted military personnel and their families stationed at bases in the Old Dominion in-state tuition rates. Because many CNU students belonged to military families, the provision hurt the college's enrollment. With out-of-state tuition rates three times higher, these students either attended less expensive community colleges or deferred their undergraduate studies altogether. To cope, Santoro ordered hiring freezes, halted library and equipment purchases, and stopped funds for faculty development and research.[112] He also relied more heavily upon

---

[111] "College's Board Counters Article, Supports Santoro," *Richmond Times-Dispatch*, 31 January 1991; "CNC President, Board Will Get Inquiry Report, *Daily Press*, 2 March 1991; "Report on CNC Boss Sent to Panel, *Daily Press*, 28 March 1991; "CNC President Wins Faint Praise; Criticism Heaped on Santoro in Employee Survey," *Daily Press*, 6 April 1991; "CNC Gives President Its Strong Support," *Richmond Times-Dispatch*, 25 April 1991; "CNC Tuition, Fees Will Increase by 16%; Board Accepts Review of Confidential Report," *Daily Press*, 25 April 1991. See also "CNC Students, Faculty, Staff Quiz Santoro at Forum," *Daily Press*, 1 December 1990; "Santoro Speaks Out on Policy Changes, Faculty Senate, Off-Campus Campus Activities," *Captain's Log*, 24 January 1991. Unfortunately, the senate report is not in the University Archives and is only obliquely mentioned in Faculty Senate Minutes.

[112] "Colleges Hope to Absorb Cuts, Keep Faculty Intact," *Daily Press*, 4 August 1990; "Education Programs Likely to Bear Brunt of Proposed State Budget Cuts," *Daily Press*, 18 August 1990; "Va. Schools Will Feel Crunch of Budget Ax," *Daily Press*, 14 September 1990; "CNC Staff Escapes State Budget Crunch," *Daily Press*, 15

part-time adjunct professors who were cheaper than hiring new full-time faculty. By the 1992–93 academic year, 40 percent of CNU classes were taught by part-time instructors. The president even cut the university's basic maintenance and repair budgets. To assist the school through this difficult period, some student organizations pitched in to do maintenance work themselves. The English Honor Society, Sigma Tau Delta, and its faculty advisor Douglas Gordon actually painted classrooms in McMurran Hall one Saturday as "a way of trying to help the school during tough financial times."[113]

Such belt-tightening measures, though, could not compensate for all of the lost state revenue, especially when additional higher education cuts came in 1991–92 and 1992–93. The General Assembly's actions dropped Virginia to forty-third in the nation in terms of funding its public colleges and universities. They also forced CNU officials to enact significant tuition and fee hikes: 15 percent in 1991–92, 25 percent in 1992–93, and 12 percent in 1993–94. By 1993, in-state students paid $3,196 per year while out-of-state students' annual costs jumped to $7,867 (compared to $1,830 and $3,560 respectively in 1990).[114] As the hikes took effect and the state shifted the burden of education upon the students themselves, some balked. Margaret Murphy, a mother of four studying at CNU to become a high school mathematics teacher told the *Daily Press*, "We just can't take any more money out of our pockets." Already deeply in debt with student loans, she concluded, "If financial aid

---

September 1990; "Peninsula Tightens Purse Strings, *Daily Press*, 29 December 1990; "Budget Cuts Cause Rough Times at CNC," *Captain's Log*, 10 October 1991; "Wilder Targets Military Tuition: Says Eliminating Discount Could Save Millions," *Daily Press*, 18 January 1992; Santoro interview with Hamilton, 24 March 2009.

[113] "At 25 More, CNU Still a Steal," *Daily Press*, 23 April 1992; "Honor Society Paints Classrooms," *Captain's Log*, 2 March 1992. See also "College Chiefs Asked to Recommend Cuts," *Daily Press*, 3 September 1993. In the early 1990s, colleges across the nation deferred basic maintenance, just as in the 1970s; see Thelin, *History of American Higher Education*, 350.

[114] "CNC Board Raises Costs to Attend," *Daily Press*, 27 April 1990; "Virginia Leads in College Aid Cuts," *Daily Press*, 4 July 1991; ""Va. Colleges, Universities are Still Strapped for Funds, *Daily Press*, 29 June 1991; "At 25 More, CNU Still a Steal," *Daily Press*, 23 April 1992; "Tuition Increase Produces Mixed Emotions," *Captain's Log*, 27 April 1992; "CNU Funding Comes and Goes," *Captain's Log*, 2 November 1992; "College Presidents Dispute Report on Education Funding," *Daily Press*, 16 December 1992.

doesn't pick up the extra, it means I don't get to go to school next year." Other students took more direct action and traveled to the state capital to protest. In January 1992, 100 students (including many from Christopher Newport) crowded into an education committee meeting and shouted at the delegates, "Let us learn! Let us learn!" In the capital for biennium budget negotiations, President Santoro supported the students and said, "The point has been reached where irreparable harm is being done to the education process."[115]

Santoro and CNU officials had additional causes for complaint. During the early 1990s, the university received the lowest amount of funding per student in the state. In 1993, for instance, the University of Virginia received $10,328 in public funds for every student enrolled, with the overall funding average standing at $5,669 per pupil; however, CNU only received $2,488 for each full-time enrollee. Santoro frequently traveled to Richmond to strongly protest the school's treatment in the state's budget negotiations. Sometimes his defense of the school was so strong, however, that rumors circulated that he had argued with and alienated both Hunter Andrews and Alan Diamonstein over these matters. Although the legislative leaders and other prominent Hampton Roads citizens often and publicly came to CNU's defense, the lack of adequate funding over these years sapped the morale of students, staff, and faculty alike.[116]

In addition to the dour budget situation, CNC's declining enroll-ment levels were yet another cause for alarm. In the fall of 1991, the school's numbers had peaked with 5,034 students taking classes. But then enrollment drifted downward with steady and disturbing regularity. In 1992, only 4,860 signed up for classes; two years later, the number had declined even further to 4,705 and then bottomed out in the

---

[115] "College Students Protest Cuts, Higher Tuition," *Daily Press*, 29 January 1992; "Tuition Increases, More Faculty in Future," *Captain's Log*, 13 April 1992; "At 25 More, CNU Still a Steal," *Daily Press*, 23 April 1992; see also "Tuition Hikes Could Hurt Area," *Daily Press*, 27 January 1992; "College Presidents Throw Out First Pitch for More Money," *Daily Press*, 14 January 1994.

[116] "A Cut Too Deep? CNU Makes Good Case Against Reduction in State Aid," *Daily Press*, 10 October 1993; "SGA Develops Petition to Address Funding Problem," *Captain's Log*, 11 October 1993. On prominent civic leaders coming to CNU's defense, see "CNU: the Working Class Learning the Value of a Dollar," *Daily Press*, 3 October 1993; "Give Universities What They Gave the U.S.," *Daily Press*, 3 October 1993.

fall of 1995 with 4,555 students present at the start of the semester. Although the reasons for the decline seemed murky at the time, they became clearer with hindsight. Since the mid-1980s, the number of high school graduates declined nationwide from a peak of 3,100,000 in 1982 to only 2,342,000 ten years later. This drop in potential college students was felt not only at CNU, but at other Virginia colleges as well. Clinch Valley College and Radford College both saw student enrollments drop by 5–6 percent in the mid-1990s.[117] At the time, however, CNU's 10 percent decline over five years renewed fears that the college might be about to enter a "death spiral," as Jack Anderson had once put it a decade before.[118]

Many of these problems crystallized in 1994–95 when the university opened its new dormitory and moved into the old Ferguson High School. While both events should have been causes for celebration, they seemed to demonstrate that Christopher Newport was a school in decline. The long-anticipated dormitory opened its doors in the fall of 1994 with much fanfare. While many celebrated the accomplishment, only half of its rooms were occupied. Although the dormitory had 430 beds, only 210 students had signed-up to live on campus. The reasons were not hard to discover. Room and board cost students $4,750 per year—roughly the same as the University of Virginia. CNU officials explained that they had to charge the students that rate in order to offset the costs of the brand-new construction. Furthermore, though the building (which consisted largely of two-room suites for four students each) had many state-of-the-art amenities, residents disliked the

---

[117] On the decline in enrollment at CNU and elsewhere, see "Local Colleges Face Record Enrollment," *Daily Press*, 22 August 1991; "College Gaining Accessibility," *The Sun*, 29 March 1992; "Student Admission Down from 1991," *Captain's Log*, 28 September 1992; "CNU Budget: $1 Million in Red," *Daily Press*, 12 November 1994; "Enrollment Decline Puzzles CNU: 1995 Freshman Class Largest in History," *Daily Press*, 20 September 1995; "CNU Retention Rates Fall," *Captain's Log*, 25 September 1995; "How Area Schools Fared in State Budgeting," *Daily Press*, 15 November 1995. On number of high school graduates see U.S. Department of Education, National Center for Educational Statistics, "Number and Enrollment of Regular Public School Districts, 1979–2007," http://nces.ed.gov/programs/digest/d08/tables/d08_088.asp (accessed 29 August 2009).

[118] "Students Can't Leave Fast Enough; Students say SCHEV Stats Don't Give Whole Picture," *Captain's Log*, 27 February 1995; "CNU Increases Recruitment," *Captain's Log*, 22 February 1993.

university's strict rules and regulations, especially its visitation policy which required all guests to leave by midnight. Emotions became so strained that at one "town hall" meeting that autumn President Santoro and students got into "a shouting match" over their differences, especially after the president accused some of them of sneaking alcohol into their rooms. With the dormitory only half-full, the university decided to move faculty and staff into the empty rooms. But it also had to dip into $447,000 of its "rainy day" fund to cover the building's annual bond payment. At a time of constrained state budgets and dropping university enrollments, this proved an enormous and unexpected expense.[119]

The acquisition of Ferguson High School also, ironically, seemed to demonstrate CNU's faltering status. The $10.8 million deal with the city of Newport News was finally completed in February 1995, and officials expected its additional classrooms and labs to be available the following autumn. After officials and board members toured the building and thoroughly reviewed its facilities, they realized that millions in additional funds were needed to make the space usable. Indeed, Ferguson needed a new roof and had to be wired for phones and computers. The cost estimates for these basic renovations alone were $3 million. Interior walls, moreover, could not be disturbed for fear of releasing the asbestos used in the building's construction in 1957. After seeing the building close-up, Lewis McMurran III, eldest son of Lewis McMurran, Jr., told the *Daily Press* that Ferguson was "a piece of junk." Board member Manuel Deese proposed tearing the entire structure down and starting from scratch. Remembering Hunter Andrews's

---

[119] "Residence Hall Preparations Continue," *Captain's Log*, 6 September 1993; "CNU Ready to Be Home Away from Home," *Daily Press*, 18 May 1994; "New Dorm at CNU Has Vacancies, School to Spend $450,000 to Cover Projected Losses," *Daily Press*, 8 June 1994; "Students Discover New Home at CNU," *Daily Press*, 25 August 1994; "Resident Students to Head Quality of Life Commission," *Captain's Log*, 10 October 1994; "Meeting Mayhem," *Captain's Log*, 14 November 1994. To try and fill the dorm in 1995, the school required all students who lived more than 75 miles from Newport News to live in the building, see "CNU Freshmen Must Live in Dorm," *Daily Press*, 15 April 1995. For more information about the building and opening of the university's first dormitory, see Zeh Hale, "Santoro Hall: The Long Process to Get the First Dorm," unpublished undergraduate research paper, "Researching CNU" history seminar, Spring 2008, University Archives.

admonition about asking for more money, Santoro warned that money for new construction would not be forthcoming from the General Assembly anytime soon. Therefore, he felt CNU should live with the school as it was despite the fact that Ferguson was "a typical 1950's high school" building.[120]

Tensions between the faculty and administration, moreover, hit bottom in late 1994 when news broke that, despite CNU's financial and enrollment difficulties, the board of visitors had approved an 11.9 percent raise for President Santoro. By contrast, the faculty received only 3.5 percent raises (and these came after several years of no raises whatsoever). Public comments by Rector David Peebles, then chairman of Ferguson Enterprises, a nationwide plumbing-supply business, made matters significantly worse. When the Daily Press queried Peebles about the president's raise, he explained that Santoro was doing "a good job" at a time "when state-supported colleges are under pressure." Noting that the president's pay hike did not seem out of line to him, Peebles added that "I'm much more concerned about the professors that are teaching two classes a week and earning $60,000 a year. If there's anybody overpaid in the system, it's the professors."[121] The remark hurt and outraged faculty members who struggled with heavy teaching loads of four classes per term, and who believed the rector neither understood nor respected their work. Richard Hunter in the department of management publicly called Peebles's remark "pathetic;" Douglas Gordon of English wrote the Daily Press that only three of CNU's 174 faculty members made more than $60,000 a year, with the average salary at only $44,584. Gordon concluded with the sarcastic admonition to the rector, "Remember to get the facts straight and think before you speak."[122] Undaunted by the criticism, Peebles later questioned the

---

[120] "School Purchase Boosts CNU Size," Daily Press, 16 February 1995; "Finally, Ferguson's Ours," Captain's Log, 27 February 1995; "Ferguson Changes Costly," Daily Press, 15 November 1995; "What's the Big Deal?" Captain's Log, 4 December 1995.

[121] "William & Mary Head's Pay Raise Less than Statewide Peers," Daily Press, 1 December 1994; "Raises Stir Student Resentment," Captain's Log, 5 December 1994. On Peebles' appointment to the CNU board, see "New CNU Board Members Appointed by Governor," Daily Press, 16 September 1993.

[122] "Letters to the Editor—CNU Rector Under Fire" [Hunter letter], Daily Press, 11 December 1994; "Letters to the Editor—Think Before Talking" [Gordon letter], Daily

efficacy of faculty research. "At a school like CNU," he asked, "why do we have to be doing a lot of research?" Santoro, meanwhile, did not publicly come to the faculty's defense, but remained silent in both instances.[123]

As CNU dealt with these internal tensions, a university restructuring plan ordered by the new governor, George Allen, was submitted to State Council of Higher Education and embarrassingly rejected. In the spring of 1994, the governor had told all public college and university presidents to prepare comprehensive proposals to make their institutions more cost-effective and more responsive to student needs. Those schools that submitted unacceptable plans were told they would have their budgets cut. Working throughout the summer, Christopher Newport administrators proposed increasing the school's reliance on computer technology. Indeed, the proposal's centerpiece was to greatly expand CNU On-Line so that Internet courses in multiple disciplines could run throughout the calendar year. Officials hoped the plan would attract those local part-time nontraditional students who had left the school in recent years, as well as attract students from outside the Hampton Roads area who would have access to CNU through their computers. The restructuring plan, moreover, called for increasing the number of masters programs in order to attract CNU alumni who wished to pursue graduate studies. Finally, all CNU faculty members would be contractually employed year-round instead of only for nine months so that they would be always available for students both on campus and online. In fact, the entire school would be nicknamed "CNU: the ContiNuous University."[124] SCHEV bluntly rejected the university's proposal in November 1994, stating that CNU's plan lacked "specific information," especially in terms of articulating "the financial benefits of

---

Press, 29 December 1994. See also "Letters to the Editor—CNU Duties Outlined," *Daily Press,* 15 December 1994.

[123] "CNU Provost Plans to Quit; Speculation Swirls Around Decision," *Daily Press,* 21 April 1995.

[124] "CNU: the Continuous University" [University publication], University Archives; "Six State Colleges Comply with Streamline Efforts," *Virginian-Pilot,* 11 May 1994; "CNU, ODU Study Ways to Cut Costs," *Daily Press,* 2 September 1994; "Colleges Submit Reports On Ordered Restructuring," *Richmond Times-Dispatch,* 2 September 1994; "University Charts New Course," *Captain's Log,* 31 October 1994; Summerville interview with Hamilton, 8 January 2008.

[its] restructuring steps." The rejection also meant that the school lost an additional $600,000 in state funds.[125] The State Council later approved a heavily revised proposal, but only after Governor Allen's cuts had been submitted to the legislature. Thus, budget concerns continued into 1995. Due to ongoing enrollment declines and funding shortages that spring, the university had to cancel forty-six already-scheduled classes, much to the distress of the students previously enrolled in them. Many expressed their displeasure with their feet. Indeed, when the spring semester began, a "sharp decline" in registrations occurred with frustrated students going elsewhere for their college course work. With even fewer tuition dollars available, everyone on campus feared "another round of cuts" was right around the corner.[126]

By the spring of 1995, the board of visitors let it be known that it was increasingly unhappy with these developments. In March, board members even set up an ad hoc committee in order to allow "more open and direct communications between the board and mid-level administrators." One member of the committee was former Senator Paul Trible, who had joined the board of visitors in 1994 and who had immediately become active in learning about the school's affairs. The following month, Richard Summerville, Vice President for Academic Affairs and Provost for thirteen years, suddenly resigned stating, "it has become evident that a new perspective will be required of this office." Rumors swirled that the board of visitors—unhappy about the restructuring plan, declining student enrollment, and vacancies in many key administrative positions (such as Dean of Students and Director of Admissions)—had forced Summerville out. Although Santoro declined

[125] "CNU, NSU Restructuring Plans Inadequate," *Daily Press*, 4 November 1994; "Education Panel Threatens Budget Cuts at CNU, NSU," *Daily Press*, 9 November 1994; "CNU May Be Caught in VA Budget Crunch; School May Lose $600,000," *Daily Press*, 6 December 1994. See also "Pinch from Cuts May Miss CNU: Funds Will Be Restored, Confident President Says," *Daily Press*, 7 December 1994.

[126] "Budget Shortfall Forces Large Number of Class Cancellations," *Captain's Log*, 21 November 1994; "State OK's CNU Restructuring; But Shortfall in Funds Looms," *Daily Press*, 11 January 1995; "Budget Problems Continue to Plague CNU," *Captain's Log*, 30 January 1995.

the rumors, several board members publicly stated that they supported Summerville's decision to go.[127]

Two months later, it became apparent that President Santoro's days were numbered as well. A *Daily Press* article of 8 June 1995 explained that the president was considering resigning because of dwindling support among the board of visitors. Indeed, Peebles now refused to publicly back Santoro. When contacted by a reporter for the story, he said, "Eight years is a long-time to be a university president" and "[i]f that's his wish—to step down or move aside—we have to respect that." The piece also explained how Santoro had "angered many people over the years" with his fiery temper, including such important figures as Alan Diamonstein. Finally, the article described the faculty's increasingly "strained" relationship with the president.[128] Five days later, on 13 June, Santoro announced his resignation to become effective on 30 June 1996. He said in a letter to the board of visitors that he wished to join the history department to teach courses in his areas of specialty, particularly Byzantine and German history. Santoro later recalled that he had "accomplished most of what I had wanted to do" as president and genuinely "felt that CNU was ready for new ideas." He acknowledged, moreover, that the composition and politics of the board had changed, especially with the 1993 election of George Allen.[129]

The board accepted Santoro's resignation, but publicly bestowed enormous praise upon him. Rector Peebles said the president's "accomplishments dwarfed anything by his predecessors" and, to honor him, the board of visitors unanimously voted to name the university's

---

[127] "Board Strives for More Direct Communication," *Captain's Log*, 27 March 1995; "CNU Provost Plans to Quit Speculation Swirls Around Decision," *Daily Press*, 21 April 1995; "Summerville Steps Down After 13 Years," *Captain's Log*, 24 April 1995; Summerville interview with Hamilton, 8 January 2008. Dr. Jouett Powell was named "acting provost" after Summerville's resignation. Summerville took a one-semester sabbatical and returned to teaching as professor of mathematics in the spring of 1996, see "CNU Dean Named Acting Provost Replacement Search to Begin this Fall," *Daily Press*, 16 May 1995.

[128] "CNU Chief Santoro Considers Resignation," *Daily Press*, 8 June 1995.

[129] "Santoro Resigns as CNU President: Historian Plans Returning to Teaching," *Daily Press*, 14 June 1995; Santoro communication to Hamilton, 23 February 2009; Santoro interview with Hamilton, 24 March 2009.

dormitory the Carol K. and Anthony R. Santoro Residential Hall.[130] Two months later, the board also negotiated a generous separation package, which included an eighteen-month sabbatical at Santoro's annual presidential pay of $113,379, plus a $2,400 monthly housing and car allowance. Moreover, when Santoro finally joined the history department, he would possess the titles of "President Emeritus" and "Distinguished Professor" as well as enjoy a lower teaching load compared to the regular faculty. News of the separation package angered some in the community and on campus. Faculty senate president Robert Doane, for instance, openly questioned the package's generosity. He even speculated about what specific research project Santoro would be working on during his eighteenth-month sabbatical. Reflecting the lingering bitterness between the president and the faculty, he asked sarcastically, "I don't understand why if a person has risen to the ranks of distinguished professor, he needs that much time to return to undergraduate teaching."[131] The controversy, however, soon passed and the university community began the much more important task of searching for a new president.

Between 1980 and 1995, as Christopher Newport evolved into a more mature institution, it had experienced both remarkable development and significant growing pains. Presidents Jack Anderson and Anthony Santoro had certainly had turbulent administrations with the school continually searching for funds, students and political support, which, by 1995, all seemed in short supply. Nevertheless, despite their difficulties, both presidents had significant accomplishments. Anderson had strengthened Christopher Newport's internal administration and

---

[130] "Santoro Resigns as CNU President," *Daily Press*, 14 June 1995; "Santoro Resigns," *Captain's Log*, 19 June 1995; "Dedication Honors Presidential Team," *Captain's Log*, 18 September 1995. See also the *Daily Press's* positive editorial about Santoro's tenure as president, "The Santoro Era: CNU Made Remarkable Strides Under Activist President," *Daily Press*, 15 June 1995.

[131] "Santoro's CNU Contract Extends Paid Sabbatical," *Daily Press*, 15 December 1995; Jim Spencer, "CNU's Santoro a Pro at 'Let's Make a Deal,'" *Daily Press*, 20 December 1995. For more information about Santoro's presidency, see Chris Allen, "Santoro's Presidency: Controversy and Achievements," and Hunter Snellings, "Developing a Legacy for Success: A Comparison of the Santoro and Trible Presidencies," unpublished undergraduate research papers, "Researching CNU" history seminar, Spring 2008, University Archives.

academic bureaucracy, which allowed the school to expand in the future in a rational and orderly manner. Under Santoro's leadership, CNU had acquired Ferguson High School and its thirty acres, achieved university status, and successfully constructed its first dormitory. Although many questioned these accomplishments in 1995, all would prove crucial to the school's development in the years ahead. Finally, both presidents had maintained CNU's core commitment to high-quality classroom instruction and providing students with positive and meaningful academic experiences. Still, as Santoro prepared to leave the presidency, many wondered what lay in the future for the university.

PART III

TRANSFORMATION (1996–2011)

5

A New Vision and New Directions

On 4 December 1995, Christopher Newport's Board of Visitors voted unanimously to name Paul Trible as the university's fifth president. A former US congressman and senator, the forty-eight-year-old lawyer had himself been appointed to the board of visitors the previous year by Governor George Allen. In that capacity, Trible increasingly saw *both* the institutional challenges CNU confronted and its enormous potential as a university. When the former senator assumed the office the following month, he immediately began a program of controversial changes that profoundly altered CNU's historic role as a commuter college serving the local population. Indeed, Trible sought to remake CNU into a highly selective liberal arts college which focused on three things: 1) attracting superb students from throughout the Old Dominion, 2) providing them with rigorous and challenging classroom instruction, and 3) creating a dynamic campus environment that would be both meaningful and memorable for students and the community. Trible also transformed the Shoe Lane campus itself and ushered in an era of building and construction that left the old campus unrecognizable.

The first five years of "the Trible era" transformed CNU in numerous ways. Because of the former senator's political skills and acumen, additional financial resources (especially from Richmond) flowed to the university, and high quality students drawn from all corners of the state arrived on campus. Furthermore, observers in Hampton Roads were in awe of the number and quality of the new academic and student buildings that were proposed and built. Indeed, the school took on the appearance of a well-endowed private liberal arts college rather than an under-funded and struggling public university.

Nonetheless, many faculty members who had been at CNU since the Cunningham and Windsor eras lamented these changes. While everyone appreciated the new resources, many perceived that the school had abandoned the local population, especially nontraditional Peninsula students for whom the college had opened in 1961. The local community surrounding CNU, moreover, watched warily as the school changed, especially as its residential-student population grew more numerous. They, too, saw these transformations as potentially negative ones. Traditional-aged college students were well known as being stereotypically loud and occasionally disrespectful to neighbors and local residents. Homeowners near campus, therefore, wondered if their old neighborhoods would survive as CNU's buildings expanded upward and the campus expanded outward. By 2001, after five years at the helm, Paul Trible led a school that was very different from the one he took over in 1996—indeed, many new opportunities were in place, yet many new challenges also lay ahead.

Trible's Appointment and New Directions

On Tuesday, 27 June 1995, a *Daily Press* article on CNU's search for a new president began with the sentence: "For those who think big changes are right around the corner at Christopher Newport University in the wake of CNU President Santoro's resignation, [Rector] David L. Peebles has this message: forget about it." The university's rector explicitly said he did not want a transformative leader in the position. As head of the presidential search committee, Peebles argued the school needed a leader with a modest vision. Indeed, the successful candidate should focus on just two things: 1) improving on CNU's long-standing mission of being a "teaching university" and 2) squeezing inefficiencies out of the school's administrative structure. Toward this end, Peebles himself had proposed "reducing the number of [CNU's] colleges and ... merging academic departments." Faculty and staff, however, were eager for dramatic changes after years of financial hardship and clashes with administration figures. Although faculty members did not know exactly what changes the new president should implement, most believed he or she should at least attempt to recover the nontraditional, part-time students who had drifted away in the early 1990s. The State Council for

Higher Education reported, moreover, that such students were growing in number in the state. Thus, everyone felt that the university's new leader should recommit him- or herself to CNU's traditional mission and actively seek to attract and enroll older working adults.[1]

Five months later in early December, expectations of slow and modest changes came to a sudden end when the board of visitors selected Paul Trible as CNU's fifth president. The selection of a former US senator with no experience in higher education stunned the campus and the Hampton Roads community. Trible's first public statements, moreover, indicated that he intended to move CNU in a dramatically new direction. Trible *was* an unlikely choice as president. Born in 1946, he remembered how his parents had instilled in him a sense of public responsibility, service, and leadership. He attended Hampden-Sydney College as an undergraduate student and afterwards went to the law school at Washington and Lee. Trible's public career began in 1974 when voters elected him county prosecutor of Essex County on Virginia's Middle Peninsula. Two years later, he ran for Congress as a Republican from the state's First District after incumbent Thomas Downey of Newport News stepped down. Trible campaigned tirelessly against Democrat Robert Quinn of Hampton, a more experienced and better-known candidate. The race included nearly thirty debates across the district—including one at CNC—and, on election night 1976, Trible eked out a narrow victory by a margin of fewer than 1,500 votes out of the 150,000 cast. He won reelection to the House twice more (in 1978 and 1980) and served over the years on the Armed Services and Budget Committees. In 1982, Trible ran for the US Senate and won, despite the year being a difficult one for the Republican Party overall. His one-term in Congress' upper-chamber included service on the Foreign Relations Committee, which brought him national television exposure, especially during the hearings on the Iran-Contra affair. Trible decided not to run for reelection in 1988, stating that he wished to spend more time with his wife, Rosemary, and their two young children. The following year, however, Trible ran for Virginia governor and lost in the Republican

---

[1] "CNU Chairman Wants to Focus on Efficiency," *Daily Press*, 27 June 1995; "College Students Grow Older, Stay Longer; Typical Freshman a Rarity, says Survey," *Daily Press*, 7 September 1995.

primary. At that point, most observers considered his meteoric political career to be over. After spending a year as a teaching fellow in the Kennedy School at Harvard, Trible started a Washington, DC- lobbying firm called the Jefferson Group.[2]

Around this same time, George Allen won the governorship of Virginia. Allen was the first "Reagan Republican" to enter the Old Dominion's governor's mansion and, starting in 1994, he began appointing several "heavy-hitters" to CNU's board of visitors, including David Peebles and Paul Trible. Although prominent local leaders had previously served on the board, Allen's selections that year reflected a new level of political importance and it was noticed throughout the Peninsula. Trible later recalled that as soon as he arrived on Christopher Newport University's campus, he "fell in love with the potential of this place" and, therefore, he became an active and energetic board member. In May 1994, furthermore, he delivered the university's commencement address where he somberly warned graduates about the nation's decline in basic academic knowledge. Excellence, he lamented, had not been a priority in recent years. "Our nation's strength and prosperity depend on an educated populace." Thus, he concluded, "We must do better."[3]

After Santoro announced his retirement the following year, David Peebles asked Trible to serve on the presidential search committee along with several other board members, administrators, and faculty. The former senator readily agreed. One of the committee's first actions was to commission a report from an outside consultant to assess CNU's institutional strengths and weaknesses. The consultant also assembled a profile of the key qualities the ideal presidential candidate should possess. The search committee received the report on 30 October 1995, and it stressed that CNU desperately needed a president with proven leadership experience as well as political savvy in order to deal with state legislators in Richmond. Because the president must also carve out a new vision for the school, the consultant said that the ideal candidate might not—and perhaps should not—come from within the academic

---

[2] Paul Trible interview with Phillip Hamilton, 31 August 2009; "Paul S. Trible: Life Goes On for Private-Citizen Trible," *Daily Press*, 19 April 1993.

[3] Trible interview with Hamilton, 31 August 2009; Richard Summerville interview with Phillip Hamilton, 8 January 2008; "CNU President: 'Your Task is to Heal a Broken World;' Trible Decries Violence in U.S.," *Daily Press*, 16 May 1994.

world. Committee members instead ought to look at applicants with governmental and/or business experiences. After reading the report, Trible told his wife Rosemary that he thought he might qualify. She immediately encouraged him to apply. Two weeks later on November 13, the search committee met again—this time to discuss the eighty-four applications that had so far arrived. Toward the meeting's end, Trible announced to everyone "I'm considering applying for the presidency and I want you to tell me if this is something I should consider." The committee sat stunned and initially no one said a word. Associate Vice President for Planning and Development Cynthia Perry remembered, "Everyone just sat across the table and stared at each other." Rector Peebles later confessed, "I was dumbfounded like everyone else." After a few moments of silence, Trible said he should probably leave and quickly exited the room. A week later, Peebles called and said, "Paul, we have met three times and we think you should be the next president of CNU. We have disbanded the Search Committee and are prepared to recommend your selection to the Board of Visitors." On 5 December, the rector announced to the press that the board had unanimously selected Trible as CNU's fifth president.[4]

That same day, the rector personally introduced Trible to the university community. At a campus meeting of two hundred people in Gaines Theater, the new president immediately let it be known that he had big changes in mind. Under his leadership, he announced, more students would be recruited, more dormitories and academic buildings would be built, and more financial resources would flow to the school. "We will immediately engage new friends in Richmond and Washington," Trible pledged. He asked, moreover, for help from faculty, staff, and students "to communicate with passion and persuasion the vision and good work of CNU." Finally, the new president proclaimed, "It is time to think and act like winners.... We will not tolerate those that

---

[4] "CNU Names Trible President; Ex-Senator Takes Office on January 2," *Daily Press*, 5 December 1995; "Trible Charts New Course as CNU's Fifth President," *Daily Press*, 6 December 1995; "CNU's Trible Returns to the Spotlight," *Daily Press*, 6 December 1995; "High Profile—Paul Trible: from Private Life to Public Service CNU Hopes Trible's Political Ties Work to School's Advantage," *Daily Press*, 11 December 1995; Cynthia Perry interview with Phillip Hamilton, 3 June 2009; Trible interview with Hamilton, 31 August 2009.

say it can't be done." Two weeks later, Trible signed a lucrative
compensation contract that included an annual salary of $150,000. While
significantly higher than Santoro's last pay package, Rector Peebles said,
"When you're looking for a miracle worker, you've got to pay a miracle
worker."[5]

Although several faculty members expressed "disbelief" at Trible's
appointment due to his lack of academic experience, most were willing
to give the ex-senator a chance and some thought a number of factors
actually made him a strong selection. Virginia's decentralized system of
higher education certainly was one factor in his favor. Unlike many other
states (California, Florida, New York, and Georgia, for example), no
centralized state education agency governs the Old Dominion's system
of colleges and universities. Rather each public institution is largely
independent with its own separate board of visitors appointed by the
governor. The flat hierarchy of the state system, therefore, encourages
institutional diversity and avoids the "one-size-fits all" mentality
common at other more highly centralized state systems. This freedom to
innovate would permit a dynamic president with a different vision and
different ideas to change an institution's direction. Thus, Trible's many
years of leadership and political experience as well as his prominence as
a former US senator were seen as significant assets by board members
anxious to secure both a new direction as well as more adequate funding
from the state.[6]

During his time as a board member, Trible certainly saw the need
for CNU both to secure more state funds and to dramatically change
direction. He also understood that Christopher Newport had a long and
impressive reputation for high-quality teaching by faculty members who
cared deeply about their students. But the university's open-admissions
model aimed at serving local nontraditional students no longer worked
in the school's favor. By the mid-1990s, other universities viewed the
Peninsula as fertile ground for recruiting both traditional and
nontraditional students. The College of William and Mary, for instance,

---

[5] "Trible Charts New Course as CNU's Fifth President," *Daily Press,* 6 December
1995; "Trible to Get $150,000," *Daily Press,* 20 December 1995.
[6] Richard Summerville communication to Phillip Hamilton, 10 December 2007;
Summerville interview with Hamilton, 8 January 2008.

Paul and Rosemary Trible on Dec 5, 1995 at the ceremony formally announcing his appointment at president of CNU.

(above) CNU freshmen and upper-classmen on "move-in day" at Santoro Hall.
(below) Six thousand students and other fans crowded into CNU's new stadium on
September 1, 2001 to watch the Football Captains play Salisbury State University.

(above) Faculty members processing toward graduation ceremonies in 2002. Taken from the top floor of the Admin Building, this photograph reveals the beatification efforts undertaken by the administration. McMurran Hall is on the upper right. (below) Professor Bill Brown performing with the CNU jazz ensemble. Brown and his students played for Newport News school children annually during the Ella Fitzgerald Jazz Festival.

French Professor Susan St. Onge with Governor George Allen after winning the state's "Outstanding Faculty Award" in 1997

Barry Wood, as the senior member of the faculty, carrying the university mace at the December 2000 graduation held in the new Freeman Center. A member of the original faculty of 1961, Wood retired in 2002.

Rector Robert "Bobby" Freeman Jr speaking at an academic ceremony in the early 2000s.

had opened its "Peninsula Center" for adult learners at Oyster Point in 1995 and Old Dominion University followed soon afterwards with its Peninsula Graduate Education Center. Moreover, with the advent of Internet-based online instruction, a number of other institutions had opened up "store-front operations" near CNU, including the George Washington University, Averett University, Florida Tech, and St. Leo's University. These schools catered to working adults who beforehand had come to Christopher Newport for additional training during evening classes. Because of these fundamental shifts in higher education, Christopher Newport would likely never get these students back.[7] Furthermore, Trible saw that CNU's political base was simply too narrow. Although the university had long received strong backing from local General Assembly members like Alan Diamonstein, the school was not on anyone else's political radar. Indeed, few delegates outside the Hampton Roads area really knew or cared much about CNU because they had few or no constituents who attended the school. This narrow political base meant that the university's funding from Richmond would always be vulnerable.[8]

As a result, Trible realized the school had to dramatically change course. Toward this end, he wanted the school to grow from its current size of nearly 3,400 full-time students (or FTEs) to 5,000. But, he pledged, it should grow no larger. At five thousand full-time undergraduates, the university could offer a diverse array of strong academic programs, but still be small enough so that professors could get to know their students by name. He also told a newspaper interviewer soon after his appointment that CNU needed to focus its attention once more upon its liberal arts heritage. Because of the university's historic connection to William and Mary, strengthening its academic curriculum in the liberal arts disciplines made sense. Clearly influenced by his own experiences as

---

[7] Trible interview with Hamilton, 1 September 2009; Summerville communication to Hamilton, 10 December 2007; Summerville interview with Hamilton, 8 January 2008. On the opening of William & Mary's Peninsula Center, see "Strengthening Ties—W&M Opens Newport News Center—College Seeks Links With Area Business," *Daily Press*, 19 April 1995.

[8] Trible interview with Hamilton, 1 September 2009; Summerville communication to Hamilton, 10 December 2007; Summerville interview with Hamilton, 8 January 2008.

a student at Hampden-Sydney and Washington and Lee, Trible also wanted to expand CNU's residential population. By the year 2000, he said he hoped at least one thousand students would be living on campus in both Santoro Hall and a new dormitory yet to be built. Perhaps additional residential halls could be constructed beyond that if demand existed. With more residential students drawn from throughout the Old Dominion, campus life would be more dynamic, stimulating and engaging. Finally, CNU had to create "a 'students first' atmosphere," both to convince current students to stay and to attract talented new ones.[9]

Trible officially took the university's reins on 2 January 1996. During his first several weeks on the job, he regularly walked the campus, visiting with student groups and attending athletic events. He also taught an evening course that term called "Leadership in Politics." "This way," the president told the Captain's Log, "I can listen and learn." To gain an even better perspective about student views, he also ordered Dean of Students Robert Spicer to create and distribute a questionnaire asking students their opinions on a wide range of issues, including classes and academics, the registration process, tuition, and financial aid. Trible said that he wanted to make the university work more effectively and efficiently on the students' behalf.[10]

The new president, moreover, prepared for the upcoming bi-annum budget negotiations in Richmond. During his first week as president, for instance, he met with the Hampton Roads General Assembly delegation in order to explain his specific budgetary goals for the session. Governor George Allen's previously released budget proposal had included only a paltry 4.9 percent increase for the university. Trible understood that the

---

[9] "High Profile—Paul Trible: from Private Life to Public Service CNU Hopes Trible's Political ties Work to School's Advantage," Daily Press, 11 December 1995. FTE stands for "Full-Time Equivalency." In fall 1995, CNU had 2,819 full-time students and 1,739 part-time students. SCHEV calculated the total number of credit hours students were taking and said that CNU had 3,379 FTEs. These numbers are from the CNU Office of Institutional Research.

[10] Trible interview with Hamilton, 31 August 2009; "High Profile—Paul Trible: from Private Life to Public Service CNU Hopes Trible's Political Ties Work to School's Advantage," Daily Press, 11 December 1995; "CNU Welcomes New President," Captain's Log, 22 January 1996; "Family and Friends Warmly Received," Captain's Log, 13 February 1996.

school had to do better. He wanted money not only to renovate Ferguson Hall, but also to construct three brand new buildings: a new convocation/sports arena to replace Ratcliffe Gymnasium, a second dormitory for students, and a performing arts center to serve both the university and the Hampton Roads community. Trible focused much of his attention at the meeting on Alan Diamonstein, who continued to be a figure of enormous influence within the legislature especially as chair of the Education Appropriations subcommittee. The president, however, also spoke with Delegate Phillip Hamilton, a Republican of the Ninety-third District in Newport News and a rising star within the legislature. Elected in 1988, Hamilton was a former public school teacher and principal, and by 1996, he had established himself as an articulate spokesperson on education matters within the state. In addition to requesting additional funds, Trible assured the state leaders that he planned to continue CNU's fundamental mission to serve the Hampton Roads community. "They [Trible and his staff] assured us," Hamilton told the press afterwards, "that they don't want to become another ODU or VCU [Virginia Commonwealth University]."[11]

When Trible traveled to the state capital the following month, he continued his lobbying efforts, and his skills, connections, and thorough understanding of Virginia politics paid dividends. When the budget negotiations ended in March, the General Assembly gave CNU a 21.4 percent increase in funding—the largest percentage increase of any university in the state and four-and-a-half times more than Governor Allen had originally proposed. The $4.8 million in new money partially went toward long-delayed faculty raises, renovating Ferguson Hall, and the purchase of several new mainframe computers. The Assembly also gave the university the go-ahead to begin planning for the convocation center and a second residential hall. The budget session's high point came, however, when Alan Diamonstein successfully convinced his colleagues to appropriate $5 million to allow CNU to begin building a state-of-the-art performing arts center that would serve the entire

---

[11] "CNU Officials Make Plea to Legislators for Funds; Priorities Outlined at Luncheon Meeting," *Daily Press*, 6 January 1996; Trible interview with Hamilton, 31 August 2009. Trible also expressed a desire for stronger community ties in "High Profile—Paul Trible: from Private Life to Public Service CNU Hopes Trible's Political Ties Work to School's Advantage," *Daily Press*, 11 December 1995.

Hampton Roads community. "Alan carried the day for us," Trible beamed upon his return to campus.[12]

After his return from Richmond, the president also continued to put together his key administrative staff, a process he had started soon after taking over the job. He appointed Cynthia Perry to be his chief of staff. Having worked at CNU for seventeen years, including an extended term as director of planning and budget, Perry possessed a wealth of knowledge about the university as well as about financial and budgetary matters. Trible also named William Brauer as his executive vice president. Son of Christopher Newport's first rector Harrol Brauer, he had graduated from CNC in 1977 and had returned to the college in 1992 as vice president for administration and finance. Both Perry's and Brauer's long tenures with the school ensured that Trible would receive sound advice and accurate information from his top staff. On the other hand, the president asked Wendall Barbour, dean of academic services, and Robert Spicer, dean of students, to accept demotions. Both men declined and left the university. The ex-senator's one-time press secretary in Washington, DC, John Miller, also joined CNU in August 1996 as vice president for university relations. Prior to joining the school, Miller had been a television news anchor for WVEC-TV in Norfolk. As head of university relations, he marketed the school to the public, served as liaison to local, state, and federal government agencies, and lobbied on CNU's behalf in Richmond during General Assembly sessions.[13]

---

[12] CNU's Budget Outpaces the Rest," *Daily Press*, 16 March 1996; "CNU Nets $15.7 Million from General Assembly," *Captain's Log*, 18 March 1996; "CNU and the Future University Deserves Recognition as Community Asset," *Daily Press*, 22 March 1996; Trible interview with Hamilton, 1 September 2009. Trible repeated his budget success in 1998 when the General Assembly approved a 26 percent increase in funding for the school. Again, Diamonstein led the effort on the school's behalf, but he was also greatly assisted by delegate Phillip Hamilton and state senator Marty Williams of Newport News, Virginia. See "State Boosts CNU Funds 26% Increase to Help Pay Costs of Buildings, Staff members," *Daily Press*, 20 March 1998.

[13] "Two CNU Administrators Leaving in Trible Shakeup," *Daily Press*, 19 January 1996; "Trible changes in Administrative Faculty," *Captain's Log*, 29 January 1996; "Trible Shakes Up Staff Again," *Daily Press*, 30 May 1996; "Ex-TV Anchor to Speak for Christopher Newport; Miller Rejoins Trible After Stint at WVEC," *Daily Press*, 10 August 1996; "CNU Names John Miller as VP for University Relations," *Captain's Log*, 9 September 1996. On Brauer's initial hire in 1992, see William Brauer interview with Phillip Hamilton, 13 November 2008 and "CNC Has New Vice-President," *Captain's*

Major changes occurred with regard to the university's academic organization. When Trible became president, the university had four separate "colleges," each headed by a dean. The president thought that four colleges were too many for a school CNU's size. Thus, in mid-May, he combined the College of Business and Economics with the College of Science and Technology, thus creating the College of Science and Commerce. To head the new entity, Trible appointed George Webb, who was already dean of the Science and Technology school.[14] Two weeks later, the president combined the university's two other colleges. Thus, the College of Arts and Humanities joined with the Social Science and Professional Studies School in order to create the College of Liberal Arts. Trible appointed Dr. Jouett "Doc" Powell to be its new dean. Powell had been CNU's acting provost since Richard Summerville's resignation the previous year. To replace the reassigned Powell, the president named Dr. Robert Doane as his new provost. Doane had been a government professor at CNU since 1973 as well as recent president of the faculty senate. He had also been a member of the presidential search committee that had recommended Trible's appointment.[15]

Amid these staff and organizational changes, Trible publicly laid out his specific goals for Christopher Newport for the next six years in what he called "Vision 2002." On March 20, he gathered the university community together into Gaines Theater to update everyone on his work in Richmond and to announce his long-term plans for the university. As he opened his speech, he pledged to bring about a permanent and beneficial transformation to the campus. He predicted that, by 2002, CNU would have reversed its enrollment decline. Indeed, the school would have four thousand full-time students from across the state, as well as a new performing arts center, a sports/convocation building, and another dormitory. Moreover, eight hundred to one thousand students would be living on what he said would be "a stunningly beautiful

Log, 27 January 1992. Miller once taught at CNU on a part-time basis, see "Adjunct Anchored at CNU," *Captain's Log*, 3 October 1994.

[14] "CNU Fills New Job from Within; Science, Business Colleges Combined," *Daily Press*, 17 May 1996.

[15] "CNU's Trible Shakes Up Staff—Again," *Daily Press*, 30 May 1996; "Inside Trible's Team: CNU Staffers Take on New Jobs to Realize the Vision," *Daily Press*, 17 September 1996.

campus." As he concluded, Trible urged everyone to go out and tell "our story more wisely [and] more persuasively" than ever. As faculty members left the theater, they looked at one another with amazement. Professor Sam Bauer joked with his colleagues, "That guy is crazy as hell."[16]

"Telling Our Story ... more persuasively": Recruitment from 1996–2002

Paul Trible realized that to accomplish the goals he laid out in Vision 2002, he needed to take the lead in admissions and commit both time and resources to recruiting excellent students from throughout the Old Dominion. He knew, however, that CNU had little experience in the art of student recruitment. Prior to 1993, the state had actually prohibited the university from sending recruiters outside a thirty-five-mile radius from Newport News. When the campus dormitory had opened in 1994, this restriction ended, and President Santoro did send admissions personnel as far away as Massachusetts to recruit out-of-state students who would pay higher tuition rates. The results, however, were decidedly mixed. Although some non-Virginia students enrolled, most recruiting trips ended in failure. Carol Safko, a member of the admissions office in the early to mid-1990s, recalled traveling to a high school college fair in western Pennsylvania during this period. Not only did her car get stuck in a blizzard on the Pennsylvania Turnpike, but after she arrived at the fair, she was completely ignored by students and parents. No one had heard of Christopher Newport University and no one seemed very interested in attending a small college in Tidewater Virginia. Finally, when Trible took over, the position of admissions

---

[16] "Trible Sets Growth as Goal for CNU," *Daily Press*, 20 March 1996; "The New CNU: President Envisions Future," *Daily Press*, 25 March 1996; Trible interview with Hamilton, 31 August 2009. To more effectively convey CNU's changing image, the president commissioned a new more modern logo at the cost of $18,500, see "Identity Crisis: CNU Searches for a Suitable Symbol," *Captain's Log*, 19 November 1996; "New CNU Logo," *Daily Press*, 26 February 1997. In 1998, the university officially changed its address from 50 Shoe Lane to 1 University Place. President Trible explained the alteration "helps us establish our own identity and underscores that CNU is a university on the move;" see "CNU Changes Address to One University Place," *Daily Press*, 31 March 1998.

director had long been vacant and no viable candidate was on the horizon.[17]

Trible and the admissions staff got to work soon after his Vision 2002 address in March. Realizing that he needed to be out front in the process, the president began speaking directly to high school guidance counselors from throughout the state. Not only was it impressive to have a university president (much less a former US senator) speak directly to such individuals, but also Trible spoke so enthusiastically about the university's great assets—its attentive faculty, small classes, and long tradition of top-notch teaching. He furthermore explained Christopher Newport's "marvelous sense of community" where people knew one another by name as well as felt a commitment to such principles as honor and public service. Finally, the president skillfully created what he and others would later call "word pictures" in which he described the future CNU he envisioned in the years ahead—one with "a stunningly beautiful campus" that had "the look and feel of a great private school," and which inspired students and faculty alike.[18]

In addition to reaching out to new students, the president implemented policies to make the school more "student friendly" for those already enrolled—a process he hoped would halt student transfers and end the school's five-year enrollment decline. Toward this end, he told the registrar's office to streamline the class registration process in order to eliminate both long lines and student frustration. The president and the board of visitors also *lowered* tuition as well as room and board charges for the 1996–97 academic year. Although the decreases were modest, students greatly welcomed the relief after many years of rate hikes.[19] These efforts soon paid dividends. As everyone hoped, total

---

[17] "CNU's Out-of-State Push is Beginning to Pay Off," *Daily Press*, 2 April 1995; "Record Freshmen Class Makes CNU History," *Captain's Log*, 11 September 1995; Carol Safko interview with Phillip Hamilton, 15 October 2009.

[18] "Trible Sets Growth as Goal for CNU," *Daily Press*, 20 March 1996; Trible interview with Hamilton, 31 August and 1 September 2009.

[19] "New Registration Policy Greeted with Doubts," *Captain's Log*, 25 March 1996; "CNU Looks to Lower Tuition and Frees; President Reviews Proposed Cuts," *Daily Press*, 13 April 1996; "CNU Cuts 1996–97 Tuition, Room and Board Trimmed," *Daily Press*, 17 April 1996. To emphasize the university's focus on students, the president ordered the name of the Campus Center changed to the Student Center, see "Student Taking Name at the Campus Center," *Captain's Log*, 20 October 1996.

enrollment in the 1996–97 academic year rose for the first time in nearly a half-dozen years, growing from 4,558 (in 1995–96) to 4,565 (in 1996–97). The most impressive figure, however, was the jump in full-time students, which rose by 101 students (or 3.6 percent) from 2,819 to 2,920. Trible's new policies certainly contributed to this growth, but the rise in the number of high school graduates nationwide also proved to be a positive factor. In fact, several months before the fall 1996 term began, the State Council for Higher Education in Virginia (SCHEV) reported that state colleges and universities could expect a surge of new high school graduates in the years ahead, the first since members of the baby-boom generation had graduated from college approximately a decade before. Dr. Michael Mullen, SCHEV's deputy director, explained that Virginia "had just passed the bottom of the high school graduation curve." Therefore, 62,000 additional full- and part-time students would soon be attending state institutions by the year 2000.[20] Another achievement for the 1996–97 academic year was that the university filled Santoro Hall to capacity for the first time. This fact pleased everyone, not only because it meant the dorm would start to pay for itself, but the presence of more than four hundred residential students in the coming year promised everyone a more dynamic campus life.[21]

The positive recruitment numbers of 1996–97 became spectacular in the following academic years. The reasons were two-fold: SCHEV's predictions of more high school graduates nationwide attending college proved accurate and President Trible himself continued to work diligently with an increasingly professional admissions staff to host numerous campus events, college fairs, and open houses. In 1997, moreover, Patty Patten became CNU's new Dean of Admissions. Previously director of admissions at Old Dominion University and the University of West Florida, she brought a wealth of experience to the admissions office and a keen familiarity with high schools throughout the state. As a result, the university's numbers improved dramatically. In

---

[20] "Following Years of Failed Predictions, Va. Colleges Ready for Enrollment Boom, *Daily Press*, 15 June 1996; "Colleges Welcome Class of 2000," *Daily Press*, 23 August 1996; "Enrollment Increases: CNU Turns Around a Five-Year Decline," *Captain's Log*, 1 October 1996. Enrollment statistics are from CNU Office of Institutional Research.

[21] "Students Fill Dorm to Capacity at CNU," *Daily Press*, 25 August 1996.

1997, for example, the admissions office received 1,493 applications with 674 freshmen arriving on campus that fall. By 2000, the numbers were even better: applications had more than doubled, growing to 3,319 with the freshmen class of 2000–01 numbering more than one thousand students. These freshmen, moreover, came not just from the Hampton Roads area, but from throughout the state. Indeed, nearly four hundred high school seniors from northern Virginia applied to CNU in 2000, while 240 came from Richmond and its suburbs. The academic quality of the incoming students was also impressive. Every year average GPAs and SAT scores improved, rising from 2.83 and 960 in 1996–97 to 3.03 and 1072 by 2000–01.[22]

President Trible, furthermore, made sure that once these students arrived on campus their initial experiences were positive. He realized that this would help them to form a permanent bond with the university they had chosen to attend. In the fall of 1998, for example, CNU staff and student-volunteers helped new freshman arriving at Santoro Hall unload their cars. One impressed parent even wrote to the *Daily Press* about the experience:

> Last week, my son and I packed up and headed to check-in at Christopher Newport University as one of the reported large freshman class, fully expecting to experience that all too familiar crush of people unloading, dragging, waiting for elevators, etc.... We pulled right in front of the residence hall, a crew of students met us with a huge cart, helped us unload all within, then they asked us to go park while they delivered the possessions to his room. When we arrived in the room, there were all his things just waiting for him to put away.... [I]t was obvious that much

---

[22] "Ex-Chief of Staff to Speak at CNU Ceremony," *Daily Press*, 22 April 1997; "CNU Applications Rate Up 32%," *Captain's Log*, Summer 1997; "CNU Freshman Enrollment Up 43%," *Daily Press*, 29 July 1997; "State Boosts CNU Funds 26% Increase to Help Pay Costs of Buildings, Staff Members," *Daily Press*, 20 March 1998; "More Freshmen Making CNU Home; Growing School Welcomes Largest Incoming Class," *Daily Press*, 24 August 1998; "CNU Student Population Rises by Three Percent," *Captain's Log*, 14 September 1998; "Higher Standards, Better Students," *Captain's Log*, 5 October 1998; "Trible—CNU Becoming Selective in Admissions," *Daily Press*, 21 August 1999; "2000 Freshman Class Largest and Smartest Class Ever," *Captain's Log*, 5 September 2000; "Students Change with University," *Daily Press*, 12 November 2000; "Va. Colleges Become More Selective Application Boom May Hurt Students," *Daily Press*, 22 May 2001; "CNU Now Stronger Magnet for Talent," *Daily Press*, 29 August 2001.

planning had gone into making it as painless as possible. They even had cold drinks, snow cones and cotton candy. Thank you, CNU, for making our very first experience as a part of the entering class a very positive one. Perhaps other universities could take some lessons.[23]

The president and Rosemary Trible, moreover, hosted a series of "Freshmen Dinners" in their home at the start of every academic year in order to welcome the new students to campus. Faculty members also attended in order for the freshmen to get to know their professors in a more informal setting. Furthermore, the Tribles instituted "Parents Weekend" so that students' fathers and mothers could get to know the campus, their children's roommates, and some of the university's staff and faculty. Finally, some freshmen parents were annually invited to the president's home for a special reception with the Tribles in order to discuss CNU and its plans for the future. Before this event, the president always looked over the guest-list to learn as much as he could about the children whose parents were coming. When they arrived, Trible made sure he worked into his conversations how impressed he was by their children's academic achievements and/or sports performances on one of CNU's athletic teams. Former Provost Richard Summerville attended one of these receptions during the late 1990s and witnessed the president interact with several parents in this manner. He remembered that, "the impact was palpable."[24]

And the cumulative effect of all these efforts *was* dramatic. Trible later recalled how "young people came and fell in love with this place and then they went home and shared what they loved about CNU." Heather Vance, for instance, arrived at CNU from the highly regarded C.D. Hylton High School in Prince William County during the late 1990s. An excellent student and soccer player as well as Hylton's Homecoming Queen during her senior year, she was heavily recruited by the university's admissions team. Her mother, moreover, worked as one of Hylton High School's guidance counselors. After Vance came to CNU and started classes, she indeed fell in love with the university and often spoke about her experiences when home during breaks and summer

---

[23] "Letters to the Editor: Nice CNU Welcome," *Daily Press*, 8 September 1998.
[24] Summerville interview with Hamilton, 8 January 2008.

vacations. By the time she graduated, twenty to thirty students from Hylton were applying to CNU every year.[25]

"To Build a University"

To accommodate the growing number of students, many of whom wished to live on campus, Christopher Newport University not only had to build a larger network of academic buildings and dormitories, but the campus itself needed to be transformed in order to conform with the university's new mission. Indeed, Trible said time and again that he wanted to build a university that would both inspire students to do their best as well as remake the city of Newport News itself. When he became president, the most pressing issue facing the university with regard to its infrastructure also presented him with the greatest opportunity for campus and community transformation: the renovation of Ferguson High School.

Purchased in 1994, the old high school had a number of problems requiring immediate attention and funds. It needed a new roof as well as modern wiring for computers and the Internet. Asbestos installation from the 1950s, moreover, had to be removed. Beyond simply taking care of this basic maintenance, many were still asking what role Ferguson would play in Christopher Newport's long-term future. In the last days of Santoro's tenure, the board of visitors had refused to put significant amounts of new money into what Lewis McMurran III called "a piece of junk." Another board member said putting funds into an overhaul of Ferguson High School was "like putting a four-dollar collar on a two-dollar dog." Rector David Peebles agreed and wrote the *Daily Press* soon after Trible's appointment that he and other board members did not want "band-aid" approaches to the building. Rather they wished to see:

> ... a developmental process in ensuring that we pull this piece of property, which will represent one third of the CNU campus, together in an orderly manner that will reflect credit on the planning process 10 years down the road as well as now. We consider this immediate area to be a real anchor to the city of Newport News. It is a magnificent opportunity to make this an educational and cultural center for our city.... Can you

---

[25] Trible interview with Hamilton, 31 August 2009; Patty Patton interview with Phillip Hamilton, 13 December 2009.

imagine J. Clyde Morris Boulevard becoming known as the "Avenue of the Arts" coming off of Interstate 64?[26]

President Trible shared this vision of a dramatic new role for Ferguson. In fact, he wanted to remake the old high school into a spectacular performing arts center, one that would transform both the university and the Peninsula community itself. To make the vision a reality, Trible lobbied Alan Diamonstein and other legislators during his March 1996 visit to Richmond during state budget negotiations. He explained that a performing arts center had for too long been discussed by local leaders, but without concrete action. *Now* was the time to act and for the General Assembly to make a significant commitment. As a result of the president's efforts, Diamonstein sponsored legislation earmarking $5 million in state funds for construction of an arts center seating two thousand people. Estimating total construction costs at $20 million, Trible realized that additional funding sources would be essential. Therefore, he also approached the Newport News City Council for help. Explaining that a state-of-the-art performing arts center on CNU's campus would establish a permanent bridge between the university and the community as well as reshape the Peninsula's cultural life, he asked council members for an additional $5 million. Persuaded by his vision, the city voted an immediate grant of $650,000 to help CNU begin architectural planning as well as $5 million in future pledges for construction.[27]

With the cash in hand and more than $10 million pledged, the university hired the New York architectural firm Pei, Cobb, Freed, and Partners to design the center. Founded by the famous architect I.M. Pei, the world-renowned firm had previously created the plans for the Holocaust Museum in Washington, DC, the Rock and Roll Hall of Fame in Cleveland, and the expansion of the Louvre Museum in Paris. By hiring the architects, the *Daily Press* noted that CNU was "daring the

---

[26] David Peebles, "CNU's Plan for Ferguson High," *Daily Press*, 7 December 1995; see also Trible interview with Hamilton, 31 August 2009.

[27] "Art Center Dream in Spotlight Again," *Daily Press*, 27 March 1996; "Newport News Backs off $5 Million for Lee Hall; CNU Arts Center May Benefit Instead," *Daily Press*, 23 May 1996; "Rehashing Newport News's Priorities: CNU Arts Center Among Items that New Council Members Want to Discuss," *Daily Press*, 19 August 1998; Trible interview with Hamilton, 31 August 2009.

Peninsula to redefine itself." In March 1997, the university unveiled the drawings to the public. Ferguson High School would *not* be demolished to make way for the center, as many had expected. Pei, Cobb, Freed, and Partners instead had designed a hybrid building. According to its plans, a large portion of the old school would be remodeled while a new 1,750-seat concert hall would be built immediately adjacent to it. In the area where the high school's old gymnasiums stood, the firm proposed constructing two additional theaters—a five-hundred-seat Music and Theater Hall and a two-hundred-seat Studio Theater. With the center's front facing Warwick Boulevard, the architects also designed a dramatic two-story colonnade walkway in order to connect the old school to the new concert hall. Finally, the university proposed the construction of a nine-hundred-car parking garage to handle the increased automobile traffic from theater patrons on campus.[28]

Although spectacular, the Pei firm's elaborate design led cost-estimates to rise in an equally spectacular fashion. In the spring of 1997, for instance, planners estimated the building would cost $30 million. Three years later, however, estimates had further jumped to $45 million and were still climbing. Therefore, the president realized that the university had to secure more funds from the state government, local municipalities, and private individuals and corporations. Toward this end, Trible convinced the city of Hampton to give $1 million, while York County appropriated $400,000 for the performing arts center.[29] Moreover, large donations from prominent individuals and corporations started to be made. In May 1998, investor Robert Freeman, Sr., his wife Dorothy, and their two children contributed $1 million, the largest single donation to the university to date. A graduate of William and Mary, Freeman and his family had roots in Hampton Roads that stretched back generations. Four months later, Ferguson Enterprises, Inc., also pledged

---

[28] "Pei Firm to Design CNU Center for Performing Arts Complex," *Daily Press*, 22 August 1996; "A Defining Moment: CNU Performance Hall Can Transform the Peninsula," *Daily Press*, 1 September 1996; "Ferguson Plays Role in CNU Arts Center," *Daily Press*, 27 March 1997. See also "Radar Interview—CNU Leader Sets Course for Future; Trible Looking Ahead to the Next Century," *Daily Press,* 26 August 1996.

[29] "CNU Chief Asks York to Help Fund Arts Center," *Daily Press*, 15 October 1998; "York Ok's $400,000 for Arts Center," *Daily Press,* 3 December 1998; "Growing Tradition: CNU Now Caters to Full-Time Students," *Daily Press*, 12 November 2000.

$1 million to the arts center. President and CEO Charlie Banks said that, although he was very proud of Newport News' "blue collar heritage," this project represented a university and community "seeking greatness," and Ferguson Enterprises wanted to be a part of this "statement of excellence." Commenting on the Freeman and Ferguson donations, the *Daily Press* editorialized that they represented a community in the midst of a fundamental transformation and that the performing arts center was "a key element in that change."[30]

Although the fundraising overall proceeded slowly, Trible secured an additional $2.5 million from the state government in 2000, and the following year Virginia's two senators, George Allen and John Warner, acquired a $1 million appropriation in federal funds. By April 2001, sufficient dollars had been pledged for Trible to hold a "foundation placement ceremony" outside the old high school building and construction began the following January. Scheduled to open in 2004, Trible confidently predicted that the "take-your-breath-away beautiful" arts center would "transform our community and enrich the lives of all Virginians."[31]

As construction for the arts center began, CNU students and the Peninsula community were already enjoying a new $15 million sports and wellness facility. Named the Freeman Center because of the family's

---

[30] "$1 Million Donated for Arts Center: Newport News Family's Gift is Largest Ever for CNU," *Daily Press*, 8 May 1998; "The Freemans' Gift: One Family's Commitment and Challenge," *Daily Press*, 11 May 1998; "Newport News Company gives CNU $1 Million," *Virginian-Pilot*, 9 September 1998; see also "Trible Shares Vision for CNU Arts," *Daily Press*, 15 October 1998; Paul Trible, "New Center Will Elevate the Area," *Daily Press*, 16 October 1998; "School President Shouts at Stage Whispers: CNU's Planned Arts Center Has World-Class Acoustics," *Richmond Times*, 18 October 1998. In 1999, CNU signed a 10-year deal with PepsiCo, granting the corporation exclusive rights to sell its products on campus in return for $2.2 million. One million dollars of the deal was to got to construction of the performing arts center, "CNU Receives $2.2 Million by Agreeing to Sell Pepsi," *Daily Press*, 21 January 1999.

[31] "Center for the Arts is Awarded Further Funding," *Captain's Log*, 18 April 2000; "Fine Arts Center Set in Stone," *Captain's Log*, 24 April 2001; "CNU Ready to Build Arts Center with $1 Million from Campus," *Daily Press*, 9 November 2001. For more information about the Ferguson Center's renovations and design, see Jessica Achorn, "The Ferguson Center," unpublished undergraduate research paper, "Researching CNU" history seminar, Spring 2008, University Archives.

extraordinary $1 million gift to the university, the structure opened in October 2000. Its genesis, however, actually stretched back to 1993. In the spring of that year, the CNU men's basketball team was ranked number one in the South for Division III and its squad was preparing for the NCAA tournament. However, because the twenty-six-year-old Ratcliffe gymnasium could only seat one thousand spectators, tournament officials moved the event from CNU to tiny Emory and Henry College, six hours away by van in the mountains of western Virginia. After the long drive westward, the exhausted Captains were easily routed by Ohio Northern University in the tournament's opening round. After the embarrassing change of venue by the NCAA, CNU officials realized that a new and larger indoor-athletic facility was needed. The following year, therefore, the university obtained a $50,000 planning grant and the Santoro administration hired the Richmond architectural firm of Marcellus, Wright, Cox, and Smith to prepare a design. Its architects proposed a $12 million, 55,000-square-foot building to house an indoor track, three basketball courts, and seating for 2,500 spectators. Afterwards, however, university officials could not secure state funds with which to actually begin construction. Thus, the project was shelved.[32]

When Trible became president in 1996, he decided that the new athletic facility had to be a construction priority. If built on the proper scale, the center would not only enhance student life, but would also be a potential recruiting tool for new students. Therefore, working from the original plans drawn up several years before, Trible and university officials added a brick façade, a tall-square tower, and wide windows. They also expanded the structure's indoor features. In addition to the track and basketball courts, offices for athletic coaches, a food-court restaurant, and a ten-thousand-square-foot, state-of-the-art wellness center were added to the plans. Compared to Ratcliffe gymnasium, Athletic Director C.J. Woollum joked, "It's like [going from] a Pinto to a

---

[32] On the 1993 basketball tournament, see "CNU's Fate: Small Gym, Will Travel," *Daily Press*, 8 March 1993; "CNU Tries to Scale Mountain," *Daily Press*, 12 March 1993; "CNU Loses to Ohio Northern University in 83–67 Rout," *Daily Press*, 13 March 1993. On attempts to build a new gymnasium, see "CNU Gets Funding to Study New Gym," *Daily Press*, 28 April 1994; "CNU Sees Plan for $12 Million Rec. Center," *Daily Press*, 28 January 1995.

Rolls Royce."[33] The university secured sufficient money for construction through state appropriations, higher student fees, and private donations. Construction began in the fall of 1998 and took two years to complete. On 20 October 2000, the 107,000-square-foot athletic facility opened. Christened the Freeman Center, its first event was "Midnight Madness," an annual campus celebration marking the basketball squad's first practice of the season. As Trible and other officials hoped and expected, the building dazzled the students. As hundreds poured into the center for the first time, most reacted like Jamilia Benthall, who said "you can't even believe you are at CNU. It's like 'Oh my gosh, this is so nice.'"[34]

With the Freeman Center opened, renovations on the now-vacant Ratcliffe Hall began. Instead of razing the 1967 building, as some had suggested, Trible decided to transform it into greatly needed academic space. Therefore, between November 2000 and September 2001, construction workers turned the old gymnasium into two floors of faculty offices and classrooms outfitted with the latest technology. As the 2001–02 academic year began, the departments of English, government, and leisure studies and physical education moved into the renovated building. Ratcliffe did retain some ties to its athletic past, however, as coaches' offices and locker rooms for the outdoor sports teams remained located on the building's western wing, directly adjacent to the campus's sports fields.[35]

As buildings went up and as various renovations projects moved forward, the president also worked to transform the campus' appearance. Realizing that high school seniors often decided to attend a particular university on the basis of its physical appearance, Trible initially thought CNU left much to be desired. When he first walked across campus, he saw "concrete walkways that went every which way"

---

[33] "Changing the Face of CNU; $15 Million Sports Center Expected to Draw Students," *Daily Press*, 6 April 1998; "New CNU Gym Set for 2000," *Daily Press*, 17 September 1998.

[34] "CNU Names New Center After Peninsula Businessman," *Daily Press*, 21 October 2000; "CNU Center Named for Robert L. Freeman, Sr.," *Daily Press*, 22 October 2000; "Growing Tradition: CNU Now Caters to Full-Time Students," *Daily Press*, 12 November 2000.

[35] "Future of Ratcliffe," *Captain's Log*, 6 November 2000; "Moving Out, Moving In: Ratcliffe Gym Becomes Ratcliffe Hall," *Captain's Log*, 5 September 2001; "It's Official, Ratcliffe Hall Opens to Fanfare," *Captain's Log*, 17 October 2001.

and "crabgrass [lawns] that died in the summer." Throughout its existence, landscaping at CNU had been a haphazard affair. Since the 1970s, a buildings and grounds committee decided on plantings and sidewalk schemes. Two faculty members, Dave Bankes of Biology and Paul Killam of Government, had been particularly active on the committee in terms of supervising maintenance, putting jobs out to bid, and overseeing major landscaping projects. CNU horticulture students, moreover, initially grew many of the campus's plants in the university's greenhouse located next to the Science Building. In the early 1990s, though, Santoro dismissed the school's meager landscaping staff in the face of severe budget cuts. Although he contracted the work out to private companies to save money, many thought the appearance of the campus significantly deteriorated in the early to mid-1990s.[36]

Beginning in 1996, the new president announced his determination to change this and to make CNU "green, lush, and lovely." Landscaping personnel were hired again and they immediately started planting flowers and shrubs around existing buildings as well as seeding and maintaining campus lawns. Trible also hired Bob Goodhart as Director of Grounds. A retired army lieutenant colonel, Goodhart shared the president's passion to dramatically change the university's appearance. Not only did he plant a number of oak trees throughout the grounds in order to provide both beauty and shade, but he also began replacing the concrete pathways across campus with more attractive interlocking brick pavers.[37]

Some faculty members, however, wondered aloud at the investment in landscaping. Dr. Robert Sauders of the history department wrote to the *Daily Press* that, "the Christopher Newport administration has its priorities confused. The school should strive for academic excellence.... It should not be spending millions to have a pretty campus. What does it

---

[36] Trible interview with Hamilton, 31 August 2009; George and Jane Webb communication to Hamilton, 27 May 2008; "Landscaping Begun on Ships' Court," *Captain's Log*, 28 April 1983; "Landscapers Plan Face-Life," *Captain's Log*, 24 March 1997.

[37] "Trible Sets Growth Goal for CNU," *Daily Press*, 20 March 1996; "Landscapers Plan Face-Life," *Captain's Log*, 24 March 1997; "Appearance is Everything for Dedicated Grounds Staff," *Captain's Log*, 28 September 1998; Trible interview with Hamilton, 31 August 2009.

mean for a job applicant to say he/she graduated from a beautiful school?" Sam Bauer of Psychology also complained about the spending on landscaping, especially when the library still desperately needed books. Bauer went directly to the president himself to complain. In their meeting, Trible answered Bauer's criticisms with a two-fold response. First, he said "Sam, I'm going to ask a lot of you on this campus and in turn you're going to be asking a lot of students. And I want us to be in an environment that encourages people to be their very best;" secondly, "there are going to be tens of thousands of people visiting this campus [as prospective students], and I want them to fall in love with it." Trible later recalled that Bauer "cut me some slack" after their conversation.[38] The investment in landscaping paid off. By the early 2000s, CNU students and visitors regularly commented on the campus's remarkably improved appearance. Music-theater major Chad Wagner, for example, recalled that when he attended high school in Newport News in the mid-1990s, "the university's grass was yellow and flowers were few." As a CNU student in 2002, however, he now saw "landscapers working all the time." Thus "[t]he grass is green. Foliage is plentiful. Sidewalks are made of brick.... It makes you want to be at CNU," Wagner concluded.[39]

In addition to the campus's improved appearance, more students called CNU home. When the fall 1997 term began, for instance, four hundred students filled Santoro Hall; a year later, nearly six hundred students squeezed into the dormitory. Indeed, so many freshmen and upperclassmen wished to live on campus that they had to be tripled into rooms. By that point, plans for a new dormitory were well underway. To be constructed next to Santoro and named James River Hall, the L-shaped, four-story brick building was designed to house 440 additional students as well as provide a variety of possible living arrangements, including traditional suites, themed units, and apartments with kitchens for upperclassmen. After ground was broken in April 1999, W.M. Jordan

[38] "Letters to the Editor: Academics First," *Daily Press*, 3 September 1997; Trible interview with Hamilton, 31 August 2009.
[39] "Envisioning the Future," *Daily Press*, 5 May 2002; see also "Not Just Ivied Walls: CNU Landscape Has Lots of Trees to Study Under," *Daily Press*, 25 February 2001.

Company constructed the $12.7 million residence hall in record time, with the building opening for students in August 2000.[40]

As students moved into James River Hall, designs for even more dormitories were already on the table. The university, for instance, proposed building a 538-bed freshmen dormitory complex along Shoe Lane. Moreover, CNU's Educational Foundation had plans to "jump Warwick Boulevard," as the university entered into negotiations to purchase multiple properties across the street from the main campus. Once it had acquired these lands, the foundation intended to build four large student residential halls. As these new projects became public, everyone realized the transformation at work. The *Daily Press* editorialized in February 2001, "The expansion plan announced by Christopher Newport University is a great leap into the future—not just for the university, but for the city that surrounds it." Indeed, the newspaper claimed that the school had become "a major factor—visually, psychologically, and economically—in a demonstrably improving midtown Newport News." Most importantly, the university was "poised to play an even more important role" in the city's ongoing development in the future, especially once construction workers completed the performing arts center.[41]

Change and Continuity: Academic Life in the late 1990s–early 2000s

When Paul Trible became president, he realized that many things about Christopher Newport University *had* to change. On the other hand, aspects of the school *had* to remain intact. Regarding the latter, Trible certainly believed that CNU's decades-old tradition of excellent teaching and close attention to students needed to remain front and center of academic life. Indeed, throughout the late 1990s and into the new millennium, the university's professors continued to provide students with meaningful and substantive classroom experiences. Faculty also produced important works of scholarship. These strengths were

---

[40] "CNU to Build Upperclassmen Residence Hall," *Daily Press*, 1 September 1998; "New Residence Hall to Be Built," *Captain's Log*, 5 April 1999; "New Residence Hall Opens," *Captain's Log*, 5 September 2000; see also "CNU Raising Out-of-State Tuition, Dorm Fees Beginning this Fall," *Daily Press*, 7 April 1998; "Students Claim Territory in New Residence Hall," *Captain's Log*, 29 February 2000.

[41] "Editorial: Where the Newspaper Stands," *Daily Press*, 25 February 2001.

illustrated in 1996 when the Southern Association of Colleges and Schools (SACS) reaccredited the university for another ten-year period. In its final report, the SACS visiting team uniformly praised the dedication and effectiveness of CNU faculty members.[42]

The faculty's strengths and commitment to students and teaching were demonstrated in other ways. In 1997, for instance, Professor Susan St. Onge won Virginia's highly prestigious Outstanding Faculty Award given annually by the State Council of Higher Education. St. Onge was one of only eleven professors from across the state to win the coveted prize that year, and she was the first CNU faculty member to win the award in the school's history.[43] Three years later, Harold Cones of Biology also garnered the state's highest teaching prize. In letters from students supporting his nomination, they noted how Cones not only made learning interesting, but he had also helped many of them turn their academic careers around. Biology major Mark Kornberg wrote how Cones had helped him to improve his GPA from a dismal 1.8 to an impressive 3.4. "What Dr. Cones really brings to his lectures," Kornberg elaborated, "is a contagious enthusiasm for what he is doing, and his students cannot help but respond with enthusiasm." The biology professor, moreover, regularly took students outside the classroom, leading them on trips to the Florida Everglades as well as the shores of Maine in order to study different coastal environments. "It's very apparent that he enjoys himself," Kornberg concluded, "and he makes it apparent we should enjoy ourselves." Observers both on and off-campus viewed these awards as signs that the State Council and others in Virginia were finally recognizing the high quality of instruction at CNU.[44]

The same year Cones won the SCHEV award, however, CNU lost Dr. Albert Millar, who died of cancer in October 2000. A professor of English and well-known since 1965 as one of that department's stalwart instructors, Millar had helped establish CNU's tradition of excellence,

[42] Trible interview with Hamilton, 31 August 2009; "CNU Must Monitor Some Staff; Accreditation Team Calls for Review of Part-Timers," *Daily Press*, 14 July 1996; "Officials Renew CNU Accreditation," *Daily Press*, 13 December 1996.

[43] "Area Professors Given State Faculty Awards," *Daily Press*, 8 February 1997.

[44] "Outstanding in His Field; State Award Granted to CNU Professor," *Daily Press*, 13 March 2000.

and he maintained a formidable commitment to his students to the end of his life. When diagnosed with the disease in February 1999, he bravely told the *Captain's Log*, "I have not missed a class in thirty-three years. Primarily I feel guilty," he said, about having to do so now.[45] Two years after Millar's death, Barry Wood retired. The last of the school's eight original faculty members, Wood had, over the decades, served as a professor, administrator and, finally, chair of the university's fine and performing arts department. An academic jack-of-all-trades, he had particularly labored throughout the late 1990s to develop and reshape the university's arts program. His serious, engaging, and occasionally eccentric teaching style informed and inspired CNU students to the very end of his career.[46]

Although teaching consumed the bulk of the faculty's time—particularly with CNU's heavy 4-4 teaching load—scholarly projects remained vitally important to many professors. In 1997, for instance, Dr. Robert Atkinson won a $700,000 grant from the Environmental Protective Agency to monitor efforts to restore the Atlantic white cedar tree population in the Great Dismal Swamp National Wildlife Refuge. Atkinson used the funds not only to oversee the restoration process, but he also hired CNU graduate and undergraduate students to aid him in his endeavors, thus allowing them to "see the real world applications of the concepts they are taught in class."[47] Psychology professor Sanford Lopater co-wrote a textbook on human sexuality with Dr. Ruth K. Westheimer, the host of a nationally syndicated cable television show called "Sexually Speaking." Collaborating closely together, the pair wrote the book in a "conversational style" in order to communicate "sexual literacy" more directly and effectively to undergraduate students. Lippincott, Williams, and Wilkins, a medical publishing company, published *Human Sexuality: A Psychosocial Perspective* in 2002

---

[45] "Admired Professor 'Determined' to Return," *Captain's Log*, 1 February 1999; "Albert E. Millar, Jr.: CNU English Professor, *Daily Press*, 15 October 2000.

[46] "Tough Act to Follow: Retiring English Professor Launched Performing Arts Series at CNU," *Daily Press*, 7 May 2002.

[47] "CNU Prof Gets $700,000 to Save Rare Virginia Cedars," *Daily Press*, 13 September 1997; "Restoration of Wetlands Sprouts from CNU," *Captain's Log*, 20 October 1997. See also "CNU Scores Big Grant," *Daily Press*, 22 September 1997; "NASA Grants CNU Atmosphere Project," *Captain's Log*, 29 September 1997

and later issued a second edition.[48] Former president Anthony Santoro, who began teaching in the Department of History in the fall of 1997, remained productive. For example, he provided "voice-over" commentary for Leni Riefenstahl's 1934 Nazi-propaganda film *Triumph of the Will* when, in 2001, it was released on DVD by the home-video company Synapse Films.[49]

Another point of continuity during Trible's presidency was steady growth in the size of CNU's faculty. During Santoro's administration, the faculty grew in number from 108 in 1987 to 164 members in 1995. Like his predecessor, Trible also saw the need for more classroom instructors at the university, especially in order to reduce class sizes and to improve students' academic experiences. Therefore, he lobbied hard in Richmond to obtain more state funds to achieve this. As a result, the professorship grew from 164 to 184 (or by 12 percent) during the first five years of his presidency, and, therefore, class sizes did start to come down.[50]

Despite these points of continuity, several important changes unfolded in the late 1990s involving academic life. As mentioned, Trible wanted to refocus CNU's academic mission upon the liberal arts. This change in mission, though, meant not just strengthening those departments in the traditional liberal arts disciplines, but also scaling back or even eliminating some of the university's vocational programs. CNU's international exchange students, for example, found the English as a Second Language program (ESL) cut in 1998. Established during Santoro's administration when CNU had attempted to attract international students, the program provided intensive English-language training to more than ninety students from Europe, Asia, and Central America. But, as the school added more faculty and classes in the traditional liberal arts disciplines, the program came to be viewed as extraneous. Provost Doane explained to the *Captain's Log* that ESL's

[48] "Lopater and Dr. Ruth Write Sex Text," *Captain's Log*, 15 February 1999; Lippincott, Williams & Wilkins, http://www.thepoint.lww.com (accessed 10 December 2009).

[49] "CNU Expert 'Triumphs' on DVD," *Daily Press*, 24 April 2001.

[50] "CNU Board OK's More Teachers, Scholarships," *Daily Press*, 26 June 1999; Trible interview with Hamilton, 31 August 2009. Statistics on faculty numbers from the CNU Office of Institutional Research.

elimination was "not a question of productivity or success, it's a question of centrality to mission."[51] Several years later in 2001, the administration also eliminated most of the university's online Internet courses. Believing that they lacked sufficient rigor as well as stood outside CNU's new mission as a liberal arts and residential institution, officials cancelled the online courses with neither faculty consultation nor discussion.[52]

As some academic programs disappeared, others were created. In 1998, for instance, Trible started "The President's Leadership Program" designed to engender within students "a love of learning" and "a sense of civic responsibility and duty." Indeed, the president hoped that participants would leave CNU determined "to lead lives of meaning and significance." To join the program, entering freshmen needed a 3.0 high school GPA and a minimum of 1000 on their combined SAT scores. After acceptance, each participant received an annual $1,000 scholarship and could remain in the program if he or she: 1) declared a Leadership minor, 2) maintained a 2.5 overall GPA, and 3) performed fifty to 100 hours of community service. Twenty students participated in the program during its inaugural year and, just before their first semester began, they all took part in a five-day sailing voyage on the Chesapeake Bay. Designed to build teamwork, the students navigated two thirty-foot sailing vessels across the great waterway—a challenge that forced them to work together. Incoming freshman Katherine Gately admitted that the trip "got stressful.... But you learn to keep your composure." All the participants also agreed that the voyage helped them to "learn about themselves." During the academic year, the students not only enrolled in leadership classes and performed community service together, but they also enlivened campus life by joining dozens of clubs and athletic teams. In 1999, the university expanded the program to sixty students, and it quickly became an important part of the campus's academic and social culture. Many students, moreover, found their own lives transformed. Jamilia Benthall, for instance, came to CNU reluctantly after she graduated from Warwick High School. Not originally part of the

---

[51] "CNU Cuts ESL Program," *Captain's Log*, 13 April 1998; "CNU Will Give Up Teaching English as a Second Language," *Daily Press*, 24 April 1998; see also "Falling Through the Cracks: Exchange Students Struggle But Find Little Support," *Captain's Log*, 12 November 1996.

[52] "General Education Classes Go Off-Line," *Captain's Log*, 12 September 2001.

Leadership Program, she hoped to transfer from CNU after her first year. But Benthall took a leadership class in the spring of 1999, and it inspired her to join the program and to become more involved in the campus's social life. By her senior year, Benthall had not only completed the program, but she had been elected vice president of the Student Government Association and had joined Delta Sigma Theta, a historically black sorority on campus.[53]

In general terms, the student body changed fundamentally during these years. Part-time students of various ages declined, while the number of traditional-aged students rose substantially. By the late 1990s, many faculty members noticed these changes at work and reflected upon the positive and negative ramifications. Some professors, for instance, noted that the university became much less diverse in the late 1990s in terms of students' ages, races, and socio-economic backgrounds, and they saw this growing lack of diversity as a loss. Ronnie Cohen recalled that, before Trible's presidency, "many faculty felt [they] were really making a difference and opening doors for students who might not have a lot of options." Professor Cheryl Mathews, moreover, remembered that most of CNU's older, nontraditional students had always seemed to understand that "education was a privilege" and, therefore, sought to make the most of their classroom experiences. Yet most of the faculty also grasped the beneficial changes that the younger students brought to the classroom. Susan St. Onge, for instance, explained that the students who started to arrive in the late 1990s were clearly "better qualified" as well as "more focused ... than our typical students used to be."[54] In this environment, several true stars began to emerge. One of the first mathematical students former Provost Richard Summerville taught after his sabbatical in 1996 was James Rossmanith, who took his abstract

[53] "Lead or Follow, Students Sail Onward," *Daily Press*, 2 February 1999; "CNU Board OK's More Teachers, Scholarships," *Daily Press*, 26 June 1999. See also "Senior Leaders 'Part of the Fabric of CNU,'" *Daily Press*, 13 May 2000; "PLP Develops Official Contract," *Captain's Log*, 29 January 2003. The President's Leadership Program had antecedents. In 1988, CNC sponsored the "Student Leadership Institute" which sought to foster leadership skills among participants, see "Institute Makes Better Leaders," *Captain's Log*, 13 October 1988.

[54] Ronnie Cohen communication to Phillip Hamilton, 5 March 2008; Cheryl Mathews communication to Phillip Hamilton, 6 June 2008; Susan St. Onge communication to Phillip Hamilton, 25 February 2008.

algebra class. A young man of remarkable ability, he eventually earned a PhD from the University of Washington in applied mathematics and later became a professor of mathematics at the University of Wisconsin. Another such student was Heather Hoffman, who came to CNU in 1997. She also majored in mathematics and enjoyed an equally extraordinary academic career. Graduating first in her class in 2001 with a 3.99 GPA, she afterwards attended the Medical College at Virginia Commonwealth University where she earned a PhD in biostatistics. Following the completion of her doctorate, she became a research professor at the George Washington University School of Public Health. Hoffman, moreover, had been preceded at CNU by her sister Lisa, who also had graduated first in her class and who later attended dentistry school.[55]

The growing quality of the student body combined with the university's ongoing focus on solid teaching and classroom instruction led *US News and World Report* in 1999 to rank CNU number two in the South as "a top regional public liberal arts college." That same year, the Kaplan-Newsweek College Catalog labeled the university one of its "hidden treasures"—that is, one of a select number of "terrific colleges that aren't as well known as they should be." Kaplan-Newsweek stressed that such colleges are especially unique because they "offer [students] the maximum amount of individual academic attention" and excelled at "providing a good liberal arts education." After the announcements, Trible told the *Daily Press* "we have changed the paradigm" in terms of the university's academic mission. "With each passing day," he continued, "CNU will look less and less like ODU and more like JMU [James Madison University]."[56]

---

[55] "Laughter, Joy, Frustration and Friendship: CNU Graduates Class of 2000," *Daily Press*, 14 May 2000; "Dole's Humor Livens CNU Graduation," *Daily Press*, 13 May 2001; Summerville communication to Hamilton, 10 December 2007. Rossmanith returned to CNU in the spring of 2007, where he gave a colloquium on fluid dynamics to mathematics majors and faculty.

[56] "Letters to the Editor: CNU Ascending," *Daily Press*, 9 September 1999; "Moving Up in the World," *Captain's Log*, 13 September 1999; "CNU Gains National Recognition with Trible: Students, Faculty Praise Leadership," *Daily Press*, 26 September 1999.

Life on Campus — Student Culture and Activities

Unlike the university's academics, improving campus life posed more of a challenge for Trible and his staff. Throughout the late 1980s and early 1990s, most CNU students stayed away from campus outside of attending classes. Thus, almost all student-organized events were lightly attended. In 1995, a transfer student named Sara Williams said that she found CNU's "social scene" pretty grim, "especially if you are not involved in a Greek organization." Therefore, in order to turn the situation around, Trible and other administration officials realized they had to put together a dedicated student life staff as well as develop an array of engaging student activities.[57]

One strategy Trible adopted was actually to expand the number of Greek organizations on campus. During the Santoro years, Greek life had grown stronger in part because of new alcohol restrictions at campus dances and other university-sponsored events. In order to enhance student experiences overall, Trible wanted this trend to continue. A member of Lambda Chi Alpha during his undergraduate years at Hampden-Sydney, the president wished to see membership expand among existing chapters and he encouraged the establishment of new fraternities and sororities. Thus, he periodically spoke at membership meetings where he explained the life-long benefits of Greek friendships and service. The president also envisioned CNU eventually building the "most impressive" fraternity and sorority houses in the state.[58] In addition to recruiting new members during these years, CNU's Greek chapters continued to perform charitable work within the community and they provided important social networks and friendships for new students, especially for those from outside the Hampton Roads area. By 2002, the university's six fraternities and three sororities were at maximum membership with a growing number of students anxious to pledge. Therefore, the university hired a full-time

---

[57] Trible interview with Hamilton, 31 August 2009; "Transfer Students Prefer CNU," *Captain's Log,* 13 November 1995.

[58] "President Trible Speaks to the Brothers of CNU," *Captain's Log,* 23 January 2002.

Greek advisor to work in the Office of Student Life overseeing existing chapters and helping to establish new ones.[59]

The administration also encouraged the establishment of other new student clubs and organizations. And, again, it had great success. In fact, a "[f]ierce competition" for office space in the Student Center developed in the late 1990s due an increasing number of active student groups. While many new organizations appeared at CNU during this period, others returned to campus after long hiatuses. Circle K, for instance, revived in spring of 1996. The largest college-service organization in the world, a Circle K chapter had been present at CNU for many years. But it had folded in the early '90s due to low membership and a general lack of interest. With Trible's new focus on traditional-aged high school graduates, though, a new and younger generation became interested in the club's mission, and, hence, they restarted the chapter. Thirty-five students belonged to Circle K by 2000, all of whom were involved in service projects throughout Hampton Roads, such as mentoring local elementary school children, visiting the elderly in nursing homes, and taking part in an annual 5K "Crop Walk" dedicated to ending hunger on the Peninsula.[60] Reflecting the changing attitudes of the era, a group of students founded the Gay/Straight Student Union in 1998. Its members held monthly meetings to socialize with one another, but they also worked with the Office of Student Life to arrange for programs and seminars to educate the entire university on gay, lesbian, and bisexual issues.[61] By 2002, CNU not only officially recognized more than sixty student clubs, but the school held its first annual "Club and

---

[59] "New Sorority Seeks to Diversify Greeks," *Captain's Log*, 24 April 2002; "Sorority Expansion to be Sooner Than Later," *Captain's Log*, 11 September 2002. See also "The Rush is On: Sororities Celebrate New Members After Fall Recruitment," *Captain's Log*, 17 September 1996; "CNU Considers an InterFraternity Council," *Captain's Log*, 17 February 1997; "Greek Week 1999: A Splashing Success," *Captain's Log*, 29 March 1999.

[60] "Crowded and Crying: Student Clubs Compete for Office Space," *Captain's Log*, 9 September 1996; "Going Full Circle: The Return of Circle K," *Captain' s Log*, 8 October 1996; "Circle K Prepared to Serve: mentoring Program Excels," *Captain's Log*, 11 October 2000.

[61] "The Gay/Straight Student Union Aims to Promote Acceptance and Tolerance," *Captain's Log*, 26 October 1998; "Vigil Sheds Light on Message of Common Decency," *Captain's Log*, 9 November 1998.

Organization Fair" to help incoming freshmen get more easily plugged into the school's developing campus scene.[62]

The most important and significant change to student life during these years came with the rapid rise in the campus's residential population. As mentioned, between 1997 and 1999, students filled Santoro Hall to capacity and even beyond, with most rooms housing three residents each. In 2000, James River Hall's opening eased the pressure for space, but only temporarily. Indeed, more students wanted to move onto the campus with each passing year. Therefore, the university started to purchase some of the existing houses surrounding campus in order to lodge those students who could not be squeezed into one of the dorms. For several years, the university even leased rooms from a privately owned hotel called The Relax Inn across the street from campus in order to accommodate everyone who wanted to take part in campus life. By 2001, the number of residential students had grown to 1,454.[63]

The presence of so many students on campus also required the administration to dramatically expand its food services throughout the academic year. Harbor Lights served as the university's main dining facility. Adjacent to Santoro Hall and filled with neon-lighted signs and nautical-theme décor, it provided residential students with three meals every day, mainly served buffet-style.[64] In 2000, the university opened the Discovery Café in the Student Center, which replaced The Terrace (the restaurant that had opened with the building in 1973). Serving both residential and commuter students, "DisCo" (as it was soon nicknamed

---

[62] "CNU Holds First Annual Club & Organization Fair," *Captain's Log*, 11 September 2002. See also "Centered on Diversity: CNU Multicultural Director Reveals Plans for Making All Students Feel at Home," *Daily Press*, 21 March 1996; "CNU Students Want Pagan Club," *Daily Press*, 7 February 1999; "New Student Political Group Seeks to Offer 'Third Way,'" *Captain's Log*, 2 October 2002.

[63] On students in the Relax Inn and homes near campus, see "Freshmen Squeeze into CNU," *Daily Press*, 21 August 1999; see also "Students Flustered Over On-Campus Housing Shortage," *Captain's Log*, 26 March 2001. On the number of CNU residential students in 2001, see "Enrollment History," Office of Institutional Research, CNU.

[64] Christopher Newport University Web site, 4 October 2001 (accessed 19 December 2009 on Internet Archive Wayback Machine: http://web.archive.org/web/20010501200707/www.cnu.edu/information/ctour/vtour).

by students) was set up as a food court that featured items from national restaurant chains such as Chick-Fil-A and Pizza Hut.[65] That same year, the university opened an upscale coffee bar in the Smith Library called "Einstein's." President Trible himself developed the idea when he and Rosemary visited their daughter at school in South Carolina. Visiting such a coffee shop on campus and liking its atmosphere, the president asked his staff if this concept could work at Christopher Newport. When told that it could, he ordered plans to be developed and for the shop to be placed in the library. Opening in February 2000, Einstein's served milkshakes, croissants as well as Starbucks coffee to CNU students, faculty, and staff.[66]

While the administration expanded the university's food services, it increasingly restricted the availability and use of alcohol. With a greater number of younger students on campus and a growing residential population, administration officials believed more stringent policies were necessary. Growing pressure from the state government in Richmond, moreover, led to new limitations. In the fall of 1997, five Virginia college students (none from CNU) died in alcohol-related incidents. The spate of deaths led the state Attorney General's office to convene a taskforce of college and university presidents, parents, and state officials. In response to its recommendations, CNU decided to ban the sale of beer and wine at the Student Center and prohibit all alcoholic beverages from campus-sponsored events. With the student body in the midst of fundamental change, Dean of Students Maury O'Connell explained, "We don't want alcohol to be the binding social ingredient on campus." Students' reaction, however, was mixed. Some agreed that books and alcohol did not mix, while others argued the decision would do nothing to halt the misuse of alcohol. Junior Amy Ragan said she

---

[65] "The Terraces' Lunch Line Grows as Christopher's Closes," *Captain's Log,* 13 September 1999; "Details of Terrace Renovation Clearer," *Captain's Log,* 21 March 2000; Christopher Newport University Web site, 12 November 2001 (accessed 19 December 2009 on Internet Archive Wayback Machine http://web.archive.org/web/20011112171352/www.cnu.edu/admin/cnuaux/dining/).

[66] "Campus Coffee Shop to Stir Collective Genius," *Captain's Log,* 4 October 1999; "Einstein's Brews Up Business," *Captain's Log,* 7 February 2000; Christopher Newport University Web site, 12 November 2001 (accessed 20 December 2009 on Internet Archive Wayback Machine http://web.archive.org/web/20011227215523/www.cnu.edu/admin/cnuaux/dining/einstein/home/html).

thought the ban simply would "encourage students to go elsewhere" to drink off-campus. Many students felt the same way. Nonetheless, the administration put the policy in place and CNU officially became a "dry campus" in 1998.[67] Although students generally obeyed the new rules, a significant portion of them continued to feel that, if of legal age, they should be free to consume alcoholic beverages on campus. Therefore, three years afterwards, CNU's Student Government Association formed a committee to review the policy and, if necessary, request certain alterations. Following its examination, the committee collectively recommended relaxing the original policy. In particular, it proposed that limited beer and wine sales be permitted in the Discovery Café after 5pm to adults twenty-one and older. Realizing the university benefited by being a "dry campus," especially among some prospective students and their parents, Trible pointedly rejected the recommendations. He explained that, in his view, the alcohol policy was "working well," the campus was "safe and secure," and, as a result, "[t]he issue is closed for now."[68]

Despite the restrictive alcohol policy, campus life continued to develop in a positive way. By the early 2000s, many seniors noted the dramatic changes that had occurred during their four years at the university, a number of which they themselves had initiated. When the first cohort of the President's Leadership Program students graduated in

---

[67] "Battle of the Binge Begins: Va. Colleges Try New Anti-Alcohol Programs," *Daily Press,* 24 August 1998; "Drying Out: CNU Ends On-Campus Beer Sales," *Daily Press,* 27 August 1998; "Alcohol On Campus Has Evaporated," *Captain's Log,* 7 September 1998. See also "Va. Colleges Weigh Law on Drinking Notification," *Daily Press,* 16 October 1998; "CNU Adding Programs to Curb Student Drinking," *Daily Press,* 12 December 1998. For more information about the evolution of CNU's alcohol policy, see Jenna Heggie, "When A Three Letter Word is Not Enough: A History of ... the Alcohol Policy at Christopher Newport University," unpublished undergraduate research paper, "Researching CNU" history seminar, Spring 2008, University Archives.

[68] "University May Reconsider Alcohol-Free Policy," *Captain's Log,* 12 February 2001; "Alcohol Committee Formed," *Captain's Log,* 19 March 2001; "CNU Rebuffs Attempt to allow Alcohol: Trible Says College Will Remain Dry," *Daily Press,* 20 June 2001; see also "Where the Newspaper Stands," *Daily Press,* 30 June 2001. Although the policy generally worked, students were occasionally caught with alcohol. In 2000, for instance, six students were expelled when caught drinking beer in the James River dormitory, see "James River Residents Expelled," *Captain's Log,* 11 September 2000.

2002, for instance, most of them had led various student organizations such as fraternities and sororities and/or had begun popular campus programs. For instance, PLP student Jesse Gray of Spotsylvania started "CNU Tonight," a weekly campus variety show held in the Student Center and patterned after the television program *Saturday Night Live*. Other students worked to expand the university's community service and volunteered with local charities. Pamela Todd said the Leadership Program "gave me that instant connection to people," while other participants claimed it provided them with "the confidence to change CNU." With a greater number of student organizations and activities up and running, fewer residential students went home on weekends.[69] Another indication of success came with the emerging tradition of Family Weekend. When the Tribles held the first Family Weekend in 1996, the school's student body was still predominantly commuter and, thus, only 130 people attended. Six years later, however, with 2,058 residential students, more than one thousand parents, siblings, and guests visited the campus, met with President and Rosemary Trible and attended a variety of weekend events.[70]

The theater and music programs expanded during these years as well and provided not only additional artistic opportunities and campus events for students, but also created important outreach to the Hampton Roads community. The Nancy Ramseur Memorial Concert Series, for instance, begun by Barry Wood and Rita Hubbard in the early 1970s, continued to run annually in the Student Center's Gaines Theater. The theater program, moreover, produced superb shows throughout the 1990s and into the new millennium. In 2000, for instance, Professor George Hillow directed Gilbert and Sullivan's *The Mikado*. The *Daily Press's* theater critic attended one performance and afterwards wrote, "From beginning to end, this was a polished performance of a show that's not easy to pull off." The critic finished by stating that Hillow and

---

[69] "CNU Graduates Grow into Leaders; First Students Finish Program," *Daily Press*, 11 May 2002.

[70] "York River, CNU Apartments Open to Family and Fanfare," *Captain's Log*, 25 September 2002; Trible interview with Hamilton, 31 August 2009. The growth of the residential student population meant growing concerns over student safety and the need for a larger campus police force, see "CNU Police Evolve Along with School," *Daily Press*, 3 August 2002.

CNU "deserve high marks … [for] treating the community to such a strong show."[71]

In 1997, the university teamed with the City of Newport News to co-sponsor the first Ella Fitzgerald Music Festival. Its purpose was to honor the world-renowned jazz singer and Newport News native who had died in June 1996, as well as to enhance cultural life throughout the Peninsula. Initially envisioned as a weekend of jazz music performed by some of the nation's best musicians, it eventually turned into a weeklong celebration of the musical genre, during which CNU hosted some of the world's premier jazz artists and musical pioneers. In 1998, for example, Phil Woods and Cassandra Wilson performed to sold-out crowds in the Gaines Theater. Hampton Roads community leaders were thrilled with the festival's contribution to the region's cultural life. Jae Sinnett, a radio host on the Peninsula's NPR station exclaimed, "I think it's awesome…. This is the closest to a true artistic festival as I have seen in many years." Rob Cross, director of the Virginia Waterfront International Arts Festival, not only agreed, but he saluted Christopher Newport's contribution. "CNU has a real vision for what they are trying to do on the Peninsula," he said, "They are thinking big—and progressive." Although the high-profile performances grabbed most of the headlines, one of the festival's fundamental missions was to bring jazz music to young school children of Newport News. During the festival in 1999, more than 2,500 fourth graders came to campus for two days of music workshops and concerts. The following year (and in the years thereafter), CNU music Professor Bill Brown took the university's jazz ensemble to middle schools throughout the city in order to host all-day jazz clinics and to play concerts.[72]

---

[71] "CNU's 'Mikado' was a Gem," *Daily Press*, 5 March 2000. The theater department also sponsored visits from prominent actors. In 1998, film star Danny Glover along with director Felix Justice spoke to students and Peninsula community members; see "The Stage as Platform for Change, Glover, Justice Tell CNU Crowd," *Daily Press*, 19 April 1998. For more information about the theater program over the years, see Kimberly Burbank, "Theater CNU," unpublished undergraduate research paper, "Researching CNU" history seminar, Spring 2008, University Archives.

[72] "CNU Pitches Idea to Honor Fitzgerald," *Daily Press*, 17 February 1997; "Peninsula Has All that Jazz: Ella Fitzgerald Jazz Festival Brings Top Acts to CNU," *Daily Press*, 8 May 1998; "Ella Festival is a Real Credit to CNU," *Daily Press*, 4 April 1999; "Diane Schuur, Ramsey Lewis to Close Jazz Festival Saturday," *Daily Press*, 30

Christopher Newport's athletic teams performed strongly throughout the late 1990s under the exceptional leadership of long-time athletic director and men's basketball coach C.J. Woollum. Indeed, in 1998, the university's sports program was ranked fourteenth among more than three hundred NCAA Division III schools in the annual competition for the prestigious Sears Cup. That same year, the men's basketball team won thirty-five straight games and was crowned Dixie Conference champions for the seventh time in the school's history.[73] Not only were CNU's squads successful and thriving, but Woollum also lobbied to establish even more intercollegiate teams, especially in women's sports. This was due partly to comply with Title IX and NCAA gender-equality requirements, but also because by the late 1990s, 60 percent of CNU's student body was female. Thus, women's soccer was added in 1997 and, in September 1999, Woollum announced that the university would launch two new female sports teams—field hockey and lacrosse—for the 2000–01 school year.[74]

At the September press conference announcing the new women's squads, a reporter asked the athletic director about rumors then circulating concerning football coming to CNU. Woollum scoffed and said that such stories were "all speculation."[75] Less than two weeks later, however, President Trible announced at another press conference the formation of a university committee to study the feasibility of a football team at Christopher Newport. The president said, "There is strong support for football among the members of the Board of Visitors and alumni." In talking further to reporters, Trible himself made no secret

April 1999; Mark Reimer, email communication to Phillip Hamilton, 20 October 2009. For more information about CNU's music program in general, see Kate Judkins, "The History of Christopher Newport University's Music and Band Program," unpublished undergraduate research paper, "Researching CNU" history seminar, Spring 2008, University Archives.

[73] "CNU Men Go Undefeated in the Dixie," *Captain's Log*, 16 March 1998; "CNU Athletics Has Best Year Ever," 7 September 1998. Woollum was appointed athletic director in December 1987; see "CNC Names Woollum Athletic Director," *Daily Press*, 11 December 1987.

[74] "CNU to Add Field Hockey, Woman's Lacrosse in 2000," *Daily Press*, 11 September 1999.

[75] Ibid. Former Athletic Director Bev Vaughan was asked in 1984 about why no football at CNC and he too scoffed at the thought, see "Why Don't We Have a Football Team?" *Captain's Log*, 29 November 1984.

that he too supported taking such a step; football, he argued, would enhance student life, aid recruitment, and increase the number of students who wished to live on campus. Furthermore, two of CNU's competitors in the Dixie Conference—Averett and Shenandoah—had just announced plans to launch football teams of their own in fall 2000. Douglas Gordon of the English department, who was also the university's NCAA faculty athletics representative, was appointed to chair the new committee.[76]

During the fall 1999 term, Gordon and eleven students, staff, and faculty members explored football programs at other mid-sized Division III institutions and held public forums to solicit views from the broader community. Most students and faculty who voiced their opinions supported the move. One residential student named Rusty Goodsell said football "gives people a chance to show their enthusiasm. I sit in my dorm room on Saturday afternoons and watch the games on TV and think that I really wish CNU had this." Some individuals, however, expressed doubts and concerns. Women's soccer coach Jen Clark argued, "I have seen what occurs when football teams arrive. They are placed in a higher position than any other sport, and they tend to take over the field's other sports use, just like that."[77]

The committee's final report, though, unanimously recommended the creation of a football program, stating that it would likely improve the quality of student life and university's collegiate environment. Indeed, it would bring excitement to campus, carry CNU's name across the state, and assist in ongoing student recruitment efforts, especially if a university marching band was created. The program, moreover, was financially feasible. Estimating start-up costs of $1.3 million and annual expenses of $450,000, the committee said money could partly come from

[76] "CNU is Talking Football," *Daily Press*, 22 September 1999; "Football Feasibility Committee Formed," *Captain's Log*, 27 September 1999; see also "Interest in Football Team Growing," *Captain's Log*, 16 November 1998; "Editorial: CNU Football," *Daily Press*, 9 October 1999.

[77] "Speakers at CNU Forum Voice Support," *Daily Press*, 15 October 1999; "Feasibility Committee Tallies Positive Response," *Captain's Log*, 19 October 1999; "Feasibility Committee Hears New Views," *Captain's Log*, 1 November 1999. Some local neighbors of the university expressed their concern about traffic and noise created by games; see "What Will CNU Football Bring? Neighbors Concerned about Crowds, Traffic," *Daily Press*, 18 December 1999.

a $2.2 million deal the university just struck with the Pepsi Corporation giving the soda company exclusive marketing privileges on campus. Student fees could also be modestly raised to support the team. With the committee's report in hand, the board of visitors unanimously voted on 16 December 1999 to create the new football program. The board also scheduled its inaugural season for the fall of 2001. "It will be one more commitment to an outstanding liberal arts college," Trible told the *Daily Press* after the vote.[78]

The following May, CNU hired Matt Kelchner as head coach of the team. Originally from Pennsylvania and from a football family himself, Kelchner proved to be a natural fit for the position. His father had been the head football coach at Mansfield University, and Kelchner himself had been assistant head coach at William and Mary for sixteen years. Working in one of the most widely respected football programs in Division I-AA, Kelchner had served as the team's recruiting coordinator and had performed many administrative duties associated with the job. Therefore, he was well prepared to build a program from the ground up.[79]

Throughout the remainder of 2000 and into 2001, Kelchner hired coaches, recruited players, and purchased equipment in preparation for the 2001 season.[80] Meanwhile, the university moved forward with plans to build a football stadium. It hired Magoon & Associates Architects of Williamsburg to design a $2.5 million facility to seat approximately three thousand people. When the university made the plans public, Trible promised the community, "It's going to be a Division I type football

---

[78] "Panel's Report Endorses CNU Football in 2001," *Daily Press*, 10 December 1999; "CNU Explores Football's Cost, Impact on School," *Daily Press*, 16 December 1999; "CNU Agrees to Tackle Football; Trible Says Team May Play in 2001," *Daily Press*, 17 December 1999; Douglas Gordon interview with Phillip Hamilton, 6 June 2008. On the deal with Pepsi Corporation, see "'I Dew,' Trible Exchanges Vows with Pepsi," *Captain's Log*, 1 February 1999.

[79] "CNU Names First Coach," *Daily Press*, 10 May 2000; "Kelchner's Road to Head Job for New Football Program," *Daily Press*, 10 May 2000; see also "CNU Sets Timetable for New Football Program," *Daily Press*, 8 April 2000.

[80] In March 2001, the *Daily Press's* Sports Division began a monthly series on the program's progress; see especially "CNU Football Hopefuls Building Team Unity," *Daily Press*, 25 March 2001; "Pace Quickens at CNU; Football Has Athletics Department Scrambling with an Eye Toward September 1," *Daily Press*, 27 May 2001; "The Devil is in the Details Before Kicking Off," *Daily Press*, 26 August 2001.

stadium, not in size, but in quality." Before construction could begin near the intersection of Prince Drew Avenue and Moore's Lane, five acres of woods had to be cleared. Once that was completed, workers got started. Designed to be built over two years, the stadium would contain stands with 650 chair-back seats, as well as several thousand general admission bench seats. The stands themselves were finished by the start of the 2001 season. Following that first season, stage two of construction began. Construction workers enclosed the stands in brick, and added a press box and special reception suite.[81]

As opening day 2001 approached, excitement built throughout Newport News. Trible and Kelchner spoke to numerous civic and community groups, explaining the program's progress and urging all to support the Captains' new squad. The publicity efforts paid off. When season ticket sales began in July, the chair-back seats sold out in less than three weeks. On opening day, moreover, more than six thousand fans squeezed into the new stadium to see the Football Captains play Salisbury University. Although CNU lost the game 21–6, the team played well, the stadium's facilities operated according to plan, and those in attendance enjoyed themselves, both beforehand tailgating in the parking lots as well as during the game itself.[82] Most importantly, the football program continued to succeed throughout the remainder of the 2001 season. While everyone's mood turned deeply somber following the September 11 terrorist attacks on New York City and the Pentagon (which led to the cancellation of CNU's second home game), Kelchner's team grew stronger as the autumn progressed. Indeed, it finished the year with a regular season record of 5–3 *and* it won the Dixie Conference championship. Although the team lost in the Division III playoffs to powerhouse Widener University, everyone was thrilled with the

[81] "CNU Takes Wraps Off Football Stadium Plans," *Daily Press*, 1 May 2001. In 2002, CNU sold the naming rights of the stadium to Pomoco Auto Group for 10-years for $1 million, see "CNU Sells Stadium Naming Rights for $1 Million," *Captain's Log*, 11 September 2002.

[82] "CNU Football Tickets Selling Well," *Daily Press*, 19 July 2001; "'A Wonderful Day for CNU:' Despite Loss, Football Tradition Gets Underway Without a Hitch," *Daily Press*, 2 September 2001.

program's initial success and looked forward to the team's second season.[83]

Changing Midtown: Widening Warwick Boulevard,
Closing Shoe Lane, and Establishing Campus East

In 1995, motorists driving past CNU along Warwick Boulevard—one of the city's main traffic thoroughfares—saw a motley hodge-podge of buildings and small businesses, including the Lotz Realty Company and an enormous "Jesus is Coming" sign planted next to its non-descript two-story headquarters. One thing drivers did not see, however, was Christopher Newport University. Indeed, since the establishment of its campus in midtown Newport News, the university was invisible to the thousands of residents who traveled past it every day. When Paul Trible became president, he decided that he would change both the school's visibility from the street as well as the appearance of things along Warwick Boulevard.[84]

Fortunately for the university, the president's plans to improve this section of town coincided with the long-term goals of both the state and the city. In 1992, for instance, the state government first proposed widening Warwick Boulevard from four to six lanes along a congested two-mile stretch that included the area in front of CNU. Although constrained budget conditions slowed the project's progress, plans again moved forward in early 1995. That February, public hearings laid out the project's details to the general population. The state's Department of Transportation called for the widening in order "to improve traffic conditions ... and to make the area more attractive." The state also wanted to widen the median, add trees, and create more space for

---

[83] On the football teams first season, see especially "Sky High at CNU: Captains Earn Playoff Bid," *Daily Press*, 11 November 2001; "Widener Teaches Captains a Lesson in 56–7 Playoff Loss," *Daily Press*, 18 November 2001; "CNU Players Coach Earn Dixie Conference Honors," *Daily Press*, 20 November 2001. The Dixie Conference's name was changed in 2003 to USA South Athletic Conference. For more information about the creation of the football program and its initial season, see Dan Moore, "CNU Football: Adding More than Just Another Sports Team to the Campus," unpublished undergraduate research paper, "Researching CNU" history seminar, Spring 2008, University Archives.

[84] "Leaving Sign Not Upsetting Move for Lotz," *Daily Press*, 25 February 2001; Trible interview with Hamilton, 31 August 2009.

pedestrians and bicyclists. Newport News City Manager Edgar Maroney said the street expansion "would create a true 'boulevard' effect" along Warwick. The project, however, required the purchase and demolition of nineteen buildings, including a gas station, an apartment complex, and even the First Baptist Church Morrison headed by the Rev. Marcellus Harris. While those who possessed properties slated for destruction were outraged, CNU officials were quietly pleased. Then-president Santoro said that he certainly wanted to be "sensitive to our neighbors," but CNU was also interested "in the beautification of the city and high-profile visibility for the university."[85]

When Trible became president the following year, he, too, maintained discreet support for the project. Not wanting to appear as if he were forcing out Warwick residents and business owners, he said that greater visibility for the university and "the tree-lined medians and bike trails would be agreeable." How those things were accomplished, however, were "not a matter for me to resolve." Nonetheless, when the Department of Transportation (VDOT) held a public hearing on the project at nearby Warwick High School in September 1996, then-Vice President for University Relations Chris McDaniel attended with fifty students who came to voice their support. Ten months later, in June 1997, the city council voted unanimously to proceed with the two-mile widening project, and Mayor Joe Frank predicted that VDOT would begin construction in 2001 and finish by 2003.[86]

At that same council meeting, the city also approved an even more controversial road project associated with CNU—closing the eastern terminus of Shoe Lane at Warwick Boulevard. The project had first been proposed a year beforehand in order to eliminate that section of the road that separated Ferguson Hall from CNU's main campus. It aimed to

---

[85] "Warwick Proposal Threatens Church," *Daily Press,* 15 February 1995; "Street Widening Could Help CNU Plan; May Enhance Entrance, Visibility," *Daily Press,* 18 February 1995; "Warwick Widening Proposal Could Benefit CNU, Big Time," *Captain's Log,* 6 March 1995; see also "Warwick Widening Strikes Again," *Daily Press,* 12 May 1995.

[86] "Warwick Businesses Are Again Up in Arms; Merchants Blame City, CNU for Putting Stores in Jeopardy," *Daily Press,* 8 August 1996; "Widening Warwick Open Up Boulevard to CNU, *Daily Press,* 8 September 1996; "Hundreds Question Warwick Proposal: Residents Wary of 'Grandiose Boulevard,'" *Daily Press,* 19 September 1996; "Battle Over a Wider Warwick," *Captain's Log,* 24 September 1996.

redirect traffic from the Riverside neighborhoods southward behind Ferguson and directly to the intersection of J. Clyde and Warwick Boulevards. The alteration had much to recommend it. It promised to entirely reconfigure CNU's campus by creating a more dramatic and park-like entrance. It also aimed to increase safety for students and faculty who had to cross Shoe Lane each time they traveled between the main campus and Ferguson Hall.[87] Finally, the project would ease potential traffic snarls before and after concerts and theatrical shows once the performing arts center opened at the Ferguson location several years in the future.[88]

In preparation for the city council vote on the Shoe Lane reroute, Trible pulled out all the stops. CNU employees who lived in the Riverside neighborhood wrote letters to the press voicing their support. Vice President of University Relations John Miller, moreover, visited individual classrooms and requested that students sign petitions backing the project. One city council meeting held in May 1997, furthermore, was filled with CNU students, faculty, and staff, including President Trible, all of whom sported lapel buttons saying "Yes, the new Shoe fits." According to press accounts, the president was the project's "most emphatic supporter." Not only did he greet people at the door, but he also spoke for fifteen minutes about the "take-your-breath-away-beautiful" campus he envisioned and how the Shoe Lane reroute would benefit both the university and community.[89]

Despite the administration's efforts, opposition from many Riverside residents was fierce. They worried that the Shoe Lane closure as well as CNU's expansion plans would *cause*, rather than relieve, traffic back-ups as well as undermine their old neighborhoods. Some residents began a petition drive of their own to condemn the plan, and it quickly

---

[87] "City Plans Changes for Shoe Lane: Closing Street at Warwick Considered," *Daily Press*, 29 August 1996; "Newport News Approves Widening Warwick," *Daily Press*, 11 June 1997.

[88] On the traffic issues involved, see Bobby Freeman's letter to the editor in the *Daily Press*, 21 April 1997.

[89] Lucy L. Latchum, "Letters to the Editor: Favors Shoe Lane Plan," *Daily Press*, 11 March 1997; "Shoe Lane Petitions Draw Ire CNU Goes Too Far in Rallying Support for Rerouting, Critics Say," *Daily Press*, 10 May 1997; Julia Ahern, "Letters to the Editor: A Sorry Spectacle," *Daily Press*, 29 May 1997.

had nearly 1,700 signatures. At one public forum, opponents even dressed in costumes—with one as the "Dragon CNU" and the others representing the "Guardian Angels of Shoe Lane"—to protest the university's proposals.[90] Notwithstanding these complaints, the city council had solid reasons for supporting the project, especially those having to do with pedestrian safety. Thus, members voted unanimously to proceed with the Shoe Lane reroute in June 1997.[91]

Although the start of both the Warwick Boulevard and Shoe Lane projects were several years off, university officials now knew they would eventually be completed and, thus, could plan accordingly. As a result, CNU started to purchase and then demolish buildings along the west side of Warwick Boulevard. These acquisitions and actions accomplished two things: 1) they increased the school's visibility from the street and 2) they improved the overall appearance of midtown Newport News. Indeed, for years, residents had viewed the diverse collection of apartment buildings, stores, and gas stations as eyesores and embarrassments. CNU's first purchases along Warwick were a law office, a realty building, and a four-story bank and office structure. While the university immediately put the latter building to use as classrooms and office space, it razed the other structures. Afterwards, motorists started to see the university from the street. "The more people see us," Trible pointed out at the time, "the more they will appreciate us."[92] Nevertheless, many determined business owners resisted CNU even after these initial purchases. Tommy Gardiner, owner of a heating and air-conditioning firm, angrily said he had heard someone claim that "Newport News deserves more than these 'God-forsaken' buildings." He told the *Daily Press*, however, "The bad part about that is these little God-forsaken buildings are people's livelihoods." Other business owners

[90] Dawn Young, "Letter to the Editor: Shoe Lane Precedent," *Daily Press*, 15 September 1997; "Safer Shoe Lane Approved by City Council," *Captain's Log*, Summer Issue 1997; "Shoe Lane Proposal Draws Ire," *Daily Press*, 30 October 1998; "Shoe Lane Showdown," *Captain's Log*, 2 November 1998.

[91] "Shoe Lane to Be Rerouted: Residents Keep Up Fight," *Daily Press*, 11 June 1997; "Newport News Approves Warwick Widening," *Daily Press*, 12 June 1997. In 1998, the Council reaffirmed its decision, see "Newport News Council Votes Again to Close Shoe Lane," *Daily Press*, 11 November 1998.

[92] "CNU Buys Warwick Buildings," *Daily Press*, 8 January 1997; "CNU Buys Buildings, Shops for More," *Captain's Log*, 27 January 1997.

also admitted that, although "the street is not exactly an eye pleaser," most of the businesses were "money maker[s]."[93]

Despite this opposition, the university pressed ahead. In 1999, it demolished two small apartment buildings it had recently purchased, thus giving the university even more prominence on Warwick.[94] Two years later, CNU purchased ten additional properties on the *east* side of Warwick Boulevard for $6.6 million. These properties included the Lotz Realty building (with its "Jesus is Coming" sign) as well as the old Warwick Motel and a housing complex called Barclay Apartments. The university purchased the properties on the east side of the boulevard for a number of reasons. Owning the Barclay Apartments and the Warwick Motel allowed the university to house an additional three hundred students on campus. As the president explained, "We're buying this property because we care about the development [of Warwick Boulevard]" and "we want to have some influence over the renewal of these properties."[95] CNU announced soon afterwards that it planned two major constructions projects to continue the revitalization of both CNU and midtown Newport News: first, a $13.2 million, five-building apartment complex on the newly purchased properties on the east side of the boulevard to house 350 juniors and seniors in two-, three-, and four-bedroom apartments; and, second, a new $34 million dormitory on the campus's west side near Shoe Lane to be called York River Hall and designed to house more than five hundred freshmen. When the two new housing complexes opened in August 2002, more than two thousand

---

[93] "CNU's Grand Plan; Trible Widens Scope with New Buildings," *Daily Press,* 17 August 1997; see also "Station Owner Says Exxon, CNU are Squeezing Him Out," *Daily Press,* "Budget Allocation for CNU Short on Land Acquisitions Funds," *Daily Press,* 20 December 1997; "Some CNU Neighbors Not Happy with Growth," *Daily Press,* 12 November 2000.

[94] "A Time-Line of CNU's Expansion Efforts," *Daily Press,* 21 February 2001.

[95] "CNU Jumping Warwick," *Daily Press,* 21 February 2001; "Leaving Sign Not Upsetting Move for Lotz," *Daily Press,* 25 February 2001; "CNU to Expand Across Warwick," *Captain's Log,* 27 February 2001. The displacement of long-time residents from the Barclay Apartments did cause some negative press; see "CNU Expansion Uprooting 'Community' at Barclay," *Daily Press,* 19 March 2001.

students (approximately 40 percent of the student population) would then be living on CNU's campus.[96]

On 29 August 2001, the *Daily Press* ran three highly positive articles about CNU's development since Paul Trible had taken over as president. The headlines themselves spoke to the profound alterations at work— "CNU Now Stronger Magnet for Talent," "New Buildings Dot CNU," and "... Commuter Campus Fading Away as [CNU] Builds for the Future." The trio of pieces collectively illustrated the enormous amount of work that had been achieved since 1996. Students themselves noticed and appreciated the ongoing changes. A student interviewed for one of the articles was senior Jonathan Janis. He said that things just got "better and better" throughout his years at the university both in terms of the quality of the academics and the school's facilities. "The [number] of students who consider CNU a vital part of their life has changed dramatically," he added. Though some might complain about construction, Janis concluded "[T]he overall feeling is excitement and appreciation." By no means, however, was the university approaching the end of its transformations. As all three articles made clear, President Trible was a forward-looking leader who rarely glanced backward. When interviewed by the *Daily Press* that summer, for instance, he spoke not about his recruiting successes of the past, but about recruiting even stronger students in the future. He also enthusiastically ticked off the new and revamped buildings he looked forward to opening in coming years: the I.M. Pei-designed performing arts center, a new state-of-the-art library, a multipurpose student center, a parking garage, and even a "fifth and sixth dorm." Clearly, in the summer of 2001, CNU's overhaul was by no means over.[97]

---

[96] "York River to Expand On-Campus Family," *Captain's Log*, 21 October 2001; "CNU Students' Apartments Slated for 2002 Construction of 5-Building Complex Begin in September," *Daily Press*, 8 November 2001; see also "Crossing Warwick a Huge Dilemma," *Captain's Log*, 5 September 2001.

[97] "CNU Now Stronger Magnet for Talent," *Daily Press*, 29 August 2001; "New Buildings Dot CNU," 29 August 2001; "CNU Greets Class of 2005, Commuter Campus Fading Away as it Builds for the Future," *Daily Press*, 29 August 2001.

Working With and Clashing With the Faculty

Throughout the first five years of his presidency, Paul Trible experienced a generally positive—though occasionally tense—relationship with CNU's faculty. As soon as he arrived, many instructors embraced his long-term vision for the school. Professors greatly appreciated, moreover, the raises he obtained from the General Assembly as well as a growing number of new faculty positions. In 1997, for example, Trible and the board of visitors secured a 5 percent across-the-board payraise for all instructors, and the following year, they obtained funds to hire ten additional full-time professors. From 1996 to 2001, moreover, the president generally refrained from interfering in faculty matters; rather, he repeatedly praised their dedication to their students, lauded their teaching skills, and celebrated their scholarly achievements. He furthermore refrained from meddling with the university's curriculum and general education requirements. Nonetheless, some faculty members voiced concerns about the dramatic shift away from CNU's historic mission to provide high-quality education to local Peninsula students. Some also disliked what they perceived as the president's heavy-handed decision-making style on broader university matters, which initially involved neither faculty participation nor consultation. Part of the problem likely stemmed the new president's unfamiliarity with the academic world (from any other perspective than as a student) and its tradition of shared institutional governance.[98]

The first serious clash between the administration and faculty came in the spring of 1997 with the surprising dismissal of Dr. David Wall from the faculty. Wall had joined CNU in 1992 to teach geography. Over the years, he had received solid teaching evaluations from students as well as positive peer-reviews from faculty colleagues. In 1997, however, Provost Robert Doane rejected a recommendation by the university's Faculty Review Committee that Wall be granted tenure, citing overall "institutional considerations" as the reason. President Trible supported the provost's action and refused to overturn it. Outraged at the decision, four members resigned from the committee in protest. Those who quit told the *Daily Press* that they left not only because of Wall, but also due to

---

[98] "CNU Board Approved New Budget Funds; Will Support Additions to Staff," *Daily Press*, 30 June 1998; Trible interview with Hamilton, 31 August 2009.

the fact that Doane had previously disregarded other recommendations the faculty committee had made by "promot[ing] and grant[ing] tenure to faculty members who don't publish [their] research often enough." As a result of these conflicts, many untenured faculty members suddenly felt vulnerable. One such professor, who requested anonymity from the press, said, "I don't want to leave CNU ... but I know now it would be irresponsible of me not to look around to other universities."[99]

Three years later, another controversy erupted when the administration proposed to eliminate two of its graduate programs—environmental science and applied physics/computer science—due to their heavy costs and low enrollment. Because no prior discussion or consultation about this move had taken place with the faculty, professors were dumbfounded. And they (and many students) immediately rallied to save the programs. Students started a petition drive and staged a "sit-in" protest in the Administration Building. The faculty senate meanwhile unanimously voted to support the imperiled academic programs.[100]

In addition to these actions, several prominent and well-respected faculty members wrote "letters to the editor" disputing the administration's plans and also its data. Chair of the Department of Physics, Computer Science, and Engineering, Randall Caton, specifically chastised Doane for making the decision to eliminate the program based on incorrect enrollment figures. "Bad data," he concluded, "result in bad decisions." Biology department chair Harold Cones explained that the faculty senate had explicitly "warned" the administration that its data on graduate student enrollment were incorrect. But, Cones asserted, officials had stubbornly refused to correct the numbers. In stark contrast to the administration, the Department of Biology, Chemistry, and Environ-

---

[99] "CNU Dismissed Beloved Professor: Students and Faculty Launch Protests," *Captain's Log*, 29 April 1997; "4 Resign from CNU Promotion Committee," *Daily Press*, 1 May 1997. See also "Letter to the Editor: Geography Slighted," *Daily Press*, 5 May 1997.

[100] "Graduate Programs' Fate in Question: Decision to Be Made November 1st," *Captain's Log*, 2 October 2000; "On a Mission: Students Rally to Save Programs," *Captain's Log*, 23 October 2000; "CNU May Cut Programs; Students Protest Plan to Trim Two Masters Degree," *Daily Press*, 11 October 2000; "Programs Get Support; CNU Students, Faculty, Protest Proposed Cuts," *Daily Press*, 28 October 2000; "CNU Faculty Supports Keeping Threatened Graduate Programs," *Daily Press*, 3 November 2000.

mental Science had *always* provided honest information. "Being honest, it just seemed the right thing to do," Cones finished. Lora Friedman of the education department pointed out that, if the administration spent as much effort developing these "viable, successful graduate programs" as it did "on finding financial support for the [new] building, sports, and beautification projects," CNU might "excel even beyond the neighboring institutions of Old Dominion University and the College of William and Mary." Faculty protests received a boost when, in the midst of the controversy, the American Institute of Physics named CNU's masters program in applied physics as one of the nation's top twenty such programs.[101]

Surprised by the resistance from the faculty and students, the administration defended its position and worked toward a compromise. University Rector Robert Freeman, Jr., for instance, published a guest editorial in the *Daily Press* declaring that he was "disheartened" by the tone of the "community conservation" then taking place. Critics, he asserted, had simply focused on saving the two graduate programs, but had said nothing about the reasons for CNU's "recent success" in terms of its qualitative growth and expansion. Freeman pointed out that when he joined the board of visitors in 1995, "CNU was in a serious downward spiral" and "in serious jeopardy." To save the school, the administration and board "developed a very focused vision: to become a great undergraduate liberal arts university...." CNU's success in recruiting more full-time students and residential undergraduates over the years clearly demonstrated the wisdom of this move. However, Freeman stated that the school's "graduate program offerings do not fit into the new vision for CNU." Moreover, they were relatively small (compared to the undergraduate population) and expensive in terms of the money and faculty resources they consumed. Thus, Freeman said, "We simply cannot achieve our goals of being a great undergraduate university ... by diverting our attention and limited resources to graduate programs that serve small numbers of students." He concluded that whatever action

---

[101] Randall Caton, "Letters to the Editor: Bad data, decision," *Daily Press*, 22 October 2000. The *Daily Press* editorial board, which generally supported Trible, criticized him for the proposed elimination, saying that "Trible went a step too far," see "Where the Newspaper Stands," *Daily Press*, 15 November 2000; see also "National Asset Could Be Destroyed," *Daily Press*, 12 November 2000.

the president and the board took, it would be in the best interests of *the entire university.*[102]

On 14 November 2000, two days after Freeman's editorial appeared, President Trible released a fourteen-page memo outlining a compromise that would allow both programs to continue, but which also called for specific reforms to deal with his concerns. Beginning with the numbers controversy, the president explained that the true number of enrolled graduate students "doesn't matter." Acknowledging that there were different methods of counting, he asserted that the graduate programs were still too small whichever figures were used. More troubling from his perspective was that CNU graduate students were not performing well academically; he pointed out that over half of them had grade point averages below 3.0. He demanded, therefore, that the two programs work to make their admissions standards more rigorous as well as aggressively recruit more talented students from among CNU's undergraduate population. Furthermore, the biology and physics departments had to raise private funds to support additional graduate assistantships. Once these actions had been taken, the administration would reexamine the environmental science and applied physics programs to see if they were academically, numerically, and fiscally sound. In the meantime, their faculty had to pay more attention to undergraduate students. The president eliminated the standard course-release professors had previously received whenever they taught a graduate course, and he required that full-time faculty henceforth *must* teach all introductory courses to undergraduates. Noting that, while tenured and tenure-track professors had been teaching "graduate courses to a handful of students, ... we are assigning over 1,000 high-ability undergraduate students to biology classes averaging 80 students and to physics classes ranging in size from 51 to 95, and [with] many [sections] taught by adjuncts." "This is not putting students first," he finished.[103]

---

[102] Robert Freeman, Jr., "Debate at CNU: Focus Should Be on Undergraduates," *Daily Press*, 12 November 2000.

[103] Paul Trible Memo to CNU Faculty, 14 November 2000, University Archives. The president's memo was reprinted in its entirety by the *Daily Press*; see "CNU's Undergraduate Students Will Come First," 19 November 2000. See also "CNU's President Says Keep Programs Mission to Increase Quality, Number of Graduate

Trible's compromise temporarily eased tensions between the faculty and the administration, but new strains emerged seven months later when the administration again acted unilaterally and without consultation. In June 2001, the president consolidated of the university's two colleges—Humanities and Science & Technology—into a new school called the College of Liberal Arts and Sciences. The new entity was to be headed by former Provost Richard Summerville. Summerville was to be assisted, moreover, by Douglas Gordon of English and Dorothy Doolittle of Psychology, both of whom the president promoted to associate deans. Trible said the opportunity for the restructuring presented itself when Dean of Humanities Christina Ramirez-Smith unexpectedly resigned. Consolidating all departments into one college, the president pledged, would streamline academic administration and prevent separate departments from competing for resources. The elimination of the Science & Technology College, however, also eliminated George Webb's position as academic dean. As a result, Trible appointed him special assistant to the president for technology. In this capacity, he wanted Webb to strengthen the university's technological capabilities as well as oversee the redesign of CNU's Web site.[104]

The university's reorganization stunned both students and faculty, particularly the dissolution of the Science & Technology College and Webb's reassignment. One former student, Barry Price, said that George and Jane Webbs' instruction was the reason he had become an engineer. "Their enthusiasm was contagious," he explained, "and the caring manner they used to reach out to each student, pulling them into the excitement of learning made a huge difference in my life." Price viewed Webb's reassignment as a "real loss" to "the future students of CNU."[105] Price was not alone. Many Science & Technology faculty were also

Students," *Daily Press*, 15 November 2000; "Board Ok's Continuance of Grad Programs; CNU's Trible Hopes to End the 'We and them' Mentality," *Daily Press*, 16 November 2000; and "CNU Set Sights on Graduate Students; Improvement Sought in School's Program," *Daily Press*, 15 July 2002.

[104] "CNU Soon to Become 1 College," *Daily Press*, 28 June 2001; "CNU Faction Challenges Merger; Students, Faculty Doubt It's Needed," *Daily Press*, 22 July 2001; "And Then There Were Two: a New, Single College of Liberal Arts and Sciences," *Captain's Log*, 5 September 2001.

[105] Barry Price, "Letter to the Editor: Passionate Professors," *Daily Press*, 19 July 2001.

distraught especially because they considered themselves "a large family." Indeed, the Webbs had long encouraged both professional and social interaction among the college's professors, ranging from "building an exemplary undergraduate research culture" on campus to organizing potluck dinners in their homes.[106] Several faculty members publicly stated that Webb's reassignment was in retaliation for his defense of the environmental science and applied physics graduate programs the previous autumn. Others argued that the restructuring itself was inappropriate as there had been no consultation with the faculty in general. Trible rejected both charges. Concerning Webb's reassignment, he stated, "If it was retaliation, I certainly wouldn't be giving George Webb an opportunity of even greater service to the university." As to the appropriateness of the consolidation, the president said, "This is a decision about the structure and organization [of the university], and that is quite appropriately an administrative decision." Finally, regarding the discontent among some instructors, Trible simply pointed out, "It's very difficult to keep 200 faculty members happy."[107]

Despite the president's statements, the administration's move had created angst among the faculty. Although classroom instruction remained untouched by the reorganization, some professors lamented what they saw as repeated instances of poor communication and a lack of concern for shared university governance. Chemistry professor Gary Hammer told the press, "If you don't respect your boss, that affects the way you do things in the college." Other departments also complained. In late 2001, the new College of Liberal Arts and Sciences sponsored a report on CNU's "academic culture." The history department's report bluntly stated, "The only way to 'develop a sense of common purpose and shared responsibility' is for the administration to respect the proper role of the faculty in the shared governance of the institution."[108]

---

[106] "Reassignment of CNU Dean Broke Up Sciences 'Family,'" *Daily Press*, 22 July 2001.

[107] "CNU Faction Challenges Merger; Students, Faculty Doubt It's Needed," *Daily Press*, 22 July 2001.

[108] Ibid. The history department's concerns are contained in Shumet Sishagne's memo to Dean Richard Summerville, 5 October 2001. This memo is contained in the College of Liberal Arts and Science's "Report on CNU Academic Culture" dated 6 November 2001.

As CNU entered the new millennium, and as Paul Trible began his sixth year as president, CNU was in the midst of enormous changes. Indeed, the school in 2001 had become dramatically stronger in four important respects. First, its population decline had reversed, with thousands of highly qualified and talented students now applying each year for the one thousand freshman slots available. Secondly, the campus was undergoing a complete physical transformation in terms of the addition of new dormitories, a new performing arts center, and the new Freeman Convocation Center. Furthermore, more university buildings were in the advanced stage of planning and were on schedule to be built in the coming decade. Third, the state government in Richmond supported CNU more fully during Trible's presidency. Indeed, instead of being at the bottom of the public university system in terms of funding, the university received strong financial support either in line with or exceeding support given to other state institutions. And fourth, President Trible had brought with him a new and ambitious vision to make Christopher Newport into one of the finest public liberal arts colleges in the nation. Because of his leadership, the university community was on its way to make this vision a reality.

Nevertheless, challenges remained. As the controversies of 2000–01 revealed, a number of faculty members resented the administration's management style, which appeared to shun shared governance and collaboration. Other instructors were also unhappy with the shift away from CNU's decades-old mission of serving local students from Hampton Roads. Moreover, many neighbors surrounding campus—both residential and commercial—remained uneasy with the changes occurring around them, especially as these changes seemed to threaten their homes and livelihoods. Finally, in late 2001 and early 2002, the nation headed into a severe economic recession following the September 11 terrorist attacks on New York and the Pentagon—a recession that threatened to undo the progress made to date.

6

A University for the Twenty-First Century

Christopher Newport senior Anthony Colosimo shared the Ferguson Center Concert Hall's grand stage with famed Italian tenor Andrea Bocelli on 20 October 2005. Before a sold-out audience of 1,700 people, and with Bocelli standing at his side, the twenty-two-year-old music major sang a beautiful rendition of "La Serenata." The invitation to sing with the internationally known vocalist had come the day before at a luncheon where Colosimo and a William and Mary student had received music scholarships from the National Italian American Foundation. During the meal, Rosemary Trible mentioned to Bocelli that Colosimo and the Christopher Newport Chamber Choir were heading to Italy for a concert tour the following spring. Bocelli smiled at the news and asked if the choir could perform with him onstage during his Ferguson appearance the next evening. Turning to her husband, Rosemary asked if that could happen. After a quick phone call, President Trible was told that the thirty-member choir was too big to appear onstage with Bocelli and the Virginia Symphony (which was to accompany the tenor). The famed singer then asked Colosimo if he would appear onstage with him alone.

After a brief rehearsal, Colosimo performed "La Serenata" the following evening and received a rousing ovation from both the audience and Bocelli himself. The CNU senior and aspiring high school teacher breathlessly told a reporter afterwards, "I was scared. I don't remember anything until I left the stage. Bocelli told me I sounded good." Once he collected his thoughts, Colosimo added, "I feel so fortunate that I'm here at CNU now for all these things to have happened." The Bocelli concert was the tenor's only performance in the

United States in 2005 and, after nearly a decade of planning, the concert was part of the Ferguson Center Concert Hall's inaugural season. Rosemary Trible also spoke to reporters that evening and said that Bocelli's show and Colosimo's appearance made it "a transformational moment" in the university's history.[1]

The Bocelli concert, including Colosimo's performance, *was* a transformational moment for the university. In many respects, it epitomized all of the profound changes at work at Christopher Newport University during the first decade of the new millennium. When Paul Trible took over as president in 1996, he said he was not interested in incremental changes. Indeed, he wanted CNU's faculty and staff to help him create an entirely new liberal arts university that would provide unmatched educational opportunities for students who would find their minds enlightened and their lives changed forever. The president also wanted to transform Newport News itself by making CNU into an educational and cultural jewel that would bring the world's best musicians, performers, and scholars to this one-time blue-collar industrial town. By the early 2000s, CNU had made significant progress. Applications for enrollment had skyrocketed over the previous five years, and the school grew increasingly selective in its admissions. The faculty, moreover, grew both in number and scholarly accomplishments. Finally, the university's campus changed in unimaginable ways as long-planned buildings and facilities were completed and opened.

Nonetheless, challenges remained as the school approached its fiftieth anniversary. State funding from Richmond proved notoriously uneven and unpredictable throughout the decade. Periodic reductions in public funds led to several spending freezes as well as cuts in programs and personnel. Students also had to endure repeated hikes in tuition and fees in order to maintain the budget. Divisions within the university between older and newer faculty, moreover, sometimes caused tension on campus, with the former lamenting CNU's altered mission and what they perceived as the administration's heavy-handed management style. Despite these difficulties, the university community collectively

---

[1] "Andrea Bocelli at CNU—A Night to Remember," *Daily Press*, 21 October 2005; CNU Web page, 23 October 2005, http://web.archive.org/web/2005102315638/ http://www.cnu.edu (accessed 10 May 2010).

overcame many of these problems and moved forward toward fulfilling its liberal arts mission. Thus, at the decade's end, as people looked back upon a half-century of service to the Old Dominion, almost everyone recognized CNU's numerous contributions to Hampton Roads and Virginia. Furthermore, as people looked forward, they saw a dynamic institution in place, ready to educate the commonwealth's future leaders and citizens.

The Budget Crisis of 2002–03

Although the new millennium's first decade was one of significant accomplishment and progress, its early years proved exceptionally difficult for CNU, the state of Virginia, and the country. Indeed, the university experienced multiple challenges, particularly after the state and nation suffered the trauma and tragedy of the September 11 terrorist attacks. While devastating in terms of lost lives, the attacks also caused an immediate economic downturn that produced a yawning deficit in the Old Dominion's state budget. Even before September 11, however, Virginia's budget situation had been darkening. Part of the problem stemmed from Governor Jim Gilmore's economic policies enacted during the late 1990s in which he and the General Assembly cut taxes and increased spending. Gilmore also convinced the General Assembly to cut tuition at Virginia colleges and universities by 20 percent in an effort to make higher education more affordable. The state government, moreover, prohibited public institutions from raising their tuition in the future. By early 2001, however, these policies had led to a significant shortfall in state revenues. To deal with the situation, the General Assembly slashed the state budget, including in higher education. In 2001–02, for example, CNU lost $1.5 million in promised funds equaling a 7 percent cut. The university, therefore, imposed an immediate hiring freeze and halted all travel and equipment purchases in order to cope.[2]

---

[2] "More Cuts for Higher Education: CNU Freezes Spending, Hiring to Avoid Layoffs," *Daily Press*, 2 March 2001; "College Presidents Try to Save Projects," *Daily Press*, 13 March 2001; "Where the Paper Stands," *Daily Press*, 17 March 2001; "In-State Undergrads to Pay 5.4% More," *Daily Press*, 19 April 2001. On Governor Gilmore's 20% cut in tuition, see "Gilmore Seeks 20% Cut in Virginia College Costs," *Daily Press*, 13 December 1998; "Governing Higher-Ed," *Daily Press*, 27 September 2001.

(above) CNU Senior Anthony Colosimo after his performance at the Ferguson
Center in October 2005. Italian tenor Andrea Bocelli is standing on the right
(Courtesy of the *Daily Press*) (below) The Ferguson Center for the Performing Arts

The 1,700 seat Concert Hall in the Ferguson Center

The main atrium inside the David Student Union which opened in September 2006.

(above) President Paul Trible speaking at the opening of the new "Paul and Rosemary Trible Library" in January 2008. Rosemary Trible is on the right. (below) A scene from the Theater CNU production of "Actus Fidei." Written by Prof. Steven Breese, it was performed in the Ferguson Music and Theater Hall in 2007.

(left) Long-time basketball coach and CNU athletic director, C. J. Woollum before a game in the Freeman Center. (right) Dean Douglas Gordon in the late-2000s, shortly before his retirement.

CNU's revamped central campus and "Great Lawn" in 2010—Trible Library on the left; David Student Union in the center; New McMurran Hall is in the distant right.

When Governor Mark Warner took over as Virginia's chief executive in January 2002—five months after September 11—the budget situation had only worsened. Soon after his inauguration, Warner announced a projected $3.8 billion shortfall in state revenues over the next two-and-a-half years. To manage the grim fiscal picture, Warner proposed a series of tax hikes and "extraordinary reductions in spending," including additional ones in higher education. Thus, the new governor imposed an immediate 3 percent cut for the current fiscal year for all public colleges and universities to be followed by a 7 percent cut in 2003 and an 8 percent reduction in 2004. To deal with the 3 percent cut, CNU extended its hiring and purchasing freeze as well as laying off 130 of the school's 170 part-time adjunct faculty members. In order to cover already scheduled classes, full-time faculty members were asked to teach an extra course without compensation, thus creating a five-course teaching load for the spring 2002 term. Although some professors complained that they were "forced" into the extra class, many accepted the task with remarkable understanding. Political science professor Gary Green, for instance, volunteered to cover an additional introductory criminal justice course, saying, "It's sad but unavoidable." President Trible saluted the university's professors for their reaction to the crisis, telling the *Daily Press*, "The faculty has really responded heroically ... to help us meet this state budget crisis."[3]

Despite the president's words, tensions between the administration and faculty were rising, in part due to the growing financial strains, but also because of the lack of faculty involvement in university governance. In the same article in which he praised CNU's professors, for instance, the president also predicted that the university would inevitably have to lay off some full-time faculty members in the coming academic year in order to handle the future reductions in state funds. Trible's statement that faculty cuts were coming came as a complete shock to everyone and set off a wave of anxiety and anger across campus. Indeed, some professors felt not only uninformed, but that they were unfairly suffering

---

[3] "CNU Tightens Its Belt: College Lays Off 130 Adjunct Faculty Members," *Daily Press*, 16 January 2002; "130 Adjuncts Lost in Budget Crisis," *Captain's Log*, 23 January 2002; "Letters to the Editor—"Share the Budget Pain at CNU," *Daily Press*, 29 January 2002.

the brunt of the budget cuts. Timothy Morgan, a thirty-year veteran of the CNU history department, sent an email to the entire faculty, stating that he had seen many budget crises over the years, but this was "shaping up to be the worst that I've lived through." And, instead of "spread[ing] the pain across the board ... this time, the crisis seems to be heading straight for the faculty."[4]

Professors on the faculty senate were particularly shocked by the president's announcement. Mario Mazzarella said the state budget crisis had been approaching for a long time, but the administration had simply not taken proper actions. The faculty, moreover, "had no idea what was going on" until university policies were announced in the paper. Physics professor Peter Knipp agreed and further pointed out that the faculty senate had passed resolutions calling upon President Trible "to involve faculty in academic decisions." "These resolutions," Knipp concluded, "seemed to have no effect upon CNU's administration." Barry Wood, who was then in his last year of teaching in 2002, sadly acknowledged that everyone felt "anxious," particularly younger untenured faculty members who considered themselves placed in a "very vulnerable position."[5]

Due to the severity of the state's cuts, and recognizing the need for more faculty input, President Trible created the Budget Advisory Committee (BAC) during the spring 2002 semester. A committee of five senior faculty members and five top administrators, it was tasked with looking at the university's budget and finding ways to implement the state-mandated cuts. Trible later acknowledged that he needed the faculty's input, particularly during such a challenging period. "The faculty has helped me appreciate the importance of consultation," he recalled, "and I understand that leadership is a flowing back and forth of energy and ideas. And two minds are better than one." In mid-February 2002, after a series of long and difficult meetings, the new BAC proposed

---

[4] "Full-Time Faculty Members At Risk," *Captain's Log*, 30 January 2002.

[5] "Some Professors Favor Pay Cut Over Loss of Adjuncts," *Captain's Log*, 6 February 2002; "Information on College Cut Delayed: Governor Will Review Proposals from Schools," *Daily Press*, 8 February 2002; "Letters to the Editor—Faculty Frozen Out of Decisions," *Daily Press*, 15 February 2002. For a public defense of the administration from Professors Timothy Marshall and Thomas Berry, see "Letters to the Editor—CNU Faculty Will Excel, Despite Cuts," *Daily Press*, 6 February 2002.

several measures to resolve the situation: it called for a 9 percent tuition hike, increasing the size of the 2002 freshman class by 100, continuing the already-imposed hiring and traveling freezes, as well as eliminating a dozen administrative staff positions. Questions about whether or not the state government would permit the tuition increase, however, made the plan's viability uncertain. When the BAC announced its proposals, Trible said the school needed to see what the General Assembly would do in this regard and he admitted that "[f]urther reductions may be necessary."[6]

While the university dealt with these challenges, Trible also made another major change in administrative leadership. He asked Richard Summerville to become the university's provost once more. Robert Doane had long wanted to return to the classroom, and CNU needed an experienced budget and financial expert who knew the university inside and out, and who could deal effectively with officials in Richmond. Two months after Summerville's appointment in April 2002, the budget crisis appeared solved when the General Assembly repealed the state's tuition freeze, which allowed CNU to increase its tuition. This increase, along with the BAC's proposed cuts, allowed CNU to finally balance its budget.[7]

In August 2002, however, Governor Warner shattered everyone's complacency when he announced that the state's budget situation had unexpectedly worsened over the summer as revenue collections had come in significantly below estimates. Thus, a new $1.5 billion shortfall had opened up (on top of the earlier $3.8 billion state deficit) leading the governor to call the budget crisis "the worst since the state began compiling records forty years before." To close the gap, he ordered all

---

[6] "CNU to Reduce Spending, Balance Budget," *Daily Press*, 23 January 2002; "CNU Could See More Students, Less Staff," *Daily Press*, 16 February 2002; "Tuition Blues," *Daily Press*, 27 March 2002; Paul Trible interview with Phillip Hamilton, 31 August 2009. Amid the tension over the budget, another controversy arose in the Spring 2002 term over salary raises given in the year 2000 to administrators which were significantly higher than corresponding raises given to the faculty, see "Some Received Pay Increases Prior to State-Mandated Cuts," *Captain's Log*, 13 February 2002.

[7] "CNU's Provost, Robert Doane, Resigns to Return to Classroom, *Daily Press*, 16 February 2002; "Doane Steps Down as Provost," *Daily Press*, 20 February 2002; "CNU Raises Tuition and Fees to Offset Losses," *Daily Press*, 30 April 2002.

state agencies to submit three new possible budget plans containing further cuts of 7 percent, 11 percent, and 15 percent. Warner said that Richmond would evaluate the proposals and then decide which level of cuts to implement.[8]

As the Budget Advisory Committee worked to put together the new budget proposals, President Trible warned the campus community that the cuts this time would be "brutal" and would definitely contain staff and faculty layoffs, as well as many fewer classes for students. After the plans were submitted and when the state government issued its final budget-figures, CNU's share of the burden was nearly as bad as everyone expected; on top of the 7 percent cut imposed the previous academic year, the state slashed CNU's budget in 2002–03 by 8.3 percent *and* by 10 percent in 2003–04. These cuts brought the university's total budget reduction to more than $7 million. To deal with these stark realities, members of the administration and BAC realized that they could not avoid deep personnel cuts. Unlike William and Mary and the University of Virginia, CNU had no substantial endowment to call upon to cover budget shortfalls in times of emergency. The only question was whether to cut all departments across the board or to create a plan of targeted program cuts. Trible later recalled that he and members of the BAC realized during their internal deliberations that "if you cut *across the board*, you're diminishing the quality of your programs *across the board*. So we said, we're going to do what they do in the real world in terms of our values and what we want to become. We're going to see what programs are good programs but are not essential to our success and that perhaps we cannot afford." Thus, the BAC recommended to the board of visitors that three departments be eliminated: education, nursing, and leisure studies/physical education. None of the three programs fit with CNU's new institutional focus on the liberal arts, and those students who majored in these disciplines had nearby institutions they could attend to pursue such degrees. Therefore, the board of visitors officially approved the terminations on 16 October 2002. The next day, President Trible publicly announced the elimination of the three programs as well as the termination of sixteen tenured and tenure-track

---

[8] "'More Layoffs'—Warner Paints Bleak Picture of State Budget," *Daily Press*, 20 August 2002.

professors and six part-time instructors at the end of the academic year. To reach $7 million in needed savings, the BAC also recommended that twenty-five administration and classified employees be laid off.[9]

The campus community was indeed stunned by the actions. The dismissed faculty members were particularly shocked because word of their terminations had leaked to the press the evening before and thus appeared in the next morning's newspapers before the president's official announcement. Nursing professor Roxanne Lord said, "I found out from the paper this morning that we were fired." Lord followed up by saying that she was "more concerned" about her students, especially 113 sophomores and juniors who now could not finish their nursing degrees. Students in the affected programs were also upset and angry. Erin Keough was "furious" because she "never thought they would cut education." Freshman Scott Henning said, "I don't understand how they're building new buildings but cutting back on teachers and programs." One student, Shannon Bertrand, predicted many would leave CNU, even those students in departments unaffected by the cuts. Laying the blame squarely at President Trible's feet, she said, "He wants to make this into a liberal arts college, where only the elite go. But CNU was set up to help the community." Another student held up a sign at a student protest several days later reading "Just because this is CNU, does not mean they will come."[10]

Although some people attacked the president in frustration, many others blamed the state government and especially former Governor Jim Gilmore for his tax and spending policies. Freshman Christina Wheeler protested, "Gilmore made the tax cuts that everyone loved. However,

[9] "Budget Crisis Reaches CNU Personnel," *Captain's Log*, 25 September 2002; "Trible Warns Community About Budget Cuts," *Captain's Log*, 9 October 2002; "Nursing Program to be Cut at CNU," *Daily Press*, 16 October 2002; "CNU Faces Tough Choices, Tough Times," *Daily Press*, 12 November 2002; Trible interview with Hamilton, 31 August 2009; see also "Budget Woes Force CNU to Cancel Non-Credit Classes," *Daily Press*, 30 August 2002.

[10] "CNU Education, Nursing Programs Gone," *Daily Press*, 17 October 2002; "Sen. Warner Visits CNU to Garner Bond Support" and "CNU Students Want Answers," *Daily Press*, 23 October 2002; "CNU Budget Slashed," *Captain's Log*, 23 October 2002; "Students, Faculty Gather to Give Governor Message," *Captain's Log*, 30 October 2002. There were a number of letters to the editor about the cuts; see those published in the *Daily Press* on 27 October, 4 November, and 6 November 2002.

did he ever take into account where they were going to replace the money?" Professor Jane Carter Webb chimed in to blame the state government as well as Virginians in general for not understanding that higher education is not free. Writing an op-ed piece entitled "Welcome to the Starving Times," Webb lambasted "taxpayers who believe you can have something for nothing" and state politicians who avoid telling the truth and do things only "to please the voters," however unwise.[11] The *Daily Press* agreed. In an editorial, the paper wrote, "Quibbling about whether CNU should have made these cuts or some others misses the point of whether it should be forced to cut at all given that it and all state colleges were underfunded to begin with."[12] To make up some of the lost dollars and to prevent further cuts, the board of visitors voted in December 2002 to impose a mid-year tuition increase of $250 on all full-time students. The increase brought in nearly $900,000. Nonetheless, the administration refused to consider reinstating the eliminated programs. Referring to the new dollars coming in, the president said, "This is insurance against further reductions in programs or people."[13]

Despite the uncertainty over exactly who was to blame, the campus remained divided, and bitterness characterized the remainder of the academic year. Some professors pleaded with the faculty senate to petition the administration not to eliminate the programs. Most refused to go along, however, arguing that the administration's decisions were correct and that the university had to move forward. Faculty members in the eliminated departments were especially bitter as they completed their teaching contracts. Leisure studies and physical education professor Robert Cummings, a twenty-seven-year veteran of the university, openly admitted that he was furious. Immediately prior to the budget crisis, he had made a $100,000 donation to CNU in order to

[11] "Letters to the Editor—All Gov. Gilmore's Fault," *Daily Press*, 23 October 2002; "Welcome to the Starving Times," *Daily Press*, 22 October 2002.

[12] "CNU Cuts," *Daily Press*, 23 October 2002; see also "Trible Blames VA Lawmakers," *Daily Press*, 27 October 2002. Former CNU Rector Stephen D. Halliday wrote a letter to the editor supporting President Trible's actions; see "Higher Ed Declined," *Daily Press*, 2 January 2003.

[13] "Cost of Tuition to Rise at CNU," *Daily Press*, 7 December 2002; "Faculty Senate Refuses to Endorse Reinstating Depts. With Tuition Increase," *Captain's Log*, 5 February 2003.

establish a sports-science laboratory. After discovering his department's elimination, Cummings ordered his will changed in order to halt the transfer of the remaining $40,000 of his gift.[14] Many students, also angry, left CNU and transferred to other institutions such as Old Dominion University and William and Mary. Indeed, at least 150 residential students left after the fall 2002 semester and another two hundred exited following the spring term. Some local schools even recruited CNU students. Virginia Wesleyan College of Norfolk, for example, took out a half page ad in the *Captain's Log* saying, "CNU Education and Recreation, Sports, and Wellness Management students: We've got room for you!"[15]

A "Remarkable" Recovery –– CNU from 2003 to 2005

"I think the most painful time of my [twenty-seven] years of service was the 2002–03 academic year [when] we had to eliminate academic programs and ... faculty positions," Richard Summerville wrote shortly after his retirement in 2007, "I was (and am) proud of the way this awful job was done; but it was awful nevertheless." Summerville finished his recollections about this difficult period with the observation, "It is remarkable that the University recovered from it so quickly."[16] The provost's opinion about CNU's recovery was shared by many. The 2002–03 academic year had been difficult and painful—but the university community recuperated in a *remarkable* fashion and moved forward to accomplish significant things during the remainder of the decade. Many factors accounted for the school's resurgence, including the successful completion of numerous building and campus projects, as well as ongoing success in recruiting outstanding students from throughout

---

[14] "CNU Faculty Votes No on Reinstating Departments," *Daily Press*, 1 February 2003; "CNU Teacher-Donor Gets Budget Lesson After $100,000 Gift, Professor is Losing Job and Department," *Daily Press*, 6 April 2003; "Bid to Save CNU Programs Can't Draw a Crowd," *Daily Press*, 19 March 2003.

[15] "Housing Consolidates," *Captain's Log*, 26 February 2003; "Displaced CNU Students Run to Local Colleges; ODU Sees Surge in Transfer Applications," *Daily Press*, 25 April 2003. See also "Budget Cuts Hurt CNU's Athletes; One-Fourth of Sports Participants Must Change Their Majors or Transfer," *Daily Press*, 26 October 2002; "Education Majors Rush to Finish," *Daily Press*, 22 January 2003; "CNU Nearly Loses Funds in [Newport News] Council Vote," *Daily Press*, 12 February 2003.

[16] Richard Summerville communication to Phillip Hamilton, 10 December 2007.

Virginia and excellent new faculty members from throughout the country. Above all, recovery came because faculty and administrators remained focused on the university's new mission and found creative ways to implement this charge.

One of the first areas of the university to recover was teacher training. The elimination of the education department had been the most controversial part of CNU's budget cuts in fall 2002. CNU-trained elementary and secondary teachers had always been highly regarded and eagerly employed by Hampton Roads school districts. The Newport News public school system, for instance, hired sixty-one CNU graduates as teachers in the spring of 2002 alone (20 percent of the school's system's new hires that year). Community anger for eliminating teaching training, therefore, was palpable. The Newport News City Council even discussed possibly halting its financial contributions to CNU for construction of the performing arts center (the council vote, however, deadlocked at three votes for and three against.).[17]

To resolve the situation and ease tensions, President Trible began meeting with members of the Newport News School Board in December 2002. From their conversations came the idea for CNU to create a new five-year Masters of Arts in Teaching (MAT) program. To turn the idea into reality, Trible helped organize an ad hoc committee of CNU faculty members and Newport News school officials. Meeting throughout the spring 2003 semester, the committee modeled its new five-year program on the University of Virginia's successful masters degree in education. During students' first four years, they would earn their bachelors degrees in a traditional discipline (such as English, government, or history, for instance); and in their fifth year, they would then take graduate courses (taught by CNU faculty and Newport News school teachers holding advanced degrees) as well as complete their student-teaching at a Peninsula public school. Not only did the new MAT cost "significantly less" than the undergraduate education program, but

---

[17] "CNU Nearly Loses Funds in [Newport News] Council Vote," *Daily Press*, 12 February 2003. The number of CNU's graduates hired by the Newport News Public School is contained in Paul Trible email communication to CNU faculty and staff, 12 December 2002.

graduates would also start their teaching careers at higher salaries.[18] Approved by the Virginia Board of Education in the summer of 2003, the program began in fall 2004. Under the direction of Dr. Marsha Sprague, it quickly attracted many excellent students and proved a notable success. In 2005, nineteen MAT students graduated, almost all of whom found jobs either before they received their degrees or immediately afterwards. The following year, forty-three students were awarded the MAT while another ten received state teaching licenses. And the number of graduates continued to increase every year thereafter. In 2010, for example, the program produced eighty-six MAT graduates. Not only did these students find themselves in demand, but most stayed and taught in the Hampton Roads area.[19]

The ongoing success of the admissions office under Patty Patten's leadership also helped CNU recover from its 2002 nadir. Due to the budget and program cuts (and the bad publicity in the press), the admissions staff had to step up its recruitment and marketing efforts in 2003. Patten's team, therefore, organized twenty-eight recruiting events both on campus and throughout the state, including college fairs in Charlottesville, Fredericksburg, and Northern Virginia. CNU recruiters also traveled outside the Old Dominion as far away as New York and New Jersey. The staff's aim was not just to attract *more* students, but *more talented* ones who possessed stronger SAT scores and higher GPAs. As a result, the freshman class grew from 1,190 students in 2002 to 1,215 in 2003. GPA and SAT averages rose as well. The school also broadened the geographical diversity of its students with 41 percent of applicants coming from Northern Virginia, 15 percent from the greater Richmond area, and 14 percent from outside the state. On the other hand, only 12 percent of applications came from high school graduates on the Peninsula. The recruiting efforts that year culminated with a *Washington*

[18] Trible interview with Hamilton, 31 August 2009; Paul Trible email communication to CNU faculty and staff, 12 December 2002; "Education Program Will Return," *Captain's Log*, 5 February 2003; "NN Schools, CNU Join To Train Teachers Program to Award Master's Degree," *Daily Press*, 22 May 2003.

[19] "Master of Arts in Teaching Program Approved," *Captain's Log*, 3 September 2003; "CNU Teacher Program Gets Mixed Marks," *Daily Press*, 31 May 2005; Marsha Sprague, "Letters to the Editor-Teacher Education," *Daily Press*, 9 August 2006; Marsha Sprague email communication to Phillip Hamilton, 23 May 2010.

Post article naming CNU one of "20 undiscovered gems" among colleges in the mid-Atlantic region. The piece pointed out that these "gems" were excellent institutions that deserved more attention from talented students. The *Post* article particularly highlighted Christopher Newport as an "up and coming small state school with a caring faculty."[20]

In addition to the new MAT program and strong undergraduate recruitment, the university forged a new strategic plan in 2003. Trible had several purposes in launching this effort at this time. Not only had the prior strategic plan expired the year before, but a new and more substantive articulation of Christopher Newport's long-term goals would help the university community see past the difficult and painful budget cuts of the previous year. Faculty, staff, and students were involved in laying out specific objectives and aims designed to create a more selective liberal arts university, and local Newport News leaders also joined in discussions about how CNU could become a stronger asset to the entire Hampton Roads community. Released in 2004 and entitled "Vision 2010," the final plan articulated several vital priorities: recruiting better and more talented faculty and students, designing a rigorous curriculum to meet the global challenges of the twenty-first century, and creating a beautiful yet functional campus that would inspire all members of the campus community.[21]

As the university's strategic planning moved forward, it also modernized its general education program—a step many felt was long overdue. In early 2002, Trible had created a thirty-member faculty task force with professors from a broad range of disciplines, and he charged them to produce a thoroughly revised core curriculum—one modeled on the best curricula at the best colleges and universities in the United

---

[20] "Twenty Undiscovered Gems—Harvard Schmarvard," *Washington Post*, 3 April 2003; "CNU Admissions Evolve," *Daily Press*, 28 April 2003; "Colleges Score Big Freshmen-Class: Quality, Diversity Up Across State," *Daily Press*, 11 September 2003; Patty Patten interview with Phillip Hamilton, 13 December 2009.

[21] "Where the Newspaper Stands—Let's Talk," *Daily Press*, 29 November 2003; Richard Summerville and Virginia Purddle email communication to CNU community, 26 February 2004; "History of 'Vision 2010,'" CNU Web site, http://web.archive.org/web/20060908075755/vision2010.cnu.edu/history2010.pdf (accessed 25 May 2010).

States.[22] Frustration with the rigidity of the existing general education requirements—most of which dated back to the 1960s—had been building for years. After September 11, for instance, faculty members realized the university could not offer courses on Islamic history, religion, or politics geared for the general student population. Government professor Quentin Kidd, co-chair of the task force, later explained, "[W]e couldn't [offer such courses] because our general education was so rigid. The courses are all set in stone."[23] The taskforce completed its work in 2004, and the new curriculum plan was approved by the faculty senate and board of visitors that spring. The new system, which took effect in 2006, established a program that gave students more options in fulfilling their writing, mathematical, science, foreign language, and other requirements. As at many selective colleges, instead of placing students into most of their required courses, the university gave them a menu of classes dealing with a range of general topics and issues from which to choose. To help freshmen adjust to college life and academic work, moreover, the core program required all incoming students take specially designed first-year seminars. Although course topics varied according to professors' specialties and disciplines, all of them introduced freshmen to the practical realities and expectations of academic life. Although the history department formally protested the elimination of a six-credit-hour global history requirement that had been adopted during Santoro's presidency, most faculty members supported the updated core program.[24]

Christopher Newport also expanded its faculty and boosted salaries in 2004. Progress in both these areas came largely because the state's budget crisis had mostly subsided by that point in time. Thus, the General Assembly and governor restored a good deal of higher education funding that had been previously cut. In the budget

---

[22] "Trible Moving Toward Inclusion; CNU President Seeks Faculty Involvement," *Daily Press*, 23 January 2002; "CNU Raises Tuition and Fees," *Daily Press*, 30 April 2002.

[23] "CNU Adds Some Zing to Course Offerings," *Daily Press*, 22 February 2004.

[24] "Task Force Attempts to Update Core Curriculum," *Captain's Log*, 10 December 2003; "Curriculum Will Affect Freshmen Class of 2006," *Captain's Log*, 15 September 2004. The first-year seminar requirement became optional for the freshman class of 2010.

negotiations that spring, for instance, the state granted CNU a 16 percent increase and those new funds, combined with increases in tuition, permitted the university to hire forty-seven new professors for the 2004–05 academic year. An additional thirty tenure-track hires, moreover, were scheduled for 2005–06. While some of these new lecturers were to replace retiring professors, this significant expansion in the middle part of the decade brought the size of the faculty to nearly 240 members and permitted average class sizes to drop. This growth, furthermore, allowed professors to give students more time and attention both inside and outside the classroom. The additional state funds also allowed the university to raise salaries across the board. Due to the strained financial circumstances of the early 2000s, faculty and staff raises had been few and far between. This had made retaining the best professors difficult, and several had left for higher paying jobs elsewhere; therefore, to stem these losses and to reward instructors, all returning professors in 2004 received pay raises averaging 14 percent.[25]

The influx of such a large number of new faculty, many from the nation's premier graduate programs, combined with the substantial raises boosted morale on campus considerably and helped to complete CNU's "remarkable" recovery. The new professors, who made up nearly one-third of the faculty by 2005, fully subscribed to the university's goal of becoming a premier liberal arts university. Because many of these junior faculty members were recent PhDs, they also brought with them ambitious research and publication agendas as well as innovative approaches to teaching their students. Meanwhile, as these new professors entered the classroom, the physical transformation of CNU's campus continued.

A "Breathtakingly Beautiful Campus" — From "Word Pictures" to Reality

During the late 1990s and early 2000s, President Trible and other university officials often had to verbally paint what they called "word pictures" to describe the campus they envisioned in the future. In 2004,

---

[25] "CNU Raises In-State Tuition," *Daily Press*, 1 May 2003; "State Funding Boosts CNU Employment," *Daily Press*, 20 June 2004; "University Boosts Salaries," *Daily Press*, 14 September 2004.

these "word pictures" finally started to become reality. Indeed, as construction workers completed and opened one building after another, a fundamentally different CNU campus emerged. The most important— and certainly the most spectacular—new building to open in the middle years of the decade was the long-planned performing arts center. Administration officials had worked tirelessly on planning and raising funds for the center from 1996 onward. President Trible himself viewed the art center as the linchpin to CNU's transformation, understanding that it would dramatically improve and enrich campus life and student experiences. Construction on the center had begun in 2001 at the site of the old Ferguson High School and progress continued even during the budget crisis of 2002. In late 2003, officials announced that phase one of the building would be completed by the following September when the university would open the "Music and Theater Hall," an intimate venue seating 440 patrons, as well as the two-hundred-seat Studio Theater. Phase two would be completed in the fall of 2005 when the 1,700-seat concert hall would open for concerts and other performances. At the same time CNU provided this timeline, it also publicly announced that the building itself would be named the Ferguson Center for the Performing Arts in recognition of Ferguson Enterprises' extraordinary $1 million donation to the project. The new name additionally honored the leadership provided by the corporation's senior officers. Indeed, former CEO, David Peebles, had served as CNU's rector for several years. Moreover, another former Ferguson CEO, Charlie Banks, had spearheaded the university's fundraising efforts for the arts center. Finally, not only did Ferguson Enterprises' current president and CEO, C.S. "Chip" Hornsby, then serve on CNU's board of visitors, but he had also attended Ferguson High School as a youth.[26]

To manage the new building and to schedule performers, the university hired William "Bill" Biddle to serve as the Ferguson Center's executive director. A native of New Jersey, Biddle had previously been the director of the Miller Auditorium at Western Michigan University in

---

[26] "CNU Art Center Gets Name; Ferguson Enterprises to be Honored for Contributions, *Daily Press*, 6 December 2003; "All in a Name," *Daily Press*, 8 December 2003; "Ferguson Open, Departments Settling In," *Captain's Log*, 1 September 2004; see also "Serious Play to Open New Space," *Daily Press*, 8 October 2004, which discusses the opening of the Ferguson Center's experimental theater, the 200-seat "Black Box."

Kalamazoo. While in Michigan, Biddle had revived the Auditorium's
sagging attendance by developing a highly varied performance schedule
that included Broadway shows, symphonic concerts, and appearances by
popular artists. One of the biggest stars Biddle had brought to Michigan
was the legendary signer Tony Bennett. As he settled into his job at
CNU, Biddle thought that Bennett would be the perfect star to open the
Ferguson Center's Music and Theater Hall.[27] Using his contacts with the
performer's agent, Biddle scheduled the concert for 1 September 2004.
On that day, and before the evening performance, the *Daily Press*
editorialized about the meaning of the Ferguson Center's opening not
just to CNU, but also to the entire Hampton Roads community:

> Newport News will be a different, better place because of the
> Ferguson Center for the Arts at Christopher Newport University. Flash
> forward 100 years, and the impact will still be felt. Not just in Newport
> News, but across the region. This is not an exaggeration. Universities are
> centers for learning and culture. They are engines of economic growth.
> Christopher Newport is growing, as anyone with eyes to see can tell
> driving down Warwick Boulevard where it passes the campus.... The
> Ferguson Center for the Arts is an extraordinary structure, one that is
> proof that true beauty is more than skin deep. The center's dramatic,
> sweeping front is a sufficient statement that this is a special place.... The
> finished lobby is easily one of the most beautiful interior public spaces in
> Hampton Roads. The 440-seat music and theater hall, where Bennett will
> perform tonight, will be worthy of the finest talents in music and
> theater....[28]

That evening, Bennett indeed dazzled audience members with his
showmanship and elegant flair; but the Ferguson Center itself, with its
beautiful open lobby and the theater's superb acoustics, also enormously
impressed the four-hundred-plus patrons. One guest at the show was
Barry Wood, who had retired from CNU two years before. Not only was
Wood among CNU's first faculty members, but he had also organized
the school's first classical concert series in 1973. As he looked around the
new facility, he joked, "I hoped we'd go somewhere, but I never thought

---

[27] "CNU Art Center Lands a Director," *Daily Press*, 11 January 2004; Bennett's
opening appearance was announced in June 2004; see "Opening Night: Venue Has
World-Class Potential," *Daily Press*, 1 September 2004 for timeline.
[28] "Where the Newspaper Stands—Applause!" *Daily Press*, 1 September 2004.

we'd go this far."[29] Other audience members were equally impressed. The fine arts reporter and reviewer for Norfolk's *Virginian Pilot* wrote:

> The center is impressive, from its expansive, cacophonous lobby with Italian marble floors to its plush, library-quiet music and theater hall. Pei's firm is well known for its museum designs, notably the see-through pyramid on The Louvre in Paris, Cleveland's Rock and Roll Hall of Fame and the National Gallery of Art's angular east wing in Washington. Liberal use of glass and natural light is a hallmark of the work of the firm he founded, Pei Cobb Freed & Partners. Ferguson Center features skylights, glass walls with wavy patterns and a glamorous glass entrance, which attracts like a lantern in the evening. When the concert hall is finished, an even more commanding windowed entry—five stories high—is expected to become an icon for Newport News.[30]

Twelve months later, workers completed phase two of the Ferguson Center, and Michael Crawford with the New York Pops inaugurated the 1,700-seat concert hall before another sell-out crowd. Once again the accolades poured in, but Crawford's performance at the Ferguson was only one of many impressive shows that first season. Indeed, the 2005–06 season also included performances of the Broadway show *Miss Saigon* as well as concerts by the Three Irish Tenors and Bruce Hornsby. The season was further highlighted by thirteen concerts by the Virginia Symphony, which made the Ferguson Center one of its regular performing venues.[31] The Andrea Bocelli concert, however, proved to be the high point of the season. Although the $300 ticket price did not begin to cover the tenor's $500,000-plus fee, the show was well worth it. Not

---

[29] "CNU Arts Center Hosts First Concert," *Daily Press*, 2 September 2004; "Bennett Opens Ferguson," *Captain's Log*, 8 September 2004; Barry Wood communication to Phillip Hamilton, 15 March 2008.

[30] "Curtain Rises on a Gem of a Space," *Virginian Pilot*, 12 September 2004. At the same time that Phase I of the Ferguson opened, an adjacent parking garage opened up for students during the day and theater patrons in the evening; see "Deck Compensates Loss of Lots," *Captain's Log*, 1 September 2004.

[31] "A Dramatic New Presence," *Daily Press*, 11 September 2005; "Where the Newspaper Stands—Bravo!" *Daily Press*, 12 September 2005; "CNU's Ferguson Center; Hall Takes Its Bow," *Daily Press*, 13 September 2005; "Ferguson Phase II Finalized," *Captain's Log*, 14 September 2005. On the Virginia Symphony making Ferguson one of its regular playing arenas, see "Classics at CNU," *Daily Press*, 25 January 2005; "Where the Newspaper Stands—Welcome Home," *Daily Press*, 18 September 2005.

only was the performance Bocelli's only appearance in North America that year, but publicity about the concert also generated ticket sales for the Ferguson's other shows. Bocelli himself also lauded the hall's extraordinary sound. In fact, the tenor pronounced the acoustics so good that he publicly performed a song without amplification for the first time in his singing career. And, finally, Anthony Colosimo's appearance onstage with Bocelli permitted the university to publicize both the new facility and the extraordinary academic experiences offered to students.[32]

As predicted, the Ferguson Center transformed cultural life at CNU and on the Peninsula. During its first full season, more than 136,000 patrons attended performances, including many students who purchased deeply discounted tickets ranging from $5 to $25. Attendance rose even further during the 2006–07 season, with more than 198,000 people attending a wide variety of performances, concerts, and shows. Looking back on his efforts to build the $60 million facility, President Trible pointed out that there are "few if any schools in America that [can] rival the Ferguson Center." Although the project consumed extraordinary amounts of time, work and money, it proved well worth the effort. Indeed, the president later said that it was essential to "build buildings of civic proportions" in his efforts to change the university. "Our job is to instruct and inspire," he continued, "and there's nothing that inspires more than great art and great architecture. Buildings such as the Ferguson Center underscore the seriousness of our purpose and the reach of our dream."[33]

While spectacular and transformative, the Ferguson Center was only one of many building projects completed during the decade's middle years. In the fall of 2004, for example, the university finished a

[32] "CNU Lands World-Class Tenor – A $500,000-Plus Performance," *Daily Press*, 19 October 2005; "Ferguson Center Perfect for Bocelli," *Virginia Pilot*, 20 October 2005.

[33] "Little Bit of Everything in Newport News—Ferguson Center Announces Its 2006–07 Lineup," *Daily Press*, 11 May 2006; "Attendance Up But Revenues Down," *Daily Press*, 14 September 2007; Paul Trible interview with Hamilton, 31 August 2009. See also Paul Trible, "CNU Arts Center Brings the World to Newport News," *Virginian Pilot*, 22 February 2006. Because of his work to make the Ferguson Center a reality, President Trible was honored in late-2005 with an Alli Award, given annually to local leaders who strongly support the arts and culture in Hampton Roads, see "Supporters of the Arts Honored," *Daily Press*, 7 November 2005.

new 482-bed dormitory named Potomac River Hall.[34] Because demand for campus housing had grown so significantly over the years, the administration gave high priority to this building's completion. Begun in the summer of 2003 on the campus's west side along Moore's Lane, the co-ed upperclassmen facility cost $23 million and, like York River dormitory, featured four-person suites.[35] The following fall, 2005, a mixed residential-retail complex called CNU Village opened on the east side of Warwick Boulevard. Like other residential halls, this $23 million, 398-bed dormitory was co-ed and had a variety of two-, three-, and four-bedroom suites. CNU Village's ground floor was dedicated to retail space, with room for ten to fifteen stores. Eventually a variety of businesses occupied the first floor, including the Panera Bread Company, Subway Sandwich Shop, and Schooners, a sports bar/restaurant featuring nautical décor. Theo Gouletas, co-owner of Schooners, pointed out that his restaurant and the other businesses gave CNU students a place to "hang out." CNU Village added considerable vitality to campus life and brought the number of students living on campus to nearly 2,800—or almost 60 percent of the total student population.[36]

Despite the rapid growth in student housing, demand for dorm rooms continued to outstrip supply, forcing the university to occasionally scramble to find space. In fall 2005, for instance, CNU purchased the old motel along Warwick Boulevard called the "Relax Inn." Renaming the facility "Warwick River Suites," the university repainted and refurnished its thirty rooms, which allowed an additional

---

[34] "Rain and Budget Impasse Delay Construction," *Captain's Log*, 1 September 2004.

[35] "James River Hall II?" *Captain's Log*, 26 February 2003; "New Residence Hall Construction Begins," *Captain's Log*, 13 June 2003; "CNU Aims to be Better, Not Bigger," *Daily Press*, 28 August 2004; "Potomac Still Incomplete," *Captain's Log*, 1 September 2004.

[36] "CNU Plans Retail, Apartment Complex," *Daily Press*, 4 September 2003; "Housing and Retail Combine in CNU Village," *Captain's Log*, 10 September 2003; "CNU Plans New Buildings and Additions," *Daily Press*, 11 March 2004; "Constructing the Future—CNU Complex to Have Its Villagers by Fall, *Daily Press*, 9 June 2005; "CNU Gets More Like a Village: A Hangout and More," *Daily Press*, 19 October 2005. Number of residential students is from the CNU Office of Institutional Research.

100 students to live on campus.[37] The following year, due to the fact that CNU guaranteed new freshman as well as sophomores university housing, more than three hundred juniors and seniors had to be waitlisted after they had applied to live in the dormitories. Two students, angered that younger classmen received preferential treatment, started a Web site called "CNUhousingsucks.com." Although housing officials were able to place all the waitlisted students—by tripling up some dorm-rooms as well as by purchasing several houses along Prince Drew Road and Meritt Circle—the demand told everyone that more residential halls would be needed in the future.[38]

The opening of both the David Student Union in fall 2006 and an expanded Smith Library in spring 2008 continued the transformation of CNU's campus. Located on the Great Lawn at the center of CNU's campus, both buildings were the fruition of years of planning and construction. Discussions about a new student center had actually begun early on in Trible's presidency. Although the existing campus center was still functional, it had been showing its age for years. Serious planning for a new student facility began in 2000 when a committee of students, faculty and administrators began working with architects to sketch out a new 116,000-square-foot structure. To be financed in part through higher student fees, the building was especially designed to serve the needs of a residential student body. Plans for the center were made public in 2001, but the project ran into delays, including the 2002–03 budget crisis. After the financial emergencies ended, problems then arose in obtaining adequate amounts of steel and other essential building materials. When

[37] "Relax Inn to House Students Next Year," *Captain's Log*, 30 March 2005; "Trading Spaces: A New Name Change for the old Relax Inn," *Captain's Log*, 31 August 2005.

[38] "No Vacancy," *Captain's Log*, 29 March 2006; "Three's Company—Or Just a Crowd?" *Captain's Log*, 5 September 2007. Housing officials particularly had to scramble just weeks before the Fall 2006 semester when lightening struck Madison Hall during a late-summer storm, igniting a ruinous fire. Although no one was hurt, the university had to arrange for students to live at the Point Plaza Hotel, located three miles from campus. Madison Hall's ruins were razed and the dormitory was rebuild in time for the 2007–08 academic year; for more information on the fire, see "CNU Dorm Burns," *Daily Press*, 5 August 2006; "University Dormitory a Total Loss after Fire," *Richmond Times-Dispatch*, 6 August 2006; "CNU Transfers Displaced Students, *Daily Press*, 15 August 2006; "A Strike of Bad Luck for CNU," *Captain's Log*, 30 August 2006.

the $36 million facility finally opened in September 2006, however, visitors were again dazzled by what they saw. Student government president Molly Buckley called the neo-Georgian brick building "just phenomenal" due to its beauty and functionality. Buckley particularly noted the center's impressive design with a dramatic three-story interior atrium inside the main foyer and second- and third-floor balconies that looked down upon the ground floor entrance. The entire building, the student president concluded, "draws students together." The university named the center the David Student Union (DSU) after the Edward "Buddy" David family because of its generous support to the university over many years (particularly in shaping and strengthening CNU's Educational and Real Estate Foundations). Quickly becoming a central part of CNU life, the building hosted more than 1,500 campus events, lectures, and meetings during its first year of operation alone.[39]

Like the old student center, the Smith Library had been showing its age for many years. Most students and faculty thought the building cramped, filled with outdated technology, and an even more out-of-date book collection. President Trible, therefore, made the construction of an entirely new library a university priority in late 1998. He called for the construction of a twenty-first-century facility that would be twice the size of the old library, possess an inspiring design, and contain "fully wired" study spaces for students and professors. As with the David Student Union, however, state budget cuts from 2001 to 2003 delayed design and construction.[40] As the economy recovered in 2003, plans again moved forward. After reviewing a variety of designs, the

[39] "The New Student Center is Coming," *Captain's Log*, 17 October 2001; "Absent Funding, CNU Dreams of a New Student Center," *Daily Press*, 20 October 2001; "New Student Center Will Open by Fall 2005," *Captain's Log*, 9 April 2003; "CNU Projects Delayed," *Daily Press*, 30 November 2005; "Stumbling Stones for Student Union," *Captain's Log*, 1 February 2006; "Student Union Opens at CNU," *Daily Press*, 21 September 2006; "High Traffic Hits CNU's 'Main Street,'" *Daily Press*, 23 September 2006; "David Student Union," CNU Web site, http://cnu.edu/dsu/index.asp (accessed 7 June 2010).

[40] "CNU President Lists Top 3 Priorities," *Daily Press*, 26 September 1998; "News About CNU Library 'Wows" Students, Faculty," *Daily Press*, 31 January 2001; "Library Receives Major Funding for Improvements, New Facilities," *Captain's Log*, 5 February 2001; "Panel Prepares a Wish-List for New, Improved Library at CNU," *Daily Press*, 20 October 2001.

administration decided not to tear down the Smith Library, but to significantly rehab the existing structure. Plans called for expanding the building to 110,000-square-feet and for the construction of a dramatic brick façade with columned entrances on three sides. Finally, 140-foot high, white-and-bronze cupola would top the new structure. Building began in 2004, but work proceeded slowly in part due to the same material shortages that delayed the David Student Union. In addition, progress was further slowed because the project was a rehab, which essentially required workers to fit the new sections of the building onto the existing structure.[41]

The new library finally opened in January 2008 with fireworks, fanfare, and celebration. Indeed, the building—now renamed "The Paul and Rosemary Trible Library" by the board of visitors to honor the couple's many contributions to Christopher Newport—impressed everyone and made a powerful statement about the academic changes at work at the university. The cupola, visible from all parts of campus, marked the building's central role in CNU's intellectual life. A marbled-floor foyer, moreover, lay just inside the new structure underneath a two-and-a-half-story rotunda. A grand double staircase led upstairs to two elegant reading rooms, a pair of classrooms, the university's "Media Center," and an array of study rooms. The library's books were placed on compact shelving in the building's original wing and the university budgeted new funds in order to add to the book collection. The coffee shop "Einstein's," which had temporarily been relocated in Gosnold Hall during construction, returned to the library in a larger and more stylish setting.[42]

The Trible Library also had a new university librarian named Mary Sellen, who had previously worked in the library system at the State

---

[41] "Library On Track for '04 Ground-Breaking," *Captain's Log*, 19 March 2003; "Library Construction Behind Schedule," *Captain's Log*, 11 February 2004; "CNU Projects Delayed," *Daily Press*, 30 November 2005; "View From the Top: New Construction at CNU," *Daily Press*, 3 July 2006.

[42] "New Library: From Sailor to Senator," *Captain's Log*, 17 January 2007; "Gold Dome Caps CNU's Library Addition," *Daily Press*, 30 October 2007; "New Face, Space for Library," *Captain's Log*, 23 January 2008; "Einstein's Celebrates Its Homecoming," *Captain's Log*, 23 January 2008; Mary Sellen email communication to Phillip Hamilton, 10 June 2010. On naming the library after the Tribles, see "CNU Library Named for Tribles," *Daily Press*, 9 December 2006.

University of New York, Albany. Like President Trible, Sellen wanted to make the new building the true intellectual center of campus. Therefore, she encouraged faculty members to share their teaching and scholarly needs with the library's staff and she tried to make the building and its resources as accessible as possible to students. Toward this latter end, Sellen helped to create a large reading room on the building's ground floor that would be open twenty-four hours a day, with both computers and a technician available to help students with any technology problems. Within weeks of its opening, the library became immensely popular with students (as well as with many faculty) who flocked to the facility in order to work on papers and projects as well as to meet with friends.[43]

As the new buildings went up, CNU's campus changed in other ways. In fall 2004, for instance, the city completed the rerouting of Shoe Lane. The $2.8 million project closed the street's exit onto Warwick Boulevard and channeled local automobile traffic along a new street leading to the main intersection of Warwick and J. Clyde Morris Boulevards. In order to highlight the performing arts center, the City of Newport News named the new roadway "Avenue of the Arts." With the eastern end of Shoe Lane now closed and covered with sod, the Ferguson Center became directly linked to CNU's main campus. A new traffic circle, moreover, was built in front of the Trible Library connecting the new terminus of Shoe Lane to the Avenue of the Arts. Soon after the rerouting project ended, construction crews began the long-delayed widening project of Warwick Boulevard's four lanes into six along a two-mile section. Aimed at easing growing automobile congestion, the project proceeded slowly, delayed by weather and other construction problems. As it moved forward, however, old and unattractive buildings disappeared, and the land in front of campus was cleared and seeded with grass, thus making CNU's main campus completely visible from Warwick Boulevard.[44]

---

[43] "Gold Dome Caps CNU's Library Addition," *Daily Press*, 30 October 2007; Mary Sellen email communication to Phillip Hamilton, 9 June 2010; see also "Einstein's Open 24/7," *Captain's Log*, 23 April 2008.

[44] "New Shoe Lane Opening Will Alter Traffic Patterns," *Daily Press*, 23 August 2004; "Traffic Rerouted Off Shoe Lane," *Daily Press*, 22 September 2004; "Don't Let

Sculptures and statues, moreover, increasingly dotted the campus. In 2008, for instance, former Rector Bobby Freeman and the Newport News Public Arts Foundation arranged for the sculpture "Elements" to be placed at the center of the new Shoe Lane traffic circle. The abstract work of white, Italian marble was sculpted by Norwegian artist Inger Sannes, who said that he wanted the piece to be "suggestive of wind, water, and waves."[45] The previous year a more controversial statue had appeared at the university's new main entrance at the intersection of Warwick Boulevard and Avenue of the Arts—a twenty-four foot tall, 7,500-pound bronze rendition of Captain Christopher Newport. Commissioned for CNU by the North Carolina philanthropist, Irwin Belk, the piece was sculpted by artist Jon Hair. After it was placed on campus in June 2007, everyone discovered that Captain Newport (who had lost his right arm in 1592 in combat with the Spanish) had two arms! When local history buffs loudly protested the inaccuracy, Hair defended himself by asserting that the university had approved a model of the statue with both arms and, he added, "We always depict our heroes in their prime." History professor Mario Mazzarella replied, however, that the British had proudly placed Admiral Horatio Nelson atop the great column in London's Trafalgar Square with only one arm. Although something of an embarrassment, the complaints soon faded and the enormous statue remains at the university's main entrance.[46]

Academic Life and Scholarship in the 2000s

The new buildings and the beautified campus that emerged in the middle part of the decade were only the top-most reality of CNU's ongoing development. As construction proceeded, the university's

---

Traffic Circle Make You Dizzy," *Daily Press*, 6 December 2004; "Part of J. Clyde Now 'Avenue of the Arts,'" *Daily Press*, 18 August 2005.

[45] "New Sculpture at CNU to Be Dedicated Sunday," *Daily Press*, 29 October 2008; Newport News Public Arts Foundation Web site, http://nnpaf.org/CNUElements Project.htm (accessed 21 June 2010).

[46] Mary Sherwood Holt, "Letter to the Editor—Newport's (Un)likeness," *Daily Press*, 6 May 2007; Mario Mazzarella, "Letter to the Editor—Capt. Christopher Newport," *Daily Press*, 17 July 2007; "University's Statue Has History Buffs Up in Arms," *Virginian-Pilot*, 19 July 2007; "Captain Christopher Newport Statue Installed Amid a Sea of Controversy," *Captain's Log*, 5 September 2007.

academic life also improved with ever-more-talented students coming to CNU taught by a growing number of gifted and accomplished faculty. Indeed, the recovery that began during the 2003–04 academic year picked up momentum in the decade's latter years. Under Patty Patten's leadership of the admissions office, applications to CNU continued to grow. In 2007, for instance, 7,400 high school students applied for CNU's 1,200 freshmen slots; two years later, that figure had grown to 8,400. Not only were more students applying, but their academic quality also improved. The 2009 freshman class had a combined SAT score average of 1,119—29 points higher than in 2007 and 239 points higher than the 1996 average. Grade point averages rose as well. New students entering the university in 2009 had an average 3.64 GPA, much higher than the 2.8 freshman average of thirteen years before.[47] More out-of-state students enrolled in the university during this period. Of the 1,218 freshmen of 2009, for example, 114 (or 9.3 percent) were from outside the Old Dominion. Overall, 350 out-of-state students attended CNU at the decade's end, and some officials thought about pushing that number as high as 750 or 15 percent of the total student population. The administration pushed for more out-of-state students for two reasons—first, they possessed experiences and perspectives different from the bulk of the student body, which remained overwhelmingly Virginia-born and bred; and secondly, they paid higher tuition than in-state students.[48]

As the number of out-of-state students increased and the overall enrollment picture brightened, the university nevertheless struggled to attract talented minority students. In 1996, 23 percent of CNU's undergraduates came from a minority background. African-American enrollment was particularly strong. Indeed, nearly eight hundred black students took classes at CNU in the mid-1990s, comprising over 17 percent of the total student population. By 2003, however, with higher

[47] "Class of 2011 Breaks Records in Size, Academics," *Captain's Log*, 5 September 2007; "New Freshman Numbers Show Academic Growth, *Captain's Log*, 3 September 2008; Paul Trible, "State of the University Address," 17 August 2009; Patten interview with Hamilton, 13 December 2009.

[48] "Low Out-of-State Tuition Hike Concerns Some at CNU," *Daily Press*, 26 April 2006; "Out-of-State Enrollment May Rise," *Daily Press*, 18 September 2009; Trible, "State of the University Address," 17 August 2009. In 2009, out-of-state students paid an annual tuition of $14,930 compared to in-state tuition of $7,550.

admissions standards for entrance and the program cuts in education, nursing, and leisure studies/physical education, that figure had dropped to 480, or 10.2 percent. Even more troubling, the freshman class that year included only sixty-seven African-American students or just 5.7 percent of the overall total. Although the university established a committee of faculty and administrators to examine the problem and suggest solutions, minority enrollment proved to be a challenge throughout the entire decade. In 2009, for instance, black enrollment had dropped to a little over 8 percent of the general student population.[49]

Despite these difficulties, the variety of academic opportunities and experiences offered to all CNU students multiplied in the 2000s. The President's Leadership Program (PLP), for example, continued to expand and attract some of the university's best students. In fact, the program grew from twenty participants in 1998 to 315 in the freshman class of 2009. These latter undergraduates, moreover, brought stellar academic records to campus (with average SAT scores of 1,240 and GPAs of 3.8) as well as a great deal of intellectual energy and ambition. CNU's Honors Program also grew throughout these years. Under the direction of English professor Jay Paul, the university strengthened both the program's core offerings and opportunities for students to engage one-on-one with faculty mentors in academic research projects. Furthermore, like the PLP students, participants in the Honors Program received scholarship money and the option to live in specially designated group housing.[50] The most exciting scholarship opportunity for students came in 2007 when CNU partnered with Canon USA, Inc., and Canon Virginia, Inc., to create twenty-five annual scholarships for outstanding CNU freshmen. Not only did these students—designated as Canon Scholars—participate in the PLP program, but they each received annual tuition scholarships of five thousand dollars per year for four years as well. Finally, the university expanded travel-abroad opportunities for all

[49] "Where the Newspaper Stands: CNU—Challenge," *Daily Press*, 19 January 2004; "Minorities Get Minor Role at CNU," *Captain's Log*, 26 September 2007; "Retention Up for Some, Not All," *Captain's Log*, 17 October 2007.

[50] Trible, "State of the University Address," 17 August 2009; "President's Leadership Program," CNU Web site, http://presidentsleadership.cnu.edu/ (accessed June 24, 2010); "Honor's Program," CNU Web site, http://honors.cnu.edu/ (accessed June 24, 2010).

students. It sponsored for several years, for instance, a special study-abroad semester for twelve-to-fifteen students in the Czech Republic led by different CNU faculty members each term. Outstanding students, moreover, were given the chance to study at Oxford University in a unique, ten-day summer seminar while in residence at Harris Manchester College.[51]

With the development of such opportunities at home and abroad, Christopher Newport produced an ever-increasing number of outstanding graduates with a variety of intellectual interests and aspirations. Philip LeClerc was one such student. LeClerc graduated in 2009 as a double major in psychology and economics as well as a participant in the university's Honors Program. During his years at CNU, he developed a passionate interest in global affairs and social justice. His interests were sparked not only by his course work, but also by a joint CNU-US State Department student-exchange program in which he participated in 2006 and 2007. The program brought together twenty Muslim students from North Africa and twenty CNU undergraduates, including LeClerc. In the summer of 2006, the North Africans (who came from Morocco and Algeria) traveled to Virginia in order to study American history and culture; the following summer, the CNU students went to North Africa to learn about the region and its Islamic-based civilization. LeClerc continued to expand and develop his intellectual horizons during the 2007–08 academic year when he traveled to Tanzania as a Rotary Ambassadorial Scholar. While in residence in Africa, he studied the impact of AIDS on the continent as well as served as a good-will emissary of the United States. Before graduating in 2009, LeClerc founded "Citizens of the World," a nationwide student

---

[51] "Canon, CNU Team Up to Aid Students," *Daily Press*, "Canon Leadership Scholars Program," CNU Web site, http://leadership-scholars.cnu.edu/ (accessed 24 June 2010); "International Initiatives and Fellowship," CNU Web site, 3 April 2007, http://web.archive.org/web/20070403022821/iif.cnu.edu/prague.html (accessed 24 June 2010); Paul Trible, "State of the University Address," 17 August 2009. The study abroad semester in the Czech Republic was eliminated due to reductions in state funding in the wake of the 2008 recession.

organization dedicated to the advancement of international affairs and human rights.[52]

Lauren Conner was another remarkable student from the late 2000s. Legally blind due to Leber congenital amaurosis—a disease that damaged her retinas and caused near-total vision loss—Conner nevertheless graduated in 2007 at the top of her class with a 3.98 GPA. Throughout her academic career, she not only persevered through her own academic work—using only a magnifying glass and portable Braille machine in classes—but she also helped teach special-education children at nearby Riverside Elementary School. After she finished her degree at CNU, Conner attended William and Mary in order to pursue a graduate degree in education. The same year Conner graduated, Anne Zagusrky walked down the commencement aisle with a degree in religious studies. Zagusrky was the youngest of five siblings, all of whom had attended and graduated from the university between 1993 and 2007. After graduation, Zagusrky and her brothers and sisters presented their parents with a giant "fake honorary degree" to thank them for all the sacrifices they had made over the years.[53]

Faculty scholarship and accomplishments also significantly improved during the decade, reflecting the campus's increasingly dynamic intellectual climate as well as the growing size of the faculty itself. The history department's accomplishments illustrate many of these positive changes. When Paul Trible became president in 1996, the department consisted of only five full-time faculty members, most of whom had been long-time members of the university. To help teach the then-required six credit hours in world history, the department had to rely on a large number of part-time adjunct instructors. In the late 1990s-early 2000s, however, the number of history majors grew significantly, and President Trible wanted to reduce CNU's dependence on part-time faculty. As a result, the history department grew rapidly. By 2002, there were ten tenure-track members, and by 2010, the department had

---

[52] "Across the Great Divide —From North Africa to CNU," *Daily Press*, 27 July 2006; "CNU Student Named Rotary Ambassadorial Scholar," *Daily Press*, 1 March 2007; "Honor's Program," CNU Web site, http://honors.cnu.edu/ (accessed June 24, 2010).

[53] "CNU Grad Has Hurdled Her 'Little Obstacle,'" *Daily Press*, 13 May 2007; "CNU Commencement End of an Era for One Family," *Daily Press*, 14 May 2007.

expanded to fourteen full-time professors who taught a wide variety of core curriculum classes as well as upper-level courses for its three hundred majors. Not only did the department grow in number, but the new historians also came from some of the nation's most prestigious PhD-granting institutions, including the University of Michigan, University of Chicago, and University of North Carolina, Chapel Hill. The new faculty, furthermore, all possessed ambitious research agendas and published important monographs with major academic presses. Dr. Xiaoqun Xu, for instance, came to CNU in 2004 to teach Asian history. An expert in early twentieth-century China and possessing a PhD from Columbia University, Xu already had one book published by Cambridge University Press when he arrived on campus. In 2008, Xu published a second book with Stanford University Press entitled *Trial of Modernity*, which examined China's judicial system after the fall of the last emperor.[54] Recognizing that such scholarly productivity significantly raised the university's profile and reputation, the administration wanted to encourage more such work. Therefore, it lowered the standard faculty-teaching load from 4-4 to 4-3 in 2007–08, with the ultimate aim of enacting a 3-3 load by 2014. It also modestly increased the number of faculty sabbaticals in order to provide professors with the time and opportunity to pursue major research projects.[55]

Although CNU's new faculty members energetically pursued their research, they also recognized their fundamental role as teachers. The history department again illustrates this point. In addition to teaching large numbers of students during the regular academic year, many department members led academic trips off-campus and abroad to such locations as the United Kingdom, Germany, France, and Italy. In 2006, moreover, Professor Xu designed a special summer course on Chinese history for CNU students, which he taught at the University of Shanghai. Not only did Xu and twelve students live on the university's campus during the three-week class, but he also led them to various historical sites throughout the country, including the capital city of Beijing and the

---

[54] "History Department, Faculty Profiles," CNU Web site, http://history.cnu.edu/profiles.htm (accessed 24 June 2010). Xu's first book is entitled *Chinese Professionals and the Republican State*.

[55] Three courses per semester is the standard teaching load at most public colleges and universities of CNU's size and reputation.

Great Wall. Other members of the history department led undergraduates to historic sites within the United States. Given the enormous interest in the Civil War among students from Virginia, several faculty members began in 2006 to lead annual "Spring Break" trips to the Gettysburg National Military Park in Pennsylvania for members of the History Club. These yearly trips allowed professors to get to know their students better as well as provided their undergraduates with memorable and meaningful academic experiences.

By no means, though, was the history department unique in its activities. Many academic departments possessed outstanding teachers and scholars who provided their students with important academic experiences, both in and out of the classroom. Tracey Schwarze of the English department, for example, taught British literature and was a scholar on Victorian literature. Coming to CNU in 1999, she immediately proved her skills as a demanding classroom instructor as well as an expert in her field of study. In 2002, she published an important book on the Irish writer James Joyce entitled *Joyce and the Victorians.* Indeed, on the strength of her scholarship, the prestigious International Joyce Summer School at University College, Dublin invited Schwarze in 2005 to lecture on their campus. Before heading over, Schwarze arranged to bring five English majors with her so that they could attend the school. While in residence on campus and in between lectures, Schwarze directed these students in their own research projects at the National Library of Ireland. As a result of both her scholarship and commitment to her students, Schwarze became in 2007 the third CNU professor to win the state of Virginia's Outstanding Faculty Award.[56]

In 2010, moreover, Edward Brash of the physics and computer sciences department won a $650,000 National Science Foundation grant to fund CNU's ongoing undergraduate research program at the nearby Thomas Jefferson Accelerator Facility where he and other scientists from around the country studied and explored the fundamental nature and behavior of subatomic matter. In addition to Brash's work, Tarek Abdel-

---

[56] "CNU Professor Receives 2007 Outstanding Faculty Award," CNU Press Release, 8 February 2007; Mark Padilla email communication to CNU faculty, 2 August 2010. Sadly, Professor Schwarze died of cancer in 2010. She remained a leader on campus throughout her career, serving as president of the faculty senate and then as vice provost for the university.

Fattah headed up CNU's Applied Research Center at the Jefferson Labs. The center not only provided space for CNU science faculty to conduct innovative experiments in such areas of biomedicine, alternative energy, and environmental remediation, but it also allowed the professors to directly involve their students in all aspects of their investigations. Derek Loftis, for instance, worked with Abdel-Fattah for several years at the laboratory conducting experiments in electrochemistry. After Loftis received his BS degree in biology, he enrolled in CNU's environmental sciences master's program where he continued to conduct research at the lab as well as present his work at conferences with Professor Abdel-Fattah.[57]

Other developments during the decade further pointed to the university's evolving academic reputation. In 2005, the Business School earned accreditation from the American Association to Advance Collegiate Schools of Business. The prestigious recognition—possessed by only one in three collegiate business schools in Virginia—took years of work and preparation, largely under the leadership of Dean Donna Mottila. Mottila came to CNU in 1999 as dean of the Business School, and she immediately strengthened its program by eliminating several academic tracks with low enrollment, raising GPA standards for admittance, and tightening the curriculum requirements for business, economics, and marketing majors.[58] Six months after the school's accreditation, Smithfield Foods, Inc., donated $5 million to CNU, the largest single donation ever made to the university. The corporation made this gift because it wanted its charitable gifts to directly benefit the Hampton Roads area, and the firm's board had been deeply impressed by CNU's overall progress as an academic institution. Upon receiving the contribution, CNU's board of visitors renamed the Business School

---

[57] "Faculty Member Wins National Science Foundation Grant," CNU Press Release, 28 April 2010; CNU-Applied Research Center Homepage, http://arc.cnu.edu/index.htm (accessed 23 July 2010).

[58] "Seeking Collegiate Stamp of Approval; Business School Attempting to Gain National Accreditation," Daily Press, 16 October 2003; "CNU Business School Earns Accreditation," Daily Press, 28 January 2005; "Other Voices: A New Honor for CNU," Daily Press, 28 February 2005.

the Joseph W. Luter III School of Business after Smithfield's chairman of the board.[59]

In addition to the creation of the Luter School of Business, CNU entered into an important partnership with its long-time neighbor, the Mariners' Museum. In 2007, President Trible and Mariners' Museum President Timothy Sullivan announced that the museum's world-renowned research library would be housed in the new Trible Library. The 1.7 million-item collection—the third largest maritime history and culture collection in the world—needed a new home as its original facility was badly outdated. Unable to raise sufficient funds after the completion of its $30 million USS Monitor Center (which houses the original gun-turret and other items from the famous Civil War battleship), Sullivan and other museum officials approached Trible about the possibility of placing the collection at CNU. While president of William and Mary from 1992 to 2005, Sullivan had forged an excellent relationship with Trible, and that personal tie helped to secure the institutional partnership. The university provided the museum with 23,000 square feet or one-quarter of the Trible Library's space. In order to facilitate the research library's integration into CNU's academic community, University Librarian Mary Sellen was also named director of the Mariners' Museum Library.[60]

The research library's presence on campus invigorated the university's general intellectual life in several ways. Faculty members, particularly in the history department, used the museum's extensive collections to teach majors not only about "public history" (the study of how history is presented to the general public), but also about the ins and outs of archival research and the scholarly work of research libraries in general. Writers and scholars on maritime subjects, moreover, increasingly appeared both at the museum and on campus giving

---

[59] "Smithfield Food Gives CNU $5 Million," *Daily Press*, 31 August 2005. Four million dollars of the donation went into the university's endowment and $1 million was designated for academic scholarships for students; see also "Ex-CNU Dean Stayed Busy; Now Ready to Leave School," *Daily Press*, 12 July 2007.

[60] "Maritime History Library to Set Sail for New Port," *Daily Press*, 20 September 2007; "Mariners' Museum Library Collection to Come to CNU," *Captain's Log*, 26 September 2007; see also "First Dance: The Mariners' Museum and CNU Could Go Far Together," *Daily Press*, 23 September 2007.

lectures to the university community on such varied historical maritime topics as ancient Greek triremes, the 1609 shipwreck of the *Sea Venture* on Bermuda, and the fate of the World War II submarine, the USS *Tang*. Sellen explained that the placement of the collection within the Trible Library "greatly improved the university's intellectual resources and opened CNU to a world community of scholars and not just in maritime studies. The rare books and manuscripts go well beyond maritime subjects." The new partnership paid particular dividends in 2010 when the university and the Mariners' Museum co-sponsored the Fifth Annual Virginia Forum, a scholarly conference that brought nearly two hundred professors, graduate students, and researchers from across the nation to campus to present papers on Virginia's maritime heritage and other aspects of the Old Dominion's history.[61]

Student and Residential Life

The ongoing improvements in CNU's academic life were mirrored in the middle to later years of the decade by significant changes in students' campus experiences. Indeed, because a greater proportion of the student body attended school full time and came from outside the Hampton Roads area, CNU's undergraduates turned in ever-increasing numbers to intercollegiate sports, Greek life, and greater participation in campus affairs. As a result, activities related to student life expanded in scope and variety, thus becoming more satisfying to all. Nevertheless, challenges remained. Although CNU's retention and graduation rates improved significantly during the Trible-era, both statistics were still too low to satisfy the administration and faculty. The Wall Street financial crisis at the decade's end, moreover, led the nation into yet another recession and a new round of budget cuts from Richmond. Therefore, as the decade ended, CNU had to tighten its financial belt as it attempted to place the school in the strongest possible position as an up-and-coming public liberal arts university.

---

[61] Sellen email communication to Hamilton, 9 June 2010. For more information about the Mariners' Museum Research Library, see http://www.marinersmuseum.org/library; for information about the Fifth Annual Virginia Forum, see http://www.virginiaforum.org/conference.html.

The university's athletic program enjoyed ongoing success throughout the 2000s. Under the direction of long-time Athletic Director C.J. Woollum, CNU's twenty-two sports teams collectively served as a model Division III NCAA program, with winning records, successful coaches, and student-athletes who did well both on the field and in the classroom. In fact, the school won the "President's Cup" every year during the decade for having the top athletic program in the USA South Conference. The university also invested in superb playing and training facilities which added to the students' positive athletic performances. In 2004, for instance, CNU constructed new athletic playing fields on the western side of campus. Not only were new practice fields installed, but "Captain's Park" was also built. The latter facility included two new stadiums—one for the men's baseball team and the other for the Lady Captains' softball squad. The university also constructed a new playing field for the lacrosse and field hockey teams that sported state-of-the-art synthetic turf, lighting for nighttime games, and seating for seven hundred spectators.[62]

On these fields, the teams themselves proved extraordinarily successful. The football Captains under Coach Matt Kelchner won six USA South Conference titles during the decade and sported a winning record every year but one.[63] The men's soccer team under its long-time coach, Steve Shaw, won four conference championships between 2003 and 2009, and twice (2008 and 2009) his team reached the NCAA Elite Eight in the Division III national championships. The men's and women's basketball teams also earned winning records over the years. In the 2009–10 season, for example, the Lady Captains, led by Coach Carolyn Hunter, went undefeated during the regular season with a 28–0 record and then advanced to the Sweet Sixteen of the Division III

---

[62] "Neighbors Respond to Baseball Field," *Captain's Log*, 4 February 2004; "CNU Starts on Men's Lacrosse Foundation," *Daily Press*, 24 February 2007; "CNU Athletic Facilities," CNU Web site, http://www.cnusports.com/sports/2010/2/18/GEN_0218100142.aspx?tab=facilities (accessed June 15, 2010).

[63] In 2004, CNU started a marching band program which began playing during half-time at CNU home football games, see "CNU Plans to Start Marching Band," *Daily Press*, 7 April 2004, and Kate Judkins, "The History of Christopher Newport University's Music and Band Program," unpublished undergraduate research paper, "Researching CNU" history seminar, Spring 2008, University Archives.

championship. The team's key player that remarkable season was junior Chelsie Schweers who averaged 24.5 points per game and became one of only ten Division III players in the nation to be named All-American by the Women's Basketball Coaches Association.[64]

C.J. Woollum, meanwhile, successfully led the men's basketball team until the end of the decade. Indeed, he won his five-hundredth victory as head coach against Greensboro College on 23 February 2010. Several days later, he announced to the university that the time was right for him to step down at the conclusion of the 2009–10 season (although he continues on as CNU's athletic director). During his twenty-six-year coaching career, Woollum amassed an outstanding 502–221 record; his teams, moreover, won thirteen conference titles and played in seventeen NCAA tournaments. Most importantly, Woollum served as a mentor and role model for his players. Lamont Strothers—probably the most talented basketball player in CNU history—remembered how Woollum taught him to be an upright team player both on and off the court. When Strothers had initially balked at some of the team rules when he played in the late '80s and early '90s, Woollum gave him a stern but decisive ultimatum: "I don't care how good your are," the coach said, "you either start listening and work within the confines of the program or you're gone." Strothers got the message and straightened up. Another former player, Tiron Matthews especially appreciated how Woollum always "treated us like adults" by insisting that squad members play up to their potential and take responsibility for their actions.[65]

In addition to the university's athletic teams, campus life outside the classroom continued to develop and improve. During the 2008–09

---

[64] "CNU Women's Basketball," CNU Web site, http://www.cnusports.com/index.aspx?tab=basketball2&path=wbball (accessed 20 June 2010); "Perfect Season Comes to An End," *Daily Press*, 13 March 2010.

[65] "Fortune 500," *Daily Press*, 24 February 2010; "End of CNU Era," *Daily Press*, 22 April 2010; "Lasting Blueprint," *Daily Press*, 25 April 2010. For more information about Woollum's tenure as basketball coach, see Jeff Eckert, "A Brief History of CNU Basketball," unpublished undergraduate research paper, "Researching CNU" history seminar, Spring 2008, University Archives. John Kirkorian replaced Woollum as head basketball coach. Kirkorian had been the head coach of the US Merchant Marine Academy's team; for more information, see "CNU Men's Basketball," CNU Web site, http://www.cnusports.com/index.aspx?tab=basketball&path=mbball (accessed 3 July 2010).

academic year, for example, nearly six hundred students took part in Greek life, belonging to one of six fraternities and five sororities on campus—the largest number ever in CNU history. As in past years, Greek-affiliated students annually participated in a variety of social and charitable activities.[66] In addition to Greek organizations, CNU students belonged to a wide variety of other clubs and social groups on campus, ranging from academic honor societies to special interest clubs to service organizations.[67] A large and growing number of students participated in TheaterCNU, especially after the theater department moved into the Ferguson Center and regularly performed its major productions in the Music and Theater Hall. In 2007, for instance, TheaterCNU director Steven Breese wrote and directed an original play entitled "Actus Fidei" (meaning "Act of Faith"). Set in the turbulent maritime world of the seventeenth century, the drama focused on the life of the university's namesake, Captain Christopher Newport, who was one of the great mariners of his age. The play featured an enormous cast and was one of several cultural contributions CNU made to the state's commemoration of Jamestown's four-hundredth anniversary.[68]

The growing presence of residential students, above all, increasingly shaped and defined the university's student life. During the latter years of the decade, the university's residential population averaged 2,816 students, approximately 60 percent of the school's total. With the opening of the Ferguson Center, the David Student Union, the expanded Trible Library, and CNU Village, there was simply much more activity on campus during weeknights and over weekends. Fewer and fewer

[66] The numbers of CNU students involved in Greek life are from "Greek Life," CNU Web site, http://www.cnu.edu/studentlife/current/greek.asp (accessed 3 July 2010). For a sampling of articles on Greek life on campus during these years, see "New Sorority Recruits a Base," *Captain's Log*, 17 September 2003; "House Purchased for Greeks," *Captain's Log*, 1 October 2003; "Greek Life Expands at CNU," *Captain's Log*, 25 February 2004; "Creating Breast Cancer Awareness," *Captain's Log*, 9 November 2005; "Sigma Tau Gamma Returns after Five Years," *Captain's Log*, 27 September 2006.

[67] For more information on student organizations, see "Student Organizations," CNU Web site, http://www.cnu.edu/studentlife/current/organizations.asp (accessed 3 July 2010).

[68] "Captain Newport Inspires Play," *Daily Press*, 30 July 2004; "'Actus Fidei' Brings Virginia History Alive," *Virginian Pilot*, 31 March 2007.

students, therefore, went home on Friday afternoons. The presence of special unit housing—such as "Quest Housing" for Honors students—further developed this social atmosphere.[69]

As mentioned, demand for university housing grew so heavy that the school typically had more students who wished to live on campus than available rooms. To deal with the situation, the university added an "Off-Campus" housing link to its Web site in 2005, providing upperclassmen with information on local properties for rent. Many students, moreover, chose to live off-campus because they found the university's rules, especially concerning alcohol usage, too restrictive. In 2005, a private firm sought to take advantage of this growing demand by constructing an apartment complex three miles from CNU called "University Suites." The apartments became popular with many students, especially because it served as a location for many weekend parties. Unfortunately, Newport News police frequently were called by nearby residents because of loud noises, under-aged drinking, and fights.[70]

The neighborhoods immediately surrounding campus also were transformed by the off-campus students, and not always for the better. Located just south of campus, Paddock Drive especially became a haven for CNU renters during 2007 and 2008. Although most students behaved responsibly, the street rapidly became well known for its off-campus social activities. As at University Suites, city police were sometimes called to deal with loud noises, intoxicated students, and trash-strewn yards. To put a stop to such behavior, CNU worked with the city to let student renters know that they *had* to be good neighbors and respect those living around them. Indeed, the administration informed students that a serious complaint against them regarding off-campus activities could lead to their dismissal from the university. Students got the message and, by the spring of 2009, the situation along Paddock had quieted down and considerably improved. Dawn Young, a thirty-year homeowner on the street, said with relief, "We have peace. Our street is

---

[69] The numbers of residential students are from the Office of Institutional Research, CNU; see also "Honors Program, Quest Housing," CNU Web site, http://honors.cnu.edu/quest.htm (accessed 3 July 2010).

[70] "Police Tired of Trouble at NN Suites," *Daily Press*, 4 May 2006.

happy once more." Trible went further, though, to deal with the growing number of disturbances and incidents with police. He told the *Daily Press*, "Perhaps what we need to do is require all students to live on campus. I am prepared to recommend that to my board." As a result, the board of visitors passed a new resolution in 2009 requiring all CNU freshmen, sophomores, *and juniors* to live in university housing on campus starting with the incoming class of 2010.[71]

Life at CNU continued to change throughout the decade, not only with the arrival of new students, but also because of the new values and attitudes they brought to campus. In the fall of 2003, for example, CNU's Gay-Straight Student Union called for sexual orientation to be included in the university's policy of non-discrimination on campus so that gay, lesbian, bisexual, and transgender individuals would be treated as a protected class. Although gay students stressed that they already felt comfortable and accepted at Christopher Newport, they believed that the addition was needed to reflect changing values on the subject nationwide. Working with the Student Government Association, students convinced the faculty senate to approve the addition. But the board of visitors initially balked and voted to table the motion in the summer of 2004, saying it needed more information on the subject. Students, however, continued to press for the change. Because of their persistent lobbying, the board finally approved the measure in February 2007 by a unanimous vote.[72]

---

[71] "Residents Tired of Unruly CNU Students," *Daily Press*, 30 September 2008; "CNU Off-Campus Students in NN Council's Radar," *Daily Press*, 8 October 2008; "Community Complaints Addressed" and "Paddock Residents Strive for Improved Image," *Captain's Log*, 5 November 2008; "'Peace' Returns to Notorious Student Party Neighborhood," *Daily Press*, 2 February 2009; see also "Letters to the Editor—CNU Renters Affect Neighborhoods," *Daily Press*, 15 September 2007. CNU's alcohol policy remained largely in place from 2002–10. The only change came in 2007 when some special functions sponsored by student organizations were permitted to serve alcohol to those 21 and over; see "ATF Rejects Residential Booze 10–2," *Captain's Log*, 24 January 2007.

[72] "Faculty Senate Discusses Non-Discrimination Policy," *Captain's Log*, 8 October 2003; "Resolution for Sexual Orientation Passed," *Captain's Log*, 12 November 2003; "CNU Students Want Policy to Protect Gays, Lesbians," *Daily Press*, 5 December 2003; "Gays at CNU Seek Protection in Official Policy," *Daily Press*, 11 November 2006; "Gays Guarded at CNU," *Daily Press*, 24 February 2007.

The War on Terror certainly had an impact on students and faculty, especially the long conflicts in Iraq and Afghanistan. Debates over the wisdom of the Bush administration's policies, particularly its justification of the Iraqi war, consumed much attention in classrooms and on campus in the Spring 2003. But after the conflict bogged down, the campus community largely turned to other matters. For students with loved ones in harm's way, however, the War on Terror proved an ever-present reality. In 2007, senior Audrey Copeland told the *Captain's Log* that she was constantly afraid for her brother who was deployed in Fallujah, Iraq. Anna Nordin, a junior with a husband also stationed in Iraq, felt the same way. To help cope with the pressures of having loved ones at war, Nordin and Copeland together organized several university drives to assemble care packages for US troops deployed in the Middle East. The Iraq war actually brought Stephanie Patterson back to campus in 2007. Patterson had been completing her senior year at CNU in 2003 when her husband was transferred to Camp Lejeune. To keep her family of three together, Patterson left the school and moved to North Carolina. Eventually deployed to Iraq, her husband was killed by an IED in January 2005. Therefore, Stephanie returned to CNU under the military's Survivors and Dependents Educational Assistance Program and completed her degree in 2008.[73]

One faculty member who left CNU due to the War on Terror was anthropology professor Marcus Griffin. Griffin had come to the university in 2000, but took a leave of absence in 2007 in order to participate in a US Army program called Human Terrain Systems (HTS). Embedded as a civilian advisor in Iraq with the Second Brigade of the First Infantry Division, his mission was to help the brigade's commander and subordinate officers understand the cultural landscape of the country and to better communicate with the Iraqi people. The HTS program sparked enormous debate within the anthropological community nationwide. Many anthropologists at other universities strenuously objected to scholars directly assisting the US military in its pacification efforts. Griffin took part in these debates and strongly defended the program as an effort to reduce bloodshed on both sides.

---

[73] "War Hits Home for Students," *Captain's Log*, 5 December 2007.

After one year in Iraq, Griffin wanted to continue his work within the HTS program and, therefore, permanently left CNU in 2008.[74]

The growth of student life combined with CNU's more rigorous academic program led to significant improvements in the university's overall graduation and retention rates during the first decade of new millennium. In 1997, for instance, CNU's graduation rate for freshmen that had entered six years previously stood at only 31 percent. Part of the problem was that in the 1990s part-time and commuter students together comprised the bulk of CNU's overall population. Both types of students typically held outside jobs and/or had other off-campus commitments. Therefore, the possibility of graduating within the normal four- to six-year pattern was simply not an option for many. Equally as problematic, CNU's overall student-retention rate during that same period stood at only 43 percent, due to similar factors.[75]

Although both figures had improved by 2002, the large number of students who left the college after the elimination of the education, nursing, and leisure studies/physical education programs led CNU to take more direct steps to improve the situation. In 2004, the university formed a Retention Planning Team composed of faculty, current students, and administrators. Led by physics professor David Doughty, it examined why many students either did not complete their degree in a more timely fashion or transferred elsewhere after their freshmen and sophomore years. From interviews and surveys, the team found that students left CNU for many reasons: they wanted to transfer to more prestigious and older institutions such as University of Virginia; they felt that CNU's "dry campus" was too restrictive; or they had academic problems and/or did not believe their academic advisors truly understood their majors and other requirements needed for graduation. To help students become more academically and socially engaged right from the start, the Retention Team proposed the creation of "Learning

---

[74] "From the Classroom to the Battlefield," *Captain's Log*, 5 December 2007; Marcus Griffin, "Research to Reduce Bloodshed," *Chronicle of Higher Education* 54, no.14 (30 November 2007).

[75] "CNU Retention Rates Fall," *Captain's Log*, 25 September 1995; "CNU Has 2nd Lowest Grad Rate," *Daily Press*, 14 June 1997. See also "CNU Graduation Rate Second Lowest in State," *Captain's Log*, 29 January 2001; "SCHEV Releases College Report," *Daily Press*, 17 July 2002.

Communities" for freshmen. Initiated in 2005, Learning Communities pulled together groups of twenty new students who all lived in the same dormitory and took at least two classes together. The aim was to provide these freshmen with an identifiable peer group at the beginning of their college careers. CNU also worked with faculty to strengthen academic advising, especially in terms of better guiding students in the selection of their coursework as well as in helping them to identify scholarships and career opportunities.[76] As a result of these efforts, both graduation and retention figures improved by the decade's end. In 2009, for example, CNU graduated 58 percent of those freshmen who had entered campus six years before. Student retention rates also pointed to success as the number of freshmen returning for their sophomore year averaged 81 percent between 2007 and 2010.[77]

Looking Backward, Looking Forward

Former CNU Rector Alan Witt wrote a *Daily Press* op-ed article in late 2005 in which he said that when he moved to Newport News in 1971 friends told him "the then-Christopher Newport College was a diamond in the rough, an undervalued asset that would develop over the years into a major force in our community." After seeing CNU's transformation during the early 2000s, Witt remarked, "Never did I think those words so prophetic." He noted that Christopher Newport's new buildings and vibrant intellectual climate "are changing the image of our community." The economic impact on the Peninsula was equally considerable. Taking into account the financial contributions of CNU employees, construction workers, and students living on campus, Witt argued that "the impact is huge." The annual "economic value created by CNU was more than $736 million, which generated more than 9,000 jobs with a payroll over $300 million." The former rector finished his

---

[76] "Retention Rate Falling," *Captain's Log*, 27 October 2004; "University Retention Low," *Captain's Log*, 2 February 2005; "Many CNU Freshmen Don't Graduate," *Daily Press*, 22 February 2005; "Learning Communities to Be Instituted," *Captain's Log*, 13 April 2005; see also "CNU Wants to Rank Higher; Magazine's List Spurs Self-Study," *Daily Press*, 13 February 2004.

[77] "Most 4-Year Colleges See Graduation Rates Increase," *Virginian Pilot*, 28 May 2006; "Va. College Graduation Rates Better than Average," *Richmond Times-Dispatch*, 3 June 2009; "Applications to CNU Top 8,400," *Daily Press*, 29 April 2010.

article by stating, "When you take into account the social, cultural, educational, and economic influence of this jewel, you can't help but realize how fortunate we are in having CNU in our community."[78] Most people on the Peninsula in the middle to later years of the decade agreed with Witt's assessment. As the university approached its fiftieth anniversary, however, numerous people recognized Christopher Newport not only for its current contributions, but also for its many past accomplishments. Indeed, because the year 2011 would mark fifty years since CNC opened in the Daniel School, many Peninsula residents wanted to look backward as well as forward.

The passing of some of the school's most revered figures encouraged such reflections; in July 2007, Christopher Newport's first president H. Westcott Cunningham died at the age of 86. After leaving CNC in 1970, he had served as headmaster of the Pingry School in New Jersey for twelve years before returning to the Peninsula to work once more at the College of William and Mary, this time as vice president of the school's Alumni Association. His successor as president, James Windsor, pointed out at Cunningham's funeral what many already recognized: "All the significant growth and development at Christopher Newport University over the years rests on the foundation envisioned and created by Scotty Cunningham."[79] The sudden death of CNU's third president John "Jack" Anderson in 2009 at the age of 77 led to more reflections. Long-time members of the faculty and college community greatly respected Anderson for his service as president from 1980 to 1986 when he instituted critical administrative and financial reforms that placed the university in a much stronger position for long-term growth. Colleagues also remembered Anderson for his many years as a dedicated faculty member in the School of Business, during which he taught many students, served for several years as a department chair, and mentored a number of younger CNU professors.[80]

---

[78] Alan Witt, "Other Voices: CNU is Now the Sparkling Jewel of Our Community," *Daily Press*, 3 December 2005.

[79] "First President of CNC Dies," *Daily Press*, 26 July 2007; "Rite Set for H. Westcott 'Scott' Cunningham: First Head of What's Now Christopher Newport University Dies at 86," *Richmond Times-Dispatch*, 28 July 2007.

[80] "John E. Anderson, Jr.," *Daily Press*, 30 August 2009.

Toward the decade's end, several long-time members of the administration who had had a tremendous impact on CNU's development retired. Richard Summerville, for instance, stepped down as university provost in June 2007. Having served in that position first from 1982–1995 and again since 2002, Summerville was instrumental in advancing many of the university's initiatives over the years, and he proved a steady hand when important decisions had to be made and when presidents needed honest and straightforward counsel. Trible called Summerville a "marvelous human being" who had helped to make CNU a stronger and more academically rigorous institution. To honor his contributions, the board of visitors named one of the large reading rooms in the Trible Library "the Richard Summerville Reading Room." After a national search, the university hired Dr. Mark W. Padilla to replace him. Having served as provost at the University of North Carolina, Asheville from 2002–2007, Padilla brought to CNU considerable experience as the academic head of a public university. A scholar of classical studies and the holder of a PhD in comparative literature from Princeton University, the new provost particularly wanted to help CNU faculty members become more productive scholars as well as to assist Trible in the ongoing implementation of the university's vision.[81]

Dean Douglas Gordon's retirement also came late in the decade. Involved in just about every aspect of teaching, research, and administration over a twenty-nine-year career at CNU, Gordon was affectionately known across campus as "Dr. Dog" because of his research on dogs in literature. Serving as dean of the College of Arts and Sciences during his final years on campus, Gordon provided important leadership to the university community, and he especially mentored and assisted new and younger faculty members within his college, helping them to adjust to what were (for many of them) their first academic positions. In honor of his contributions, Gordon gave the university's commencement address in the Spring 2009 where he urged graduates to use the skills and knowledge they had gained at CNU "in the service of human liberty." Reminding them that they sat within ten miles of the

---

[81] "CNU Provost Says It's Time to Say Goodbye, Again," *Daily Press*, 4 January 2007; "CNU Committee Selects New Provost," *Daily Press*, 8 May 2007.

Yorktown battlefield where Americans had won the Revolution, the outgoing dean stressed that the new graduates must serve the nation as teachers, soldiers, and public leaders if they wished to preserve the ideals and freedoms the Founders had embraced and won more than two hundred years before.[82] Gordon's departure, however, left big shoes to fill. Indeed, after his retirement was announced, President Trible and Provost Padilla decided the College of Liberal Arts and Sciences was simply too large—with more than 200 of the university's 240 professors within it—to stand alone. Therefore, after consultation with the campus community, they proposed (and the faculty later approved) dividing CNU's academic departments into three separate colleges of roughly equal size—Arts and Humanities, Natural and Behavioral Sciences, and Social Sciences.

Beyond providing leadership on campus throughout the decade, President Trible broadened his work in higher education during the decade. In addition to periodically writing newspaper op-ed articles on college and university matters,[83] he was elected in 2005 to the Division III Presidents' Council of the National Collegiate Athletic Association (NCAA). The fifteen-member council serves as the governing body for 419 Division III college and university sports programs. Upon joining the group, Trible worked to enact NCAA policies that would lead to student success both on the playing field and in the classroom. Moreover, Trible served three times during the decade as chair of the Council of Presidents—the group representing the heads of Virginia's two- and four-year public higher education institutions. In this capacity, he consistently championed the cause of higher education throughout the Old Dominion. Under his leadership, for instance, the college and university presidents collectively adopted a statewide capital building initiative that Trible had proposed and then, working with General Assembly leaders, he had helped to usher through the legislature.[84]

---

[82] Douglas Gordon interview with Phillip Hamilton, 6 June 2008; "Rain Doesn't Dampen Spirits," *Daily Press*, 18 May 2009.

[83] For example, see Paul Trible, "Cease Fire! Profs and Pols Must Work Together for America's Future," *Free Lance-Star (Fredericksburg)*, 2 August 2005.

[84] "Trible Joins NCAA Committee," *Daily Press*, 13 December 2005; Trible interview with Hamilton, 1 September 2009. See also "Successes, Failures Greeting Nonacademic College Leaders," *Virginian Pilot*, 20 March 2005.

Construction on campus—long a staple of CNU life—continued unabated at the decade's end. In the spring of 2009, Paul and Rosemary Trible moved into a new seven-thousand-square-foot presidential home. The CNU Real Estate Foundation had long-planned the new presidential residence to replace the outdated home purchased during Jack Anderson's presidency. The $4.4 million, fourteen-room Georgian-style house was located a mile west of the main campus. Overlooking the James River, the house resembled the eighteenth-century plantation homes built on the river around the time of the American Revolution. As soon as it opened, the Tribles began hosting numerous student groups and faculty events as well as special receptions for university donors and other VIPs.[85]

Nine months later, the new Lewis Archer McMurran, Jr., Hall opened amid much fanfare. Anchoring the west end of the university's Great Lawn, the 86,000-square-foot brick building became the academic home of CNU's liberal arts departments as well as of the graduate-teaching and honors programs. The building featured thirty state-of-the-art classrooms, ranging from a 150-seat lecture hall to multiple seminar rooms for smaller classes of fourteen to eighteen students. Within weeks of the new building's January 2010 opening, the original McMurran Hall, which had served the school for forty-six years, was quietly (and without fanfare) torn down.[86]

Soon after the new McMurran Hall opened, the city and state finally completed the widening of Warwick Boulevard from four to six lanes. First proposed in 1991, the $42 million project helped to complete the transformation of midtown Newport News into an area now largely dominated by Christopher Newport. Not only did occupants of the 47,000 cars per day who drove up and down the thoroughfare see a

[85] "Funds Buy Trible New Property," *Captain's Log*, 17 January 2007; "A Grand Space for CNU," *Daily Press*, 21 September 2009. The riverfront lot cost $1.96 million and the construction of the mansion itself cost $2.4 million. For more information on the long search for a new presidential home, see "CNU Pays $1.45M for Waterfront Home," *Daily Press*, 26 February 2005; and "Trouble Housing Trible: A Third Home for CNU's President," *Daily Press*, 14 December 2006.

[86] "University Expansion Continues," *Captain's Log*, 21 January 2009; "CNU Celebrates Newest Hall," *Daily Press*, 12 January 2010; Christopher Newport University Press Release, 11 January 2010, http://cnu.edu/news/newsarticle/01-12-10mcmurran.asp (accessed 3 July 2010).

beautiful university campus from an unobstructed setting, but with better sidewalks and crossing lanes, students also traversed the busy roadway more safely.[87]

In July 2010, the *Daily Press* ran an extended article entitled "Growth Spurt at CNU." The piece informed the Peninsula community that even more buildings and construction lay in Christopher Newport's future. A new $78 million 156,000-square-foot science building, for instance, was rapidly going up on the northern edge of the Great Lawn. Named the Mary Brock Forbes Hall, it honored the mother of Dr. Sarah Forbes who was a major donor to the university. Mary Brock Forbes had been a pioneer for women in education throughout much of the twentieth century. Not only did she hold a bachelor's degree from the University of North Carolina Chapel Hill (at a time when relatively few women attended college), but she also enrolled at Columbia University to earn a master's degree in progressive education. Starting in 1932, she taught in the Newport News public school system where she earned wide recognition as an outstanding classroom instructor and school administrator. Dr. Sarah Forbes later donated $1 million to CNU as a way to honor her mother's legacy as well as to give back to the community that had given her a great deal. Scheduled to open in two phases, the building's first-wing is to be completed in fall 2011 and the second in spring 2012. The large structure resembles the other neo-Georgian buildings on the Great Lawn and will feature multiple classrooms and laboratories as well as faculty offices for members of the College of Natural and Behavioral Sciences. Construction also continued on a $26 million expansion of the Freeman Center. Designed to double the center's usable space, the plan called for a second gymnasium, a larger fitness-center, and a new four-hundred-seat Gaines Theater to replace the original one, which had been torn down with the demolition of the first student center in 2008. The article, furthermore, laid out an array of other new buildings to be constructed after 2011, including a third academic building where Wingfield Hall once stood, a university chapel, and an additional five-hundred-bed dormitory. The aim of this new construction, the president insisted, was not to be bigger. As CNU headed into its second half-century of existence, Trible emphasized that

---

[87] "Warwick Wrapping Up," *Daily Press*, 4 May 2010.

the ongoing campus transformation—which would total $1 billion in renovations and new buildings when completed—was to better serve CNU's five thousand students in terms of creating a more dynamic learning environment and a more animated social atmosphere.[88]

Of course, shaping students' minds in order to have a meaningful and permanent impact on their intellects, lives, and careers has always been the real goal. Christopher Banks, a member of the graduating class of 2010, exemplified this larger and more important mission. Indeed, Banks's story demonstrates the tremendous impact that CNU has had on students over the decades whether they attended in the 1960s or early 2000s. Christopher Banks came to Christopher Newport in 2006 after leading a difficult and somewhat nomadic childhood, including a period when he and his family were homeless. "We skipped from home to home," he recalled shortly before the 2010 commencement ceremonies. Determined to succeed, however, he graduated from nearby Warwick High School with a respectable 3.25 GPA and then enrolled at CNU on several academic scholarships. Banks thrived after he arrived on campus. He became a star on the track and field team in the hammer, discus, and shot put. In fact, he set several university records during his four years of competition. With support from coaches, faculty, and college friends, Banks also succeeded in the classroom. While he admitted there were several "rough times" academically speaking when things were "not easy," he completed his degree in four years while holding down two jobs as well as volunteering on a regular basis at the local Boys and Girls Club. After he graduated, Banks planned to go to graduate school with his long-term goal being to teach at the university level and to coach track and field. He especially hoped, however, to help at-risk young men and women like he had once been.[89]

Paul Trible's first fifteen years as president marked a permanent change in Christopher Newport University's history. Indeed, the wide

---

[88] "Growth Spurt at CNU," *Daily Press*, 3 July 2010; Sarah Forbes interview (by phone) with Phillip Hamilton, 23 September 2010. For more information about the presence of a chapel on CNU's campus, see "Trible Announces Chapel at CNU," *Captain's Log*, 30 January 2008, and "Funding Raised through Private Donations for Chapel," *Captain's Log*, 11 February 2009.

[89] "Once Homeless, New College Grad," *Daily Press*, 14 May 2010. The author instructed Chris Banks in a First-Year Seminar class in Fall 2006.

range of new student and academic buildings, as well as the innovative improvements to the university's curriculum, promised to shape CNU throughout the twenty-first century. Furthermore, the city of Newport News itself (especially its now-thriving midtown region) had significantly changed for the better during Trible's decade-and-a-half at the helm, especially with the opening of the Ferguson Center for the Arts. In 2011, therefore, everyone recognized that Paul Trible's contributions to both the university and the Hampton Roads area would be long lasting and considerable.

Christopher Newport University, however, has always been an institution caught up in the throes of change and transformation. In fact, all of CNU's presidents have initiated important changes during their tenures, starting with the remarkable Scotty Cunningham. In the 1960s, Cunningham built the college literally from nothing. After Lewis McMurran sponsored and ushered through the General Assembly the legislation creating the college, Cunningham almost single-handedly hired the faculty, recruited the students, and designed the curriculum in time for the college's opening in September 1961 in the Daniel School. He oversaw, moreover, the establishment of the Peninsula campus on Shoe Lane and the construction of CNC's first five academic buildings. While Cunningham, Trible and the school's three other presidents—James Windsor, Jack Anderson, and Anthony Santoro—each brought about significant changes that helped the school grow, mature, and develop, their actions took place within the larger context of momentous transformations within American higher education in general as the number of colleges expanded nationwide and the number of students pursuing higher education exploded.

CNU's faculty members, on the other hand, have typically embraced continuity more than change throughout the decades. From 1961 to 2011, hundreds of instructors have taught at the university, and almost all of them have brought to campus similar commitments: a love of learning, a scholarly passion for their discipline, and a dedication to their students in terms of providing them with meaningful and substantive experiences, both inside the classroom and beyond. The tradition of outstanding instruction started the very first year the college opened in 1961—marked by such exceptional professors as Robert Usry and Barry Wood—and that tradition continues to the present among the university's 240 faculty members.

Although CNU students have certainly changed over the years, they have also all shared important qualities regardless of when they attended. During the first three decades of the school's existence, for instance, most students came from the Peninsula and many were nontraditional working adults attending part-time while holding down outside jobs and dealing with family responsibilities. Since the mid-1990s, however, CNU began drawing the bulk of its student body from throughout the entire state of Virginia. Today, moreover, the university's five thousand students are predominately recent high school graduates between eighteen and twenty-two years old who want a more "traditional college experience." Despite these differences, many impressive students have attended CNU each and every decade— students who were (and are) determined to make the most of the academic opportunities presented to them. Indeed, they range from James Cornette who, in 1960, saw Christopher Newport as a marvelous educational opportunity that had landed in his lap, thus leading him to become the college's first admitted student (he currently teaches in CNU's English Department today), to Christopher Banks, who flourished at the university in the twenty-first century because it presented him with multiple academic, sports, and social opportunities that helped develop his mind and character. As Christopher Newport University enters its second half-century of existence, this service to the people and students of the Peninsula and the Old Dominion promises to continue.

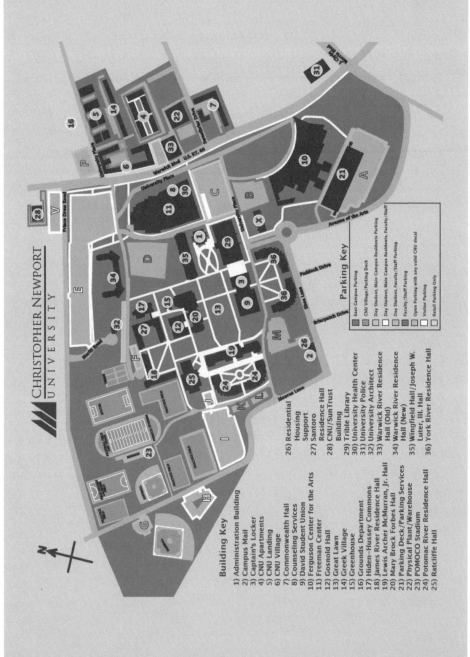

CHRISTOPHER NEWPORT
UNIVERSITY

Building Key

1) Administration Building
2) Campus Mail
3) Captain's Locker
4) CNU Apartments
5) CNU Landing
6) CNU Village
7) Commonwealth Hall
8) Counseling Services
9) David Student Union
10) Ferguson Center for the Arts
11) Freeman Center
12) Gosnold Hall
13) Great Lawn
14) Greek Village
15) Greenhouse
16) Grounds Department
17) Hiden–Hussey Commons
18) James River Residence Hall
19) Lewis Archer McMurran, Jr. Hall
20) Mary Brock Forbes Hall
21) Parking Deck/Parking Services
22) Physical Plant/Warehouse
23) POMOCO Stadium
24) Potomac River Residence Hall
25) Ratcliffe Hall
26) Residential Housing Support
27) Santoro Residence Hall
28) CNU/SunTrust Building
29) Trible Library
30) University Health Center
31) University Police
32) University Architect
33) Warwick River Residence Hall (Old)
34) Warwick River Residence Hall (New)
35) Wingfield Hall/Joseph W. Luter, III. Hall
36) York River Residence Hall

Parking Key

East Campus Parking
CNU Village/Parking Deck
Day Student, Main Campus Residents Parking
Day Student, Main Campus Residents, Faculty/Staff
Day Student, Faculty/Staff Parking
Faculty/Staff Parking
Open Parking with any valid CNU decal
Visitor Parking
Retail Parking Only

Christopher Newport University Enrollment – 1961-2009

	Total	Full-Time	Part-Time
2009	4952	4722	230
2008	4904	4656	248
2007	4884	4531	353
2006	4793	4408	385
2005	4699	4272	427
2004	4681	4168	513
2003	4812	4103	709
2002	5391	4311	1080
2001	5388	4083	1305
2000	5314	3851	1463
1999	5164	3561	1603
1998	5004	3400	1604
1997	4878	3218	1660
1996	4565	2920	1645
1995	4558	2819	1739
1994	4705	2907	1798
1993	4756	2915	1841
1992	4880	2935	1945
1991	5034	2906	2128
1990	4861	2881	1980
1989	4832	2758	2074
1988	4647	2385	2262
1987	4411	2052	2359
1986	4089	1857	2232
1985	4152	1922	2230
1984	4268	1954	2314
1983	4398	1968	2430
1982	4289	2019	2270
1981	4098	1931	2167
1980	3897	1814	2083
1979	3918	2379	1539
1978	3839	2295	1544
1977	3717	2262	1455
1976	3344	2078	1266
1975	3035	1903	1132
1974	2660	1647	1013
1973	2524		
1972	2305		
1971	2068		
1970	1770		
1969	1340		
1968	1071		
1967	1093		
1966	1106		
1965	1026		
1964	804		
1963	615		
1962	499		
1961	179		

*Source: CNU Office of Institutional Research

INDEX

Index

316 Serving the Old Dominion

Raspberry, William, 169
Ratcliffe, John (mariner) 49
Reagan, President Ronald, 162
Reid, Henry J.E., 10
Rich, Mike, 163
Richard Bland College 16
Riverside Hospital, 35, 77, 155
Robb, Governor Charles, 152
Rollins, Alfred B., 142
Rossmanith, James, 232-33

Sachs, Larry, 104
Safko, Carol, 214
Sanderlin, Stephen, 132
Sannes, Inger, 282
Santoro, Anthony, 140, 214, 230;
    attaining university status, 181-83;
    appointment as president, 169-70;
    building first campus dormitory, 178-
    79, 199; and campus
    construction/landscaping, 184, 225;
    controversies during presidency, 187-
    89, 194-95; creating graduate
    programs, 171, 179-81; creating
    Japanese Studies Program, 175-76;
    hiring faculty, 171-74; negotiating
    with General Assembly, 170, 189-91;
    President's London Seminar, 177;
    proposal to create Faculty Senate, 172
    ; purchase/refurbishment of
    Ferguson High School, 185-86, 193-
    94, 199; resignation/separation
    agreement, 197-199 ; and students,
    187-88, 193; structuring the
    curriculum, 170-71,; teaching in
    history department, 197, 230; vision
    for the college, 170-71,
Santoro, Carol K., 169,
Saunders, Robert, 104, 115, 225
Scammon, Jean, 58
Schwarze, Tracy, 288
Schweers, Chelsie, 293
Scott, Robert "Bobby," 172
Scozzari, John 3, 9-10
Seats, Lillian, 64
Sellen, Mary, 280-81, 290-91

Serviceman's Readjustment Act(G.I.
    Bill), 5, 68
Shaner, Donald, 111, 113
Shaner Report, 111-14, 137
Shaw, Steve, 292
Shenandoah University, 242
Shoe Lane Area Civic League, 51
Shoe Lane, rerouting of, 245-48, 281
Shoe Lane Controversy (1961-63), 34-46
Sinnett, Jae, 240
Sishagne, Shumet, 173
Smiley, Frank, 136
Smith, John (explorer), 50
Smith, Robert B. 42-43
Smithfield Food, Inc., 289-90
Southern Association of Colleges and
    Universities(SACS), 72, 153, 228
Spicer, Robert, 210, 212
Sprague, Martha, 269
St. Leo's University, 209
St. Onge, Susan, 98, 100, 103, 138, 157,
    228, 232
State Council of Higher Education in
    Virginia (SCHEV) 10, 93, 111-13, 114,
    127, 128, 135, 146, 151, 155, 175, 195,
    204, 216, 228
Strothers, Lamont, 160, 293
Stuckley, Grace, 173
Students; academic/classroom
    experiences 24-26, 29-30, 98-102, 115-
    16, 157-58, 186-87, 196, 227-32, 250,
    268-69, 284-86, 290-91; alcohol, use of,
    124-25, 127, 162-64, 237-38 ; Alumni
    Society, 130, 182; campus jobs, 56-57,
    101; clubs, 60-62, 66, 116-18, 121-22,
    125-26, 163, 165-66, 190, 235-36, 293;
    composition of student body, 52-53,
    68, 95-96, 98-99, 112-13, 115-16, 154-
    55, 165, 171, 217, 232-33, 241, 269,
    283-84 ; dress habits 26, 67-68 ;
    extracurricular activities 26-7, 59-63,
    116-22, 124-27, 158-59, 161-65, 234-39,
    293-94; graduation rates, 291, 298-99;
    Greek life, 164-65, 234-35, 294; "Miss
    Christopher Newport College"
    contest, 60; reasons for attending
    Christopher Newport 23, 53;